AF541064

VALOUR AND HONOUR

VALOUR AND HONOUR

Indian Army through the Ages

EDITED BY

MAJ GEN IAN CARDOZO, AVSM, SM (RETD)

&

MAJ GEN JAGATBIR SINGH, VSM (RETD)

First published 2024

This publication is an account based on data collected from various sources available in the public domain. Attributability for the content lies purely with the authors.

Published by
Pentagon Press LLP
206, Peacock Lane, Shahpur Jat,
New Delhi- 110049, India
Contact: 01126490600

ISBN 978-93-90095-90-2

Disclaimer: The views and opinions expressed in the book is the individual assertion of the suthor. The publisher doesnot take any responsibility for the same in any manner whatsoever. The same shall solely be the responsibility of the Author.

www.pentagonpress.in Follow us: @pentagonpress

Contents

List of Tables vii
Preface ix

1 Indian Army: An Overview 1
Neha Kohli, Col PK Gautam (Retd), and Maj Gen VK Singh (Retd)

2 Indian Army in the Pre-Independence Era: The World Wars and Small Wars 43
Neha Kohli

3 Post-Independence Wars I: 1947–48 Kashmir Conflict and 1962 Sino-Indian Conflict 93
Maj Gen PJS Sandhu (Retd)

4 Post-Independence Wars II: 1965 India-Pakistan War and 1971 India-Pakistan War 127
Team USI

5 Indian Army and Operations Other than War, 1948–1999 177
Neha Kohli and Maj Gen VK Singh (Retd)

6 Low-Intensity Conflicts and Counter-terrorism 215
Col Vivek Chadha (Retd)

7 Indian Army and UN Peace Operations 235
Maj Gen (Dr) AK Bardalai (Retd)

8 Indian Army: Ethos, Values and Training 255
Maj Gen Ian Cardozo, AVSM, SM (Retd)

9 Gallantry and War Memorials 273
Neha Kohli

About the Authors 309
Index 313

Tables

1.1 Presidency Armies around 1796 3
1.2 Composition of Armies in the mid-Nineteenth Century 3
1.3 Composition of Armoured Regiments 25
1.4 Composition of Infantry Regiments 25

2.1 Social Composition of the Indian Army in 1912 45
2.2 New Communities Recruited Under Pressure of World War I 46
2.3 Imperial Service Troops in World War I 49
2.4 Order of Battle of the Original Indian Army Corps (IEF A) 54
2.5 Units of the Indian Army and Indian State Forces that Served in Mesopotamia, 1914–18 58
2.6 Units of the Indian Army, Indian Volunteer and Indian State Forces that Served in East Africa 62
2.7 Indian Army and Indian State Forces Units that Served in Egypt and Palestine During the Great War 66
2.8 Units of the Indian Army that Served in the Dardanelles Campaign, 1915 70
2.9 Indianisation During the War 76

5.1 Chronology of the Kargil War 209

9.1 Victoria Cross Awardees from the Indian Army
9.2 Param Vir Chakra Awardees from the Indian Army
9.3 Ashoka Chakra Awardees from the Indian Army
9.4 List of War Memorials in India 298

Preface

In 2005, the Centre for Armed Forces Historical Research (now the Centre for Military History and Conflict Studies) at the United Service Institution of India (USI) published *The Indian Army: A Brief History*. The book was an attempt to give readers a brief idea about the Indian Army, its evolution and its contribution to national development. The narrative was meant to reach out to readers beyond the Army and make them aware of the rich legacy of this fine institution, with a focus on easy readability. Within two years of its publication, the second edition of *The Indian Army: A Brief History* was also published, indicating the growing interest in the popularity of the Army.

History is not static and neither is the story of the Indian Army. The current volume—*Valour and Honour: Indian Army through the Ages*—is the result of an initiative to publish a readable history of the Indian Army. As with the 2005 publication, this volume covers important issues, but in a simple narrative so as to make it accessible to a wider readership. Readers will see that each chapter can be read as a self-contained piece, yet is interconnected to others, so as to have a running narrative throughout the book. While the chapters are thematic, the analysis and research within each is set chronologically, so as to present to readers a wide, yet in-depth analysis of the subject.

Readers may find that there are many issues/subjects that have not been touched upon here. A detailed history of the Indian Army would require not only multiple volumes but also access to primary material and archives. It is hoped that such archival material is made available to researchers and scholars in the near future and that the Indian Army then begins the process of writing detailed histories using those archives.

Coming back to the current volume, the chapters reflect both individual as well as collaborative efforts and have been authored by a mix of those with intimate knowledge of the Army, having served in it, and young researchers with an interest in military history. Each author has his/her unique approach to the subject and writing style, yet have aimed at making the subject easy to read and understand for anyone interested in the rich legacy of this great institution.

Hope that the book brings the Indian Army closer to the citizens of India.

Maj Gen Ian Cardozo, AVSM, SM (Retd)
Maj Gen Jagatbir Singh, VSM (Retd)

1

Indian Army

An Overview

NEHA KOHLI, COL PK GAUTAM (RETD), AND

MAJ GEN VK SINGH (RETD)*

Origins

The origins of the modern Indian Army can be traced to the armies of the East India Company (EIC), which was formed in the year 1600 via a royal charter that granted the company the rights to trade with India and East and South East Asia.[1] At the time, the EIC was one of many such European Companies jostling with each other for lucrative trade opportunities in these regions.

By the end of the seventeenth century and in the early eighteenth century, it was primarily the British and the French that were engaged in attempts to gain control in the Indian Subcontinent, especially in the twilight of the once-mighty Mughal Empire. 'The outbreak of war with France in 1744 (War of Austrian Succession 1742–1748)...led to a prolonged military and diplomatic conflict in which the English and the French vied to gain the upper hand in the Carnatic and Hyderabad by intervening or taking opposing sides in local dynastic rivalries.'[2] Beginning with control of Bengal after the Battle of Plassey in 1757, the British had, by the end

*In this co-authored chapter, the segment titled 'Regimental System of the Indian Army' has been authored by Col PK Gautam (Retd), and the segment on 'Contribution to Freedom Struggle' has been authored by Maj Gen VK Singh (Retd).

of the century, wrested control of the Peninsula after the defeat of Tipu Sultan and the French in the Anglo-Carnatic Wars. Thus, at the end of the eighteenth century, the British were the dominant European power, with 'two discoveries' being 'central to their ultimate success: first, a few disciplined British troops could defeat large but disorganized Indian armies; second, Indians themselves were amenable to discipline.'[3]

The earliest British Forces in India were largely private, raised by the forerunners of the EIC.[4] It was the French, however, rather than the British that were the first to train and use Indians in European methods of war. The lineage of the present Indian Army can be traced back to the mid-1700s, and the East India Company units which were raised by Major Stringer Lawrence[5], who emulated French practices and 'established regular Companies which were led by British officers....The British recruited additional sepoy units until a total of 9,000 were in use in 1765, grouped into atleast seven Battalions, and divided into numerous Companies of atleast a hundred men.'[6] Indian Battalions were formed into Brigades, with Indian troops and British or European officers. Indian officers in the ranks of Subedar, assisted by a Jamadar, were allowed to command the Companies, while power and responsibilities remained with British officers above them.

The three Presidencies of Bengal, Madras and Bombay had their own armies with their own areas of recruitment. In 1796, a reorganisation of these was undertaken, and the numbers are as given in Table 1.1.[7]

The 1796 reorganisation saw the formation of the Indian Cavalry 'into a Cavalry Brigade and declared a distinct service...'[8] The Regimental system also came into existence with the Infantry undergoing the formation of double Battalion Regiments; the existing 36 Regiments of the Bengal Army, for example, were 'formed into 12 Regiments of two Battalions each.'[9] Artillery Battalions were also formed, which were composed mainly of European gunmen and Indian lascars and syces.

In the first half of the nineteenth century, the British consolidated their position in India further. Wars were fought with the Marathas, the Nepalese and the Sikh Empire led by Maharaja Ranjit Singh. The British adopted a policy of co-opting troops that the British had fought in these wars, after the cessation of conflict. For example, after the Anglo-Nepalese War/s in 1815, Gurkhas began to be recruited into the Army. The Sikhs were similarly recruited after the Anglo-Sikh Wars and the death of Maharaja Ranjit Singh. Over time, Punjab became one of the key areas from which the British recruited troops into the Army.

By mid-century, a large part of the subcontinent was, directly or indirectly, under British control. 'The strength of the armies [too] had grown substantially [in the first half of the nineteenth century], and by early 1857 were as given in Table 1.2.[10]

In this time, there was further reorganisation and change in areas of recruitment depending on particular situations. After the Vellore Mutiny in 1806 in the Madras Presidency, in which Infantry Battalions mutinied over the introduction of leather

Table 1.1 Presidency Armies around 1796

Composition	Number
European Soldiers (King's and Company's)	13,000
Indian Soldiers (Bengal Presidency)	24,000
Indian Soldiers (Madras Presidency)	24,000
Indian Soldiers (Bombay Presidency)	9,000

Table 1.2 Composition of Armies in the mid-Nineteenth Century

Composition	Number
Bengal Army	1,37,500
Additional local contingents	40,000
Madras Army	49,000
Armed Police	39,000
Bombay Army	48,000
Total	3,13,500
Total European Troops	38,000

headgear, the British began to recruit in large numbers from the areas of Awadh and Bihar/Bengal, which is reflected in the size of the Bengal Army as given in Table 1.2. Patterns of recruitment, however, differed in the three armies. According to Cohen, the Bengal Army saw significant recruitment of 'high-caste Hindus' and before the Mutiny had '74 regular Infantry Battalions recruited mainly from Bihar, Oudh and Agra, with a few Gurkha units. Madras had 57 Infantry Battalions which were drawn entirely from the Presidency of Madras. Both in Madras and Bombay troops were of all castes, heterogeneously mixed together.'[11]

The uprising of 1857, also termed by some historians as the First War of Independence, began with the revolt of troops at Meerut on 10 May 1857, ostensibly owing to rumours that the cartridges being used in the new rifles were greased with cow and pig fat, both of which were anathema to Hindu and Muslim troops in the Army. This led to the outbreak of other rebellions and mutinies across Northern and central India, especially the region of the Indo-Gangetic plains, from where the Bengal Army was recruited. The uprising's end in 1858 saw a number of administrative changes taking place in India. The rule of the EIC came to an end and the governance and administration of India was formally taken over by the British Crown.

Reorganisation of the Presidency armies was but inevitable in the aftermath of 1857. The 'distinction between the "royal troops" (loaned to the [EIC]) and the [EIC's] own troops' was to be done away with and these troops were to be amalgamated into the British Army as Regiments.[12] The Peel Commission in 1858 suggested that the Indian Army be composed of Indian troops, but the proportion of these troops to British troops was to be 2:1. The Artillery was to remain in British hands. 'The Commission envisaged an Army of a maximum of 190,000 Indian troops and 80,000 British troops...after the reorganization was complete in 1863, the actual number were 135,000 Indian troops and 62,000 British troops.'[13] The proportion remained until the First World War in 1914. Recruitment patterns, too, became concentrated from those areas that had not rebelled in 1857. Punjab remained a major recruiting area for the Army. The experience of 1857 meant that the British increasingly built in a number of checks and balances to ensure that such an event would not occur in the future.

From the mid-1800s till World War I, the Indian Army was engaged in a number of conflicts in service of the British Empire. Increasingly, as the British expanded the frontiers of empire in the subcontinent and beyond, Indian soldiers of the Army participated in a number of campaigns and expeditions in China, Abyssinia, on the North West Frontier, and in Afghanistan (see Chapter 2). According to Kaushik Roy and Gavin Rand, the 'Indian Army... played a crucial role in projecting and asserting British imperial power beyond South Asia...'[14] The Indian Army allowed the British to consolidate the empire. While 'Colonial recruiting drew from a pre-existing military labour market...the scale and duration of the Raj's demand for military labour helped to incentivize and also to concretize the martial identities of various South Asian communities, including the Sikhs, Gurkhas and Pathans.'[15]

By the end of the nineteenth century, there were tentative moves towards Indianization. The first move towards recruiting Indians as commissioned officers was taken in 1901 with the establishment of the Imperial Cadet Corps. Members of Princely and noble families were imparted training for the purpose and the Royal Indian Military College (the present Rashtriya Indian Military College [RIMC]) was established for the purpose. A total of 78 Imperial Cadets were trained from various princely states until the disbandment of the Corps in 1914.[16]

> In 1902-03, a further restructuring of the Army took place under the leadership of General Horatio Herbert Kitchener, Commander in Chief of the Indian Army from 1902-1909, which remained in place till 1914. Briefly, the changes brought about by Kitchener included the following: One of [Kitchener's] first reforms was to reequip the Indian Army with the Lee Enfield Mk.1 .303 magazine rifle. With an acknowledgment of the Indian Army's requirements along the Afghan frontier, he also replaced the old 2.5-inch mountain gun with the new 2.75-inch mountain gun, a mobile gun that fired a heavier 10-pound shell 6,000 yards and broke up into five mule-transportable loads. In addition to equipment changes, Kitchener restructured the Army into nine Divisions,

> divided between two Commands, Northern and Southern, the latter having four Divisions and the former five. He renumbered the Regiments, eliminated defective ones, and dropped the old designations of Bombay, Calcutta, and Madras from the regimental titles.[17] He initiated Brigade- and division-scale weeklong training maneuvers with senior Commanders in attendance to supervise the training.[18]

'In 1906, during a meeting to coordinate the practices of the British Home Army and the Indian Army, many members of the Army Council favoured dividing the British and Continental armies into larger Divisions similar to those in India since they were regarded as being more flexible and better suited to the British military's imperial requirements.'[19] The Indian General Staff was established in 1910; by 1911, it was decided that military training would be standardised throughout the British Empire.

Kitchener's tenure coincided with that of Lord Curzon as Viceroy and was witness to a bitter civil-military dispute. According to Cohen, Kitchener and Curzon 'disagreed sharply' over the military's role in India. '[Both] attempted to reconcile civilian control with military efficiency, but proceeded to argue from very different assumptions...The overt point of disagreement...was the relative power and influence of the Military Member of the Viceroy's Council.'[20] According to Cohen, the British legacy was 'a theory of civil-military relations which placed great stress on "separate spheres" of military and civilian influence, while ultimate civilian control was always acknowledged.'[21] 'The critical weakness in British civil-military relations in India [however] was the failure to set down firm guidelines defining the military sphere and the civilian sphere, and determining *who* is to indicate when the line between civil and military has shifted.'[22] The ramifications of this continue to be felt in independent India, in the Higher Defence Organisation that evolved Post-Independence and in civil-military relations.

In the lead-up to World War I in 1914, the Indian Army numbered some 150,000 men. It was a professional, organised and disciplined force. Its mandate was limited to participating in Colonial projects of the empire beyond the subcontinent, as has been mentioned above, and to police the North West Frontier, beyond which Britain was engaged in a 'Great Game' with the Russian Empire. Kitchener's reforms in the first decade of the twentieth century had '...organized the Army into nine Divisions under two command headquarters. About a fifth of the Army was Cavalry.... The Infantry were experts at mountain warfare...but lacked experience of modern war. [They] were equipped with rifles, a generation behind that of the British Army and had only two machine guns per Battalion. There was no regimental system as at present... [and] had no Artillery other than a few mountain batteries. There were Pioneers and Sappers but not much of the other arms and services. There was no motor transport and the Army depended on animal transport for carrying its stores.'[23]

The assassination of the Archduke Franz Ferdinand, the heir apparent to the throne of the Austro-Hungarian empire in Sarajevo on 24 June 1914 was the trigger for the war. Among its long-term causes were a series of political and military alliances in the aftermath of the Napoleonic Wars in Europe, the emergence of a unified Germany that sought to race other European powers for colonies, a military arms and naval race between European powers, increasing industrialization and growing economic and military power, and political crises in the Balkans. Great Britain formally entered the war on 04 August 1914. And with it, so did its empire.

The Indian Army went to war in 1914, and served in Europe in France and Belgium, in Gallipoli, East Africa, Mesopotamia, Egypt and Palestine, Persia and in North China. By the end of the war, the Army of 150,000 men had expanded to over one million men. The war thrust the Indian Army into the modern age and it distinguished itself over the course of the next four years. In the aftermath of the war, the Army was reduced in size and went back to its policing duties in the subcontinent. In 1939, the Indian Army was once again called to war as World War II broke out in Europe. Over the next six years, the Indian Army fought in every major battle and campaign in Europe, North Africa, Burma and Indo-China. It was the largest volunteer Army ever to fight in a war with over two and half million men recruited during the war. The impact of World War II on the Indian Army was significant. The war saw the '…rapid expansion of the Army and led to the theory of "martial classes" being discarded; recruitment was thrown open to the whole of India. Recruitment to the officer cadre was also thrown open and Indianisation gained a fillip.'[24]

By 1947, a mere two years after the end of the war, India had moved towards gaining Independence from Great Britain. But with Independence came the partition of the subcontinent and the emergence of two successor states: India and Pakistan. Along with territorial partition and the subsequent movement of masses of people across new borders, the modern, professional and battle-experienced Army would also be divided between the two new nations.

The Indian Army Since 1947

The end of World War II in 1945 signalled the beginning of a new era. It was apparent during the course of the war that Britain would no longer be able to hold on to its empire/dominions in the aftermath of the war. The first of its colonies to declare Independence was India, which gained Independence formally from the British Empire in August 1947. Independence, however, came at a cost—the subcontinent was to be partitioned into two nations, India and Pakistan. Along with the partition, the armed forces were also to be divided between the newly independent countries of India and Pakistan. This was to take place simultaneously with the movement of masses of civilian population between the two countries, a time of great strife.

The division of the Indian Army itself was a task of mammoth proportions. It was agreed that by 15 August 1947, India and Pakistan should each have, within their territories, effective forces predominantly of non-Muslims and Muslims, respectively, under their own control. A large portion of the Army consisted of mixed classes and involved a major re-Organisation of practically all units, which were cantoned on an all-India basis. Both Dominions selected Commanders-in-Chief (Cs-in-C) of the Army, Navy and Air Force from amongst British officers, to be directly responsible to them and to exercise executive control of all forces located in their territory after 15 August. The Navy and the Air Force did not pose a serious problem due to their small size, but the Indian Army had swelled during the Second World War to a massive 2.5 million men.

An Armed Forces Reconstitution Committee, with representatives of India and Pakistan, was set up under the Chairmanship of Field Marshal Auchinleck for the purpose, to divide the units and stores in the ratio of 2:1 between India and Pakistan, respectively. As the Supreme Commander of the Pre-Independence Indian Army, Auchinleck was made responsible for the division and dispatch of units and stores to reach their allotted dominions on a timed programme. Most of the Army units contained men of different classes and religion at the sub-unit level. Under the Army Partition Scheme, a Muslim soldier/officer domiciled in Pakistan and a non-Muslim domiciled in the rest of India had no choice other than to serve his respective dominion. A Muslim from India or a non-Muslim from Pakistan could, however, elect which dominion he would serve. The task was stupendous and time woefully short. Moreover, given the size of the new countries, the proportion of armed forces retained by each was in the ratio of 2:1, with India retaining the larger chunk of both officers and soldiers at the end of the division.

It was soon clear that the task of moving troops and stores could not be completed by 15 August 1947. The time schedule was further delayed due to complete breakdown of law and order in the aftermath of Independence, the unforeseen mass migration of minorities in Punjab and Bengal, and the inadequacy of the railways. The problem was compounded by large numbers of demobilised soldiers who retained the combat experience they had gained during the war. And almost immediately, India was embroiled in a 14-month long conflict with Pakistan over the territory of Jammu & Kashmir (J&K). Soon after Independence in 1947, hordes of tribals ('lashkars') from the North West Frontier Province (NWFP) in Pakistan, were infiltrated into J&K as part of Operation Gulmarg. By late 1947, the lashkars were virtually at the gates of Srinagar. The actions by Pakistan led the ruler of J&K, Maharaja Hari Singh, to sign the Instrument of Accession with India and seek New Delhi's help in dealing with the situation. The Indian Army, along with the Indian Air Force, was dispatched to Srinagar to deal with the situation.

The war in 1947–48 is a saga of bold actions led by aggressive and highly professional Commanders (see Chapter 3). The reactions of the Indian Army were spontaneous, quick and responsive to a highly fluid situation, reflecting on the skill, motivation and morale of a fledging and nascent Indian Army, called to save its motherland at its very inception. Although the actions in 1947–48 were predominantly Infantry-led, Commanders were innovative in their use of Artillery and tanks/Armoured cars, like the amazing feat by 7th Light Cavalry in crossing the Zoji La Pass.

In the past seven decades, the Indian Army has seen phases of consolidation, Organisational restructuring, operational and doctrinal reorientation, increased variation of roles owing to regional factors.

1950s: Consolidation

The decade of the 1950s can be viewed as a phase of consolidation for the Indian Army. With the coming into force of the Constitution of India on 26 January 1950, India became a sovereign democratic republic, with the President of India as the Supreme Commander of the Armed Forces. As with the newly independent nation, its Armed Forces too looked forward to a new beginning. In the 1950s, the Indian Army looked to expand and build structures and institutions keeping in mind the threat from Pakistan as well as the myriad needs of state building. This was also the time of a renewed focus on the Higher Defence Organisation (HDO). Newly independent India's 'strategic thinking rested on four pillars: to maintain conventional military superiority over Pakistan; to maintain friendly relations with China; to stay free of Cold War politics and entanglements; and to promote solidarity and cooperation among developing countries.'[25] This formed the context for the Army's consolidation phase.

The decade started with the successful Defence of J&K from Pakistani designs. India had also taken the momentous step of declaring itself a constitutional republic in 1950, thus setting out a clear agenda of the future. In its strategic outlook at the time, 'India's principal threat perception was from Pakistan…'.[26] At the same time, the Indian Army too was moving ahead from its pre-war role, which was in service of empire, to its role of guardians of the nation's borders in the face of a belligerent enemy. The Indian Army during World War II was a volunteer-driven Army, and its expansion at the time was necessitated by the demands of a war that spanned the globe. However, in the immediate aftermath of the war, it was downsized. In the 1950s, however, fresh from a war with Pakistan immediately upon gaining Independence from British rule, the Indian Army underwent another expansion in light of the immediate security concerns in the subcontinent. However, owing to the diplomatic endeavours of the Government of India both regionally as well as globally in the first half of the decade, 'apart from Pakistan, Indian leaders did not perceive a direct military threat to India's security from any other neighbouring state, including China.'[27]

This decade also saw India's foray into peacekeeping activities under the aegis of the United Nations (UN). The UN was formed just after the end of the Second World War, the most destructive conflict of the twentieth century at the time. India, though still under the British Crown, was an original founder member of the UN and a signatory to its charter in 1945. Its armed forces have been participating in UN Peacekeeping missions since the inception of the first UN peacekeeping mission in 1948. In the 1950s alone, the Indian Army participated in three major peacekeeping operations: Korea (1950–54), Indo-China (1954–1970), and West Asia (1956–67).[28] A few peacekeeping missions are discussed in detail in Chapter 6.

The decade of the 1950s were, however, not entirely uneventful. With the Cold War in play, the decade saw instances of conflict across the globe. Closer home, India increasingly moved towards a situation of potential conflict with the People's Republic of China (PRC). The Chinese People's Liberation Army (PLA) marched into Tibet in 1950 taking control of the region. India acknowledged Chinese control of the region in 1954 and recognised Tibet as an 'autonomous' region of China. However, as the Chinese 'gained a stranglehold on Tibet, the Dalai Lama fled to India in 1959 where he was welcomed and settled in Dharamshala. After that, relations with China deteriorated and culminated in the 1962 war.'[29]

1960s: Conflict on Two Fronts

The decade of the 1960s saw the Indian Army fight two wars on different fronts, terrains, with different outcomes for both and lessons learnt. Sino-India relations in the 1950s deteriorated considerably by the end of the decade, especially after India gave sanctuary to the Dalai Lama. Furthermore, India had inherited from the British un-demarcated boundaries with Tibet in the North and the East, which increasingly became a point of concern over the course of the decade. India and China saw border clashes in 1959 and failed diplomatic negotiations thereafter in 1960. 'In late 1961, however, the Government of India opted for…the so-called Forward Policy decision. By the middle of 1962, small numbers of lightly armed Indian Infantry established several 'forward posts' deep inside unoccupied but disputed border areas.'[30]

While the 1962 Sino-Indian conflict officially began with Chinese attacks in October of that year, events earlier in the year foretold the conflict. In early June 1962, India had established an Assam Rifles Post called 'Dhola' in the area of Bridge III on the Southern bank of Namka Chu. The Chinese reacted in September and surrounded the Indian Post. The troops of both countries ultimately came to blows resulting in casualties on both sides. Subsequently, 7 Infantry Brigade moved forward from Tawang to Namka Chu on the Indian side, with orders to evict the Chinese from Thagla Ridge. On the Chinese side, the attacking troops were already on the move to their assembly areas. The stage was now set for the events for the breakout of war on 20 October 1962 (see Chapter 3).

Soon after the war was over, Pakistan saw an opportunity to exploit the situation. By this time, Pakistan had joined the Central Treaty Organisation (CENTO) and the South East Asia Treaty Organisation (SEATO) and was firmly ensconced in the US-led bloc. Sino-Pakistan relations began to deepen in the aftermath of the 1962 war, with both seeing a common adversary in India. In 1963, Pakistan allowed China access to the Shaksgam Valley, further bolstering ties between the two countries. By 1965, the Pakistan Army felt it was opportune to attempt to wrest Kashmir from India's hands. 'The operations in J&K in August–September 1965 were preceded by the operations in Kutch which commenced in February of that year. The terrain offered advantage to Pakistan to launch offensive operations, which were soon brought to a halt by the Indian Army. As a strategic response, the Indian Army deployed on the border in Punjab and captured three Posts in Kargil on 16 and 17 May 1965. A ceasefire agreement was signed on 01 July 1965.'[31]

The main war was fought between the two countries in August-September 1965 and the Indian Army found itself stretched, for the first time, on two fronts. Operation Gibraltar was conceptualised with the objective of creating large-scale disturbances in J&K. The plan was to send about 8,000 Pakistani soldiers and Razakars into J&K disguised as guerrillas. The first phase was to create a shock wave by launching raids on selected targets, thereby preparing the ground for a civil uprising due to the chaos and consternation that would be caused in the state. The second was the fusion of the civil uprising with the infiltration operation. Operation Gibralter was combined with Operation Grand Slam, which was the plan for an Armoured thrust across the ceasefire line (CFL), with a view to capture Akhnoor, thereby threatening the line of supplies from India to Srinagar. The plan, in principle, was accepted by Field Marshal Ayub Khan in May 1965[32] and put into action in July 1965. This is discussed in greater detail in Chapter 3.

The losses incurred during the 1962 war as well as the 1965 war made the government realise the need to modernise the Army and to expand it to be able to face the threat on two fronts, Pakistan and China. Plans were thus initiated to expand the Army with six new Divisions, which would also entail increase in the manpower from 5.5 lakh to around 8.25 lakh. Scout Battalions were raised for deployment on the China border, in the Northern and Eastern Sectors. Of the six new Divisions raised initially, four were designated as Mountain Divisions and an existing Plains Division was converted into a Mountain Division. With the help of the United States (US) and the United Kingdom (UK), equipment modernisation also commenced, particularly of small arms and signal equipment. An emphasis on mountain and jungle warfare was laid. To allow for greater attention to the Eastern frontiers, Headquarters Eastern Command was moved to Calcutta (Kolkata) and a new Central Command was raised at Lucknow to cater for the threat from China. To address the need for increased requirement of officers, a scheme for Emergency Commissions was started and Officers Training Schools were opened at Madras (Chennai) and Pune to train the increased intake.

Within Army Headquarters (HQ), three important Directorates were also reorganised to entail greater efficiency. 'The Weapons and Equipment Directorate was shifted from the Master General of Ordnance to the General Staff Branch as was Military Survey from the Engineer-in-Chief Branch.'[33] Intelligence, which had emerged as a key area of concern, especially in 1962, was also addressed.

The 1965 operations had shown voids in the plains orbat, particularly in Armour, Artillery and Engineer support. The raising of the necessary units and formations was now taken into hand. The 1965 operations of the Armoured Division had brought out the incompatibility of infantry mounted on trucks accompanying tanks into battle. Steps were taken to obtain Armoured Personnel Carriers (APCs) and by 1969 the Infantry Battalion in the Armoured Division and Independent Armoured Brigades were receiving these. These Battalions are the genesis of the Mechanised Infantry Regiment that was formally raised in 1979.

On the training side, stress was laid on realistic individual and collective training. The lessons of both 1962 and 1965 were incorporated into syllabi of the various courses at schools of instruction. The Mountain formations were trained to operate on man pack and animal transport basis for limited periods and to sustain themselves when isolated. In the plains, training stressed ability and skills required to deal with Armoured attack and in Infantry-tank cooperation. The improvement in battle inoculation practices and in Army, air cooperation had already been put into practice. 'A Directorate of Combat Development was established under the General Staff Branch to review tactical concepts; develop Organisations and materials in light of new tactical concepts; and for conduct of trials in formations and experimental formations.'[34]

As a follow up of lessons learnt from the 1965 war a number of manufacturing facilities were set up; the most prominent of these were the Heavy Vehicle Factory at Avadi, near Madras to manufacture the Vijyant Main Battle Tank, and Bharat Electronics Ltd at Bangalore to manufacture communication equipment. In effect, by the end of the 1960s, the Indian Army had begun the necessary organisational changes that would take it greater heights in the coming decade. Weapons and equipment were also sought to be modernised, with moves to induct the 7.62 mm self-loading rifle, introduction of short and medium range mortars, and mountain guns with high-trajectory firing capability.

1970s: Victory and Move to Modernise

In the late 1960s, developments especially in East Pakistan, foretold of yet another war in the subcontinent. From 1947 till 1971, Pakistan comprised territories in the Western and Eastern part of the subcontinent that were culturally and linguistically different. Moreover, the population of East Pakistan was far greater in number than in the West. Elections held in December 1970 in Pakistan gave a majority to Sheikh Mujibur Rahman. The Pakistani establishment viewed with alarm the rise of Bengali nationalism in the East and moved to supress it. The Pakistan Army put into action Operation Searchlight on 25 March 1971. A genocide was conducted by the Pakistani government and Army against their own citizens. Over the course of the year, and till the outbreak of war in December, 10 million refugees poured into India, escaping the excesses of the regime. India, on its part, began preparing for war while putting in considerable diplomatic efforts to bring the events in its neighbourhood to the attention of the world. The last major war between India and Pakistan was fought from 03–16 December 1971 and led to the creation of Bangladesh (see Chapter 3). This was the Indian Armed Forces' finest hour, in particular that of the Indian Army, which had managed to throw off the yoke of defeat less than a decade previously to emerge triumphant.

Soon after the 1971 Indo-Pakistan war, Commanders down to unit level got down to review performance and conduct of operations to analyse the performance of both sides so that they could learn from the experience of victory and defeat, and to build on strengths and eliminate weaknesses. Among the major lessons that were learnt were the need for obtaining continuous intelligence about one's adversaries; the requirement for visualising the various contingencies that may arise in which the armed forces may get involved in; the need for planning and training for such contingencies in peace-time; ingenuity of plans and their dynamic execution; the use of unexpected axes of advance, outflanking envelopment including vertical envelopment of the enemy; the use of technology to improve logistics and administration and to upgrade weapons and equipment; the importance of inter-service cooperation and closer interaction with the civil services; and, most important of all, improvement in the training and morale of the officers and men of the Army. The importance of outstanding civil and military leadership was obvious.

In 1975, the Government of India constituted what came to be known as the 'Experts Committee' to go into the future of the Defence of the country, essentially undertake a long-term perspective planning exercise. The purpose behind constituting the Committee was to carry out an analysis of the changing world scenario; the need for requisite Defence preparedness to maintain credibility; the escalating Defence budget; greater sophistication of weaponry and equipment; the concurrent increase in manpower costs; the 'ad hoc' manner in which Defence matters were dealt with; and, finally, the need for ensuring maximum cost effectiveness while endeavouring to improve the fighting capacity of the Defence forces. The Experts Committee had as its Chairman Lieutenant General (Lt Gen) KV Krishna Rao with Major Generals (Maj Gen) ML Chibber and K Sundarji as members, and Brigadier (Brig) AJM Homji as secretary. The Committee was constituted with effect from 01 November 1975 and was to submit its report within nine months. The Committee decided that the time-frame for consideration should be sufficiently far ahead and should cover a period of 25 years, that is, from 1975 to 2000.

The Committee's report comprised nine volumes and covered all important aspects of Defence preparedness; threats to national interests; future strategy; force levels over different time-frames; future battlefield environment; acquisition and production of sophisticated equipment; improvement of command and control and intelligence; and measures to re-deploy resources for an improved and more cost-effective utilisation. The report's recommendations resulted in considerable improvement of the teeth-to-tail ratio and ultimate attainment of a reasonable deterrence capability, a saving of about 1 lakh personnel and 20,000 vehicles of all types within the Army, and, in the process, leading to a saving of Rs 200 crore on the initial and Rs 100 crore on the recurring expenditure.

The Experts Committee Report was, however, not properly implemented. It is only when Lt Gen KV Krishna Rao, the Chairman of the Committee, was posted as Deputy Chief of Army Staff that the recommendations began to be implemented and were dove-tailed with the 1979–84 Five Year Plan and subsequent Five Year Plans. The net effect of measures taken by Rao as Deputy Chief of Army Staff was that the teeth to tail ratio improved by approximately 70:30 and the amount spent on the Army's modernisation went up from 3 per cent to 20 per cent.

The institution of the Expert Committee in 1975 brought out for the first time the need for deliberate long-term planning. Till this time, expansions were carried out intermittently to meet unforeseen contingencies and crisis situations. The following conclusions emerged in respect of the long-term needs of the Army:

1. Adequate Infantry formations would be required to hold the Defences, take the initial brunt of the enemy's attack, contain his thrusts, and inflict maximum attrition. Sufficient mobile reserves would be needed. In the plains, they would have to be based on Armour and mechanised Infantry.
2. Sufficient strike capability based on integrated teams of Armour, Mechanised Infantry, Air Defence Artillery, Assault Engineers, and Armed Helicopters would need to be developed. Adequate vertical envelopment capability would also be required with the strike forces.
3. Close air-support, closely integrated, for both offensive and defensive operations.
4. Adequate air transport for airborne operations as well as for strategic move of troops.
5. Amphibious capability for carrying out limited amphibious operations.

6. Electronic Warfare capability to include acquisition and surveillance, guidance of weapons and communications as well as electronic and counter-counter measures and satellite surveillance.
7. Enhanced night fighting capabilities to make night fighting as efficient as that by day.
8. Logistic support to match mobility of the forces.

1980s: Challenges of Modernisation and Domestic Turmoil

Subsequent to the recommendations of the Lt Gen Krishna Rao-led Expert Committee, the Indian Army moved towards mechanisation of its forces. This was further aided by the increase in Defence expenditure. One of the first moves was the raising of the Mechanised Infantry Regiment on 02 April 1979. By the end of the 1980s, especially during the tenure of General (Gen) Sundarji as Army Chief, twentythree Mechanised Infantry Battalions had been raised, equipped with Infantry Combat Vehicles; moreover, [Sundarji's] tenure also provided moorings for the employment of these forces.'[35] The Army Aviation Corps was raised in 1986, in keeping with the requirements of modernisation and technological innovation. Additionally, the decade saw the induction of the 155mm Bofors gun, for the Infantry Division as an Air Assault Division and [the] raising of Reorganised Army Plains Infantry Division (RAPID) with an enhanced component of Armour and mechanised Infantry.'[36]

The 1980s saw the implementation of futuristic Organisational changes in the Indian Army. 'The impact of [Gen] Sundarji's drive, strategic vision and close working relationship with the [Government] created substantial changes in the Army's Organisational structure. Besides the acquisition of assets, it laid the foundation for mobile warfare and simultaneously propelled a change in the thinking of the Army's leadership. These were based on a change in the Army's doctrine as well. This shifted from defensive deterrence, witnessed prior to the 1971 war, to "deterrence by punishment" during the 1980s, bordering on compellence. This shift reflected the signs of a changing strategic culture in the Army, which was injected by offensive thinking and a more robust approach to potential adversaries.'[37]

The tenure of Gen Sundarji as the Chief of Army Staff also saw the beginnings of what would eventually evolve into the 'Cold Start' doctrine.[38] In 1986, the Army undertook a massive exercise in the Western Sector—Operation Brasstacks—to gauge the viability of this doctrine. This was in line with a more assertive approach of the Army as a whole, reflecting both in the long-term planning undertaken by HQ and the modernisation undertaken at the Organisational level.

India's extended neighbourhood saw turmoil in this decade, with the Iranian Revolution in 1979 followed by the eight year-long Iran-Iraq War. The year also saw the Soviet Union invade Afghanistan ostensibly to aid the Communist Government in Kabul in its fight with anti-Communist guerrillas. The war in Afghanistan would lead to the eventual disintegration of the Soviet Union as also provide Pakistan with the means and ability to rebound from its defeat in 1971. Domestically too, events were occurring that had a profound impact on the Indian Army in the twentieth century. By the late 1970s, reports began to emerge of Pakistani activities in the region of the Siachen glacier and the surrounding mountains. Meanwhile, in J&K itself, a movement had started for the establishment of madarsas teaching a fundamentalist version of Islam as opposed to the Sufi tradition based on a tolerant Islam, which was prevalent till then in the Valley. There was also a growing resentment and disillusionment with the government led by Farooq Abdullah. In Punjab, militancy was at its peak. In the North-East, the All Assam Students Union started an agitation against 'foreigners', that is, any non-Assamese residing in the state as also for greater autonomy. In neighbouring Sri Lanka, long-standing political differences between the Sinhala and Tamil populations led to the start of a violent movement for Tamil Eelam or Tamil homeland in 1975. While still at a reasonably low-key level in 1981, this Tamil movement had numerous sympathisers in Tamil Nadu. In 1987, under the mandate of the Indo-Sri Lanka Accord, India undertook a peacekeeping operation in Sri Lanka with the aim to disarm various military groups that were involved in the conflict. The Indian Army was a key part of the Indian Peace Keeping Force (IPKF). The IPKF was soon involved in a battle with the LTTE in contravention to its initially envisaged role (see Chapter 5).

One of the most significant operations that the Indian Army was involved in in this decade was the control of the Siachen Glacier (Operation Meghdoot, see Chapter 5). In April 1984, reports of Pakistani attempts to control the glacier was countered with Indian troops landing near Bilafond La, a pass on the Saltoro ridge, West of the Siachen glacier. The origin of the dispute lies in differing interpretations by both sides of the alignment of the un-demarcated portion of the Line of Control established by the Shimla Agreement signed on 02 July 1972 after the 1971 Indo-Pakistan War. In January 1985, Pakistan launched an attack to try and capture Bilafond La but failed. A similar effort in February 1985 to occupy the heights overlooking Sia La was also foiled. In late March/early April 1987 the Pakistani Special Services Group (SSG) occupied a position overlooking the Bilafond La area at a height of 21,156 ft atop a vertical cliff. The occupation came to light when Indian helicopters approaching Bilafond La came under fire from the post, which was called the Quaid Post. The Indian Army launched an operation to wrest control of the post. On the night of 25–26 June 1987, a force of one JCO and six other ranks inched forward and attacked the post with grenades and small arms fire. Naib Subedar Bana Singh of 8 JAK LI who led the assault was awarded the Param Vir Chakra and the post was renamed as Bana Post.

In 1987, a standoff ensued between Indian and Chinese troops at Sumdorong Chu. In the midst of the standoff, the Indian Army conducted Operation Chequerboard, a high-altitude military exercise along the Sino-Indian border in the North-East of the country. The exercise involved ten Divisions of the Army as well as a number of Indian Air Force (IAF) Squadrons. There was a de-escalation by both sides and the resumption of dialogue between India and China, which had been in cold storage for over 20 years. This was followed by the visit of then Prime Minister Rajiv Gandhi to Beijing in 1988.

By the end of the decade, Pakistan had fine-tuned its strategy of 'bleeding India with a thousand cuts'. The flames of political turmoil in the Kashmir Valley were sought to be fanned and the Pakistani Inter-Services Intelligence (ISI), fresh from its successes in Afghanistan, opened a new chapter of asymmetrical warfare against India with Operation Tupac.

1990s: Internal Security Gains Momentum

The primary task of the Army is to defend India's borders, though as part of the military arm of the state it can be (and has been) called in to aid civilian authorities as well as the government in times of crisis. In light of the growing militancy in Kashmir in the early 1990s, encouraged and supported by Pakistan, in this decade the internal security (IS) duties of the Indian Army increased manifold. To address this, the Rashtriya Rifles (RR) was created to handle this aspect. 'The RR units were raised late in 1990 by the then Army Chief Gen V N Sharma with Lt Gen P C Mankotia as its first Director-General. Initially, there were six such Battalions, three in J&K and three in Punjab. Later, all the Rashtriya Rifles Battalions were moved to Jammu and Kashmir as the valley got entangled in a bloody conflict with Pakistan-trained militants creating havoc in the region.'[39] As of today, the RR has 63 Battalions.

As mentioned earlier, the Indian Army was divided in 1947 between India and Pakistan. Steven I. Wilkinson contends that the '...socioeconomic, strategic, and (especially) military inheritance that Pakistan received in 1947...' was worse than what India received. This was '...in its trained officers and officials, state institutions, Army and the stocks of capital and goods it received as part of the division of the country.'[40] Added to that were the Pakistan Army and political establishment's aims being thwarted by the Indian Army in 1947–48, 1965 and in 1971, when the country was dismembered with the creation of Bangladesh. With the coming to power of General Mohammad Zia-ul-Haq in Pakistan in 1977, the process of Islamisation of the military and society was championed. Further, given the Pakistan military's obvious asymmetry with India, with its larger and more superior military force, a policy of asymmetrical warfare against India was adopted. The thwarting of its ambitions in Siachen in the 1980s only added to the above.

Operation Topac, initiated in 1980s under Gen Zia-ul-Haq but conducted mostly after his death in a plane crash in 1988, is a military intelligence operation conceived to foment unrest in the Kashmir Valley by providing support to separatists and militants. The programme has been run by the Pakistani ISI. The stated aim was to aid separatist forces in the Valley. The operation took advantage of political turmoil in the Valley in the late 1980s. 'The aim was to annex the state of J&K through a proxy war by infiltrating militants to foment trouble in the state under the garb of a jehad, take militancy to uncontrollable levels, and, at an opportune time, strike with regulars, if necessary to finally integrate J&K with Pakistan.'[41] Estimates suggest that around '15,000-20,000 persons exfiltrated from J&K to POK [Pakistan Occupied Kashmir]/Pakistan for arms training in 1987–1988.'[42] The intent was to support a low-level insurgency and the Pakistan Army had established contact with the Jammu and Kashmir Liberation Front (JKLF), 'which agreed to cooperate on the condition that Kashmir would be granted Independence soon after Indian control ceased on the state.'[43] As the war in Afghanistan wound down in the early 1990s, fighters moved into Kashmir adding to the growing levels of insurgency. Pakistan too scaled up the insurgency infrastructure between 1990–1994, and provided insurgents with sophisticated weaponry and training.

Beginning January 1990, militants began targeting the minority Kashmiri Pandit population, which resulted in an exodus of Pandits from the Valley. The civil administration and law and order had virtually collapsed in the state. The mantle of countering the growing insurgency in Kashmir thus fell on the Indian Army, especially on the 15 and 16 Corps. Aiding the Army in this endeavour were the RR Battalions, CRPF and BSF also contributed. Insurgency in the Valley peaked around the mid-1990s and saw a declining trend thereafter. However, India and Pakistan would soon see yet another conflict before the end of the decade.

On 11 May 1998, India conducted a nuclear test in the Pokhran range in Rajasthan. Pokharan II not only advertised India's status as a nuclear power, it impacted regional geopolitics in a major way. Pakistan, India's all-weather rival in South Asia, followed by conducting its own nuclear test. The conduct of nuclear tests in 1998 not only made South Asia a nuclearised zone, it also meant that any military conflict between India and Pakistan would now be conducted under a 'nuclear overhang'. The spectre of two nuclear armed countries going to war was a matter of deep concern both regionally and globally.

The nuclear tests of 1998 marked a significant shift in the context of conflict and warfare in the subcontinent: not only was there now a nuclear overhang, given the rapidly changing technology as well as its adoption by militaries, the character of war also underwent change. With nuclear deterrence in the fray, the likelihood of large-scale conventional wars between the two countries took a backseat. What was expected was short, localised and intense technologically-driven campaigns.

And Pakistan's actions in the summer of 1999 in the Kargil sector was a real time example.

Pakistan's domestic politics have been tenuous since its creation. Beginning in the 1950s with the military coup by Gen Ayub Khan, Pakistani politics see-sawed between civilian and military rule. After the death of Gen Zia-ul-Haq in 1988, the reins of power in Islamabad passed between the premiership of Benazir Bhutto of the Pakistan People's Party (PPP) and Nawaz Sharif of the Pakistan Muslim League (PML). In February 1999, the premiers of India and Pakistan, Atal Bihari Vajpayee and Nawaz Sharif signed the Lahore Declaration seeking to regulate the development of nuclear weapons and avoid accidental or unauthorised operational use of such weapons. However, the Pakistan Army had different plans.

In 1998, the Pakistan Army surreptitiously occupied the vacated winter posts of the Indian Army in the Kargil sector of the Line of Control (LOC). The aim was to cut the link between Kashmir and Ladakh, to isolate Indian Army troops on the Siachen Glacier, and force India to negotiate a settlement of the Kashmir dispute.[44] The Pakistani intrusions were detected on 03 May 1999, when local shepherds reported the intrusion of armed men into the area of 3 PUNJAB, the Indian Army unit stationed there. 3 PUNJAB launched a series of patrols and confirmed the intrusions. On 5 May 1999, Operation Vijay was launched to evict the Pakistanis from Indian territory. Two months of violent confrontation later, a ceasefire was declared on 26 July 1999. The Kargil intrusion was yet another attempt by the Pakistan Army, under the leadership of General Pervez Musharraf to change the position of the LOC, but was thwarted by the stellar role played by the Indian Army, along with the IAF and the Indian Navy.

Operation Vijay was virtually fought live on television. The events in Kargil not only 'captured the imagination of people in India, the conflict also raised the morale of the armed forces…firing an entire generation of soldiers.'[45]

In October 1999, a few months after seeing defeat in Kargil, General Pervez Musharraf engineered a coup against the Nawaz Sharif government. The Prime Minister was exiled to Saudi Arabia and the Pakistan Army under Musharraf again took the centre-stage in Pakistani politics.

2000s: Indian Army in the New Millennium

In the aftermath of the successful execution of Operation Vijay, some key issues, including that of intelligence and on-the-ground surveillance in the region of the LOC, emerged as areas of concern.[46] In the aftermath of Kargil, the government undertook an exercise of assessment of events in the summer of 1999 by appointing a review committee headed by K Subhramanyam, with Lieutenant General KK Hazari (Retd), BG Verghese and Satish Chandra, Secretary, National Security Council

Secretariat (NSCS) as the other members. Chandra was also designated as Member-Secretary. The terms of reference of the Committee were:[47]

1. To review the events leading up to the Pakistani aggression in the Kargil District of Ladakh in Jammu & Kashmir; and
2. To recommend such measures as are considered necessary to safeguard national security against such armed intrusions.

Since Kargil also included an element of information warfare, the Kargil Review Committee Report also evaluated '...the information and media component. This was followed by a Group of Ministers report, which addressed a number of issues that had been raised during the course of deliberations. The major ones in the Kargil Review Committee report included:

1. Enhance capacity of media cells at Army formations such as Udhampur and Srinagar.
2. Recommence the war correspondent's course.
3. Incorporate modules on information operations and perception management in courses.
4. Establishment of dedicated radio and TV channels to entertain armed forces personnel. These can also counter false propaganda of the adversary.
5. The government must evolve procedures to keep the people informed on important national security issues.
6. Need to come up with official history of the Kargil conflict and India's nuclear weapons programme.'[48]

Subsequent to other recommendations of the KRC and the Group of Ministers, the decade saw significant moves towards jointness/integration of the three Services. The Integrated Headquarters (IHQ) was established at the Ministry of Defence (MoD) as part of the reorganisation of Army HQ for closer integration with the ministry. Also established were the Strategic Forces Command, Cyber Command, Special Forces Command, and the Tri-Service Andaman and Nicobar Command. One of the recommendations of the Kargil Review Committee, and the subsequent Naresh Chandra Committee was the appointment of the Chief of Defence Staff (CDS), as a single point military advisor to the government. This was finally undertaken in 2018, with the appointment of Gen Bipin Rawat as the first CDS. Prior to Gen Rawat's appointment, the Chiefs of Staff Committee (COSC) functioned as the apex military advisory position, and was helmed in rotation by the longest serving Service Chief.

Militaries as a rule are not amenable to change in the status quo, so along with the moves to integrate there were inter-Services turf battles. It remains a fact that given India's vast and adversarial land borders, the Indian Army remains the largest of the three Services. Also, despite a renewed maritime focus since the 1990s and particularly in the 2000s, events such as Kargil and China flexing its muscles on the border with India means that the Army would continue to remain the largest and most important Service.

On 13 December 2001, a couple of months after an attack on the J&K Assembly, gun-totting terrorists attacked the Indian Parliament in New Delhi. This brought India and Pakistan to the brink of war with the launch of Operation Parakram. This was the largest mobilisation of Indian forces, especially on land, since Operation Brasstacks in the 1980s. Operation Parakram continued for a period of 21 months but at the end both sides backed down.

2010–2020: Looking to the Future

Technology has a momentum of its own. This is especially pertinent to military technology as obsolescence sets in rapidly. It is a dictum that the Army is trained to fight the previous war and this becomes an area of urgent consideration in light of the rapidity with which warfare is becoming technology-driven. Pre-1991, a large segment of military technology manufactured indigenously and also used by the various Services was of Russian origin. While a significant push was given to indigenisation in this decade, the dependence of the Indian military on Russian hardware continues. Yet, in this decade we see an increased variation in the import of technology and military hardware, and a greater leaning away from Russia and towards the West.

The Army, in particular, moved from a defensive orientation to a more aggressive posturing. This was both necessitated by operating in the grey zone as well as directed by clear political direction. The 2016 surgical strikes are an example of this changed mindset. China continues to be the key adversary for India on the Northern front, as evidenced by various instances of its trying to alter the status quo on the Line of Actual Control (LAC), the most recent of which took place in Galwan in 2020, at the height of the Covid-19 pandemic.

In terms of HDO, structurally, the move towards integration has received a fillip. With the appointment of the CDS in 2018, a new Department of Military Affairs was created in the MoD. Military thinking and doctrinal outlook today increasingly points towards integration, as stated in the 2017 Joint Doctrine for the Indian Armed Forces, prepared by HQ IDS.

This decade also saw the raising of 17 Corps, headquartered at Panagarh in West Bengal. This is a Mountain Strike Corps built as a quick reaction force and a counter to China. On the side, the debate continues on the scaling up of the Army in light of the increasing threat from China and downsizing caused by adoption of and improvement in technology as well as budgetary constraints.

Following the brief introduction of the Indian Army's history and evolution into a modern fighting force in the seven and a half decades since Independence, we will now take a look at the Organisational underpinnings and traditions that make this vast Organisation a cohesive whole. A little known, but important, part of the Army's history—its contribution to the freedom struggle—is also elucidated.

Regimental System in the Indian Army[49]

The military in any modern state is a key component of the constituent elements of that state. In the case of a multi-ethnic, plural and democratic polity like India, its armed forces, and in particular the Indian Army, mirrors the diverse society that constitutes the nation.

Factors such as Revolution in Military Affairs (RMA), precision firepower, network-centric warfare, command, control, communications, computer, intelligence and interoperability (C4I2), military-industrial complex, space, nuclear weapons and means of delivery, missile, chemical and biological Defence, nano-technologies and other emerging technologies are important 'hard' factors that are fundamental to the strength of a military Organisation. Simultaneously, the presence and use of 'soft' or non-material factors such as the human resource, composition, and Organisation are equally important.

The units of all the Regiments and Corps of the Indian Army are the building blocks of motivation and fighting spirit. It can be said that the ethos of the Regimental System is the soul of the Indian Army. This glue that binds the spirt is best known and evolved trinity of *Naam* (Honour), *Namak* (Loyalty) and *Nishan* (espirit-de-corps). All ranks are devoted to their units and perform their duties in the unique Indic philosophy of *Nishkam Karma* and propelled by the tradition of the motto of the Indian National Army's greeting of *Jai Hind* and the values of *Itteefaq* (unity), *Etmad* (confidence), and *Qurbani* (sacrifice).

Combat-Effectiveness and Structure

War demands that an Army must be capable of both maintaining Defence as well as the ability to attack in all types of terrain and conditions. Military capacity implies both firepower, manoeuvre, and sustaining of operations, thus all units of the Army must be combat-effective. Combat effectiveness is defined as an assessment of the effectiveness of a unit or formation in fulfilling its mission in battle. It is a product of its Organisation, state of weapons, equipment, training, morale and leadership. In other words, 'the only sure measure of combat-effectiveness is the performance of unit in combat'.[50]

Thus, in order to have the 'right' military capacity and effectiveness, an institution like the Army needs to be organised with the appropriate manpower, equipped with various weapon systems, and supported by services which look after the administration and logistical functions which will enable it to perform its tactical role. In a nutshell, this military system and Organisation can be divided into three categories: combat arms, combat support arms, and services. Figure 1.1 depicts the Organisational structure of the Indian Army.

Combat Arms

The combat arms comprise of the Infantry (basically a flexible foot-based Organisation armed with integral weapons systems); the Mechanised Infantry in Armoured Personal Carriers; and the Armoured Corps, with the Main Battle Tanks. The President's Body Guard and 61 Cavalry being the only Horse Cavalry unit in the Indian Army, which largely has a ceremonial role; however, it may also be used, if need be, in war-like situation.

Combat Support Arms

The combat support arms in the Indian Army comprise of Regiments and Corps such as the Regiment of Artillery, the Corps of Army Air Defence, the Corps of Engineers, and the Corps of Signals.

Services

It is axiomatic that an Army is like a society, self-contained in all respects. Thus, the famous saying that 'an Army marches on its stomach'. For the logistic and administrative needs the Indian Army has a variety of services, including Army Service Corps, Army Medical Corps, Army Dental Corps, Military Nursing Service, Army Ordnance Corps, Corps of Electronics and Mechanical Engineers, Remount and Veterinary Corps, Army Education Corps, Corps of Military Police, Pioneer Corps, Army Postal Service Corps, Defence Security Corps, Intelligence Corps, and the Judge Advocate General's Department.

Unit or Battalion Level Structure

The building block of the Indian Army is based on a 'unit'. For example, in an Infantry Battalion, or an Armoured/Artillery/Engineer Regiment (unit), three to four sub-units called 'Companies', 'Squadrons' or 'Batteries' form one unit. The sub-units

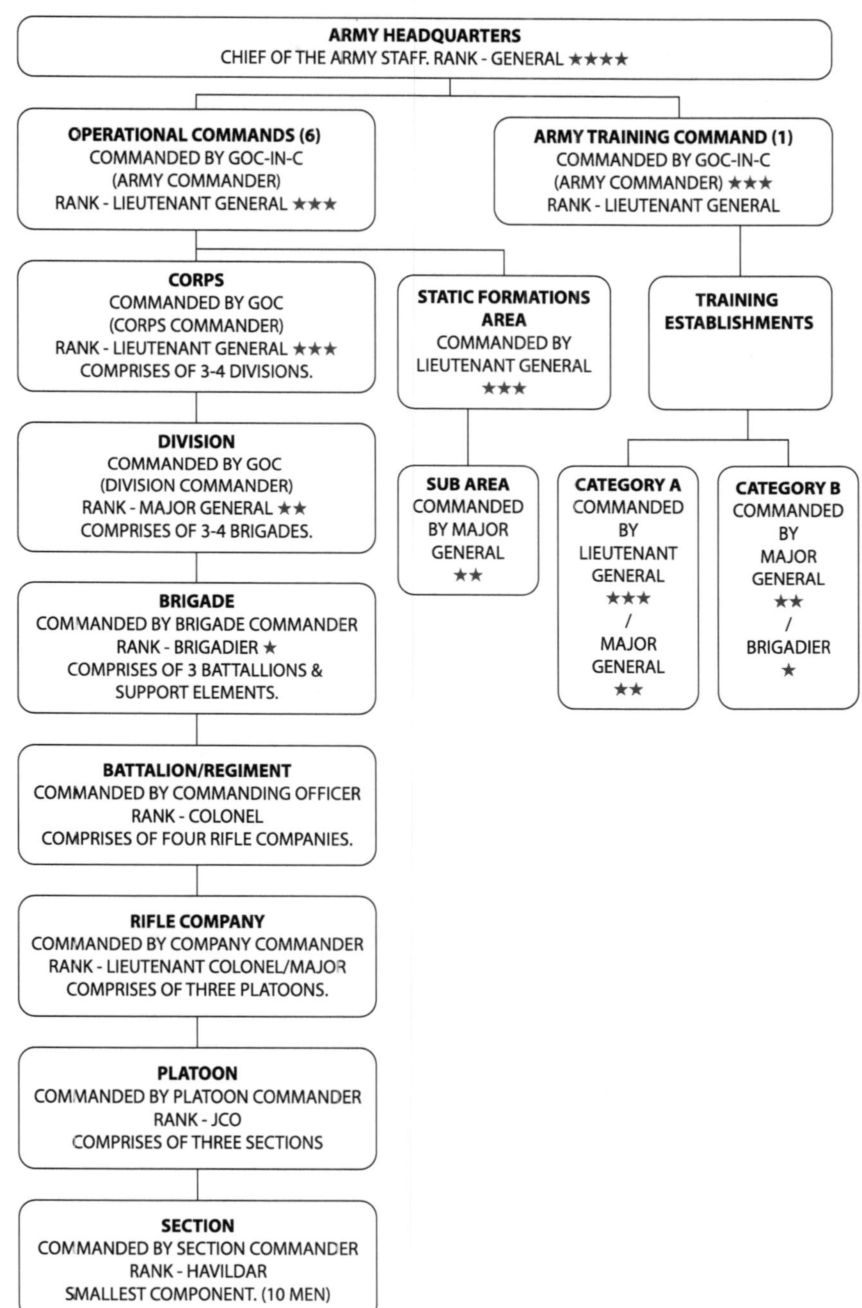

Figure 1.1 Structure of the Indian Army[51]

are commanded by Lieutenant Colonels/Majors and the units are commanded by a Colonel. A Brigade has three to four such units under its command. A Division comprises three to four Brigades along with units from other arms and services. A Corps has three or four Divisions under its command. An Army Command, for example, the Western or Eastern or Northern Command, may comprise of two or three Corps. All Army Field Commands come under the Army HQ (see Figure 1).

The strength of an Infantry Battalion (unit) is about 700 to 800 (all ranks). A rifle Company numbers about 120 soldiers. An Artillery battery comprises six guns and over 100 soldiers (all ranks). Three batteries form a Regiment (unit). An Armoured regiment has 45 tanks, divided in three sabre and one HQ Squadron, while a mechanised Infantry Battalion is equipped with 52 Infantry Combat Vehicles.

Units of the Infantry, Armoured Corps, Artillery, Army Air Defence and Engineers are based on the Regimental system, where an officer and other ranks (ORs) are assigned to a unit for their entire career. The unit moves on transfer en block. In other units, there is no permanent affiliation and personnel are rotated.

Class Regiments

The term 'class', as used technically in the Indian Army, means a type of Indian recognised as distinct from others by the Army authorities for purposes of recruitment and Organisation. The basis of the distinction may be difference of race, language, religion, caste, domicile, or any two or more of these.[52] 'In August 1947 the Government of India decided as a matter of policy that all communal and class compositions should be eliminated from the Indian Army and that all Indian nationals should have equal opportunities of service. In January 1949 orders were officially issued to abolish recruitment by classes in all arms/Services. Administrative instructions were issued in February 1949 to implement this revised policy of [the] Government, by which Artillery, Engineers and Signals were brought more and more into mixed class basis.'[53]

Later, the government made a policy decision to terminate the creation of new single-caste Regiments.[54] The policy of the Ministry of Defence (MoD) on the class composition of the Indian Army is: '[A]ttempts should be made to have "All Class" Regiments to remove imbalances which has continued due to historic reasons.'[55] The units in the Armoured Corps and Infantry (Tables 1.3 and 1.4), and Artillery are of one class, mixed class, or an all-class composition.

Recruitment and Composition

The officers in all Corps are of an all-India mixed composition. Their selection and intake is based on merit through the Combined Defence Services Exam, conducted by the Union Public Service Commission (UPSC). There is no quota system. Women officers have been recruited into the Army for some time now, mostly through the

Table 1.3 Composition of Armoured Regiments

S. No	Unit(s)	Class Composition
1	President's Bodyguard	Jats, Sikhs, Rajputs
2	1 HORSE	Rajputs, Jats, Sikhs
3	2 LANCERS	Rajputs, Jats
4	3 CAVALRY	Rajputs, Jats, Sikhs
5	4 HORSE (Hudson Horse)	Sikhs, Dogras
6	7 CAVALRY	Jats, Sikhs
7	8 CAVALRY	Jats, Sikhs, Rajputs
8	9 HORSE (Deccan Horse)	Sikhs, Jats, Dogras
9	14 HORSE (Sindh Horse)	Sikhs, Dogras
10	16 CAVALRY	South Indian Classes (SIC)
11	17 HORSE (Poona Horse)	Rajput, Jats, Sikhs
12	18 CAVALRY	Jats, Muslims, Rajputs
13	20 LANCERS	Jats, Rajputs, Sikhs
14	CENTRAL INDIA HORSE	Jats, Dogras, OIC
15	45 CAVALRY	2/3 SIC, 1/3 Others Indian Classes (OIC)
16	61 CAVALRY	Rajputs, Marathas, Kaimkhani Muslims
17	5, 6, 10, 11, 12, 13, 15, 19, 41, 42, 43, 44, 46, 47, 48, 49, 50, 51, 52, 53, 54, 55, 56, 57, 58, 59 and 60 Armoured Regiment	All India All Class
18	62 CAVALRY	Dogras, Jats, Sikhs
19	63 and 64 CAVALRY	Jats, Rajput, Sikhs
20	65 Armoured Regiment	Jats, Dogras, Rajputs
21	66 Armoured Regiment	Ahirs, Marathas, SIC
22	67 Armoured Regiment	Sikhs, Jats, Dogras
23	68 Armoured Regiment	Rajputs, Ahirs, Gujjars, Marathas
24	69 Armoured Regiment	All India All Class
25	70 Armoured Regiment	All India All Class
26	72 Armoured Regiment	Jats, Dogras, Rajputs
27	71 Armoured Regiment	Jats, Dogras, SIC
28	73 Armoured Regiment	Sikhs, Rajputs, Kaimkhanis
29	76, 77, 81, 82, 83, 84, 85, 86, 87, 88, 89, and 90 Armoured Regiment	All India All Class

Source: PK Gautam

Table 1.4 Composition of Infantry Regiments

Serial	Regiment	Class Composition	Remarks
1	Brigade of the Guards	Zonal	Zonal example: (a) Two Battalions are composed of hill tribes (b) One Battalion is composed of South Indian Classes (SIC)

(*Continued*)

Table 1.4 *(Continued)*

Serial	Regiment	Class Composition	Remarks
2	Parachute Regiment and Special Forces	Fixed class, Zonal and All India	
3	Mechanised Infantry Regiment	One class, fixed class and all India	
4	Punjab Regiment	Sikhs, Dogras	13, 14, 15 and 16 Battalions are former State Forces
5	Madras Regiment	South Indian Classes	Including former State Forces of Travancore, Cochin and Mysore
6	GRENADIERS	Rajputs, Kaimkhanis, Hindustani Mussalmans, Dogras, Gujjar, Ahir, Meena, Gujaratis, Jats	Khaimkhani companies are in 5, 6, 8, 13, 16, 17, 21 battalions. Hindustani Mussalman companies are in 4, 20 and 22 battalions. 13 Grenadiers is a former State Force
7	Maratha Light Infantry	Marathas, All -India	Some battalions have troops from all India. One has South Indian Classes
8	Rajputana Rifles	Jats, Rajputs (including Gujaratis)	3, 6 and 8 battalions have one coy each of Khemkhanis while the 9th battalion has one company of Gujaratis from Saurashtra
9	Rajput Regiment	Rajputs, Gujjars, Brahmins, Bengalis	
10	Jat Regiment	Jats	
11	Sikh Regiment	Sikhs	
12	Sikh Light Infantry	Mazhabi and Ramdasia (M&R) Sikhs	
13	Dogra Regiment and Dogra Scouts	Dogras	
14	Garhwal Rifles and Garhwal Scouts	Garhwalis	Earlier only Rajputs were enrolled, but now any domicile of Garhwal is eligible for enrolment
15	Kumaon Regiment@, Naga* Regiment and Kumaon Scouts	Kumaonis, Ahirs, Rajputs, (North-East Region)	@ Kumaon Regiment, 75% Kumaonis and 25% Ahirs * Naga Regt 50% Nagas and 50% Kumaonis
16	Assam Regiment	Nagas, Kukis, Mizos, Lushias, Assamese, Kachari, other (North-East Region).	

17	Bihar Regiment	Any person from North Bihar, Adivasis from Chottanagpur Plateau (Jharkhand and Orissa) and 5 percent Other Indian Classes (OIC)	
18	The Mahar Regiment	Mahars, All-India	Five Battalions are of pure Mahars, one battalion has troops from border regions and the balance units are on all India mixed class basis
19	Jammu & Kashmir Rifles (J&K Rifles)- erstwhile State Forces	Dogras, Gorkhas, Sikhs, Muslims	13th Battalion of JAK Rifles is composed of only Dogras hailing from Himachal Pradesh, Punjab and J&K
20	Ladakh Scouts Regiment	Buddhists, Muslims	
21	Jammu & Kashmir Light Infantry	Muslims, Hindus, Sikhs (from J&K) except one unit having Dogras, Sikhs, Buddhists, Gorkhas, others. Units are organized with 50 percent Muslims and 50 percent ethnic groups of J&K	
22	1, 3, 4, 5, 8, 9 and 11 Gorkha Rifles	Gorkhas from Nepal and India including those from Kumaon and Garhwal	In approximate ratio of 60:40. From 2020s Garhwalis and Kumaonese are also being enrolled

Source: PK Gautam

Short Service Commission. Women are now also getting Permanent Commissions, though not in the combat arms. In a small though significant move, the National Defence Academy (NDA), located at Khadakwasla in Pune, has an intake of 19 girl cadets beginning 2022—ten for the Army, six for the Air Force, and three for the Navy.[56]

Recruitment as Soldiers (Other than Officers) 'The Armed Forces epitomise the ideals of service, sacrifice, patriotism and India's composite culture. The recruitment to the Armed Forces is voluntary and every citizen of India, irrespective of his caste, class, religion and community is eligible for recruitment provided he meets laid down physical, and medical criteria. Recruitment is carried out according to the recruitable male population (RMP) of each state which is 10 per cent of the male population.'[57]

Composition of Regiments

As regards troop composition, the Armoured Corps and the Infantry, including the Mechanised Infantry, have single class units (all troops belonging to one ethnic or regional group), fixed class (Companies or Squadrons based on one class), or an all-India all class or mixed units (Tables 1.3 and 1.4). All attached elements to these one-class or fixed class units, like personnel from logistic units, clerks, and tradesmen are on all-India, all-class basis. Thus, even in a one-class or fixed class unit, one would find about 10 per cent of the troops other than that of the said class. Today, as a process of evolution, Army units of combat arms are now identified not as those based on the martial races, but on 'one-class', 'fixed' or 'mixed class', or 'all-India' basis. This, essentially, is the Regimental System: for example, one-class units are those having troops from one region, such as the Sikhs, Sikh Light Infantry, Dogras, Garhwalis, Madras Regiment (South Indian Classes), and so on. Fixed class units are those that have one linguistic or ethnic group in each Company. The Punjab Regiment, for instance, has Companies consisting of Sikhs and Dogras, or an Armoured unit like the 62nd Cavalry has a Squadron each of Dogras, Jats and Sikhs. Since 1978, all new units in the Indian Army are mixed class units raised on an all-India basis.

In the combat support arms, the Regiment of Artillery has single class units as well as mixed units. The Corps of Army Air Defence, the Corps of Signals, the Army Aviation Corps, and Military Intelligence are of all-India mixed composition. The Corps of Engineers is based on regional groupings. It has three groups: Bengal, Bombay and Madras, reflecting the old colonial EIC armies in name. The Bengal Engineering Group units have about 20 per cent Sikhs, 20 per cent Rajputs, 20 per cent troops from Bihar, West Bengal, Orissa, and Ahirs from the Indo-Gangetic plains. The balance 20 per cent are recruited from the North-Eastern states. The Bombay Engineering Group enrols 40 per cent Mazhbi and Ramdasia (M and

R) Sikhs, 40 per cent Marathas, and 20 per cent others. The Madras Engineering Group recruits, as is the case with the Madras Regiment of the Infantry or one-class South Indian units of the Artillery Regiment, from among the South Indian Classes from Kerala, Tamil Nadu, Telangana/Andhra Pradesh and Karnataka.

The Services—Army Ordnance Corps, Army Service Corps, Corps of Electronic and Mechanical Engineers, Army Medical Corps, and so on—are of all-India mixed composition.

One unique feature is that officers and troops of the Combat Arms and the Combat Support Arms (except the Corps of Signals) serve throughout their military career in the same unit of a regiment, barring instances of being posted out on extra-regimental employment.The Corps of Signals and the other Services have a fixed tour of duty for all ranks of about three years. However, this does not mean that they lack the regimental spirit when serving with their units.

The Regimental and class composition system of the Indian Army is one part of the Organisational story. In its long, rich history, the Army has adopted and evolved many customs and traditions that foster a feeling of cohesiveness and belonging to the Organisation. Further, these act as foundations for the esprit-de-corps that is essential to bringing together people from different walks of life, different regions speaking a variety of tongues, and moulding them into a formidable fighting force. In the next sections, some important customs and traditions of the Indian Army are discussed followed by the contribution of the armed forces to the freedom struggle.

Customs and Traditions in the Indian Army[58]

Military customs and traditions are important for building the esprit de corps in such organisations. They serve a significant function in engendering a sense of belonging, 'develop[ing] pride in military service and establish[ing] a strong foundation of professional and personal relations.'[59] All militaries the world over developed, over generations, certain customs and traditions that are unique to them. These are not of mere ceremonial value alone but also aid in focus and cohesiveness in functioning during times of crises or war. While the 'Indian Armed Forces have inherited many customs and traditions from the British Armed Forces, but have since then developed traditions characteristic to them.'[60] Thus, the three Services—the Army, Air Force and Navy—share some customs while others are distinctive and only applicable to the individual Service.

Post 1947, the way forward for the Indian Army was clear: it was to be a professional Army, secular and, most importantly, apolitical. The apolitical character of the Indian Army, may, however, be ascribed mostly, but not entirely, to the character of the Indian nation-state, the nature of the Indian freedom struggle and the way in which the armed forces were built up in the years since Independence.[61]

Immediately after Independence, the role played by the Indian Army and the IAF during the 1947–48 India-Pakistan conflict in Kashmir, was lauded with Indian political opinion of the Army reflecting that it had performed 'loyally, magnificently and effectively' in the period between the partition and the end of fighting in Kashmir.[62]

According to Brig SP Sinha, the evolution of the customs and traditions of the Indian Army from its colonial past to the present times must be seen from the prism of the ground realities that existed in the wake of Independence and the decades that followed. The first three decades of Independence saw India face numerous challenges. There was much to achieve on the socio-economic front. On the political, diplomatic and military front, in particular, India fought four decisive wars with Pakistan and China within 25 years of Independence along with domestic insurgencies in the North-East. The structure and traditions of the Indian Army, thus, were not tampered with much during the time. However, as with any Organisation over a span of time, the Indian Army too has changed as per the need of the hour. The discussion now moves to some key influences on the post-Independence Army as well as highlight important traditions and customs associated with it.

Field Marshal Cariappa's Influence on Customs and Traditions

The first Chief of Army Staff of the Indian Army, Field Marshal KM Cariappa, preserved and emphasised the military values that the Army inherited from the British Indian Army, and which were worthy of emulation. These included, respect for the elderly, the ladies and the seniors; drill, discipline, 'spit and polish'; strict observance of dress code, financial integrity, sanitation and hygiene and adult education. Had Field Marshal Cariappa and leaders who followed him not emphasised these values at a time when the Army had officers from different social backgrounds with varying experiences of the war and 'idea of India', the Army would have lost its inherited cohesiveness.[63]

Martial Races

In the aftermath of the rebellion of 1857, the Army saw concentration of recruitment from areas that had not rebelled during the time. Further, when Field Marshal Roberts became the Commander-in-Chief in 1885, he brought to the fore prejudices that were prevalent at the time, formed under the shadow of the Russian threat. This was the time of the Great Game between Imperial Britain and Russia, and India's North Western Frontier, along with Afghanistan, was the battlefield. According to Roberts, 'No comparison…can be made between the warlike races of Northern India and…and the effeminate people of the South.'[64] While the experiences of the Indian Army in the Second World War was the beginning of the end of such thinking, Field Marshal Cariappa drove the final nail into the coffin of this practice. 'He created a new regiment, the "Brigade of Guards" that recruited on an All-India basis, which became the official policy for future recruitment in the Services. For better or for worse, groups once designated by the British as "martial races" still tend to carry that badge with pride. Yet, a spin-off of the regimental spirit has been the absence of prejudice against any group, regardless of the unit's caste or regional composition.'[65]

A Matter of Honor

What drives the Indian Army, and the men and women who serve in it selflessly, can be encapsulated in the three words: '*Naam* (honor of the regiment, Army and the country); *Namak* (loyalty to the regiment and the country) and *Nishan* (upholding the honor of the regiment's flag).'[66] Be it the Sikhs in Saragarhi in 1897, the Dogras at Ypres in 1914, the troops at Bir Hacheim in 1942, the Gorkhas at Mortar Bluff in 1944—all blazed a trail of indomitable courage that gained greater heights after Independence. Major Somnath Sharma (1947), Havildar Abdul Hamid (1965), Lt Col Tarapore (1965), Second Lieutenant Arun Khetrapal (1971), Lance Naik Albert Ekka (1971), Captain Vikram Batra and Lieutenant Manoj Kumar Pandey (1999) are some of those who have sacrificed their lives in the conduct of duty and set the highest standards of gallantry. The Battle of Rezang La (1962) where almost the entire company of 13 KUMAON under Major Shaitan Singh, literally fought till the last man and last round against hordes of Chinese attackers has become a landmark in modern military history.

Officers' Mess

Customs and traditions in the Army are mostly centered round the officers' mess and regimental life. The outward appearance and ambience of the officers' mess conforms to a particular style: the display of mess silver, liveried waiters, the bugle calls, officers in their ceremonial dress, the protocol of sitting, drinking a toast to the President, and as a grand finale, to the proceedings a piper playing a regimental piece is still followed with justifiable pride during regimental dinner nights. While formal regimental dinner nights have been reduced in frequency, the tradition has survived as it generates a sense of dignity and helps to evoke a sense of pride and worth in the regiment.[67]

Musical Traditions

Infantry Regiments inherited a tradition for the band to play the Regimental march at the end of regimental dinner nights in the officers' mess. The regimental marches like 'Cock o' the North' or 'Highland Laddie' evoked no emotion or association and was a carryover from the past; over time Indian tunes have replaced these. The change, however, was not an act of parochialism but an assertion of our lost heritage; the musical extravaganza at the 'Beating Retreat' renders a medley of Indian and Western marches—*Sare Jahan se Accha* and *Kadam Kadam Barahai Ja* interspersed with the famous 'Colonel Bogey March'—which draw spontaneous applause from the spectators. The Retreat used to end with the soul-lifting rendering of the Christian Hymn 'Abide with Me', a tradition that drew inspiration from different sources.

Service Dresses and Accoutrements

The various Regiments in the Indian Army have individual differences in dress and idiosyncrasies. For example, the Brigade of the Guards wear buttons on their cuffs, while others wear hackles and 'pompom' on their berets. Artillery Regiments do not carry 'colours'; the gun is their 'colours'. Most such dress idiosyncrasies and differences have been carried over from the British Indian Army. If an idiosyncrasy in dress harks back to a past event in history and its association brings forth a sense of pride, nostalgia, achievement or purpose, it has been retained. In some regiment bass and tenor musicians of the regimental band wear tiger or leopard skin, a relic of the past; the origin of the custom and its association with the present remains diffused.

When the theatre of operations shifted from the West to the East in World War II, the uniform of the [British] Indian Army changed from khaki to olive green. The IAF too changed its uniform khaki to a combination of dark blue and sky blue. The identification of a particular Service with a unique uniform and style served the purpose of not just differentiating between them but also preserving their unique identity, which was reflected in the dress each Service wore. Disruptive pattern combat dress has been adopted by almost all police forces on the ground of operational requirements, which are restricted to a specific area.[68]

Sanctity of Military Customs

In modern times, the flying of flags and display of star plates on motor vehicles are in vogue in armies of most Commonwealth countries. However, every Army has its own rules that regulate this privilege. In the case of the Indian Army, only Commanders of troops and a few specified staff officers are entitled to the above privileges. These are laid down in Defence Services Regulations (Army).[69] Since the 1970s, all officers of the rank of Brigadier and above are entitled to fly a flag and display a star plate.

Inviting of Officers to JCOs Mess and JCOs to Officers' Mess

A unique tradition to invite officers to the Junior Commissioned Officers' (JCOs) Mess on Independence Day which was reciprocated by inviting JCOs to the Officers' Mess on Republic Day was introduced after Independence. This tradition is followed by all the three Services, which has contributed to harmony and cohesiveness between officers and JCOs. An atmosphere of camaraderie prevails on such occasions, where the guests and hosts interact freely.[70]

Reverence for the Dead

Most societies and militaries have solemn ceremonies to respect their dead servicemen. For example, the United States has its ceremony of flag draped coffins and salutes from the President. Reverence for soldiers' bodies is a relatively new historical development. During the two World Wars, those who died during the war were either cremated or buried in nearby locations, and there are war memorials to commemorate the same. The Maharaja of Bikaner, who was the only member of the Imperial War Cabinet during the First World War, insisted that the Hindus be cremated and Muslims be buried. During Op Pawan in Sri Lanka, the bodies of soldiers were cremated or buried *in situ*. It was during the Kargil War that instructions were issued to transport the remains of martyrs by service aircraft to an airfield nearest to their hometown for last rites.[71]

Salutation

When members of the Indian Armed Forces greet each other, they use the term *Jai Hind*. This was adopted by the Indian Army as the new form of greeting each other, civilian officials and those of the other two Services. The soldiers continue to use their regimental salutation while saluting officers.

Regimental Customs

Military customs in the Indian Army have developed primarily along regimental lines, manifesting in long-established regimental colours, insignias, crests, mottos, war cries and distinctive features of the uniform. Some elements of regimental customs, for example, replacing the crown with the National Emblem, are in keeping with the republican character of India. Over time, some customs have diluted, some have disappeared while new customs have taken root. The Indian Navy and the IAF have their own traditions, for example, many naval customs are centered around the hoisting of the flag on the ship's deck.

Since Independence, recruitment in the Army has been broad-based with comprising of soldiers from different parts of the country professing different faiths. 'A unit could have a Muslim Company, [with] all other Companies being Hindu with a sprinkling of Christians and Buddhists and more Sikhs. Such a unit is bound to have "Sarv Dharam Sthal" or a place of worship for each faith, but all under one roof with display of flags of all four faiths.'[72]

Customs and traditions in the Indian Army are not always established by regulations. For the most part, they are unwritten practices that are obeyed just the same. These are not timeless or unchanging: it is possible to change certain aspects of traditions and over time some customs have been added while others have been modified or omitted based on experiences and consultations amongst stake holders. Often, the tendency to change or introduce new customs based on the whims of the colonel of the Regiments or colonel commandants or Service Chiefs must be avoided. Customs and traditions are the building blocks for fostering esprit de corps and should not be influenced by the fashion of the time.

Contribution to Freedom Struggle

The struggle for freedom began in 1857, when Indian soldiers rose in revolt against the rule of the East India Company, termed by British historians as the Sepoy Mutiny or the Great Indian Mutiny. Though mutinies by soldiers had taken place earlier in Vellore in 1806 and Barrackpore in 1824, this was the first time when the objective of the uprising was freedom from British bondage. Hence, Indian historians had good reason to name it the 'First War of Independence'. The movement was started by sepoys in Meerut, who reached Delhi and entered the Red Fort, declaring the Mughal Emperor Bahadur Shah II as their leader. The movement soon spread to other parts of North and Central India, where it was supported by large sections of the civil population and some local rulers.

Among the historians who describe the uprising of 1857 as the first war of Indian Independence is Surendra Nath Sen, who writes:

> ...it would be wrong to dismiss it as a mere military rising. The Mutiny became a revolt and assumed a political character when the mutineers of Meerut placed themselves under the King of Delhi and a section of the landed aristocracy and civil population declared in his favour. What began as a fight for religion ended as a war of Independence for there is not the slightest doubt that the rebels wanted to get rid of the alien government and restore the old order of which the King of Delhi was the rightful representative.[73]

While the Indian Mutiny in 1857 was to an extent inspired by the desire to be free of British rule, the concept of nationalism among soldiers took root only after the birth of the Congress at the turn of the century and flowered only after the Civil Disobedience movement in 1930 and the Quit India movement in 1942. During World War II, and even earlier, many Indian soldiers with nationalistic feelings had misgivings about military service under British rule. Nonetheless, they continued to serve for many reasons. The primary role of the Indian Army was to defend India, and service in the Army could not be termed as anti-national. Moreover, the political leaders who were then heading the freedom struggle had decided to support Britain during World War I, in hope of achieving dominion status for India once it was over.

In early 1946, there were mutinies in the Royal Indian Air Force (RIAF), the Royal Indian Navy (RIN), and the Signal Corps of the Indian Army at Jubbulpore (Jabalpur). In March of that year, the Cabinet Mission led by Sir Stafford Cripps arrived in New Delhi, to confer with the principal political parties on the method of framing a constitution for a self-governing, independent India. The Viceroy, Lord Wavell, was involved in the deliberations of the Cabinet Mission, but the problem of the disaffection in the armed services caused him considerable anxiety. In a dispatch addressed to King George VI on 22 March 1946, he wrote:

> ......The most disturbing feature of all is that unrest is beginning to appear in some units of the Indian Army; so far almost entirely in the technical arms. Auchinleck thinks that the great mass of the Indian Army is still sound, and I believe that this is so. It may not take long, however, to shake their steadiness if the Congress and Muslim League determine to use the whole power of propaganda at their command to do so.[74]

On 27 March 1946, Sir JA Thorne, the Home Member of the Viceroy's Council suggested that an appreciation on these aspects be prepared by the War Department. The C-in-C directed the Director of Military Intelligence (DMI), Brigadier BPT O'Brien, to assess the present state of morale and degree of reliability of the three Indian fighting services, with special reference to the Indian Commissioned Officers (ICOs), under three conditions—in aid of civil power in widespread communal or anti-present-Government disturbances; in operations on the Frontier; and as garrisons overseas. Extracts from the DMI's Note submitted to the C-in-C on 25 April 1946, are given below:[75]

> ....Our views on the reliability of the Indian Services in widespread Congress inspired trouble are

(a) The Indian Armoured Corps, Gunners, Sappers and Infantry can in the main be depended on provided that their I.C.Os, particularly the senior ones, remain loyal and any waverers among them are dealt with firmly and immediately…
(b) The Indian Signal Corps cannot at present be considered reliable….
(c) The Ancillary Services of the Army as a whole should not be relied on to act against rioters…
(d) The Royal Indian Navy cannot at present be regarded as reliable….
(e) The Royal Indian Air Force must be regarded as doubtful…

The Cabinet Mission requested the Viceroy for an appreciation of the situation that was likely to arise if their proposals fail and for a general policy on India in that event. In a Top Secret Memorandum dated 30 May 1946, Wavell warned that if the Congress and Muslim League failed to come to terms, serious communal riots might break out, with very little warning, especially in the Punjab, UP and Bihar. Prompt action would be required to deal with the trouble, with very little time for consultations with London. In the event of serious trouble, there was a military plan which provided for holding on to the principal ports—Calcutta, Madras, Bombay, Karachi—and to Delhi. Subsequently, British troops would be transferred from Southern India to the North. Stressing the need to avoid being embroiled with both Hindus and Muslims, he suggested a 'worst case' solution—to hand over the Hindu Provinces to the Congress and withdraw to the Muslim Provinces in the North-West and North-East.[76]

Three days later, the Cabinet Mission and the Viceroy sent a 'Most Immediate' telegram to the Prime Minister, stressing the urgent need for the British Government to announce a clear policy in the event of the negotiations between the Cabinet Mission and the political parties breaking down, which could happen any time between 5 and 15 June 1946, and the line of action that the Viceroy was to adopt. The first point to be decided was whether they should attempt to repress a mass movement sponsored by the Congress and maintain the existing form of government. This was possible only if the Indian Army remained loyal, which was doubtful. It would also cause much bloodshed and achieve nothing, unless it was intended to stay on in India for another 10–20 years. At the other extreme was the decision to withdraw from the whole of India as soon as the Congress gave a call for a mass uprising. This would have an adverse impact on British prestige throughout the Commonwealth.

The appreciations of the Viceroy and the Cabinet Mission reached London while the latter were still carrying out their negotiations in Delhi and Simla. They were considered by the Defence Committee of the Cabinet, which asked the Chiefs of Staff to examine the military implications of the five courses of action listed by the Cabinet Mission, keeping in mind the short-term policy and the long-term strategic interests listed by the Viceroy. Before examining the military implications of the courses proposed by the Cabinet Mission, the Chiefs of Staff eliminated the first three, namely, withdrawal from India as soon as possible; withdrawal by a certain date; and appeal to the United Nations (UN). That left only two courses: maintaining control throughout India, and a withdrawal in phases, which they proceeded to examine. The most important factor in retaining hold over the whole country was the ability to maintain law and order, which depended largely on the loyalty of the Indian Armed Forces. The conclusions on this crucial aspect were in line with those of GHQ India:

> ....we consider that the reliability of the Indian Army as a whole, including those in garrisons outside India is open to serious doubt. This applies even to Gurkha units....The Royal Indian Navy and the Royal Indian Air Force cannot be regarded as reliable.
>
> ....A policy of remaining in India and firmly accepting responsibility for law and order would result, if the Indian Army remained loyal, in an acceptable military commitment and would safeguard our long term strategic interests.... If however, the Indian Armed Forces did not remain loyal...we would be faced with the necessity of providing five British Divisions for India, with the consequent abandonment of commitments in other areas hitherto regarded as inescapable, serious effects on our import and export programmes and world-wide repercussions on the release scheme. The only alternative to this would be ignominious withdrawal from the whole of India.[77]

The Report by the Chiefs of Staff clearly indicates that the British Government was seriously considering the option of creating Pakistan in June 1946, not because of the lack of agreement with the political parties—this was still being negotiated by the Cabinet Mission—but due to the threat of disaffection in the Indian Armed Forces. This option was ruled out only because it did not serve British strategic interests. Had the Indian Armed Forces remained loyal or there had been enough British Divisions to keep them in check, the British would not have left India when they did.

The crucial role of the Indian Armed Forces, especially the Indian Army, in the British decision to quit India has been commented on by several writers and historians. Captain Shahid Hamid, Private Secretary to General Auchinleck, made the following entry in his diary on 30 March 1946: 'Today the *Hindustan Times* commented editorially on Auchinleck's appeal to the Indian Army. "There is no doubt whatsover that if the transfer of power is not quickly brought about, the foreign rulers of India cannot count upon the loyalty of the Indian Army..."'[78]

The well-known historian, Dr Tara Chand, has written:

> The most controversial measure of the Viceroy was the decision to advance the date of transfer of power from June 1948 to 15 August, 1947. On this issue Mountbatten recorded his reasons in his conclusions appended to the Report on the Last Viceroyalty submitted to His Majesty's Government in September 1948. His Defence for expediting the transference of power to the Indians was on these lines... "Secondly, the ultimate sanction of law and order, namely, the Army, presented difficulties for use as an instrument of government for maintenance of peace..."[79]

It is interesting to reflect on the course of history if the Indian soldier had not been affected by nationalistic feelings and continued to serve loyally as he had during and before World War II. Though the freedom movement had developed considerable momentum by the time the war ended, the assumption that it would have achieved Independence on its own would be erroneous. With the vast resources at their disposal, it would not have been difficult for the British authorities in India to muzzle the movement, as they had done in 1930 and 1942. The only deterrent after 1945 was the uncertain dependability of the Army. Had the Indian soldier remained staunch, or adequate British forces been available, it is most unlikely that freedom would have come in 1947.

Notes

1. See 'East India Company: English Trading Company', https://www.britannica.com/topic/East-India-Company.
2. Lt Gen SL Menezes, *The Indian Army: From the Seventeenth to the Twenty-first Century*, New Delhi: OUP, 1999, p. 7.
3. Stephen Cohen, *The Indian Army: Its Contribution to the Development of a Nation*, New Delhi: OUP, 2001 [1990], p. 5.
4. Cohen, *The Indian Army*, n. 3, p. 5.
5. Menezes, *The Indian Army*, n. 2, p. 7; Cohen, *The Indian Army*, n. 3, p. 8.
6. Cohen, *The Indian Army*, n. 3, p. 8.
7. These figures are cited in Major General Ashok K Verma, AVSM, 'Genesis and Evolution' in Major General Ian Cardozo, AVSM, SM (ed.), *Indian Army: A Brief History*, New Delhi: USI, 2005, p. 14. The author cites a work by Lt FG Cardew, *A Sketch of the Services of the Bengal Native Army*, Calcutta, 1903, p. 67 as the source of these figures.
8. Verma, 'Genesis and Evolution', n. 7, p. 14.
9. Ibid.
10. Menezes, *The Indian Army*, n. 2, p. 157 as cited in Verma, 'Genesis and Evolution', n. 7, pp. 16–17. Cohen cites a figure of 214,000 troops (Indian sepoys) as of 1856. See Cohen, *The Indian Army*, n. 3, p. 32.
11. Cohen, *The Indian Army*, n. 3, p. 33.
12. Verma, 'Genesis and Evolution', n. 7, p. 18.

13. Ibid., p. 19.
14. Kaushik Roy and Gavin Rand, 'Introduction', in Kaushik Roy and Gavin Rand (eds), *Culture, Conflict and the Military in Colonial South Asia*, Abingdon and New York: Routledge, 2018, p. 1.
15. Ibid., p. 2.
16. Verma, 'Genesis and Evolution', n. 7, pp. 21. Also see Cohen, *The Indian Army*, n. 3, 2001 and Menezes, *The Indian Army*, n. 2, 1999.
17. Pradeep P. Barua, *The State at War in South Asia*, Lincoln and London: The University of Nebraska Press, 2005, p. 128.
18. Sir George Arthur, *The Life of Lord Kitchener*, Vol. 2, London: Macmillan, 1920, p. 168.
19. The Meeting of the Army Council, no. 278, June 21, 1906, National Archives, WOP 163/11, as cited in Pradeep Barua, *The Late Colonial India Army: From the Afghan Wars to the Second World War*, Lexington Books, 2011, Kindle edition.
20. Cohen, *The Indian Army*, n. 3, pp. 23, 25.
21. Ibid., p. 29.
22. Ibid. Emphasis in original.
23. Maj Gen VK Singh, 'The World Wars and Prelude to Independence', in Major General, Ian Cardozo, AVSM, SM (ed.), *Indian Army: A Brief History*, New Delhi: USI, 2007, p. 25.
24. Singh, 'The World Wars and Prelude to Independence', n. 23, p. 25.
25. Rajat Ganguly, 'India's Military: Evolution, Modernisation and Transformation', *India Quarterly*, 71(3), pp. 187–205.
26. Ibid., pp. 187–205.
27. Ibid., pp. 187–205.
28. 'India and United Nations Peacekeeping and Peacebuilding', at https://www.pminewyork.gov.in/pdf/menu/49151pkeeping.pdf. See also Neha Banka, '70 years of the Korean War: India's lesser-known role in halting it', *The Indian Express*, 1 July 2020, https://indianexpress.com/article/research/70-years-of-korean-war-indias-lesser-known-role-in-halting-it-6476030/.
29. Mandip Singh, 'Critical Assessment of China's Vulnerabilities in Tibet', IDSA Occasional Paper No 30, 2013, p. 12.
30. Johan Skog Jensen, 'A Game of Chess and a Battle of Wits: India's Forward Policy Decision in Late 1961', *Journal of Defence Studies*, Vol. 6, No. 4, October 2012, pp. 55–70.
31. Farooq Bajwa, *From Kutch to Tashkent: The India-Pakistan War of 1965*, New Delhi: Pentagon Press, 2014, p. 91, as cited in PK Chakravorty and Gurmeet Kanwal, 'Operation Gibraltar: An Uprising that Never Was', *Journal of Defence Studies*, Vol. 9, No. 3, July–September 2015, pp. 33–52.
32. PK Chakravorty and Gurmeet Kanwal, 'Operation Gibraltar: An Uprising that Never Was', *Journal of Defence Studies*, Vol. 9, No. 3, July–September 2015, p. 36.
33. Vivek Chadha, 'An Assessment of Organisational Change in the Indian Army', *Journal of Defence Studies*, Vol. 9, No. 4, October-December 2015, p. 25.
34. Chadha, Ibid., p. 26, citing Ministry of Defence's *Annual Report* from 1964–65.
35. Ibid., p. 28.

36. Ibid.
37. Ibid., p. 29.
38. Manvendra Singh, 'The Intellectual Origin of India's Cold Start Doctrine Lies in General K Sundarji', *The Print*, 23 February 2018, at https://theprint.in/opinion/intellectual-origin-indias-cold-start-doctrine-lies-gen-k-sundarji/37649/.
39. 'Rashtriya Rifles – Meet The World's Biggest Counter-Insurgency Battalion Of The Indian Army Deployed In Kashmir', *The EurAsian Times*, 4 May 2020, https://eurasiantimes.com/rashtriya-rifles-indian-Armys-elite-counter-insurgency-unit-vows-revenge/.
40. Steven I. Wilkinson, *Army and Nation: The Military and Democracy Since Independence*, Ranikhet: Permanent Black, 2015, p. 9.
41. Major General Ashok Krishna, AVSM, 'Counter Insurgency and Internal Security', in Major General Ian Cardozo, AVSM, SM (ed.), *Indian Army: A Brief History*, New Delhi: USI, 2007, p. 216.
42. Ibid.
43. Ibid.
44. Lt Gen Vijay Oberoi, PVSM, AVSM, VSM 'India's Wars since Independence: A Concise History', *Journal of the United Service Institution of India*, Vol. CL, No. 622, October-December 2020.
45. Vivek Chadha, *KARGIL: Past Perfect, Future Uncertain?*, New Delhi: IDSA and Knowledge World, 2019, p. x.
46. Maj Gen VK Singh, 'Times of Trial', in Maj Gen Ian Cardozo, AVSM, SM (ed.), *The Indian Army: A Brief History*, New Delhi: USI, 2007, p. 189.
47. See 'The Kargil Committee Report', at https://nuclearweaponarchive.org/India/KargilRCA.html.
48. Vivek Chadha, *KARGIL: Past Perfect, Future Uncertain?*, New Delhi: IDSA and Knowledge World, 2019, p. 83.
49. This section has made use of PK Gautam, *Composition and Regimental System of the Indian Army: Continuity and Change,* New Delhi: Institute for Defence Studies & Analysis/Shipra Publications, 2008.
50. Anonymous, *Leadership*, Revised Edn, Shimla: Army Training Command, 2004, p. 11.
51. The Official Home Page of the Indian Army.
52. *Reorganization of the Army and Air Forces in India,* Report of a Committee set up by His Excellency the Commander-in-Chief in India, Volume One, Part IV, New Delhi: Government of India Press, 1945, p. 208. The committee was chaired by Lt Gen HBD Willcox and had three Brigadiers, one Air Commodore, and one Colonel as its members. Brigadier KM Cariappa, who later became the first Indian Chief of the Army Staff, was also a member.
53. AL Venkateswaran, *Defence Organisation in India*, New Delhi: Publication Division, Government of India, 1967, pp. 187–88.
54. Venkateswaran, *Defence Organisation in India*, n. 52, as quoted in Cohen, *The Indian Army*n. 3.
55. Ministry of Defence, 'Defence Force Levels, Manpower, Management and Policy', Estimates Committee, *19th Report*, Tenth Lok Sabha, 1992–1993, p. 50.

56. 'NDA Gearing up to Admit First Batch of 19 Girl Cadets, Training in "Gender Neutral" Manner', *The Indian Express*, 22 March 2022, at https://indianexpress.com/article/cities/pune/nda-gearing-up-admit-first-batch-19-girl-cadets-training-gender-neutral-manner-7831541/.
57. See *India 2005*, New Delhi: Ministry of Information and Broadcasting, Government of India, Chapter on Defence, p. 180.
58. This section is based on Brig (Dr) SP Sinha, 'Customs and Tradition of the Indian Armed Forces', *Journal of the United Service Institution of India*, Vol. CL, No. 622, October-December 2020 (online edition) and on Maj Gen Chand N Das, *Traditions and Customs of the Indian Armed Forces*, revised and enlarged edition edited by Brigadier SP Sinha, VSM, New Delhi: CAFHR, USI, 2021.
59. Sinha, 'Customs and Tradition of the Indian Armed Forces', Ibid.
60. Ibid.
61. K Subrahmanyam, 'Indian Armed Forces: Its Ethos and Traditions', *Indo-British Review*, op.cit., n. 1, p. 127.
62. Statement of Defence Minister, Baldev Singh, in the Indian parliament. The Times of India, March 8, 1949, New Delhi, p. 9. Quoted by Fitch-McCullough, Robin James, "Imperial Influence on the post-Imperial Indian Army 1945–1973, Graduate College Dissertation Thesis. http://scholarworks.uvm.edngrades/763. Accessed on 24 April 2020
63. Sinha, 'Customs and Tradition of the Indian Armed Forces', n. 58.
64. Ibid.
65. Ibid.
66. Ibid.
67. Ibid.
68. Ibid.
69. Quote DSR Para. As per AO 46/87.
70. It is generally accepted that the tradition was formalised by Field Marshal KM Cariappa. See Sinha, Ibid.
71. Quote authority, Page 511 of the Customs and Traditions (draft), Brig SP Sinha, 'Customs and Traditions', (New Delhi: Manohar, 2020), p. 511.
72. SA Hasnain, 'Honoring Faith and Secularism in the Armed Forces: Men who Fight Together Must Pray Together', *Times of India*, 11 October 2016, as cited in Sinha, n. 58.
73. SN Sen, *Eighteen Fifty-Seven*, New Delhi: Publications Division, 1957, p. 413.
74. Nicholas Mansergh and Penderel Moon (ed.), *The Transfer of Power 1942–47* (12 Vols.), London: Foreign and Commonwealth Office, vi, pp. 1233–37.
75. Mansergh and Moon, *The Transfer of Power 1942–47*, vii, n. 74, pp. 406–07.
76. Ibid., pp. 731–37.
77. Ibid., pp. 889–900.
78. Maj Gen Shahid Hamid, *Disastrous Twilight*, Barnsley: Leo Cooper, 1986, p. 47
79. Tara Chand, *History of the Freedom Movement in India*: Vol. 1, New Delhi: Publications Division, 1961.

Troops of the Madras Presidency

Risaldar Major Ganda Singh, Sardar Bahadur, OBI, IOM, 19th Fane's Horse. Ganda Singh enlisted in 1852 in the 4 Punjab Cavalry. He saved the life of Sir Robert Sandeman near Lucknow in 1858 and later during the Second Opium War in 1860 was instrumental in saving the life of Col (later Maj Gen) Sir Charles McGregor, who subsequently founded the USI of India. Ganda Singh served on Lord Robert's staff as his Indian ADC from 1889–1892, retiring from the army in 1894
Source: USI of India.

47th Sikhs (now 5 SIKH) march through the streets of Tientsein in North China, 1906

Source: Army HQ.

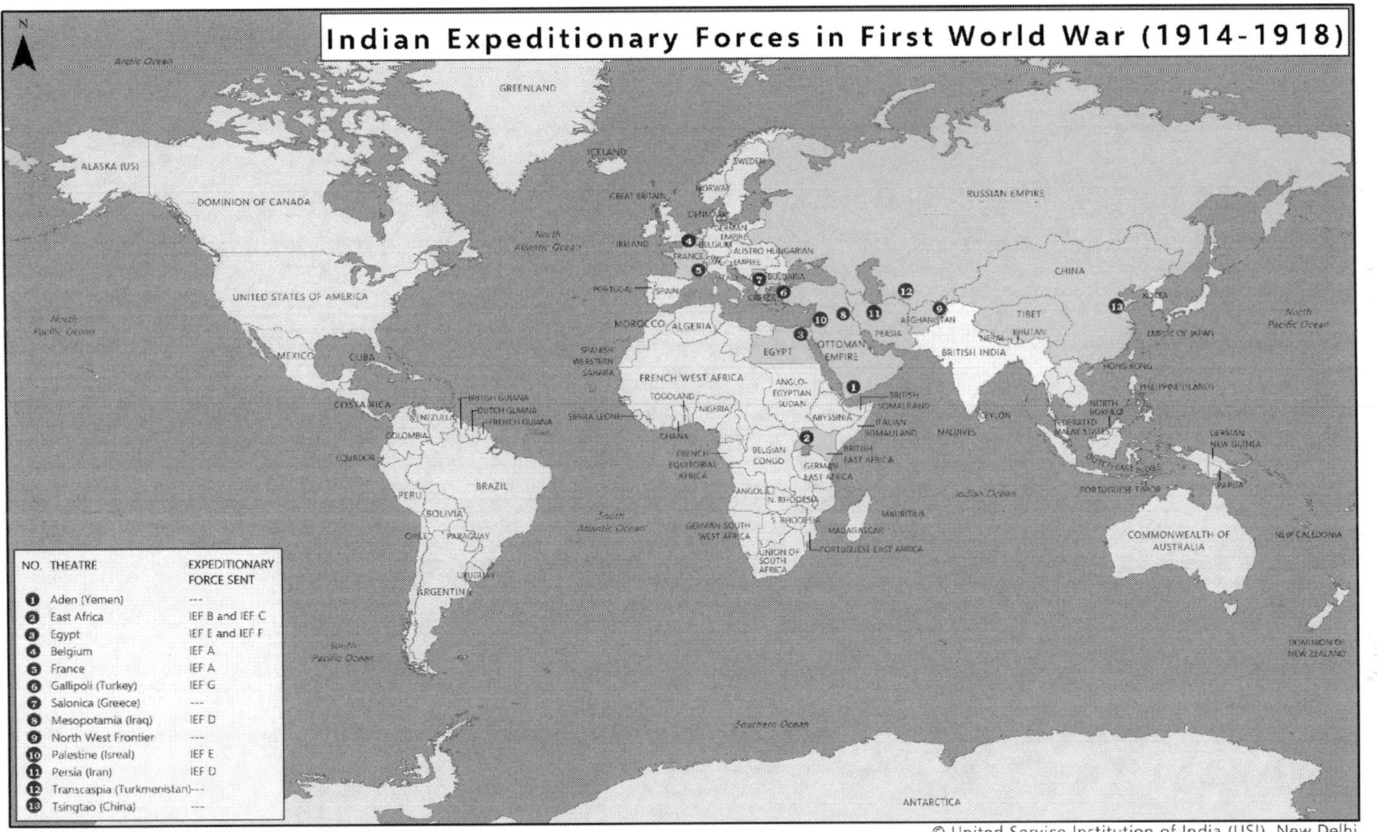

Map 1 Indian Expeditionary Forces in World War I, 1914–1918

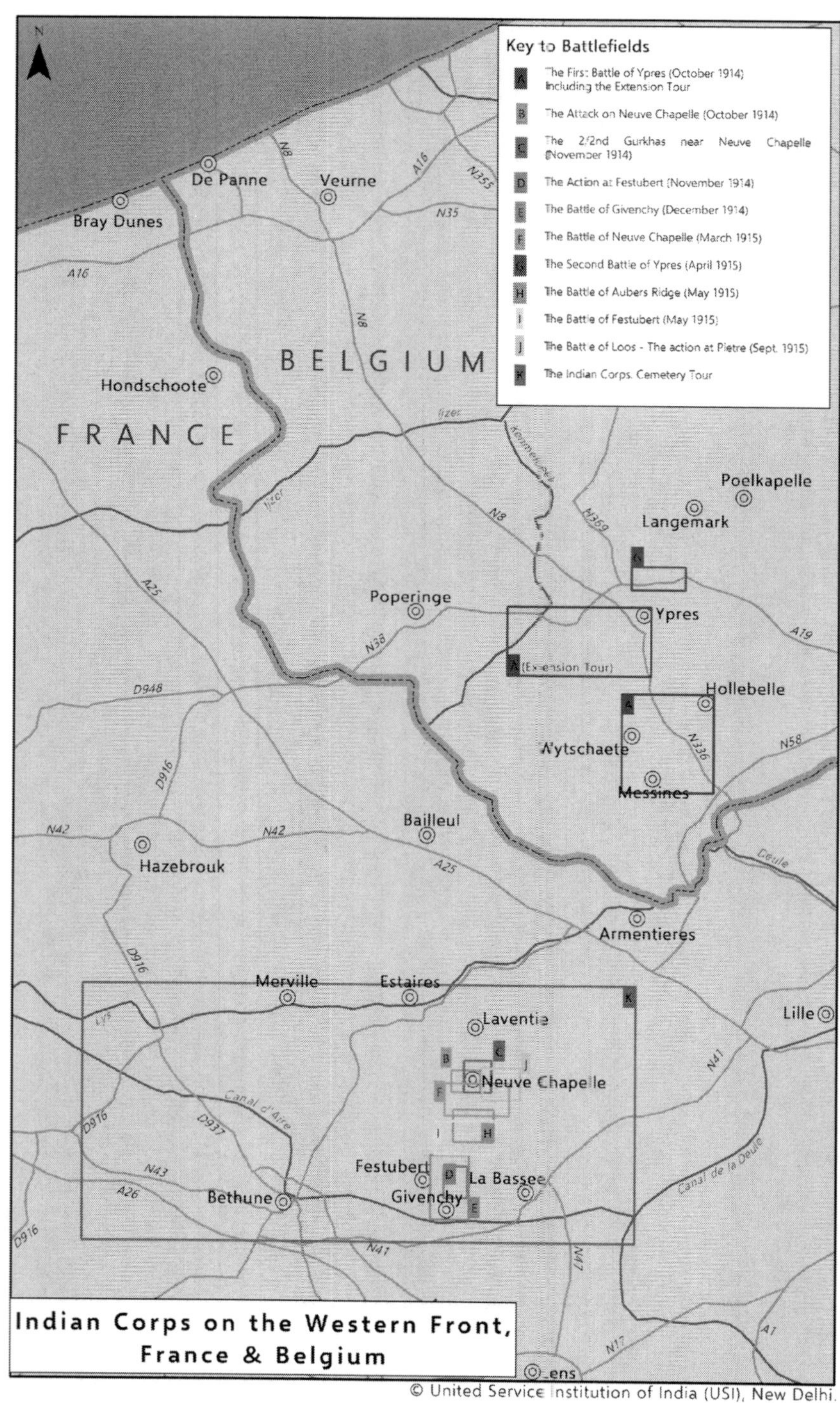

© United Service Institution of India (USI), New Delhi.

Map 2 Indian Corps on the Western Front, France & Flanders

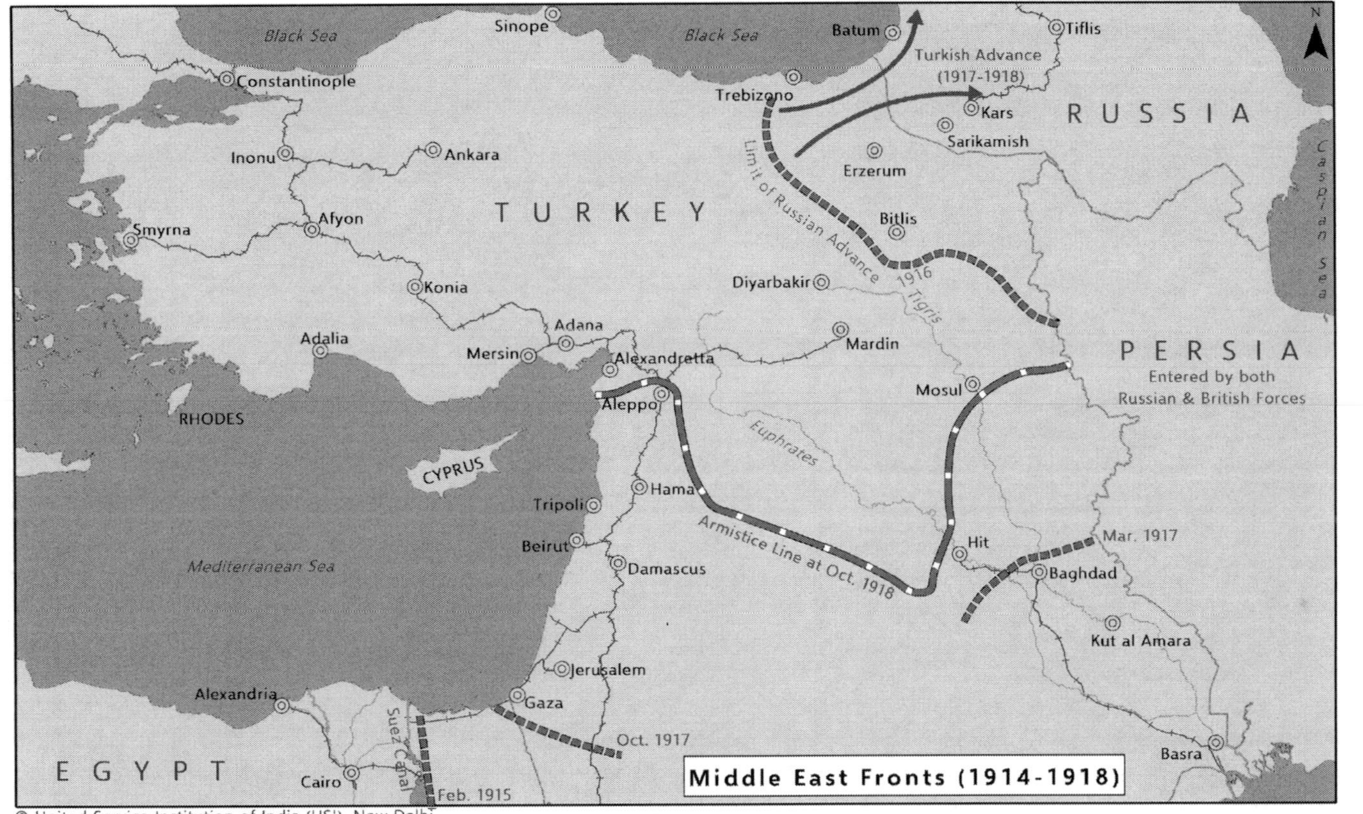

Map 3 Middle Eastern Fronts, 1914–1918

15 Sikh disembark in Marseilles, France 1914
Source: Rana Chhina.

28B: November 17th 1914, soon after the opening of the Persian Gulf campaign Subadar Sabal Singh and Lance-Naik Net Singh, of the 104th Wellesleys Rifles, gallantly stormed the outer wall of the fort, at the head of some twenty or thirty men of various units. They were the first in this part of the line to enter the enemys position, and Subadar Sabal Singh and Lance-Naik Net Singh were awarded the Indian Order of Merit for their conspicuous gallantry. Source: USI

A Hotchkiss Gun Team practising near Querrien, July 1916

The 36th Sikhs (now 4 SIKH) in Kut al Amara after the town was abandoned by the Turks in February 1917

Source: Rana Chhina.

Indian Stretcher Bearers at Gallipoli, 1915

Wounded Indian soldiers recuperate in England, 1915
Source: Private collection.

Indian soldiers provide a guard of honour for General Allenby near the Jaffa Gate

Source: Library of Congress.

Sir A Ramaswami Mudaliar, Supply Member of the Governor-General's Executive Council and leader of the delegation of India, signs the United Nations Charter, San Francisco, 26 June 1945. Source: USI

Map 4 North Africa, 1942

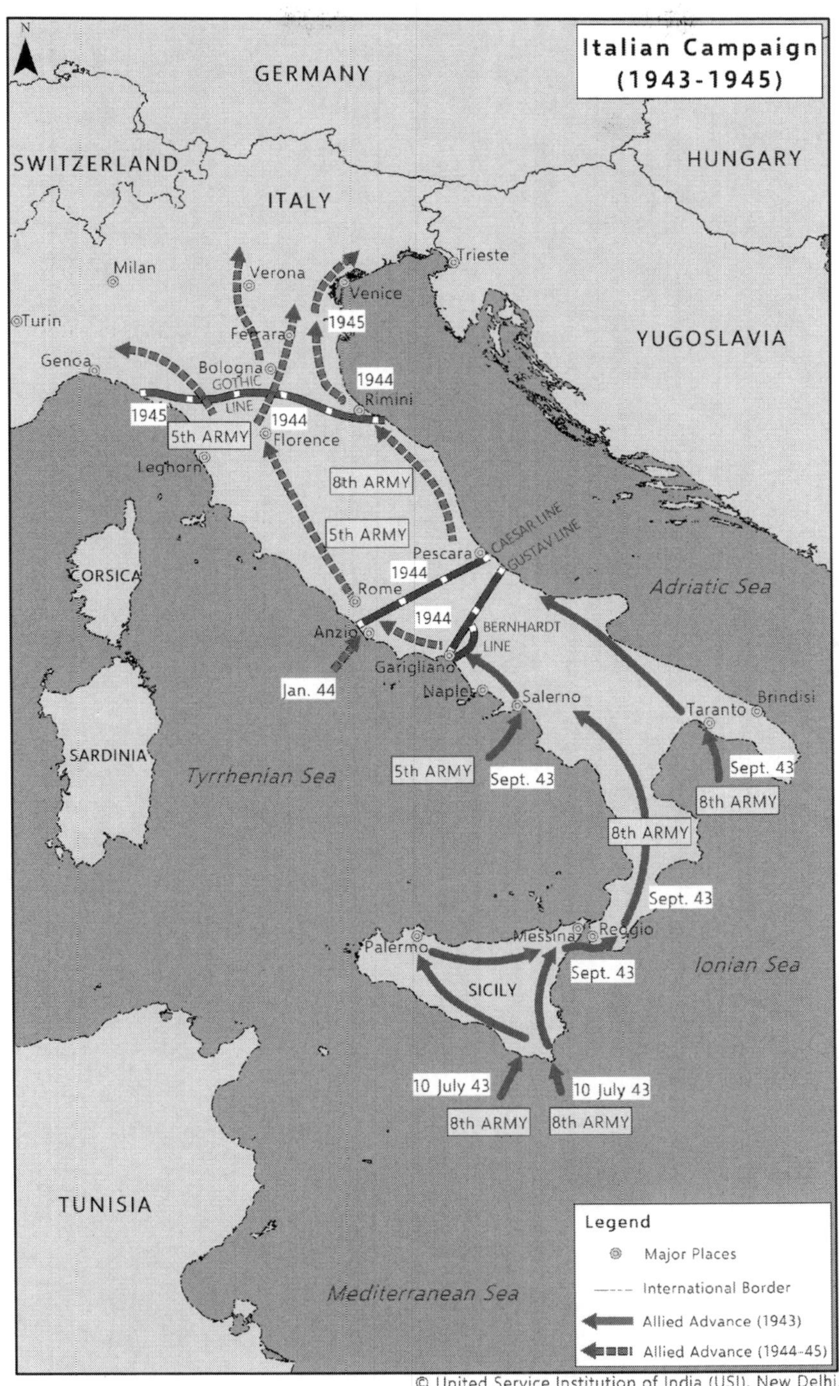

Map 5 Italian Campaign in World War II, 1943–45

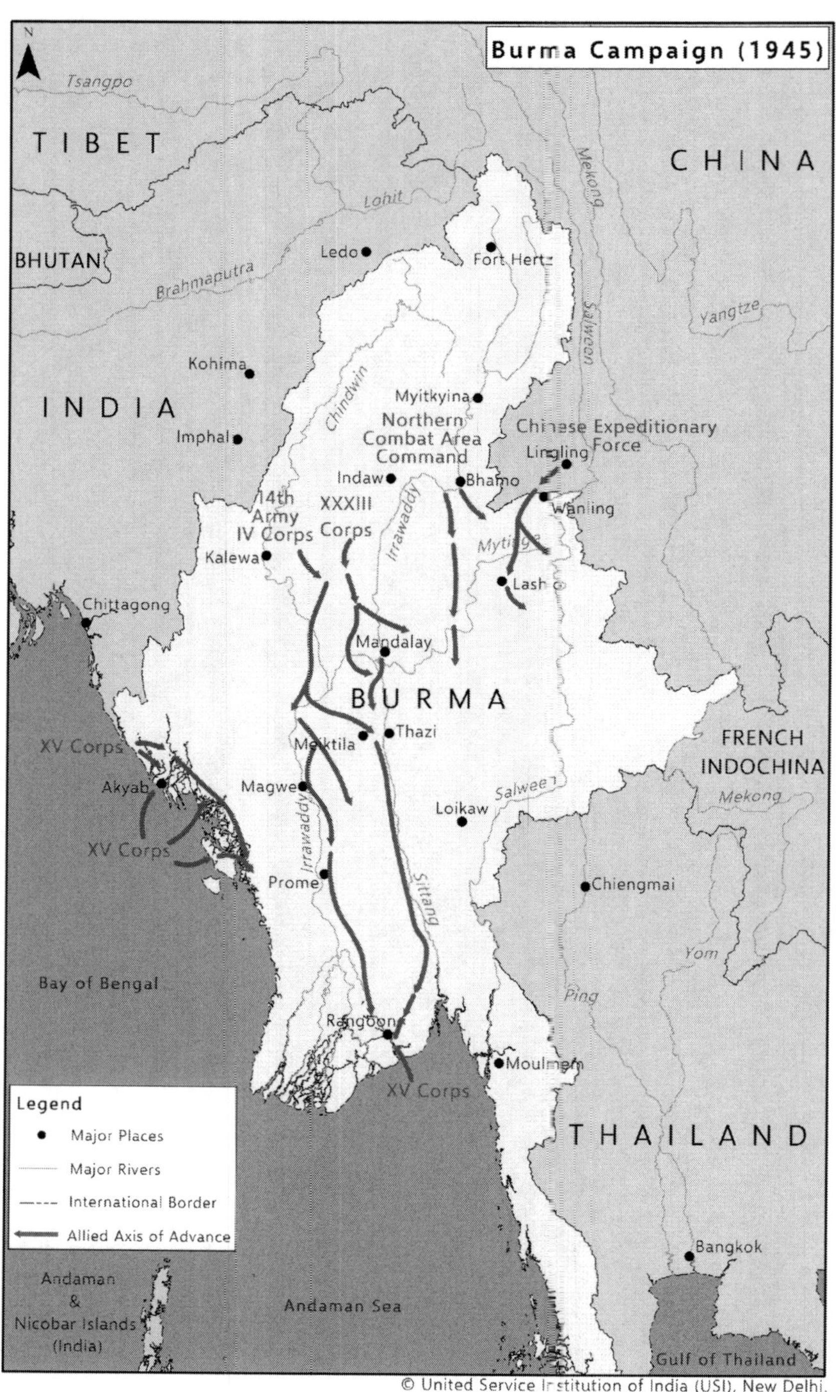

Map 6 1945 Burma Campaign

An Indian Signaler in North Africa, 1940, in the battle against the Africa Desert Korps.
Source: MoD, History Division.

An Indian Infantry Battalion prepares to embark for service in North Africa, 1940
Source: Rana Chhina.

Indian infantry clears an Italian street of German snipers during the advance to Rome, 1945
Source: MoD, History Division.

An Indian sentry guards a dangerous path somewhere on the Gothic Line in Italy, 1944
Source: USI of India.

Indian soldiers advance past a temple complex in Burma during the advance towards Rangoon
Source: MoD, History Division.

Troops of 5th Indian Infantry Division prepare to emplane for Imphal on the Burma front in a US Air Transport Command aircraft, March 1944
Source: Rana Chhina.

A historic moment, Indians from Imphal and British from Kohima meet as 4 and 33 Corps link-up at milestone 109 on the Imphal-Kohima road
Source: Rana Chhina.

End of the war for a group of German soldiers surrendering to a Jat patrol of the Central India Horse, Italy 1944
Source: USI of India.

2

Indian Army in the Pre-Independence Era

The World Wars and Small Wars

NEHA KOHLI

Overview

Following its reorganisation in the first decade of the twentieth century under Lord Kitchener, the Indian Army began to evolve into a professional, organised and disciplined force. Kitchener's reforms organised the Army into nine Divisions under two Command Headquarters (HQ), with around a fifth being Cavalry. The Infantry specialised in mountain warfare, especially along the border with Afghanistan in the North-West Frontier. They had weaponry, rifles and mountain guns, but these were a generation behind those in Europe. In addition, the Army had mostly British officers, though there were some tentative moves towards Indianisation. This Army also did not boast of a Regimental system as we see today—it included Pioneers and Sappers but not a great many arms. It was not a motorised Army and depended on animals for Transportation.

The Army had been through a few phases of expansion and reorganisation prior to Kitchener's reforms. In 1879, the Indian Army had 6,602 British officers, 60,341 non-Indian soldiers and 123,254 Indian soldiers.[1] The Eden Commission was appointed in the same year to examine the Army's organisation and structures, subsequent to which the existing Presidency Armies were abolished and a single Army HQ was created.[2] By 1885, the Indian Army's strength increased with the raising of nine new Infantry Regiments and three Cavalry Regiments.[3]

The Indian Army that served in the Great War swelled from approximately 150,000 on 1 August 1914 to nearly 1.4 million men engaged by the end of the conflict. It had a significant role to play on numerous fronts around the globe. Indian soldiers served with honour in France, Belgium, Aden, Arabia, East and West Africa, Somalia, Gallipoli, Egypt, Mesopotamia, Palestine, Persia, Salonika, Russia and even China. By the end of the war in 1918, over a million Indians had served overseas at the cost of 74,000 casualties. They earned over 9,200 decorations for gallantry, including 11 Victoria Crosses (VCs).[4]

This chapter provides a brief narration of the Indian Army's participation in two of the twentieth century's defining conflicts: World War I (1914–18), also known as the Great War; and World War II (1939–45). It also briefly discusses 'small wars' undertaken by the Indian Army.

Indian Army on the Eve of the World War I

The Army in India consisted of the British-officered Indian Army, the Imperial Service Troops (IST) and the British units deployed in India. Peacetime recruitment into the Army numbered around 15,000 men annually. At the outbreak of the Great War, the Army in India comprised of 76,953-strong British contingent and 239,561-strong Indian contingent. The British contingent included 4,744 British officers and 72,209 British other ranks (BORs). The Indian contingent included 159,134 soldiers and 34,767 reservists plus 45,660 non-combatants.[5]

According to Kaushik Roy: 'Before the First World War, there were 51 British Battalions in India, each with an establishment of 23 officers and 1,003 BORs....'[6] The Indian component of the Army had:

> 118 Indian Infantry Regiments. Of them, 95 Infantry Regiments had only one Battalion each and eleven Infantry Regiments had two Battalions each and there were twelve Pioneer Regiments of one Battalion each. Thus, in total there were 129 Indian Battalions. The eleven Indian Infantry Regiments of two Battalions each were the 39th Garhwal Rifles and the 10 Gurkha Regiments...[7]

In 1914, there were nine British Cavalry Regiments in India, each with 27 officers and 598 troopers.[8] The Indian Cavalry was organised into 39 Regiments (25,036 *sowars*).[9] 'In August 1914, the strength of the Indian Artillery was 4,160 men (including 67 British officers). The Indian Artillery comprised of 12 Mountain Artillery Batteries and one Indian Coast Artillery (immobile) Battery.'[10]

Recruitment to the Army leaned heavily towards the North and West of the Indian subcontinent, with Punjab being one of the key areas supplying troops to the Army. As the war progressed, with greater demands for manpower in its various theatres, recruitment from other regions of the country increased. Table 2.1 depicts the social composition of the Indian Army before the war.

India functioned as an imperial strategic reserve during World War I. The global nature of commitments of its Army is exemplified by none other than the 89th Punjabis, who were turned away from Gallipoli to fight the Germans in France. The Battalion had the distinction of serving in more theatres of the war than perhaps any other single Battalion in the Commonwealth: South-West Arabia, Egypt, Gallipoli, France, Mesopotamia, the North-West Frontier, Salonica, the Caucasus and finally, at Constantinople with the Army of the Black Sea.[11] Further, 'Indian society was mobilized to provide military and nonmilitary manpower as well as economic assets in order to sustain the British imperial war effort.'[12]

Since the late nineteenth century, recruitment into the Army had been based on the concept of 'martial classes'. As seen in Table 2.1, the majority of men recruited

Table 2.1 Social Composition of the Indian Army in 1912

Communities	Number	Percentage (%)
Sikhs	32,702	20.5
Punjabi Muslims	25,299	16
Gurkhas	18,100	11.5
Pathans	12,201	7.7
Rajputs	12,051	7.7
Other Hindus*	10,252	6.5
Jats	9,670	6
Hindustani Muslims	9,054	5.7
Other Muslims	8,717	5.5
Dogras	8,566	5
Marathas**	5,685	3
Brahmins	2,636	1.7
Garhwalis	1,855	1
Indian Christians/Eurasians	1,491	0.75
Burmese + Assamese + Karens	306	0.24
Jews	18	0.1
Total	158,603	

Source: *Proceedings of the Army in India Committee 1912*, Vol. 1-A, Minority Report, 1913, p. 156, quoted in Roy, *Indian Army and the First World War: 1914–1918*, n. 5.

Notes: *includes Tamils, Telegus, Ahirs, Gujars, Mers, Mians, Bhils, Pariahs and so on; and **includes Parwaris.

Table 2.2 New Communities Recruited Under Pressure of World War I

Region	Communities
Madras Presidency	Coorgis, Moplahs, Nayyars, Tiyyans and Telegus
Bombay Presidency	Berads, Bhandaris, Bhils from Khandesh, Brahmins, Chamars, Gujaratis, Indian Christians, Jamkhandis, Kathiwad classes, Kolis, Lingayats, Mahars, Sindhis and Telegus
Bengal	Bengalis
Punjab and Delhi	Arains, Baltis, Bauria Sikhs, Muslims from south-west Punjab, Bishnois, Rors, Sainis, Eurasians, Heris, Punjabi Brahmins, Hindu Aroras, Kambohs, Niazis, Kanets and Mussalis
Burma	Arakanese, Chins, Kachins, Karens, Shans and Burmese
Central Province	Lodhas, Dangis and Mahars
Assam	Jharuas, Manipuris and Sylheti Muslims
Bihar and Orissa	Ahirs and Bhumihar Brahmins
North-West Frontier Province	Bangash Miranzais, Bannuches, Marwats and Swatis of Hazara
United Provinces	Bhumihar Brahmins, Gaur Brahmins, Gwalbans Ahirs, Gadarias, Hill Brahmins, Hill Doms, Jaduban Ahirs, Kurmis, Kumaonis, Lodhas, Nandbans Ahirs, Awadh/Oudh Rajputs, Awadh Brahmins, Awadh Muslims, Pasis and Tagas

Source: 'Recruitment in India before and during the War of 1914–18, List of New Classes tried since the Commencement of War,' Appendix 13, p. 75, quoted in Roy, *Indian Army and the First World War: 1914–1918*, n. 5.

into the Army came from specific parts of the subcontinent: Punjab, Rajasthan, the North-West Frontier and the hills of modern Uttarakhand and Nepal. The long duration of World War I as well as the near-continuous need for combatants in large numbers meant that the recruitment net had to be cast over a wider population. Table 2.2 lists out the new regions and communities that saw recruitment into the Army owing to the demands of war. A major impact of the war was that it led to the beginning of the dismantling of the 'martial classes' theory; further, in the aftermath of the war, 'Indianisation' of the Army too gained a fillip.

Causes of World War I

The immediate trigger for the war was the assassination of Archduke Franz Ferdinand, the heir apparent to the throne of the Austro-Hungarian Empire in Sarajevo, on 24 June 1914, by Gavrilo Princip, a Bosnian Serb student. However, Europe had been moving steadily towards war since the nineteenth century. While the Congress of Vienna brought peace to the continent in the aftermath of the

Napoleonic Wars, the map of Europe began to change. New nation states started to emerge out of empires; the Italian and German unifications, which culminated around 1871, led to a race for colonies; increasing industrialisation and militarisation led to growing economic and military power; and an arms and naval race ensued, in particular between Britain—the foremost naval power in Europe—and Germany. In the early years of the twentieth century, there were a series of political crises in the Balkans, then a part of the large Austro-Hungarian Empire. Ultimately, the bugle call for war was sounded in Sarajevo.

It was a given that being the jewel of the British Empire, India would be involved in its conflicts. Great Britain's declaration of war on 4 August 1914 drew its colonies into the war. Even before the war began in 1914, around 10,000 Indian troops had been dispatched to Persia to ensure that the oil supplies from the region were not affected. This was significant as the British Navy, the paramount naval power in the world, had converted from coal to oil to power its ships. This was also the time that the nationalist movement in India was gathering momentum. Indians, in the early decades of the twentieth century, were calling for greater autonomy and power from Great Britain. By supporting the British in World War I, it was hoped that India would be granted dominion status.

On the eve of World War I in 1914, the British Indian Army comprised 150,000 men. It expanded sevenfold during the course of the war: 'around 1.2 million men were mobilized for the Indian Army and 0.3 million for non-combat duties.'[13]

World War I (1914–18)

When war broke out in Europe, the Indian government offered Britain two Infantry Divisions composed of three Brigades, each with one British and three Indian Battalions, and two Cavalry Divisions with three Brigades, each with one British and two Indian Regiments. Subsequent to the British government's acceptance of the offer, 'two Indian Infantry Divisions, the 3rd (Lahore Division) and the 7th (Meerut Division), along with the 9th Cavalry Brigade, embarked from Karachi and Bombay in August. The units began to arrive in Marseilles from September 26.'[14]

The Indian Army's primary war-fighting experience as well as training was for warfare on the frontiers of India, with weapons that were a generation behind that of the West. The men who went to war beginning 1914 were neither equipped nor trained to fight a war against Western armies. They had obsolete weaponry and unsuitable clothing for the extreme cold weather conditions of Europe, and were thrust into a war of attrition in trenches, something they had never faced before. Yet, they fought admirably and gained a stellar reputation for their bravery and conduct in alien terrain in a brutal mechanised war.

The Army that went to war in 1914 was divided into seven expeditionary forces overseas, with broad deployments as follows.

1. Indian Expeditionary Force (IEF) A: Northern Europe, in France and Flanders.
2. IEF B: East Africa.
3. IEF C: East Africa.
4. IEF D: Mesopotamia
5. IEF E: Egypt and Palestine.
6. IEF F: Egypt.
7. IEF G: Gallipoli.

The Indian participation in the war was not limited to fighting units alone. Apart from 90,000 combatant personnel, India sent '50,000 men from labour Companies to France'[15] alone. Additionally, 'each Regiment had followers such as Hindu and Muslim cooks, bhistis, and ward servants, ward orderlies (high-caste Hindus and Muslims), ambulance kahars (trained bearers), plus sweepers (low-caste Hindus and untouchables) for the ambulance sections.'[16]

Apart from the regular Indian Army, the armies of the Indian Princely States also contributed significantly to the war effort. A large contingent of these state troops, known as IST, took part in operations in many parts of the world (see Table 2.3).

Broadly, thus, the Indians fought in most major theatres of World War I: Northern Europe, Mesopotamia, Africa, Palestine and Gallipoli. A brief discussion of these follows next.

Northern Europe: France and Flanders[17]

The IEF A (also referred to as the Indian Corps) took part in the First Battle of Ypres in Belgium (19 October–22 November 1914); the attack on Neuve Chapelle (28 October 1914); the Battle of Festubert (November 1914); the Battle of Givenchy (16–22 December 1914); the Battle of Neuve Chapelle (10–13 March 1915); the Second Battle of Ypres (22 April–25 May 1915); the Battle of Aubers Ridge (9 May 1915); the Battle of Festubert (15–25 May 1915); and the Battle of Loos: Action at Piètre (25 and 27 September 1915).

When the war began, Germany had set into motion the Schlieffen Plan,[18] which called for the defeat of France through a sweeping manoeuvre through Belgium and northern France. However, the plan saw limited success and the war deteriorated into trench warfare; eventually, the trench lines extended from close to the English Channel to Switzerland. Warfare degenerated into attrition, with a series of attempts to break through the enemy's defences using firepower. The British Army on the ground soon found itself overstretched with no reserves. The only trained manpower available was the Indian Army, which was called upon. Simon

Table 2.3 Imperial Service Troops in World War I

Indian States	No. of Combatants Sent Overseas	Remarks
Alwar	1,502	1 Squadron of Cavalry and 1 Battalion of Infantry
Bhawalpur	326	Detachments from the Camel Corps and Camel Transport
Bharatpur	1,581	1 Battalion of Infantry and 1 transport Corps
Bikaner	444	1 Camel Corps
Faridkot	2,597	1 Sapper Company
Gwalior	1,075	2 Battalions of Infantry and Detachment of Transport Corps
Hyderabad	681	1 Regiment of Cavalry
Indore	20	1 Squadron of Cavalry and 1 Transport Corps
Idar	1,256	Despatch Riders
Jaipur	1,116	1 Transport Corps
Jhind	1342	1 Battalion of Infantry
Jodhpur	472	1 Regiment of Cavalry
Kathiawar	689	Detachments of Cavalry
Kapurthala	4,983	1 Battalion of Infantry
Kashmir	147	Detachments of Cavalry, 1 Battery of Mountain Artillery
Khairpur	520	3 Battalions of Infantry
Malerkotla	1,355	Detachments of Infantry and Transport Corps
Mysore	538	1 Company and Detachments of Sappers.
Nabha	2,695	1 Regiment of Cavalry and 1 Transport Corps
Patiala	567	1 Battalion of Infantry
Rampur	5	1 Regiment of Cavalry and 1 Battalion of Infantry
Rutlam	561	1 Battalion of Infantry
Sirmur	457	Despatch Riders
Tehri	6	2 Companies of Sappers, the second Company replacing the first which was captured at Kut-el-Amarah
Total	26,099	

Source: *India and the Great War: An Overview*, n. 4, p. 23.

Doherty and Tom Donovan describe the conditions under which the Indian Army was called to action:

> The Indian Corps came to the Western Front at a most critical point in the First World War…There was a real possibility that the Germans might have broken through the British lines and pushed the British Expeditionary Force (BEF) back to the coast. The Territorial Force was not yet ready to take to the field (with a few exceptions) and the New Army then being raised would

> take another eight months to train before any of its formations could be sent overseas. Australians, Canadians, and New Zealanders were being mobilised but none would arrive in any theatre of war until 1915. At the end of 1914 one third of the 'British' troops in France were Indians.[19]

Within weeks of the declaration of war on 04 August 1914, Indian troops arrived in France. The Lahore Division arrived in Marseilles on 26 September 1914, followed by the Meerut Division in October 1914, and hit the ground running. These were formed into an Indian Corps under Lieutenant General (Lt Gen) Sir James Wilcox, and were ordered to relieve British Divisions stretched from Neuve Chapelle to Givenchy; they held this front for the next 14 months.

The first major campaign that the Indian Army was involved in was the First Battle of Ypres, which was the culmination of the famous 'Race to the Sea'. Here, the 129th Baluchis made the first actual attack by an Indian unit on the Western Front when, on 26 October 1914, they attacked German trenches East of Hollebeke. On 31 October, the Battalion's two machine guns were eventually overrun by the Germans after a severe fight. The men kept the remaining gun in action until the German assault swept over them. Sepoy Khudadad Khan, although severely wounded, continued to fire his gun until prevented from doing so. Feigning death, he waited until dark, then managed to crawl back from the front to find his Regiment. For his brave actions, he was awarded the VC, becoming the first Indian to receive the gallantry medal.[20]

The next major engagement at Neuve Chapelle took place on 28 October 1914, where 47th Sikh, supported by 9th Bhopal Infantry and two Companies of Sappers, succeeded in capturing frontline German positions, but had to eventually pull back after heavy German counter-attacks. The Battle of Festubert in November 1914 was essentially a defensive action by the Indian Corps, consequent to a severe German attack resulting in loss of trenches. Its significance was that it was the first time that they fought together as a Corps. The lost trenches were recaptured by the morning of 24 November after heavy fighting. It was here that Naik Darwan Singh of 1/39th Garhwal Rifles became the second Indian to receive the VC.

The Battle of Givenchy took place between 16–22 December 1914. Towards the end of 1914, the Indian Corps was ordered to adopt a form of offensive defence. The Ferozepur Brigade, therefore, undertook an attack on the German lines to the North-East of Givenchy on 16 December 1914, with the aim of capturing two German saps opposite the 15th Sikhs and to use this as a firm base to undertake further operations to bite into the German defences. The attack was undertaken by the 129th Baluchis, who were eventually pushed back by strong German counter-attacks. 'Although ultimately unsuccessful, the Baluchis had fought doggedly during this attack and this was reflected in the high number of casualties—55 men killed and 69 wounded.'[21]

The Battle of Neuve Chapelle in March 2015—the first planned British offensive of the war—intended to break through the German salient round the village and move on to capture the Aubers Ridge, just over a mile away. The attack was to be undertaken on the right by the Meerut Division of the Indian Corps and on the left by IV Corps. This attack took place in inclement weather and the initial Artillery bombardment was relatively successful. However, the 1/39th Garhwal Rifles on the right of the attack unintentionally veered off to the right and lost all of their British officers and a large number of men. As a result, a gap of 250 yards opened up between the two Companies of Garhwal Rifles on the right and the 2nd Leicesters on their left, which the Germans took advantage of. The remainder of the Garhwal Brigade crossed the 200 yards of the no man's land and succeeded in capturing the German frontline and support trenches.

Both 2/3rd Gurkhas and parties of the 2nd Battalion of the Garhwal Rifles took advantage of a favourable opportunity and advanced into Neuve Chapelle, joining up with the 2nd Rifle Brigade and moving through the village. The attackers reached the Smith Dorrien Line, the old British-held trench line before the Germans captured Neuve Chapelle. Finding that this line was flooded, they dug in 50 yards to the rear. Consolidation continued for five more hours and there was no further attempt to advance until 5 p.m., when the Dehra Dun Brigade reached the Bois du Biez. The British planned to continue the attack on the Bois du Biez on 12 March 1915, but this attack was pre-empted by the Germans who opened an intense Artillery bombardment, followed by a massed frontal attack. The British and Indian troops held their fire until the German Infantry was within 200 yards range, and then opened up with a deluge of Artillery, machine gun and small-arms fire that cut swathes in the German formations. Over 2,000 bodies were counted in front of the Meerut Division alone. The following morning, Sir Douglas Haig suspended all further operations and the battle drew to a close.

The Second Battle of Ypres commenced on 22 April 1915 with a ferocious German attack North-East of Ypres, involving the use of gas. In the ensuing days, the situation remained precarious and reserves were so scant that, for the second time in six months, units of the Lahore Division were rushed to Flanders. By 1100 Hours on 26 April, the Lahore Division was in position on a 600 yard front, north of Ypres. The plan was to attack the German trenches some 1,500 yards distant on Mauser Ridge, but the exact position of the German line was unknown. In between the British and the German lines was an intermediate feature, Hill Top Ridge.

The Indians attacked at 1400 Hours. Although the attackers were protected by Hill Top Ridge for the first 500 yards, disaster lay ahead. Once they crossed the ridge, they had to advance down the other side to a small stream, in full view of the Germans, then up a bare slope for the final 600 yards. Emphasis had been placed on speed but, as soon became horrifically apparent, the enemy trenches were too far away to charge. It was impossible to stop or reorganise the attack, and the survivors were pinned down. The battle saw many acts of bravery, chief among which was Jemadar Mir Dast, 55th (Coke's) Rifles, attached to 57th (Wilde's) Rifles, who reorganised men of the shattered Battalion when no British officers were left, and later helped to carry in no less than eight wounded British and Indian officers as well as a number of men. He was awarded the VC.

It was decided to renew the attack the following day. The Germans were still well dug-in. The leading units advanced across Hill Top Ridge and into aimed machine gun and rifle fire from the Germans, meeting the same fate as the previous day. The proposed continuations of the attack were cancelled during the next two days, and on the night of 29 April 1915, the Jullundur and Ferozepore Brigades were withdrawn, leaving only the Sirhind Brigade to take an active part in the operation. On 1 May 2015, the Sirhind Brigade made advances, but the German lines remained impenetrable. Orders were issued to withdraw, and the Brigade came out of the battle in the night.

The Battle of Aubers Ridge, also known as the Rue du Bois attack, was conceived in April 1915, but postponed due to the Second Battle of Ypres. The plan envisaged a two-pronged attack either side of Neuve Chapelle. The two attacking forces, 6,000 yards apart, would break through the lines and advance concentrically, meeting on the Aubers Ridge, thereby cutting off the German forces in the triangle of Neuve Chapelle–Aubers–Fauquissart. The Germans, located opposite both 'prongs', were well dug-in and had devoted considerable effort to strengthen their lines after the Battle of Neuve Chapelle.

As the element of surprise was part of the plan of attack, the Artillery, in the preceding days, attempted to inconspicuously register targets. On the morning of the attack, there was to be a 40-minute barrage to cut the wire and destroy the strong points. Preparations were made for the attack, which began early in the morning on 9 May 1915. The attacking Battalions were mowed down by German machine guns as soon as they crossed the parapet; and in the evening, the position of the trenches was identical to when the battle had commenced. However, there were massive casualties: in the Meerut Division alone, casualties included the loss of 69 British officers, 24 Indian officers, and 1,055 British and 823 Indian other ranks; and the Lahore Division lost 122 of all ranks, bringing the total to 2,093.

The Battle of Festubert involved a plan to advance in a south-easterly direction towards the town of La Bassée, along a front of 5,000 yards, with the Meerut Division and the British 2nd and 7th Divisions on converging lines. The Indian troops involved were from the Meerut and Lahore Divisions, with the former being tasked to undertake the attack and the latter to hold their front and support the attacking troops with small-arms fire and Artillery. The attack was launched from the trenches south of the Rue du Bois at 2330 Hours on the night of 15 May 1915. The troops came under heavy Artillery and machine gun fire from the opposing German side.

By midnight, it became clear that there was no possibility of success, yet a fresh assault was ordered by the Brigade HQ to take place at 0300 Hours by the 2/3rd Gurkhas; this too came under heavy fire.

On the morning of 16 May 1915, bombardment of the German trenches resumed. At this stage, it was acknowledged that the defences in front of the Indian Corps were too strong to enable a breakthrough. It was then decided that the Indian troops should attack through the opening adjacent to them held by the 2nd Division. One section of the captured trench held by the 15th Sikhs was known as the 'Glory Hole'. The two opposing sides were separated here only by a barricade. The 15th Sikhs spent the morning of 18 May resisting heavy bombing attacks, but by the early afternoon they were running short of bombs. At 1530 Hours, Lieutenant (Lt) J G Smyth of the 15th Sikhs was ordered to take a bombing party and two boxes of bombs from the old frontline to the captured trench—a distance of 250 yards over open ground. He selected 10 Indian bombers from those who volunteered—four from the 15th Sikhs, four from the 19th Punjabis and two from the 45th Sikhs. By the time Smyth got to a shell hole within 30 yards of their objective, he had only one man left with him—the rest had been killed or wounded—and one of the two boxes of bombs. Under covering fire, they finally reached the captured trench. Smyth was awarded the VC and all the men in his party were decorated for their bravery.

The overall result of the Battle of Festubert was mixed, but it must be acknowledged that the attacking troops, including the Indian Army, largely failed to reach their objectives and suffered severe casualties.

The Indian Corps last battle was one of four holding actions that took place at a distance from the main battle at Loos. The attack was notable in that it was the first time that British troops used gas, albeit not very successfully. The attack included explosion of a mine under the enemy parapet; a gas and smoke attack immediately prior to the attack; thick smoke barrages on each side of the attacking troops; a smoke screen along the front of the attack; and finally, field guns were placed in the front parapet to destroy the enemy's parapet and machine guns. A day of gallant endeavour, some confusion and further heavy casualties—the Meerut Division suffered a total of over 3,000 killed, wounded and missing in the battle—ended with the British troops back in their start lines and no German reinforcements, other than local supports, had been drawn into the battle. Though no fault of its own, the Indian Corps failed to influence the outcome of the Battle of Loos.

The Indian Corps in France, at the battles of Ypres, Festubert and Neuve Chapelle, fought non-stop for over a year. They had reached the battlefields of France and Flanders in the month of October 1914 with a strength of 26,000. By the time they were sent to a different theatre of war after a year, they had suffered 22,000 casualties, that is, they had lost nearly 100 per cent of their original strength. Table 2.4 lists the original order of battle of the IEF in France and Belgium.

Table 2.4 Order of Battle of the Original* Indian Army Corps (IEF A)

Cavalry	Infantry	Imperial Service Troops
Mhow Division: • 2nd Lancers	Lahore Division: FEROZEPORE BRIGADE: • 129th Baluchis • 57th (Wilde's) Rifles (F.F.) • 89th Punjabis • 9th Bhopal Infantry JULLUNDUR BRIGADE: • 15th Ludhiana Sikhs • 40th Pathans • 47th Sikhs • 59th (Scinde) Rifles (FF) SIRHIND BRIGADE: • 1/1st Gurkha Rifles • 1/4th Gurkha Rifles • 27th Punjabis • 125th (Napier's) Rifles DIVISIONAL TROOPS: • 15th Lancers • 23rd Sikh Pioneers • 34th Sikh Pioneers • 20th and 21st Field Companies, 3rd (Bombay) Sappers and Miners • Indian Field Ambulance	Cavalry: • Alwar Lancers • 1st Gwalior Lancers • Indore Mounted Escort • 1st Jodhpur Lancers
Meerut Division: MEERUT BRIGADE: • 3rd Horse • 16th Cavalry • 18th Tiwana Lancers DIVISIONAL Cavalry: • 4th Cavalry • 11th Lancers	Meerut Division DEHRA DUN BRIGADE: • 1/9th Gurkha Rifles • 2/2nd Gurkha Rifles • 6th Jat Light Infantry • 28th Punjabis GARHWAL BRIGADE: • 2/3rd Gurkha Rifles • 1/39th Garhwal Rifles • 2/39th Garhwal Rifles BAREILLY BRIGADE: • 41st Dogras • 33rd Punjabis • 58th (Vaughan's) Rifles (F.F.) • 69th Punjabis • 2/8th Gurkha Rifles	SAPPERS: • Maler Kotla Sappers • Tehri-Garhwal Sappers

DIVISIONAL TROOPS:
- 4th Cavalry
- 107th Pioneers
- 2nd and 3rd Field Company, Sappers and Miners
- 4th and 5th Field Companies, 3rd Sappers and Miners
- Indian Field Ambulance
- Support Services: Supply and Transport Corps, Indian Hospital Corps, Indian Labour Corps

Lahore Division:
FEROZEPORE BRIGADE
- 7th Hariana Lancers

JULLUNDUR BRIGADE:
- 15th Lancers

DIVISIONAL Cavalry:
- 23rd Cavalry (FF

AMBALA BRIGADE:
- 30th Lancers

Poona Division:
LUCKNOW BRIGADE:
- 29th Lancers

1st Indian Cavalry Division:
- 6th King Edward's Own Cavalry
- 9th Hodson's Horse (3rd Ambala Cavalry Brigade)

TRANSPORT:
- Bharatpur Transport Corps
- Gwalior Transport Corps
- Indore Transport Corps

Source: *India and the Great War: France and Flanders*, Booklet series, New Delhi: United Service Institution of India (USI), pp. 6–7.
Note: *other units also served subsequently.

Mesopotamia[22]

Before the war began, the British government was cognizant of the fact that its oil supplies were dependent on the security of the Persian oilfields. This was particularly important for the British Navy which had switched from coal to oil to power its ships. The oil supply remained vulnerable unless the oilfields were secured. The task of securing the Persian oilfields fell to the India Office in London as the troops that were used to guard the oilfields were from India. In September 1914, a small force was dispatched to ensure the security of the Anglo-Persian Oil Company's oilfields and installations at Abadan, at the head of the Persian Gulf, and to show the flag to ensure the loyalty of the sheikdoms in the vicinity. Later, an IEF was sent from India to implement the second phase of the operation—an advance up the Shatt-al-Arab waterway. Success in the initial phases of the operation led to the capture of Basra. A further advance brought the force to the confluence of the Euphrates and the Tigris rivers.

In early 1915, an improvised Corps of two Infantry Divisions and a Cavalry Brigade was formed under General (Gen) Sir John Nixon of the Indian Army, which mounted offensives along each of the rivers. Major General Charles Townshend, General Officer Commanding (GOC) 6th Indian Division, moved up the less heavily defended Tigris and captured Kut-al-Amara in September 1915. These early successes raised British ambitions to capture Baghdad. However, they needed to capture Ctesiphon before Baghdad could be claimed. In November 1915, Ottoman forces occupied positions at Ctesiphon in order to block the British advance of the IEF 22 miles from Baghdad. In their eagerness to capture Baghdad, the British had overreached. Townshend's plan for a night march, followed by a flank attack, broke down as they had gone beyond the range of the gunboats that were supporting them from the river. His troops reached the second Ottoman position inside Ctesiphon but could proceed no further due to lack of Artillery support. By 22 November 1915, it became clear that the attack was a failure. Both sides faced heavy losses, but the British ultimately had to admit defeat. On 25 November 1915, Townshend's forces began the retreat to Kut-al-Amara.[23]

Townshend fell back at Kut-al-Amara and dug a strong defensive position in a loop of the Tigris, confident that he could sit it out until reinforcements reached him. But the Turks under the command of Gen Colmar von der Golt besieged Townshend's British-Indian force from 7 December 1915. Attempts by relief forces to link up with the garrison failed. By January 1916, supplies were running low and the garrison resorted to slaughtering their horses for food. A fresh attempt on 16 April 1916 also failed, by which time the garrison was on starvation rations. Maj Gen Townshend was given the authority to negotiate a surrender. The siege of Kut lasted five months and ended on 29 April 1916 with the surrender of British Indian forces in a humiliating defeat.

In August 1916, control of operations in Mesopotamia passed on to the War Office in London and Gen Sir Frederick Maude took over as Commander in Chief (C-in-C). Maude insisted on massive reinforcements and the establishment of an efficient logistics system before resuming the offensive in December 1916. The British retook Kut-al-Amara in February 1917 and entered Baghdad on 11 March 1917. The capture of Baghdad signalled the destruction of one of the main armies of Turkey and except for Palestine, the Turks no longer posed a serious threat to the Allies.

The campaign in Mesopotamia was fought mostly by the British Indian Army and Indian troops. Table 2.5 depicts the units of the Indian Army and Indian state forces that served in Mesopotamia during the war.

East Africa[24]

The Germans entered the race for colonies after the unification of Germany in 1871. One of the few large German colonies was in German East Africa, in what is now modern-day Tanzania. With limited road and rail infrastructure, the country was ideal for defence. The Germans were commanded by Gen Paul von Lettow-Vorbeck, who, with a force of some 16,000 local troops—known as the Askaris—kept the British at bay for four years during World War I.

Military operations in East Africa (IEF B) were officially acknowledged to be a 'subsidiary enterprise', almost wholly fought by Indian and African forces reinforced by troops from South Africa and Rhodesia. The campaign was characterised by extreme privations suffered by men and animals alike, in terrain varying from lowland coastal areas to higher ground inland, alternating between heavy rains and seasons of drought. The terrain proved difficult for the conduct of military operations and there were more casualties due to disease than battle. The outbreak of war had found the colonial authorities in Uganda and British East Africa totally unprepared. As in every previous emergency in East Africa, troops required to supplement local forces had to come from India.

The two IEFs in East Africa had the following roles:

1. IEF B was to embark for the capture of the port of Dar es Salaam, a potential hostile naval base; and
2. IEF C was to reinforce the small garrison of British East Africa.

The objective of IEF B was immediately changed to an amphibious landing to capture the German port of Tanga. The landings at Tanga and the subsequent attempts to capture the town were mismanaged from the start and were a fiasco. The 101st Grenadiers and the 2nd Jammu and Kashmir Rifles were amongst the units that saved the day, with the latter having captured two German trench lines and then covered the withdrawal.

Table 2.5 Units of the Indian Army and Indian State Forces that Served in Mesopotamia, 1914–18

Indian Army	Indian State Forces
Cavalry • 4th Cavalry • 5th Cavalry • 7th Hariana Lancers • 10th Lancers (Hodson's Horse) • 11th KEO Lancers (Probyn's Horse) • 12th Cavalry • 13th DCO Lancers (Watson's Horse) • 14th Murray's Jat Lancers • 15th Lancers (Cureton's Multanis) • 16th Cavalry • 17th Cavalry • 21st PAVO Cavalry, Frontier Force (FF) (Daly's Horse) • 22nd Sam Browne's Cavalry (FF) • 32nd Lancers • 33rd QVO Light Cavalry • QVO Corps of Guides Cavalry Artillery • 21st Kohat Mountain Battery (FF) • 23rd Peshawar Mountain Battery (FF) • 25th Mountain Battery • 26th Jacob's Mountain Battery • 30th Mountain Battery • 31st Mountain Battery • 34th (Reserve) Mountain Battery • 49th (Reserve) Mountain Battery • 50th (Reserve) Mountain Battery SAPPERS AND MINERS • 1st KGO Sappers and Miners • 2nd QVO Sappers and Miners • 3rd Sappers and Miners. Infantry AND PIONEERS • 1-1st Brahmins • 1-2nd QO Rajput Light Infantry • 1-3rd Brahmins • 1-4th PAVO Rajputs • 1-6th Jat Light Infantry • 1-7th DCO Rajputs • 1-8th Rajputs • 1-9, 2-9, 3-9 Bhopal Infantry • 1-10th Jats	Indian State Forces • 1st Gwalior Lancers • Bharatpur Transport Corps • Bhavnagar Lancers • Gwalior Transport Corps • Indore Mounted Escort • Indore Transport Corps • Kashmir Lancers • Khairpur Mounted Rifles and Camel Corps • Maler Kotla Sappers • Mysore Transport Corps • Nabha Infantry • Patiala Lancers • Sirmoor Sappers • Tehri (Garhwal) Sappers

- 1-11th Rajputs
- 13th Rajputs
- 14th KGO Ferozepore Sikhs
- 20th DCO Infantry (Brownlow's Punjabis)
- 1-22nd Punjabis
- 24th Punjabis
- 1-25th Punjabis
- 1-26th Punjabis
- 1-27th Punjabis
- 1-28th Punjabis
- 31st Punjabis
- 1-32nd Sikh Pioneers
- 1-34th Sikh Pioneers
- 36th Sikhs
- 37th Dogras
- 1-39th Garhwal Rifles
- 1-41st Dogras
- 1-42nd Deoli Regiment
- 1-43rd Erinpura Regiment
- 1-44th Merwara Infantry
- 45th Rattray's Sikhs
- 47th Sikhs
- 1-48th Pioneers
- 49th Bengalis
- 51st Sikhs (FF)
- 52nd Sikhs (FF)
- 53rd Sikhs (FF)
- 1-56th Punjabi Rifles (FF)
- 59th Scinde Rifles (FF)
- 62nd Punjabis
- 64th Pioneers
- 1-66th Punjabis
- 1-67th Punjabis
- 1-73rd Carnatic Infantry1-76th Punjabis
- 79th Carnatic Infantry
- 1-80th Carnatic Infantry
- 82nd Punjabis
- 83rd Wallajahabad Light Infantry
- 84th Punjabis
- 85th Burman Rifles
- 87th Punjabis
- 1-88th Carnatic Infantry
- 1-89th Punjabis
- 1-90th Punjabis
- 1-91st Punjabis

(*Continued*)

Table 2.5 *(Continued)*

Indian Army	Indian State Forces
• 92nd Punjabis • 93rd Burma Infantry • 1-94th Russell's Infantry • 1-95th Russell's Infantry • 1-96th Berar Infantry • 1-97th Deccan Infantry • 1-99th Deccan Infantry • 1-102nd KEO Grenadiers • 1-103rd Maratha Light Infantry • 104th Wellesley's Rifles • 1-10th and 2-10th Gurkha Rifles • 1-11th, 2-11th and 3-11th Gurkha Rifles • 1st QVO Corps of Guides Infantry LOGISTIC AND SUPPORT UNITS • Indian Medical Service • Indian Subordinate Medical Department • Army Bearer Corps • Army Hospital Corps • Survey Department • Military Accounts Department • Army Remount Department • Indian Army Postal Service • Indian Telegraph Department • Supply and Transport Corps • Indian Ordnance Department • Indian Corps of Clerks	

Source: India and the Great War: France and Flanders, pp. 6–9.

On 31 December 1914, both IEFs (B and C) were amalgamated and the combined force designated as IEF B. The force was redistributed in two Commands: the Mombasa Area, extending up to Kilimanjaro; and the Nairobi Area, including Uganda. The campaign devolved into a series of several small-scale battles and skirmishes in 1914 and 1915, later growing into a multi-divisional theatre of operations with the appointment of South African Gen Jan Smuts. Smuts forces slowly pushed the Germans back to Dar es Salaam.

> Building roads and bridges behind the advance were the engineers including the Faridkot Field Company, officered entirely by Sikhs at a time when there were no other Indians holding commissioned ranks. There were also railway Companies of the Indian Sappers repairing and running the railway.[25]

Although the strength of the Indian forces in East Africa never went beyond 15,000 at any one time, three times that number were sent from India during the course of the campaign. The war in East Africa lasted from 1914 to 1918. The key battles in 1917 were fought around Kilwa and Lindi, near the coast, where the Germans suffered a number of casualties. Von Lettow-Vorbeck captured Namakura in July 1917 and entered Rhodesia in November 1918. On 12 November 1918, the last battle of the war in East Africa was fought between Lettow-Vorbek's troops and the King's African Rifles, with Lettow-Vorbeck surrendering formally on the 25 November 1918.

The number of Indian casualties in East Africa amounted to 5,018, of which 2,972 were killed, 2,003 were wounded and 43 were declared missing. Table 2.6 lists the units of the Indian Army and Indian volunteer and state forces that served in East Africa.

Egypt and Palestine[26]

The entry of Ottoman Turkey into the war in November 1914, on the side of Germany, immediately posed a threat to the oilfields in Southern Persia and to the vital Suez Canal. The campaigns in Egypt, Palestine and Syria were thus aimed at driving the Turks out of Palestine and Syria and protecting the Suez Canal.

The initial defence of the Suez Canal was provided by the Sirhind Brigade of the 3rd Indian Division (Lahore Division), which was detached along with a Battery of Mountain Artillery from the Division as it passed through on its way to France; later, it rejoined its parent Division in France. By December 1914, the Indian forces in Egypt had built up to two Divisions, that is, the 10th and the 11th, and included the Imperial Service Cavalry Brigade of state force units, the Bikaner Camel Corps and three Batteries of Mountain Artillery. The 10th Division was made responsible for the defence of the Suez Canal. The first Turkish effort to attack the canal was in January 1915, when a force of about 20,000 men advanced towards the canal. The Turks attempted to cross the canal on 3–4 February 1915, but failed and withdrew to Beersheba. The rest of the year remained quiet for the forces in Egypt and subsequently, one Brigade was pulled out and sent to Gallipoli, while the others moved to Basra and Aden.

In March 1916, Gen Archibald Murray took command of the Egyptian Expeditionary Force. Not content with a passive defence of the Suez Canal, he decided to advance into the Sinai, simultaneously building a railway line behind his forces as they progressed. The Turks attempted to delay this advance and between April–July 1916, a number of battles were fought forcing the Turks to fall back. By 9 January 1917, the Sinai Peninsula was cleared and in British hands. On 26 March 1917, an attempt was made to capture Gaza, but a strong Turk counter-attack

Table 2.6 Units of the Indian Army, Indian Volunteer and Indian State Forces that Served in East Africa

Indian Army	Indian State Forces	Indian Volunteer Forces
Cavalry • Squadron, 17th Cavalry (January 1915–January 1917) • 25th Cavalry (FF) (August 1917–February 1918)	Artillery: • 1st Kashmir Mountain Battery (December 1916–February 1918)	• Calcutta Volunteer Battery, formed from the Cossipore Artillery Volunteers (September 1914–mid-1917) • Indian Volunteer Maxim Company (September 1914–mid-1917) • North-West Railway Volunteers Machine Gun Company (November 1914–early 1918)
Artillery • 22nd Derajat Mountain Battery (FF) (December 1916–November 1918) • 24th Hazara Mountain Battery (FF) (April 1917–August 1918) • 27th (Bengal) Mountain Battery (September 1914–January 1918) • 28th (Lahore) Mountain Battery (November 1914–January 1917)	Sappers & Miners: • 1st Faridkot Field Company, Sappers & Miners (November 1917–February 1918)	
SAPPERS & MINERS • 14th Company, 2nd QVO Sappers & Miners (February–November 1918) • 25th Railway Company, Sappers & Miners (November 1914–December 1917) • 26th Railway Company, Sappers & Miners (November 1914–December 1917) • 27th Railway Company, Sappers & Miners (April 1916–April 1918)	Infantry: • Bharatpur Imperial Service Infantry (September 1914–December 1917) • 3rd Gwalior Maharajah Scindia's Own Battalion (November 1914–December 1917) • Jind Imperial Service Infantry (September 1914–January 1918) • Kapurthala Jagatjit Infantry (September 1914–December 1917)	

- 28th Railway Company, Sappers & Miners (April 1916–September 1918)
- No. 5 Pontoon Park, Bombay Sappers & Miners
- No. 4 Engineer Field Park, Madras Sappers & Miners
- No. 3 Photo-Litho Section, Madras Sappers & Miners
- No. 4 Printing Section, Madras Sappers & Miners

Infantry

- 5th Light Infantry (March 1916–June 1918)
- 13th Rajputs (Shekhawati Regiment) (November 1914–December 1915)
- 17th Infantry (Loyal Regiment) (February 1916–December 1917)
- 29th Punjabis (September 1914–May 1917)
- 30th Punjabis (December 1916–December 1917)
- 33rd Punjabis (May 1917–February 1918)
- 40th Pathans (January 1916–February 1918)
- 55th Coke's Rifles (FF) (August 1917–February 1918)
- 57th Wilde's Rifles (FF) (July 1916–September 1917)
- 58th Vaughan's Rifles (FF), one Company (February 1918–mid-1918)
- 2nd Kashmir Imperial Service Rifles (November 1914–May 1917)
- 3rd Kashmir Rifles (Raghunath Regiment) (November 1914–May 1917)
- 1st Rampur Imperial Service Infantry (September 1914–January 1918)

(Continued)

Table 2.6 *(Continued)*

Indian Army	Indian State Forces	Indian Volunteer Forces
• 61st (King George's Own) Pioneers (November 1914–February 1918) • 63rd Palmacottah Light Infantry (November 1914–January 1917) • 98th Infantry (November 1914–January 1917) • 101st Grenadiers (November 1914–August 1916) • 127th (Queen Mary's Own) Baluch Light Infantry (August 1917–February 1918) • 129th Duke of Connaught's Own Baluchis (January 1916–January 1918) • 130th (King George's Own) Baluchis (Jacob's Rifles) (January 1915–October 1917)		

Source: *India and the Great War: East Africa*, Booklet series, New Delhi: USI, pp. 6–7.

drove the British troops back. A second effort was made on 19 April 1917, but it too failed.

Thereafter, Gen Sir Edmund Allenby was appointed to command the Egyptian Expeditionary Force, with a directive to invade Palestine and capture Jerusalem before the end of the year. With direct assaults on Gaza having failed, Allenby decided to capture Beersheba first, and then roll up the Gaza defences from that direction. The summer months were spent in improving Transport and administrative arrangements. An elaborate deception plan was employed to lull the Turks into believing that Gaza remained the main objective of the British. The attack was launched on the night of 30–31 October 1917 and Beersheba fell by nightfall on 31 October. Thereafter, Gaza fell on 7 November 1917. The attack on Jerusalem was pulled up and took place on 8 December 1917. By 11 December 1917, Gen Allenby entered Jerusalem. While the attack on Jerusalem was in progress, the XXI Corps on the coast advanced to and captured Jaffa, thus securing the seaport that would aid the receipt of supplies and reinforcements. The next phase of operations aimed at occupying the Jordan Valley and was completed by May 1918.

During this period, the Egyptian Expeditionary Force was reorganised, becoming primarily an Indian force comprising of the 3rd and 7th Indian Divisions, the 4th and 5th Indian Cavalry Divisions and some 24 other Indian Battalions.

The Allied campaign in Syria commenced in September 1918. The XXXI Corps was tasked to break through the Turkish defences, and the 4th and 5th Indian Cavalry Divisions were to break out from the gap created. The attack commenced at 0430 Hours on 19 September 1918, and by 0545 Hours, the leading troops had broken through the Turkish defences. The 4th and 5th Cavalry Divisions were immediately launched and the former advanced a 100 miles in 24 hours to secure El Afule. The 13 Cavalry Brigade of the 5th Division reached Nazareth on 20 September. On 22 September 1918, the troops reached Haifa and the only way in was through a narrow defile. The 15 Imperial Service Brigade was in the lead here, with only two units, the Mysore and Jodhpur Lancers. The Brigade launched a mounted attack on the Turks holding the defile and broke through and took the town. The Battle of Haifa was one of the last Cavalry charges into defences which was conducted using horses. On 26 September 1918, orders were issued for the advance to Damascus and the troops reached the city on 30 September 1918. Thereafter, the troops advanced to Aleppo, 200 miles from Damascus, and captured it by 25 October 1918, just before the end of World War I.

Table 2.7 lists the Indian Army and Indian State Forces units that served in Egypt and Palestine during the Great War.

Gallipoli

In November 1914, Ottoman Turkey entered the war on the side of Germany, against Britain and its ally, Russia. This move immediately threatened British interests in the Middle East, especially the vital Suez Canal.

> Turkish troops...in January 1915 actually attacked [the Suez Canal], and British India became embroiled in what proved to be a long and costly campaign in Mesopotamia, an Ottoman province. Russian requests for help in its winter campaigns against the Ottomans in the Caucasus prompted British strategists Winston Churchill and Lord Kitchener to propose a naval operation against the Ottoman capital.[27]

The naval operation that intended to force a passage through the Dardanelles for British and French warships to reach Constantinople and force Ottoman Turkey's

Table 2.7 Indian Army and Indian State Forces Units that Served in Egypt and Palestine During the Great War

Indian Army	Indian State Forces
INDIAN ARMY Cavalry • 2nd Lancers (Gardner's Horse) • 6th King Edward's Own Cavalry • 9th Hodson's Horse • 18th (King George's Own) Lancers • 19th Lancers (Fane's Horse) • 20th Deccan Horse • 29th Lancers (Deccan Horse) • 34th Prince Albert Victor's Own Poona Horse • 36th Jacob's Horse • 38th (King George's Own) Central India Horse	INDIAN STATE FORCES Cavalry AND CAMEL Corps • Bhavnagar Lancers (attached to the Mysore Imperial Service Lancers) • Bikaner Camel Corps (Ganga Risala) • Hyderabad Imperial Service Lancers • Jodhpur Imperial Service Lancers • Junagadh Lancers (specialist signallers) • Kashmir Lancers (attached to the Mysore and Patiala Imperial Service Lancers) • Mysore Imperial Service Lancers • Nawanagar Lancers (specialist signallers) • 1st Patiala (Rajindra) Lancers • Ratlam Imperial Service Despatch Riders
INDIAN ARMY MOUNTAIN Artillery • 21st Kohat Mountain Battery (Frontier Force) • 26th Jacob's Mountain Battery. • 29th Mountain Battery • 32nd Mountain Battery • 38th (Reserve) Mountain Battery • 39th (Reserve) Mountain Battery	
INDIAN ARMY SAPPERS & MINERS • 1st (King George's Own) Sappers and Miners • 2nd Queen's Own Sappers and Miners • 3rd Sappers and Miners • No. 25 Railway Company, Sappers and Miners • No. 29 Railway Company, Sappers and Miners	INDIAN STATE FORCES SAPPERS & MINERS • Tehri (Garhwal) Sappers
INDIAN ARMY Infantry AND PIONEERS • 1st Battalion, 2nd Queen's Own Rajput Light Infantry • 1st Battalion, 3rd Brahmans • 1st Battalion, 6th Jat Light Infantry • 1st Battalion, 9th Bhopal Infantry • 14th (King George's Own) Ferozepore Sikhs • 1st Battalion, 15th Ludhiana Sikhs • 1st Battalion, 17th Infantry (Loyal Regiment)	INDIAN STATE FORCES Infantry • Alwar Imperial Service Infantry (Jey Paltan) • Bahawalpur Mounted Rifles • 4th Maharaja Bahadur Battalion Gwalior Infantry • Khairpur Imperial Service Mounted Rifles • 1st Kashmir Infantry (Raghupratap Regiment) • 3rd Kashmir Rifles (Raghunath Regiment) • Patiala Imperial Service Infantry

- 2nd Battalion, 18th Infantry
- 2nd Battalion, 19th Punjabis
- 20th Duke of Cambridge's Own Infantry (Brownlow's Punjabis)
- 1st Battalion, 21st Punjabis.
- 1st and 2nd Battalions, 23rd Sikh Pioneers
- 24th Punjabis
- 1st Battalion, 27th Punjabis
- 1st Battalion, 28th Punjabis
- 29th Punjabis
- 2nd Battalion, 30th Punjabis
- 2nd Battalion, 32nd Sikh Pioneers
- 1st Battalion, 33rd Punjabis1st Battalion, 34th Sikh Pioneers
- 38th Dogras
- 1st and 2nd Battalions, 39th Garhwal Rifles.
- 1st Battalion, 41st Dogras
- 2nd Battalion, 42nd Deoli Regiment
- 46th Punjabis
- 47th Sikhs
- 1st Battalion, 50th Kumaon Rifles
- 51st Sikhs (FF)
- 53rd Sikhs (FF)
- 1st Battalion, 54th Sikhs (FF)
- 1st Battalion, 56th Punjabi Rifles (FF)
- 1st Battalion, 57th Wilde's Rifles (FF)
- 58th Vaughan's Rifles (FF)
- 59th Scinde Rifles (FF)
- 62nd Punjabis
- 1st Battalion, 69th Punjabis
- 1st Battalion, 70th Burma Rifles
- 1st Battalion, 72nd Punjabis
- 74th Punjabis
- 1st Battalion, 76th Punjabis
- 1st Battalion, 89th Punjabis
- 1st Battalion, 91st Punjabis
- 92nd Punjabis
- 93rd Burma Infantry
- 2nd Battalion, 97th Deccan Infantry
- 1st and 2nd Battalions, 101st Grenadiers
- 1st Battalion, 105th Mahratta Light Infantry
- 2nd Battalion, 107th Pioneers
- 110th Mahratta Light Infantry

(*Continued*)

Table 2.7 *(Continued)*

Indian Army	Indian State Forces
• 121st Pioneers • 1st Battalion, 123rd Outram's Rifles • 2nd Battalion, 124th Duchess of Connaught's Own Baluchistan Infantry • 1st Battalion, 125th Napier's Rifles • 126th Baluchistan Infantry • 2nd Battalion, 127th (Queen Mary's Own) Baluch Light Infantry • 1st Battalion, 128th Pioneers • 1st Battalion, 129th Duke of Connaught's Own Baluchis • 1st Battalion, 130th (King George's Own) Baluchis (Jacob's Rifles) • 2nd Battalion, 151st Indian Infantry3rd Battalion, 151st Punjabi Rifles • 1st, 2nd and 3rd Battalions, 152nd Punjabis • 1st and 2nd Battalions, 153rd Punjabis. • 3rd Battalion, 153rd Rifle. • 2nd and 3rd Battalions, 154th Indian Infantry • 1st Battalion, 155th Indian Pioneers • 2nd Battalion, 155th Indian Infantry • 1st Battalion, 1st (King George's Own) Gurkha Rifles (Malaun Regiment) • 2nd Battalion, 2nd King Edward's Own Gurkha Rifles (Sirmoor Rifles) • 2nd and 3rd Battalions, 3rd Queen Alexandra's Own Gurkha Rifles • 1st Battalion, 4th Gurkha Rifles • 1st Battalion, 5th Gurkha Rifles (FF) • 1st Battalion, 6th Gurkha Rifles • 2nd Battalion, 7th Gurkha Rifles • 1st and 2nd Battalions, 8th Gurkha Rifles • 2nd Battalion, 10th Gurkha Rifles • 4th Battalion, 11th Gurkha Rifles • 1st and 2nd Battalions, Queen Victoria's Own Corps of Guides (FF) (Lumsden's) INDIAN ARMY LOGISTIC AND SUPPORT UNITS • Indian Medical Service • Indian Subordinate Medical Department	

- Indian Army Bearer Corps
- Indian Mule Corp.
- 70th Hired Camel Corps
- Indian Supply and Transport Corps
- Indian Army Ordnance Department
- Indian Army Postal Service

Source: *India and the Great War: Egypt and Palestine*, Booklet series, New Delhi: USI, pp. 14–19.

surrender, thereby ending the war in the Middle East, failed. This failure led to the idea of landing the Mediterranean Expeditionary Force (MEF) on the Gallipoli Peninsula to capture it. However, the failed naval operation had alerted the Turks who reinforced their troops on Gallipoli to four Divisions.

The invasion of Gallipoli in April 1915 marked the start of a disastrous campaign and by the end of the year, a decision was taken to end the campaign and withdraw the remaining troops. The Army which landed in Gallipoli comprised troops from across the British and French empires, including the Australian and New Zealand Army Corps (ANZAC) and Indian troops.

> The Indian Expeditionary Force that served in the Dardanelles was not very large in numbers; barely 5,000 men in a campaign that swelled from 75,000, to nearly half a million allied troops engaged by the end of the campaign. Yet it had a significant impact upon the course of the operations, and no account of the campaign can ignore the contribution of the 14th Sikhs in the Third Battle of Krithia on the 4th of June, or the 1-6th Gurkhas in the climactic Battle of Sari Bair on the 9th of August 1915.[28]

The Expeditionary Force at Gallipoli comprised of the 7th Indian Mountain Artillery Brigade, the Indian Mule Corps, a medical establishment and the 29th Indian Infantry Brigade. It 'reflected the composition of the Indian Army at the time, largely drawn from what were regarded the "martial" peoples of India—Sikhs and Muslims…from the Punjab and especially the Gurkhas….'[29] As Indian Muslims considered the Ottoman Sultan as the Caliph, two Battalions of Punjabi Muslims were replaced by the Gurkhas. A detailed list of Indian Army units that participated in the Gallipoli campaign is given in Table 2.8.

Two Indian mountain batteries (21st [Kohat] and 26th [Jacob's]) accompanied the ANZAC on 25 April 1915, the start of the campaign. They were joined by the 29th Indian Infantry Brigade on 1 May 1915.

> The Indian gunners proved their worth by stopping heavy Turkish assaults on the ANZAC positions. They saw their heaviest action on May 19…At the precariously located Quinn's post the Indian guns fought it out with Turkish guns

Table 2.8 Units of the Indian Army that Served in the Dardanelles Campaign, 1915

Fighting Units	Administrative Units
7th INDIAN MOUNTAIN ARTILLERY BRIGADE Headquarters • 21st (Kohat) Mountain Battery (FF) • 26th (Jacob's) Mountain Battery • Mountain Artillery Section, Divisional Ammunition Column	TRANSPORT • Indian Mule Cart Train, comprising the following: • Mule Corps (each a complete Corps): 1st, 2nd, 9th, 11th, 15th, 28th, 31st and 32nd • Mule Corps (detachments from): 3rd, 6th, 7th, 8th, 10th, 12th, 14th, 18th, 19th, 20th, 21st, 22nd, 23rd, 24th, 26th, 27th, 29th, 33rd, 34th, 35th, 36th and 37th. Detachments from: • Gwalior Imperial Service Transport Corps • Bharatpur Imperial Service Transport Corps • Indore (Holkar's) Imperial Service Transport Corps
29th INDIAN INFANTRY BRIGADE Headquarters • 14th King George's Own Ferozepore Sikhs • 69th Punjabis • 89th Punjabis • Rajindra Sikhs • 1-5th Gurkha Rifles (FF) • 1-6th Gurkha Rifles • 2-10th Gurkha Rifles • 1-4th Gurkha Rifles and details • 2 Double Companies, Patiala Imperial Service Infantry (attached 14th Sikhs)	HOSPITALS • 108th Indian Field Ambulance • (with 29th Indian Infantry Brigade) • 110th Indian Field Ambulance • (Clearing Hospital) (with convalescent depot) • 'C' Section, (Indian) 137th Combined Field Ambulance (with Indian Mountain Artillery Brigade) • 'C' Section, (British) 137th Combined Field Ambulance (on a transport). POSTAL • Indian Army Postal Service (IAPS), Field Post Office (FPO) No. 34

Source: *India and the Great War: Gallipoli*, Booklet series, New Delhi: USI, pp. 6–7.

> only 350 yards away and managed to silence them…and Australian defenders freely admitted that the strategic post could not have been held without the Indian Artillery.[30]

On Cape Helles, Indian troops fought with British forces. In the Third Battle of Krithia, the 14th Sikhs '…attacked the heavily defended Turkish position at Gully Ravine' on 4 June 1915, and the Battalion lost '82 per cent of the men engaged in battle.'

The MEF was designated as the IEF G in July 1915, and took part in a fresh effort to break the stalemate with a planned assault on Sari Bair and a landing at Sulva Bay. 'The column's movement from Anzac Cove to the ridge was done at night over rocky terrain and steep gullies with no reconnaissance…' causing confusion and delay, and allowing the Turks to reinforce the strategic heights.[31] After the defeat at Sari Bair, by November 2015, orders were issued to evacuate troops from the peninsula and by mid-December, the Indian troops withdrew from Gallipoli. Out of 57,000 dead, the Indians lost 1,600 in the campaign.

Inter-War Period: Reorganisation and Indianisation

In 1881, the Government of India claimed that 'the Indian Army is required to maintain internal tranquillity rather than for employment against external foes.'[32] In 1912, a committee led by Field Marshal Nicholson reiterated the Army's primary role as 'maintaining internal security and tranquillity'. In the aftermath of the Great War, the Indian Army, which had grown to over a million men during the course of the war, was demobilised and it reverted to its primary role of internal security. At the same time, the war had brought to light glaring deficiencies in the organisation and administration of the Army and steps were taken to address these issues in earnest. In 1922, the Esher Committee recommended placing the Indian Army directly under the control of the British government, which was not viewed with favour in India. Pradeep Barua writes that the Esher Committee also recommended the reorganisation and modernisation of the Indian Army, and an increase in its 'budget beyond wartime costs'. With both the Indian and British governments looking to slash, rather than increase, spending, this was not acceptable.

> The uproar caused by the Esher Report led the Committee of Imperial Defence subcommittee to launch a new study of the Indian Army, which accepted the fact that the Indian Army's main responsibility was the defence of India and not the empire.[33] With the battle of imperial commitments temporarily won, the Indian government began to reduce the Indian Army's size and its budget. Lord Rawlinson, the Commander in Chief of the Indian Army, reduced the Army's size from 159,000 men to 140,000, between 1921 and 1925, and the budget reduced from £61.5 million to £42 million.[34]

In terms of reorganisation, a Regimental System was introduced in the Indian Army:

> [T]he existing 131 Battalions were integrated into 19 Infantry Regiments. Each of these Regiments would have five active Battalions, one training Battalion (the fore runner of today's Regimental Centres) and one Indian Territorial

> Force Battalion. Soldiers were to be recruited with a colour service liability of seven years followed by eight years in the reserve, thus providing for a trained reserve to be available permanently. The 39 pre-War Cavalry Regiments were reduced to 21 and the silladar system was abolished. In 1937, three of these Regiments were converted to training Regiments. Separate Corps of Signals and Ordnance were raised as also a Veterinary Corps. An Artillery Depot was established and steps were taken to introduce mechanised Transport. In January 1935, the 1st Field Brigade of Indian Artillery was raised with four batteries, one each of Madrasis, Punjabi Mussalmans, Rajputs and Ranghars.[35]

As part of the Army's reorganisation, an inter-departmental committee—the Chatfield Committee headed by Lord Chatfield—was set up by Whitehall to look into the modernisation of the Indian Army. A second committee was set up by the Government of India under Lt Gen Claude Auchinleck, the Deputy Chief of General Staff. The Auchinleck Committee recommended that the Army must be organised to carry out five key tasks: frontier defence; coastal and anti-aircraft defence; external defence, for example, in Persia, Iraq and Malaya; internal security; and finally, provide a mobile, general-purpose reserve. The Chatfield Committee 'recommended that London pick up part of the tab for the expanded commitments of the Indian Army, and entirely subsidize the modernization of an imperial reserve Division.'[36] Thus, on the eve of the war in September 1939, while modernisation was a point of discussion, no concrete steps had been taken to modernise the Army. As in 1914, the Indian Army went to war unprepared in many ways for the demands of war, and with almost two decades of being made to undertake a somewhat truncated, limited role.

On the subcontinent, however, events were heating up. Afghanistan was seen as a buffer state in the Great Game with Imperial Russia in the late nineteenth and early twentieth centuries. While Afghanistan had remained neutral during World War I, it went to war with British India in 1919. The Third Anglo-Afghan War began on 3 May 1919, when the Afghan Army crossed the Khyber Pass into British India and captured the strategically important town of Bagh. The Indian government responded by declaring war on Afghanistan on 6 May 1919, and ordered a general mobilisation of forces. However, with war and post-war demobilisation, the armies of both Britain and India had lost a considerable number of experienced troops. Eventually, the Afghans were forced back across the Khyber, and an armistice on 8 August 1919 formally ended the war.

The war resulted in a treaty that recognised the Durand Line as the formal border between British India and Afghanistan, and allowed the Afghans to take control of their foreign affairs. Almost immediately, the tribes in Waziristan on the North-West Frontier rose in revolt, which was ultimately over by 1921. The region continued to see periodic episodes of unrest: riots in Peshawar in 1930 that led to an uprising by the Afridis; Mohamands near Peshawar rose in revolt in 1935; and in 1936, the Fakir of Ipi gave call for a holy war and fighting against his followers continued into the 1940s. Meanwhile, in this period, the Indian Army also sent troops to Shanghai (1926) and Burma (1931). In the 1930s, with increasing Japanese militarisation and its capture of Manchuria, the Army's extra-territorial commitments increased further.

This had an impact on the Indian Army's war-fighting capabilities by 1939. Attempts at modernisation had not borne fruit, owing in part to limited finances being sanctioned. Further, the increasing 'policing' and 'internal security' role played by the Army in the inter-war years had not allowed for the necessary organisational reforms or the introduction of new technologies.

The inter-war period also saw a renewed focus on the issue of 'Indianisation' of the Army. The demand for opening up of commissioned ranks of the Army to Indians had been raised for a long time. The Imperial Cadet Corps was a start in that direction, but was limited to members of princely families. The post-war years in India saw the emergence of a new 'middle' class, which looked at military service as a career option. Moreover, the demand for entry of Indians into the commissioned ranks [had] gained greater momentum during World War I, the Congress party being most vocal about it. As a result of this, the British Government, in June 1918, issued instructions for the selection of Indian Cadets for entry into the Royal Military College at Sandhurst. The annual entry was to be ten in two batches of five each. At the same time a school to train Indian Cadets for grant of temporary commissions was founded at Indore. The first batch from this Institution was commissioned on 01 December 1919 and 33 of them were granted permanent Kings Commissions with effect from 17 July 1920.[37]

This first batch included the first Chief of Staff of the Army of independent India, Field Marshal KM Cariappa. Subsequently, to speed up Indianisation as well as to improve the standards of cadets going to Sandhurst, the Royal Indian Military College (RIMC, now the Rashtriya Indian Military College) was set up in Dehradun in March 1922 for young aspirants from notable families. The King George's Royal Indian Military Colleges were set up at Jhellum and Julundhur to train viceroy's commissioned officers (VCOs) and non-commissioned officers (NCOs).[38] Sometime later, the Kitchener College was founded at Nowgong to train cadets from the ranks so as to make them fit for entry into Sandhurst.

A number of committees examined the Indianisation question during this period. The Military Requirements Committee under the Commander in Chief, Lord Rawlinson…recommended that at least 25 [per cent] of commissions granted into the Indian Army each year be filled by Indians and that this be increased by [2.5 per cent] every subsequent year. It also recommended that an Indian Military College be opened as soon as possible and commissions granted by it be considered equivalent to those from Sandhurst.[39]

The 1925 Skeene Committee, under the Chairmanship of Gen Sir Andrew Skeene, Chief of Staff…'recommended an immediate increase of vacancies in Sandhurst from 10 to 20 per year and the opening by 1930 of an Indian Sandhurst with a capacity of 100 cadets. Thirty-three cadets were to be taken in each year for a three-year course.'[40] While this recommendation was not accepted initially by the government, in 1932, the RIMC was finally established.

According to Lt Gen VK Singh:

> In an effort to ensure that no British officer would ever have to serve under an Indian, the British started a scheme by which certain selected units would have only Indian officers after a time and the others would be officered solely by British officers. The advent of World War II and a need for rapid expansion put paid to this and by the end of the war, there were a number of units where British officers and troops were serving under Indian officers.[41]

Causes of World War II

World War I (1914–18) was the most destructive conflict the world had seen until World War II (1939–45). In World War I, though the fighting stopped in November 1918, the war formally ended with the signing of the Treaty of Versailles, on 28 June 1919, between Germany and the Allied powers led by Britain and France. The treaty laid the blame for the war on Germany, which had to pay reparations to certain countries that were part of the Triple Entente, estimated in 1921 to be 132 billion gold marks. Further, Germany had to disarm and could not retain armed forces that were capable of offensive actions. It lost significant territory, covering 65,000 sq km containing 7 million people, as well as control of the Saar coal mines for a period of 15 years. France regained the provinces of Alsace-Lorraine from Germany as the older treaties of 1871 were rescinded.

The conditions imposed on Germany by the Treaty of Versailles were particularly harsh and led to considerable resentment amongst the German people. It also bankrupted Germany, especially in the aftermath of the 1929 financial crisis. The growing resentment amongst the Germans, coupled with the ruined economy, paved the way for the rise of the National Socialist German Workers' Party (known as the Nazi Party) and its leader, Adolf Hitler. In 1933, Hitler was appointed Chancellor of Germany, a mere 10 years after failing to capture power in a putsch in Munich. Almost immediately upon coming to power, Hitler went about setting aside the provisions of the Treaty of Versailles: he took back the Saar mines; rearmed the German military and rapidly built up the war machine; and embarked on a policy of expansionism to take back the territories lost in 1919.

By early 1938, the Nazis annexed Austria; the turn of Czechoslovakia was next with the invasion of the Sudetenland with its majority German-speaking people. With no push-back from the British or the French in the Munich Conference, Hitler was further emboldened. In August 1939, Germany signed a treaty with the Soviet Union; by this time, it was clear that war was on the horizon. On 01 September 1939, German troops crossed the border into Poland. On 03 September 1939, Britain declared war on Germany and World War II began.

In the Far East, Japan had risen as a power, especially following the Meiji Restoration in the mid-nineteenth century. In 1904–05, Japan went to war with Imperial Russia and defeated the latter's forces. Though it was on the Allied side in World War I, Japan had its own imperial ambitions in the region. It invaded Manchuria in 1931, and by 1937, Japanese forces were engaged in conflict in China. It allied with the Axis Powers—Germany and Italy—in World War II. It was the Japanese Army that the Indian Army faced in the jungles of Burma in the course of the war, the details of which are discussed later in the chapter.

Indian Army on the Eve of World War II

India's entry into World War II was announced by the Viceroy, Lord Linlithgow, on 03 September 1939 from his summer residence in Simla, the same day that Britain declared war on Nazi Germany. When the war commenced, the Indian Army numbered 194,373 men, a meagre increase over its 150,000 strength in 1914. It comprised of '96 Infantry Battalions and eighteen Cavalry Regiments'.[42] As mentioned earlier, modernisation had been recommended but was yet to begin. The Cavalry was mounted on trucks and had no tanks; and the Infantry lacked mortars or anti-tank weapons. Wireless sets were available only at Brigade HQ and above. The defined role for the Indian Army continued to focus on policing duties and security of India's frontiers. However, by 1945, when the war ended, the Indian Army had expanded to a strength of over 2 million men, the largest volunteer Army in history. During the war, it was engaged in operations stretching from Hong Kong to Italy. It also provided the bulk of the forces in the Burma campaign and played a significant role in the campaigns in North Africa and in Italy.

It is to the Indian Army's credit that despite going to war with the above-mentioned deficiencies, it held its own against two of the finest armies of the world—the Germans and the Japanese. Towards the end of the war it was led by its own officers at unit and sub-unit level. Brigadier KS Thimayya successfully commanded a Brigade in operations with Indian officers commanding Battalions in the Brigade and was awarded a DSO for conduct of operations in Burma.[43]

One of the key results of the Army's participation in the war was the breaking of the 'martial classes' myth. There was forced recruitment from all classes due to

Table 2.9 Indianisation During the War

Date	Indian Officers	Ratio of British to Indian Officers
1 October 1939	396	10.1: 1
1 January 1940	415	9.7: 1
1 January 1941	596	12:1
1 January 1942	1,667	8.3:1
1 January 1943	3,676	6.9:1
1 January 1944	6,566	4.5:1
1 January 1945	7,546	4.2:1
1 September 1945	8,340	4.1:1

Source: Gautam Sharma, *Nationalisation of the Indian Army, 1885–1947*, New Delhi: Allied Publishers, 1995, p. 184.

rapid wartime expansion of the Indian Army. 'The officer cadre expanded from 1000 to 15,740. Thus by the end of World War II the Indian Army was truly representative of all areas and classes of the country'[44] (see Table 2.9). In the six years of war, the Army earned nearly 6,300 awards, 31 VCs, four George Crosses, 252 Distinguished Service Orders (DSOs), 347 Indian Orders of Merit and 1,311 Military Crosses.

After the British concession to Hitler at the Munich Conference in 1938, it was apparent that war clouds were looming on the horizon. By 1939, elements of the Indian Army were deployed overseas: '[E]ven before the British Government had formally declared war in September 1939, India had despatched nearly 10,000 troops to Egypt, Aden, Singapore, Kenya and Iraq.'[45] Headquarters 4 Indian Infantry Division and 5 Indian Infantry Brigade joined the 11th Infantry Brigade in Egypt in September 1939. The period between September 1939 and April 1940 saw little fighting and is consequently termed the 'Phoney War'. Its end, and the subsequent declaration of war on Britain by Italy on 8 June 1940, led to the beginning of intense fighting in North Africa and other war theatres. However, before moving on to discuss these actions and the linked ones in East Africa and the Middle East, a mention needs to be made of a small Indian Army detachment that took part in battles in France. There were four Animal Transport Companies that supported the British Divisions and took part in the retreat to Dunkirk. This was 'Force K6':

> [a] cluster of Animal Transport Companies that were formed in the later months of 1939 in anticipation of Transport and logistical requirements on the snowbound supply routes to military posts along the Franco-German borders and in Belgium. These Animal Transport Companies were composed largely of 'muleteers' or mule drivers and service providers such as bellows-boys, blacksmiths, hammermen, farriers, cooks, dhobis, and so on.[46]

Srinath Raghavan opines that the wartime growth of the Indian Army saw three distinct phases:

1. 'In the first eight months of the war, expansion was slow. Only some 50,000 troops were added to the pre-war number [including] the Indian territorial Battalions raised for internal security duties.'[47]
2. By May 1940, a second major phase of expansion was proposed by the Indian General Staff. Apart from being 'advanced...to offer a guarantee to Afghanistan against a Russian attack...the General Staff believed that India would be called upon...to contribute to the defence of the Middle East.'[48]
3. 'The third stage of wartime enlargement lasted from January 1944 to September 1945. By early 1944 it was obvious that the fortunes of war were turning... [thus] the focus was on training the Indian Army at its "maximum strength in maximum efficiency".[49] Training and modernization, rather than recruitment were now foremost in the mind of military planners.'[50]

In the second phase, in particular, it was proposed to raise:

> 18 Infantry Battalions and three field Artillery Regiments as well as supporting services such as engineers and signals, organizational and logistical units for six Army Divisions...Simultaneously...raise an equal number of units to replace the ones that might be sent out of the country...In August 1940, New Delhi offered to prepare four Infantry Divisions and one armoured Division for overseas deployment—if the British government agreed to equip these forces... [eventually], it was agreed that India would raise four new Infantry Divisions by December 1941 and a fifth by mid-1942.[51]

Recruitment grew considerably in the second phase, with monthly recruitment exceeding 50,000 men a month. Recruitment of technical personnel also expanded. In addition, troops from India's princely states were pressed into service in the war. 'In early 1942, 264,000 Indian troops were serving overseas, including 91,000 in Iraq, 20,000 in the Middle East, 56,000 in Malaya and 20,000 in Burma...at the end of 1942, the Indian Army stood at almost 1.5 million men...', with 'Indian state forces and British units in India [adding] up to another 1,70,000 men.'[52]

Indian Army World War II Theatres

North and East Africa and the Middle East[53]

At the beginning of World War II, the British Middle East Command stretched from the Persian Gulf to Egypt and thence along the coast of North Africa. In June 1939, Gen Archibald Wavell was appointed General Officer Commanding-in-Chief (GOC-in-C), Middle East Command. Following Italy's declaration of war against the British in 1940, the Italian forces in Libya—comprising of around eight Divisions—became a major threat to the command. The Italians were located some 250 miles from the Egyptian port of Alexandria. Apart from Libya, Italy's colonies in Africa included Somaliland and Abyssinia (Ethiopia), which Benito Mussolini had annexed in 1935.

Gen Wavell had the following troops available: the British 7 Armoured Division, later gaining fame as the 'Desert Rats'; and the 4th Indian Division, less a Brigade. The 4 Indian Division was the first formation of the Indian Army to serve on the frontline and had been in the desert since September 1939. The Middle East Command also included Brigades of the Australian and New Zealand Divisions, the first of which reached Egypt by February 1940 and were under training,

After declaring war on Britain on 08 June 1940, Italy crossed the Egyptian frontier only in early September. It had reached Sidi Barani by the end of the month and dug into a series of fortified defensive camps. Gen Wavell decided to attack the Italians with the 7th Armoured Division and 4th Indian Division, along with the 16th British Infantry Brigade and 7th Royal Tank Regiment also under his command. The attack commenced on 09 December 1940 with 11th Indian Infantry Brigade attacking the first set of camps, which were captured quickly by the 2nd Cameron Highlanders and 1/6th Rajputana Rifles. The 5th Indian Infantry Brigade followed up and captured the camp at Tumar West by the evening of the same day. On 10 December, 16th British Infantry Brigade captured Sidi Barani. On 11 December 1940, 4th Indian Division was pulled out to reinforce the troops in Sudan.

Italian East Africa (Somaliland) was important as it abutted onto the Red Sea, a major supply route, and Italian ships and submarines based at Massawa could interfere with shipping. Gen Platt, who was the C-in-C in Sudan, initially had limited forces; these were reinforced by the 5th Infantry Division in September 1940. At the end of December 1940, 11th Infantry Brigade of 4th Indian Division also arrived in Sudan, with the rest of the division coming together by the end of January 1941. Faced by these additional troops, the Italians withdrew from forward positions by mid-January, with British forces moving in pursuit and crossing the border on 19 January 1941. Second Lieutenant. PS Bhagat was the first Indian officer to be awarded the VC in the war for continuous mine clearing operations under enemy fire from 01 February to 4 February 1941.[54]

The advance halted at Keren, where the Italians made a determined stand, with severe fighting between 02 February to 27 March 1941 when Keren finally fell. Subedar Richpal Ram of 4/6th Rajputana Rifles won his VC in this operation.[55] On

08 April 1941, Massawa fell to the British and the Indians, and on 19 May, the Duke of Aosta and the remainder of the Italian forces also surrendered. After the fall of Keren, the 4th Indian Division was recalled to Egypt.

Meanwhile, the situation had changed in North Africa. The destruction of the Italian Army had compelled the Germans to reinforce this front. Gen Erwin Rommel was dispatched North Africa along with German armoured formations. Facing Rommel and the Afrika Korps in Libya were British forces comprising the 2nd Armoured Division, less a Brigade, 9th Australian Division and 3rd Indian Motor Brigade that arrived in the area in March 1941. The 3rd Motor Brigade consisted of three Cavalry Regiments—the 2nd Royal Lancers, 11th Prince Albert Victor's Own Cavalry and 18th Cavalry—mounted in un-armoured trucks, armed only with Bren guns and no Artillery support. The Brigade was ordered to hold a position at Mechili, 100 miles west of Tobruk. On 31 March 1941, Rommel launched an attack and surrounded Tobruk by 11 April 1941. The 3rd Indian Motor Brigade, by holding on to Mechili till 08 April, had delayed the German advance. Once the 4th Indian Division came back from East Africa, Gen Wavell launched a counter-attack, termed Operation Battle Axe, on 15 June 1941; however, faced with superior German tanks, the attack failed. Wavell was replaced by Gen Claude Auchinleck in North Africa.

Gen Auchinlek, on taking over the Middle Eastern Command, was exhorted by British Prime Minister Winston Churchill to go on the offensive. Operation Crusader was eventually launched on 18 November 1941; it achieved some initial success but British armour was eventually outgunned by German Panzers. The Germans then counter-attacked and the 4th Indian Division, forming part of XIII Corps, generally held on to its positions. Auchinleck continued with the attack and the Germans started falling back, with the 4th Indian Division taking part in the pursuit to El Aghelia.

Rommel struck back while the British were reorganising prior to resuming the offensive. On 21 January 1942, three German columns broke through the British defences and captured Benghazi on 29 January 1942. The 4th Indian Division was holding the area of Benghazi, with 11th Brigade detached at Tobruk. The 7th Brigade, though cut off by the Germans in the area of Benghazi, broke out and managed to get back to reserve positions. The British positions were at Gazala, with the 29th Indian Infantry Brigade of 5th Indian Division and 3rd Indian Motor Brigade deployed towards the desert flank of this position. Rommel launched his attack on 26 May 1942, with the 3rd Indian Motor Brigade being attacked on the morning of 27 May by two Armoured Divisions; it put up a strong resistance with the field Artillery playing a major role. Major (Maj) PP Kumaramangalam (later Chief of Staff of the Indian Army) extricated best of the six troops after the ammunition was over, and was awarded a DSO for his brave actions. The Brigade managed to destroy around 52 enemy tanks before it was overrun. This was followed by a month of fighting in which the 4th, 5th and 11th Indian Infantry Divisions took part. In this, 10th Brigade and half of 9th Infantry Brigade of the 5th Indian Infantry Division were destroyed and 11th Infantry Brigade of the 4th Indian Division was trapped in Tobruk and forced to surrender. The British Army retreated to El Alamein on the outskirts of Alexandria, where it decided to hold the German advance into Egypt.

Gen Auchinleck was relieved by Gen Alexander as GOC-in-C, Middle East Command, while Gen Bernard Montgomery took over as GOC-in-C of the 8th Army. Montgomery launched his attack on the Germans at El-Alamein on 23 October 1942. Though the 4th Indian Infantry Division was present here, it did not have a large role in the initial operations. When the 8th Army found itself held up by the Germans on the Mareth Line (based on a range of hills), the expertise of Indian troops in mountain warfare came in handy. The 4th Indian Infantry Division was called up to break through the Mareth Line, which it did by going through the middle of the mountains, thus surprising the defenders. It then went on to capture the Fatnassa Feature, the key to the Wadi Akarit position. For his leadership and courage during this attack, Subedar Lal Bahadur Thapa of 1st Battalion, 2nd Gurkhas, was awarded the VC.[56] By this time, the US Army had reached North Africa and were located in Tunisia. The 8th Army was closing into a junction with the Americans. The 4th Indian Division and 7th Armoured Division were transferred to the 1st British Army and took part in the final attack on Enfidaville in the Tunisia campaign. On 12 May 1943, Gen Hans-Jurgen von Arnim, C-in-C of the Axis forces in Tunisia, surrendered to Lieutenant Colonel LCJ Showers, Commanding Officer of the 1st Battalion, 2nd Gurkhas.

Events in the region of the Persian Gulf were also unfolding along with those in North Africa. In March 1941, a pro-German group seized power in Iraq. The 8th Indian Infantry Division was sent to Basra to secure the city. Once it was secured, the Division advanced to Baghdad, facing little resistance. It reached Baghdad on 30 April 1941, and the previous government was reinstated. The 8th Indian Division was joined by the 10th Indian Infantry Division in Iraq to undertake operations in Syria. During the first week of June 1941, operations were launched to secure Syria, in which 5th Indian Infantry Brigade of the 4th Indian Division participated.

In June 1941, the German Army invaded the Soviet Union as part of Operation Barbarossa. This made it imperative to secure Iran as a gateway to the Soviet Union. The ruler of Iran, Shah Reza I, was perceived to be pro-German, therefore the Soviets and the British jointly invaded Iran on 25 August 1941. The 8th and 10th Indian Infantry Divisions from Iraq formed the British compliment of the invading force. Subsequent to these events, though no actual operations took place in Syria, Iraq or Iran, six Infantry Divisions and one Armoured Division were deployed in the area for most of the war. The 203 and 204 Companies of the Royal Indian Army Service Corps manned 10-tonne trucks, conveying supplies from Baluchistan to Tabruz in

Russia through blizzards, snow and ice. The Soviets awarded the Order of the Red Star to Subedar Narayan Rao Nikkam and Havaldar Gajender Singh in appreciation of their efforts.

Southeast Asia[57]

Japan comprises of four main islands with limited natural resources. It had been modernising since the beginning of the twentieth century and had developed both a strong, modern military and economy. Its industries were dependent on outside sources for oil, raw materials and other requirements. Its imperial ambitions needed colonies to supply its industries. For this, Japan invaded Manchuria in September 1931; Inner Mongolia in 1936; and in 1937, it went to war with China (the Second Sino-Japanese War), which predates the war in Europe. Japan's entry into World War II took place on 22 September 1940 with the invasion of French Indochina; five days later, Japan signed the Tripartite Pact with Germany and Italy on 27 September 1940. On 7 December 1941, the Japanese naval fleet launched an attack on the US naval base at Pearl Harbour in the Hawaiian Islands, which brought the US formally into World War II. On 8 December, the Japanese moved in deeper into Southeast Asia, landing in Malaya. Post its attack on the US, Tokyo declared war on the US as well as on Great Britain.

Hong Kong was the nearest British outpost to Japan at the time, and was garrisoned by six Battalions. Two of the six Battalions were the 5/7th Rajputs and 2/14th Punjabis. The Japanese attacked Hong Kong on 08 December 1941. With no air support or hope of reinforcement, the small garrison fought gallantly against at least two Divisions of the Japanese before surrendering on 25 December 1941, having taken around 3,000 casualties while inflicting many more on the Japanese.

The Japanese simultaneously invaded the Malay Peninsula. Pre-war plans catered for the defence of the peninsula and Singapore against a sea-borne invasion employing a combination of naval and air power, with limited attention to land advance along the length of the peninsula. The first Indian troops deployed in Malaya were the 12th Indian Infantry Brigade, which reached Malaya in August 1939. By December 1941, two Indian Divisions were present in Malaya—the 9th and the 11th Indian Divisions, grouped under the Indian III Corps. The 9th Indian Division was on the eastern coast, with a Brigade each holding Kota Bahru and Kuantan, 150 miles to the south. The 11th Division was on the west coast of the Malay Peninsula, in the area of Jitra, to cover the Alor Star group of airfields. Both Divisions had been training for deployment in the western desert and had little to no experience of jungle warfare.

The Japanese opened their attack on night 07–08 December 1941, with landings at Kota Bahru and an advance on to Jitra by Troops landed in Thailand. At Kota Bahru, the 3/17th Dogras put up strong resistance but were finally forced out; counter-attacks to regain lost positions were a failure. On 09 December 1941, British warships—the *Prince of Wales* and *Repulse*—sailed up to Kota Bahru to try and disrupt the landings but were sunk by Japanese air attacks. As their position was now untenable, the Brigade withdrew. On the western side of the peninsula, positions of the 28th Brigade were broken when the Japanese attacked with tanks, against which the troops had no defence. By 31 January 1942, all Allied troops had withdrawn into Singapore, which fell to the Japanese on 14 February 1942. The fall of Singapore led to 85,000 British, Indian and Australian troops being taken prisoner by the Japanese. The fall was one of the largest defeats suffered by the British and, to an extent, shook the confidence of the Indian soldier in his British officers. Many of the prisoners of war (POWs) later joined the Indian National Army.

Simultaneously, the Japanese attacked Burma by advancing through the jungles on the Thai–Burma border and capturing the airfield at Victoria Point by 10 December 1941. The British forces in Burma, at the time, consisted of the 1st Burma Division with two Brigades, 13th Indian and 1Burma, and the 17 Indian Infantry Division, with 6th and 46th Indian Infantry Brigades and 2nd Burma Brigade. The 17th Indian Infantry Division was responsible for the area of the Tenasserim Peninsula, its primary task being to delay the enemy advance to Rangoon so as to allow reinforcements to be built up through the port. The natural defence line was the Sittang River, which the 17th Indian Infantry Division intended to hold. On 22 February 1942, the Japanese launched an attack on the Sittang defences. The bridge on the Sittang was demolished on 23 February to ensure that the Japanese would not capture it intact; however, the demolition left nearly two Brigades stranded on the wrong side of the river.

> Elements of these Brigades swam across during the next night but had to abandon their vehicles and equipment. All the division could muster the next day were 148 officers and 3350 men and only 1420 rifles. The enemy, nevertheless, was delayed for fourteen days giving time for the 7 Armoured Brigade to be landed at Rangoon.[58]

On 5 March 1942, Gen Sir Harold Alexander took over as C-in-C, Burma, and decided to group the two Divisions as a Corps ('BurCorps') to be commanded by Lt Gen William Slim. Rangoon was evacuated on 07 March and the retreat continued by way of Prome and then on to Yenangyaung, where the oil installations were destroyed before they could fall into Japanese hands. On 28 April 1942, orders were issued to withdraw to India and by May, the remnants of the Army in Burma had reached India.[59]

The Japanese campaign in Malaya and Burma bested the British and Indian Army, and showed up their deficiencies in terms of training and logistics, equipment and air support. A massive effort now began in India to raise new formations, as also conduct training in jungle warfare. The Chota Nagpur Plateau was the training ground and it was here that Gen Slim trained his XV Corps.

In the meantime, Army HQ ordered the 14th Indian Division to advance down the Mayu Peninsula in the Arakan; the 6th British Division was ordered to capture Akyab from the sea. The advance progressed well initially, but was held up by 6 January 1943, with unsuccessful efforts to break through the Donbaik and Rathedaung positions. In April 1943, the Japanese crossed the Mayu range using jungle tracks, and set up roadblocks behind the 14 Indian Infantry Division. The Division was forced to withdraw and by 14 May 1943, it was back to where it had started from.

> While a failure, the first Arakan campaign was invaluable in giving an insight into Japanese tactics, especially their outflanking moves through jungles to cut the lines of communication of opposing troops. From these came the directions that from now on troops cut off would not retreat but would stay and fight and they would be supplied by air.[60]

The Army raised and trained new formations throughout 1943. As its strength increased, new Corps were raised and they were grouped into the 15th Army under Gen William Slim. The IV Corps held Imphal and the border beyond it, while XV Corps held the Arakan front. In February 1943, Maj Gen Orde Wingate's first Chindit expedition was launched, boosting troop morale. In August 1943, the South East Asia Command was established with Admiral Lord Louis Mountbatten as Supreme Commander. This Command was henceforth responsible for all operations in the area, and Army HQ in India now became responsible for administration of the Army in Burma.

In November 1943, XV Corps was launched in another effort to clear the Arakan Peninsula. The 5 Indian Infantry Division advanced along the right of the Mayu Peninsula and 7 Indian Infantry Division, with 81st West African Division protecting the flank.[61] Maungdaw was captured by 10 January 1944, and a road across the Mayu range, through the Ngakyedauk Pass, was constructed. However, efforts to capture Razabil and Buthidaung did not succeed. Between 03 and 04 February 1944, the Japanese:

> infiltrated three columns through XV Corps positions to cut off various elements in the expectation that the surrounded forces would break out and withdraw as they had always done before. But these forces took up all round defence and stood fast. Among the most remarkable of these boxes was the 7 Infantry Division's Administrative Box, manned initially by Headquarter staff and a miscellany of administrative units who defended themselves stoutly till reinforced by elements of 9 Infantry Brigade of the 5 Indian Infantry Division.[62]

With air supplies beginning on 10 February, the Japanese found themselves stranded. The 26th Indian and 36th British Divisions moved up in support and by 24 February 1944, the Japanese were retreating back through the jungle.

'Even while the Arakan campaign was going on, Lieutenant General Renya Mutaguchi, Commander of the 15th Japanese Imperial Army in Burma, had been planning an offensive to secure Imphal (in Manipur) and Kohima (in Nagaland) and then to break out into the Assam plains.'[63] Mutaguchi had three Divisions—the 15th, 31st and the 33rd Divisions—and planned to cut Imphal off using the 15th Division, while the 31st Division moved on through the jungle to seize Kohima. The 33rd Division was to advance along the Tiddim–Imphal axis.[64] Imphal was the HQ and base of IV Corps, consisting of the 17, 20 and 23 Indian Infantry Divisions. Of these, 17 and the 20 Indian Infantry Divisions were operating ahead of Imphal towards Tiddim and Tamu.

The Battles of Imphal and Kohima were a major turning point in the Southeast Asian theatre of World War II. It was at these battles that the Japanese advance into India was halted. Subsequently, in 1945, the Japanese were finally driven back.

> British military historian Robert Lyman describes the importance of the twin battles: 'It is clear that Kohima/Imphal was one of the four great turning-point battles in the Second World War, when the tide of war changed irreversibly and dramatically against those who initially held the upper hand.'[65] The battles at Stalingrad, El Alamein and in the Pacific between the US and Japanese navies were the other three. In April 2013, the Battles of Imphal and Kohima were together named 'Britain's Greatest Battle' by the National Army Museum in the United Kingdom (UK).[66]

The Japanese build-up opposite Imphal was clear by early 1944. Gen William Slim, Commander of the 14th Army, decided that if Imphal was attacked it would be held and the enemy attackers destroyed as a preliminary to his own offensive into Burma. He was, however, not sure of when the enemy attack would take place and delayed orders for the outlying forces of IV Corps to withdraw to Imphal.[67]

The Japanese attack on 06 March 1944 cut off the 17 Indian Infantry Division from Imphal, which fought its way back assisted by two Brigades of 23 Indian Infantry Division that came forward from Imphal. Although the Japanese had surrounded Imphal, they were faced by a full British Corps that could still be supplied by air from airfields at Imphal and Palel.

In Kohima, a garrison of only the 1st Battalion, Assam Regiment, and a few other units was surrounded by an entire Japanese Division. On 29 March 1944, 161 Infantry Brigade of the 5 Indian Infantry Division flew into Dimapur and was immediately sent forward to relieve the garrison in Kohima. By 15 April 1944, a Brigade of 2nd (British) Division moved up and the 161 Indian Infantry Brigade relieved Kohima on 18 April 1945. The 2/5th Royal Gurkha Rifles (FF) made history in Kohima, winning three VCs, two of them on a single day. Indeed, Kohima can boast of the distinction of being one of the bloodiest battles of World War II, with Japanese and British troops virtually eyeballing each other.

Fierce fighting also continued around Imphal and the 5 Indian Infantry Division was flown in from Arakan to reinforce the garrison here. 'It was only on 08 July 1944 that General Mutaguchi accepted that his offensive had failed and ordered the remnants of his force to fall back across the Chindwin.'[68]

With the Japanese retreat, Gen Slim was ready to launch his operations to regain Burma. The XXXIII Corps and IV Corps crossed the Chindwin on 03 and 04 December 1944. The Japanese steadily retreated, with the aim of fighting behind the Irrawady River. By 14 January 1945, the 19 Indian Infantry Division had secured two bridgeheads across the river, which drew the bulk of the Japanese forces to this area, thus diverting their attention from the main crossings by IV Corps further south on 14 February 1945. Meiktila was secured on 05 March and Mandalay on 20 March 1945. The next stop was Rangoon. With lines of communication and supply stretched, only IV Corps was sent forward. The 17 Indian Infantry Division reached Pegu on 01 May 1945, but could not advance further due to the monsoon. Meanwhile, the Japanese had vacated Rangoon and the city was secured by the 26 Indian Infantry Division landing from the sea. The 50 Indian Parachute Brigade secured Elephant Point via an air-borne assault. Simultaneously, XV Corps cleared the Arakan. While mopping-up operations continued, the forces were reorganised. The 12th Army was raised for Burma and the 14th Army was pulled back to train and prepare for an amphibious assault to recapture Malaya and Singapore.

The war in Europe ended in May 1945, but that in the Southeast Asian theatre continued. It ended only after the atomic bombs were dropped over Hiroshima and Nagasaki in Japan by the Americans on 6 and 9 August 1945. On 15 August 1945, Japanese Emperor Hirohito announced the surrender of Japan and the surrender document was signed formally on 02 September 1945.

Italy[69]

Once North Africa was secured by May 1943, the Allies decided to press on to Europe via Italy. The first step in this invasion was to secure the island of Sicily. The 15th Army Group of Gen Sir Harold Alexander, which comprised the British 8th Army under Gen Bernard Montgomery and the American 5th Army under Gen Mark Clark, took part in the invasion. British and American troops landed in Sicily on 10 July 1943 and by mid-August, the island was secured. On 03 September 1943, the 8th Army landed at the toe of Italy (Operation Baytown) and on 09 September, the 5th Army landed at Salerno (Operation Avalanche). After heavy fighting, both beachheads were secured.

The 3/10th Baluchis and 3/12th Frontier Force landed as beachhead troops during the Sicilian landings, while the Jodhpur Sardar Light Infantry played a similar role at Salerno, where Major Ram Singh was awarded a DSO.[70]

The Allied advance into Italy met with stiff resistance at the Gustav Line, one of a series fortified lines intended to defend a western section of Italy, focused around the town of Monte Cassino. An important highway to Rome ran through the town, which made it a strategic target. With the Allied forces held up at the Gustav Line, the 8th Indian Division joined the 8th Army on 19 September 1943. The first operation was the successful crossing of the Trigno River on 02 November 1943, before moving on to the Sangro River. The 8 Indian Infantry Division managed to get a foothold across the river on 25 November 1943, but opposition was only cleared by 31 November. The advance then continued to the Moro River. Meanwhile, the 4 Indian Infantr Division arrived in Italy.

Monte Cassino and the monastery on top of the hill dominated the advance beyond. In January 1944, American efforts to capture this position failed. Early in February 1944, the 4th Indian and 2nd New Zealand Divisions were tasked to capture the position. The attack commenced on 16 February but they were unable to make progress, with the 4/6th Rajputana Rifles losing 196 men and the 2nd Gurkha Rifles also suffering heavy casualties. A second attack in March partially succeeded in securing some of the approaches to Monte Cassino, but the advance was stalemated by 25 March 1944. The 4th Indian Infantry Division had lost 4,000 men by this time. It was pulled back and the Polish Corps along with the 8th Indian Division and the 2nd Canadian Cavalry Brigade were brought forward. The 8 Indian Infantry Division was given the task to secure a bridgehead over the Gari River. The attack commenced on 12 May and after fierce fighting, the bridgehead was secured by 14 May 1944. It was in these operations that Sepoy Kamal Ram of 3/8th Punjabis won a VC for clearing four enemy machine gun positions.[71]

The Allies now closed in on the Gothic Line. 'The 4 and 10 Indian Infantry Divisions and 43 Gurkha Lorried Brigade took part in the battles to clear this line and the subsequent pursuit.'[72] The 10th Indian Infantry Division arrived in Italy at the end of March 1945. 'In one of these actions Naik Yashwant Gadge of 3 Marathas won a posthumous Victoria Cross for single-handedly charging and destroying an enemy position when his Company Commander and six other NCOs had been killed.'[73]

The next major action was the crossing of the Senio River on 9 April 1944, which involved 19th and 21st Brigades of the 8th Indian Division. During this attack, Sepoy Ali Haider of 6/13th Frontier Force Rifles and Sepoy Namdeo Jadhav of 1/5th Marathas were awarded VCs. Through this bridgehead, the 8th Indian Division broke through and carried out the pursuit till the end of the surrender of German forces in Italy on 3 May 1945. During this period, Rifleman Thaman Gurung of 1/5th Royal Gurkha Rifles (FF) was awarded a posthumous VC for action at Monte San Bartolo.[74]

Aftermath of the World Wars

The Indian Army went to war in 1914 and served in Europe (France and Belgium), Gallipoli, East Africa, Mesopotamia, Egypt, Palestine, Persia and North China. By the end of the war, the Army of 150,000 men had expanded to over one million men. The war thrust the Indian Army into the modern age and it distinguished itself over the course of the next four years. In the aftermath of the war, the Army was reduced in size and went back to its policing duties in the subcontinent, the focus broadly being internal security and defence of British India.

In 1939, the Indian Army went to war once again as World War II broke out in Europe. Over the next six years, it fought in every major battle and campaign in Europe, North Africa, Burma and Indo-China. It was the largest volunteer Army ever to fight in a war with over 2.5 million men recruited during the war. The impact of World War II on the Indian Army was significant. Though it entered the war somewhat unprepared for what was to come, the Army that emerged after 1945 was a mature, confident fighting force that would take on the responsibilities that came with independence. During the war, the Army rapidly expanded, and Indianised to a great extent. The theory of 'martial classes' was done away with and recruitment was no longer limited to certain geographical and demographic locations.

By 1947, a mere two years after the end of the war, India had moved towards gaining independence from Great Britain. But with independence came the partition of the subcontinent and the emergence of two successor states: India and Pakistan. The Indian Army was divided between these two states. Almost immediately, the officers and men who had fought with each other in World War II, now fought each other in their new role as armies of independent, yet hostile nations.

Small Wars

Col CE Callwell defines 'little' or 'small' wars as '...campaigns other than those where both the opposing sides consist of regular troops.'[75] He goes on to state: 'The expression small war has in reality no particular connection with the scale on which any campaign may be carried out; it is simply used to denote, in default of a better, operations of regular armies against irregular, or comparatively speaking irregular, forces.'[76] Small wars were also a reflection of the times, where irregular opponents were often deemed as 'savage' or 'uncivilized'.

The Indian Army waged numerous small wars in the second half of the nineteenth century and leading up to World War I, mainly against irregular armies. 'It usually fought alongside British Army and Imperial Service units within small Army in India expeditionary forces.'[77] It did so in Africa (Sudan) and in China. The stage of the Indian Army's small wars was mostly the 6,000 mile northern border of British India, running from the Makran desert by the Arabian Sea, past the eastern marches of Afghanistan, across the southern face of the Himalayas, and on to jungles of Assam and Burma.

The purposes of India's small wars were normally to inflict short and sharp punishment for acts against imperial authority. The policy beneath them all was ultimately defensive, that is, to safeguard imperial interests on and near the subcontinent.[78]

As the North-West Frontier was India's principal small war theatre, the Indian Army fought a particular type of small war there: 'hill warfare'.[79] Between 1851 and 1854, in particular, the British in India undertook a number of minor campaigns and military expeditions on the North-West Frontier, in which the Indian troops participated. These included operations against the Waziris in the 1850s, expeditions in the vicinity of Peshawar and a 1853 expedition against the Jowaki Afridis. The Frontier, again, was the focus of the British between 1855 and 1863.

According to George Morton-Jack, India's other sorts of small wars—in India's north-eastern jungles, on the Tibetan Plateau or in African desert and bushland—were in many respects similar to hill warfare. The ground was dense with natural obstacles; the irregular enemies avoided gathering in large numbers for decisive battles and had no Artillery; the Indian forces spread out in regions that had few roads and no railways; and the battle casualties were low.[80]

Beginning in the 1860s, there were a number of campaigns in Africa. While the scene for small wars in the early nineteenth century was the Indian subcontinent and Asia, it later shifted to Africa. In the British expedition to Abyssinia (1868), conducted in retaliation to the Absynnian emperor's imprisoning of missionaries and British government representatives as hostages, the task was given to the Army of the Bombay Presidency. The force consisted of 13,000 British and Indian soldiers, 26,000 camp followers and over 40,000 animals, including the elephants. Indian troops, such as the 23rd Punjab Pioneers, were present at the Battle of Magdala.

Indian Regiments had been sent by the British to China in the period leading up to the Opium War. The war culminated with the Treaty of Nanking in 1842, and the opening up of Chinese ports to the British.[81] Half a century later, in the Boxer Rebellion (1900–01), Chinese rebels besieged over 400 foreigners in Beijing's Foreign Legation Quarter. Again, it was troops from the Indian Army that played a crucial role in lifting the siege; and Indian troops were the first to come to the aid of the besieged foreigners.

> On August 4, 1900, a relief force of more than 3000 soldiers from Sikh and Punjabi Regiments left Tianjin, part of the larger eight-nation alliance that was dispatched to aid the besieged quarter, where 11 countries had set up legations…'[they crawled] through the Imperial sewage canals', undetected by the Boxers…Indian troops were also dispatched to guard churches and Christian missionaries, the targets of the Boxer uprisings.[82]

Later, the British deployed Sikh soldiers as law enforcement officers in ports like Shanghai and Hong Kong, where their trading Companies had set up a large presence by the early twentieth century.

In India's north-east, such small wars/expeditions included the Lushai Expedition (1871–72) into Assam; the 1888 Sikkim expedition (conducted to force Tibetan forces from the territory of Sikkim); the Anglo-Manipur War (1891); and the Anglo-Burmese War, leading to the capture of Rangoon on 14 April 1852.

In the Boer War in South Africa, the British succeeded in extending their control over the Boer republics of Transvaal and Orange Free State. The British victory was aided in large part by Indian troops. Not only did Indian troops serve in the war, but 'military bases in India were brought into service as detention camps for thousands of Boer prisoners of war (PoWs).'[83] Unlike the small wars mentioned above, the opponents in this case were the white Afrikaner (Dutch) settlers in South Africa. According to Andrew Whitehead, Britain and its colonies deployed around half-a-million combatants in the war.

> Thousands of officers and soldiers of the British Indian Army were deployed in South Africa, particularly Cavalry units which were particularly suitable for the terrain. Although these combatants were largely British, Cavalry forces require a lot of support staff: veterinary workers, grooms and farriers. It's been estimated that as many as 9,000 Indians were part of the military contingent that served in the Boer War.[84]

Notes

1. *Report of the Special Commission Appointed by His Excellency the Governor-General in Council to Enquire into the Organization and Expenditure of the Army in India* (Eden Commission), Simla: Government of India, 1879, p. 5.
2. Ibid., pp. 17, 43, 71.
3. RA Johnson, 'Russians at the Gates of India? Planning for the Defence of India, 1885–1900', *The Journal of Military History*, Vol. 67, No. 3, 2003, p. 720.
4. See *India and the Great War: An Overview*, Booklet series, New Delhi: United Service Institution of India (USI), p. 11.

5. 'Statistical Abstract of Information regarding the Armies at Home and Abroad, 1914–1920', p. 785, quoted in Kaushik Roy, *Indian Army and the First World War: 1914–1918*, New Delhi: Oxford University Press, 2018, Kindle edition.
6. Roy, *Indian Army and the First World War: 1914–1918*, n. 5.
7. *The Army in India and its Evolution: Including an Account of the Establishment of the Royal Air Force in India*, reprint, New Delhi: Anmol, 1985, p. 99.
8. Ibid., p. 61.
9. SD Pradhan, 'Indian Army and the First World War', in DeWitt C. Ellinwood and S.D. Pradhan (eds), *India and World War I*, New Delhi: Manohar, 1978, p. 51.
10. SD Pradhan, 'Organization of the Indian Army on the Eve of the Outbreak of the First World War', *Journal of the United Service Institution of India*, Vol. 102, No. 426, 1972, p. 69.
11. *India and the Great War: An Overview*, n. 4, p. 15.
12. Roy, *Indian Army and the First World War: 1914–1918*, n. 5.
13. Ibid.
14. Pradeep Barua, *The Late Colonial Indian Army: From the Afghan Wars to the Second World War*, Lanham, MD: Lexington Books, 2021, Kindle edition.
15. Corrigan, *Sepoys in the Trenches: The Indian Corps on the Western Front 1914–15*, p. ix, quoted in Roy, *The Indian Army and the First World War: 1914–1918*, n. 5.
16. War Diary IEFA Army Headquarters, India, 1–31 January 1916, Vol. 18, Appendix 44, from Deputy Adjutant General, Indian Section, Rouen, to the War Section, Army Headquarters, Telegram, 25 January 1916, WWI/176/H; Willcocks, *With the Indians in France*, p. 9, quoted in Roy, *The Indian Army and the First World War: 1914–1918*, n. 5.
17. This Section is adapted from Maj Gen Ian Cardozo, AVSM, SM, *The Indian Army in World War I: 1914–1918*, New Delhi: USI and Manohar, pp. 94–158.
18. The Schlieffen Plan was a battle plan drawn up by Count von Schlieffen, a German military strategist. It sought to ensure German military victory in the event of a two-front war against both France and Russia, with the aim of invading France from the north (and avoiding fortifications along the Franco-German border, and capturing Paris, thereby ensuring its capitulation within a short span of two months). The plan formed the basis of Germany's offensive in August 1914, with limited success.
19. Simon Doherty and Tom Donovan, *The Indian Corps on the Western Front: A Handbook and Battlefield Guide*, New Delhi: Centre for Armed Forces Historical Research, USI, 2014, p. 47
20. Cardozo, *The Indian Army in World War I: 1914–1918*, n. 17, p. 102.
21. Peter Simkins, Geoffrey Jukes and Michael Hickey, *The First World War: The War to End All Wars*, UK: Osprey Publishing, 2013, p. 93.
22. This Section is adapted from Cardozo, *The Indian Army in World War I: 1914–1918*, n. 17, pp. 94–158.
23. Gary Sheffield, *The First World War in 100 Objects*, London: Andre Deutsch, 2013, p. 108.
24. This Section is adapted from Cardozo, *The Indian Army in World War I: 1914–1918*, n. 17, pp. 94–158.

25. Maj Gen, VK Singh, 'The World Wars and Prelude to Independence', in Maj Gen Ian Cardozo, AVSM, SM (ed.), *Indian Army: A Brief History*, New Delhi: USI, 2007, p. 35.
26. This Section is adapted from ibid., pp. 33–34.
27. Peter Stanley, 'Indians, Anzacs and Gallipoli, 1915', *Journal of Defence Studies*, Vol. 8, No. 3, July–September 2014, p. 22.
28. *India and the Great War: Gallipoli*, Booklet series, New Delhi: USI, p. 4.
29. Stanley, 'Indians, Anzacs and Gallipoli, 1915', n. 27, p. 23.
30. Barua, *The Late Colonial Indian Army: From the Afghan Wars to the Second World War*, n. 14.
31. Ibid. For a more detailed discussion on Sari Bair, see *India and the Great War: Gallipoli*, n. 27, pp. 16–19 and Cardozo, *The Indian Army in World War I: 1914–1918*, n. 17, pp. 136–46.
32. David Omissi, *The Sepoy and the Raj: The Indian Army, 1860–1940*, Basingstoke: Macmillan, 1994, p. 199.
33. BR Tomlinson, *The Political Economy of the Raj, 1914–1947: The Economics of Decolonization in India*, London: Macmillan, 1979, pp. 58–59.
34. Philip Mason, *A Matter of Honor: An Account of the Indian Army its Officers and Men*, New York: Holt, Rinehart and Winston, 1974, p. 456.
35. Singh, 'The World Wars and Prelude to Independence', n. 25, p. 38.
36. Srinath Raghavan, *India's War: The Making of Modern South Asia, 1939–1945*, Gurgaon: Penguin Books, 2016, p. 36.
37. Singh, 'The World Wars and Prelude to Independence', n. 25, p. 40.
38. Ibid.
39. Ibid.
40. Ibid.
41. Ibid., p. 41.
42. Ibid., p. 42.
43. Rana Chhina, *The Last Post: Indian War Memorials around the World*, New Delhi: USI, 2014, p. 40.
44. Ibid.
45. Raghavan, *India's War: The Making of Modern South Asia, 1939–1945*, n. 36, p. 33.
46. Mahumita Mazumdar, 'The Lives of Others', *The Telegraph Online*, 4 March 2022, available at https://www.telegraphindia.com/culture/books/review-the-indian-contingent-the-forgotten-muslim-soldiers-of-the-battle-of-dunkirk-by-ghee-bowman/cid/1854383.
47. Raghavan, *India's War: The Making of Modern South Asia, 1939–1945*, n. 36, p. 63.
48. Ibid., p. 64.
49. Sri Nandan Prasad, *Expansion of the Armed Forces and Defence Organization, 1939–45*, p. 73, cited in ibid., p. 69.
50. Raghavan, *India's War: The Making of Modern South Asia, 1939–1945*, n. 36, p. 69.
51. Ibid., p. 67.
52. Ibid., p. 68.
53. This Section has been adapted from Singh, 'The World Wars and Prelude to Independence', n. 25, pp. 42–45.
54. See Singh, 'The World Wars and Prelude to Independence', n. 25, pp. 43–44.

55. Ibid., p. 44.
56. Ibid., p. 45.
57. This Section has been adapted from Singh, 'The World Wars and Prelude to Independence', n. 25, pp. 48–53.
58. Ibid., p. 50.
59. Ibid.
60. Ibid.
61. Ibid., p. 51.
62. Ibid.
63. Ibid.
64. Ibid.
65. Robert Lyman, *Japan's Last Bid for Victory*, p. 256, cited in Hemant Singh Katoch, 'The Battle of Imphal: March–July 1944', *Journal of Defence Studies*, Vol. 8, No. 3, July–September 2014, p. 102.
66. See Katoch, 'The Battle of Imphal: March–July 1944', n. 65, p. 102.
67. Singh, 'The World Wars and Prelude to Independence', n. 25, p. 51. Also see Katoch, 'The Battle of Imphal: March–July 1944', n. 65, pp. 101–120.
68. Singh, 'The World Wars and Prelude to Independence', n. 25, p. 52.
69. This Section has been adapted from Singh, 'The World Wars and Prelude to Independence', n. 25, pp. 46–48.
70. Ibid., p. 46.
71. Ibid.
72. Ibid., p. 48.
73. Ibid.
74. Ibid.
75. CE Callwell, *Small Wars: Their Principles and Practice*, 3rd edition, London: General Staff–War Office, 1906, p. 21.
76. Ibid.
77. George Morton-Jack, 'Small Wars and Regular Warfare', in *The Indian Army on the Western Front: India's Expeditionary Force to France and Belgium in the First World War*, New York: Cambridge University Press, 2014, p. 43.
78. Ibid.
79. Ibid., p. 44.
80. Ibid., p. 45.
81. See Byron Farwell, *Queen Victoria's Little Wars*, UK: Harper & Row, 1972, chapter 2.
82. Ananth Krishnan, 'The Forgotten History of Indian Troops in China', *The Hindu*, 12 July 2011.
83. Andrew Whitehead, 'How India helped Britain Win its "Dirty" War', *The Wire*, 31 May 2020, available at https://thewire.in/history/india-britain-boer-war.
84. Ibid.

3

Post-Independence Wars I

1947–48 Kashmir Conflict and 1962 Sino-Indian Conflict

Maj Gen PJS Sandhu (Retd)

1947–48 Kashmir Conflict

Historical Background[1]

The princely State of Jammu and Kashmir (J&K) had been brought under British paramountcy in 1846 via the Treaty of Amritsar, signed between the East India Company (EIC) and Maharaja Gulab Singh, the founder of the Dogra dynasty. Gulab Singh paid 7.5 million Nanakshahi rupees and bought the Kashmir Valley and the Ladakh Wazarat (comprising Baltistan, Kargil and Leh), and added it to Jammu, which was already under his rule. The Gilgit Wazarat (including Gilgit and Pamiri areas) was later conquered from the Sikhs by the Dogras. Princely J&K had five main regions—Jammu, Kashmir, Ladakh, Gilgit Wazarat, and the Gilgit Agency, which was on a 60 year lease to the British. In the nineteenth and early twentieth centuries, till the Russian Revolution of 1917, the British Government perceived Imperial Russia and, later, Communist Soviet Union as a threat to their most significant colony: India. Thus they thought it fit to administer the Gilgit Agency directly and accordingly took it on lease in 1935. As the Indian Independence Act was passed by the British Parliament on 13 July 1947 and the date of transfer of power to India and Pakistan was set to 15 August 1947, the Viceroy Lord Mountbatten decided to let go of the Gilgit Agency lease. On 01 August 1947, the administration of Gilgit thus passed back into the hands of Maharaja.

When it came to accession, the principle of geographic contiguity could not be applied in the case of J&K as it was contiguous to both India and Pakistan. The principle of the Ruler deciding accession based on the aspirations of his people was then adhered to. Sheikh Mohammed Abdullah, the foremost Muslim leader in the state and organiser of the Jammu and Kashmir National Conference (known as the National Conference), was in favour of accession to India.[2] However, the ruler of Kashmir at the time, Maharaja Hari Singh, covertly harboured visions of independence ignoring Mountbatten's explicit injunction.[3] Just three days before the announcement of independence, Maharaja Hari Singh offered a Standstill Agreement on 12 August 1947 to India and Pakistan saying that he would need some time before reaching a final decision on the status of J&K. Pakistan signed the agreement but negotiations with India were never completed.[4] By doing so, Maharaja Hari Singh tried delaying the issue of accession. Due to partition there was communal rioting in the whole of Punjab and a number of refugees moved from either side, a large number of them moving through J&K. However the state remained a safe haven for these refugees. On 3 September, a band of raiders attacked Kotha South-East of Jammu and while the raiders were securing the disposal of the state's army by the hit and run tactics, Pakistan's Government was carrying out economic blockade.

The new government of Pakistan intended to take full advantage of this situation to tilt the balance in favour of the state joining Pakistan. The leading politicians of the Muslim League and senior officers of the armed forces prepared a plan which promised a swift resolution, yet kept the risk of open conflict with India at a minimum. The plan very nearly succeeded.

Geography and Administration

Jammu and Kashmir covers an area of 222,000 sq km; its North-South extent is 640 km and East-west extent is 480 km. In 1947, the infrastructure of the state was quite primitive. The all-weather roads followed the river courses and led through Pakistani territory. From India, there were only two fair weather roads into Kashmir: the dirt road from Pathankot to Jammu to Srinagar, which ran through the Banihal Pass, however there was no bridge across the Ravi linking Jammu to Pathankot; and the caravan trail from Manali to Ladakh. Srinagar could be accessed from Muzaffarabad. Gilgit and Skardu were both accessed through the Rawalpindi-Abbottabad Road, which crossed into Gilgit agency at the 4,200 m Babusar Pass. It went on to Skardu, and further along Indus Valley joined up with Kargil. The northern road along Hunza valley led to the vassal states of Hunza and Nagar. The present Karakoram Highway is located along this alignment going further into China over the Khunjerab Pass. Only a spur of India's well-developed rail network ran into Kashmir. Jammu had a light railway railhead. The rail line ran from the Wazirabad Junction on the main Lahore-Rawalpindi line through Sialkot to Jammu. The throughput capacity of the roads and the weight bearing capacity of the bridges strictly limited the numbers, equipment and supply of the forces that could be deployed. The Srinagar and Jammu airfields were suitable for landing transport aircraft, but only in daylight.

Unlike roads or railways, the state was fairly well-provided with telegraph and wireless facilities. A network of telegraph stations covered the state, penetrating even into the wild Shyok Valley in order to send warning of floods. The most important villages and tourist resorts had telegraph offices. Wireless communications were mainly under military authorities, but Gilgit and Naushera had civil wireless and telegraph stations, which served in some measure to compensate for the lack of modern means of transport. Most of the far-flung garrisons in the state could communicate with Srinagar by wireless telegraphy, which proved a crucial advantage when the tribal hordes poured into the state in October 1947.

The administration of J&K, both civil and military, was headed by the Maharaja, who was the repository of all powers, and could lay down or amend the state's constitution by his own orders. He was the Head of Government and was the C-in-C of the State Army. The only check on his authority was the British Resident acting as the Crown Representative, and paramountcy had, in the twentieth century reached a stage where the British Resident could Command or influence every action of the State Government in any field, if the Viceroy so desired. The appointment of the Prime Minister of the J&K required the approval of the Viceroy conveyed through the Resident. The state had two capitals: Srinagar was the summer capital while Jammu was the winter capital. J&K comprised of four provinces: Jammu, Srinagar, Gilgit and Ladakh, each under a Governor. As mentioned earlier, Gilgit had been held on lease by the Government of India, and was handed back to the Maharaja only in August 1947.

Division of Armed Forces in 1947[5]

The end of British rule in India, and the partitiion of the country led to the Division of the armed forces and the civil administration. Field Marshal Sir Claude Auchinleck oversaw the Division of this force. According to the Independence of India Act, two thirds of the personnel and material resources of the armed forces were to go to India and one third to Pakistan. Around 260,000 personnel, mainly Hindus and Sikhs, went to India and 140,000 personnel, mainly Muslims, went to Pakistan.[6] Many British officers stayed on to assist in the transition, including General Sir

Robert Lockhart, India's first Commander-in-Chief (C-in-C), and General Sir Frank Messervy, who became Pakistan's first C-in-C. As the various Indian principalities had their own armed forces prior to independence, as the princely states joined either India or Pakistan, their forces were also incorporated into the two national armies. Due to the shortage of the available time a fair and equitable Division of materiel (and particularly of installations) was impossible. The airbases were mostly in Pakistani territory, but most of the training establishments were in India. The arsenals, supply dumps, repair installations and naval bases were also mostly in Indian territory.

In the division of British India's army, the new Indian Army acquired 88 Infantry Battalions, 12 Armoured Regiments, and 19 Artillery Regiments.[7] These were organised into 10 Divisions (nine Infantry and one Armoured). The Indian Air Force (IAF) was a respectable force, even after some of its equipment and personnel were transferred to Pakistan. It was equipped with modern aircraft (Tempest and Spitfire fighters and C47 Dakota transports). These forces were organised into seven fighter Squadrons and one transport Squadron. It is these two Services that featured in the war that is discussed in detail here.

Pakistan acquired 33 Infantry Battalions, six Armoured and nine Artillery Regiments at independence. In August 1947 a two-Brigade Division (the 7th) was formed in Rawalpindi. By October that year there were 10 Infantry Brigades and one armour Brigade guarding Pakistan's borders. The Brigades were organised into four Divisions in West Pakistan and one Division in East Pakistan. Three Aviation Squadrons formed the nucleus of the Pakistani Air Force (PAF). The equipment consisted of modern fighter (Tempests and Spitfires) and transport (C47 Dakota) aircraft. The Air Force was initially organised into two fighter Squadrons and one transport Squadron. As Pakistan's territory encompassed what had been British India's western border region and its initial line of defence against a Russian threat, the three Squadrons had a choice of seven airbases. The PAF played only a limited role in the course of events: Pakistan wanted to maintain the pretence of having nothing to do with events in Kashmir.

The state of J&K had its own state forces. The military administration of J&K comprised an Army HQ at Srinagar, and four Brigades. The Army HQ was headed by a Chief of Staff, who formerly used to be a retired British officer. Major General (Maj Gen) HL Scott, CB, DSO, MC, was the last British Chief of Staff, and was succeeded after independence by Brigadier (Brig) Rajendra Singh of the J&K State Force. The four Brigades were the Jammu Brigade under Brig NS Rawat (HQ at Jammu), the Kashmir Brigade with Body Guard Cavalry and 7th J&K Rifles at Srinagar Commanded by Brig Faqir Singh, the Mirpur Brigade under Brig Chattar Singh (HQ at Jhangar), and the Punch Brigade under Brig Krishna Singh in the Punch-Rawalkot area. Between them, the four Brigades had only eight Infantry Battalions, with some garrison police companies. The State Force had no artillery or armour. The force was dependent on the arsenals from Northern Command Headquarters, Rawalpindi, for arms, ammunition and equipment. There was a wireless link with

Rawalpindi, but none with New Delhi. As a part of the British Empire, Kashmir had no reason to fear a foreign invasion, therefore the state forces performed border security, constabulary and parade functions. However, they had taken part in the two World Wars and were battle hardened.

The Plan

Pakistan made its designs to force accession of J&K clear when within 12 days of agreeing to the Standstill Agreement, on 24 August 1947, it threatened Maharaja Hari Singh by writing to him that 'The time has come for Maharaja of Kashmir that he must take his choice and choose Pakistan. Should Kashmir fail to join Pakistan, the gravest possible trouble will inevitably ensue'.[8] Having sensed the Maharaja's intention to hold out on joining either of the two countries, Pakistan conceived a military plan to attack J&K to force it to accede to Pakistan; the operation was codenamed 'Gulmarg'. The British C-in-C of the Pakistan Army issued orders signed personal and top secret regarding the operation, one of which was received by Maj Onkar Singh Kalkat, then Brigade Major of Bannu Brigade.

The broad plan was that every Pathan tribe was required to enlist atleast one lashkar consisting of 1,000 tribesmen. After enlistment, these lashkars were to be concentrated at Bannu, Wana, Peshawar, Kohat, Thal, and Nowshera by the first week of September 1947. The Brigade Commanders at these locations were to issue them arms, ammunition and some essential items of clothing. Each tribal lashkar was also to be guided by a Major, a Captain and ten Junior Commissioned Officers (JCOs) of the regular Pakistan Army. The entire force was to be Commanded by Maj Gen Akbar Khan, who was given the code name 'Tariq'. He was to be assisted by Brig Sher Khan. All lashkars had to be concentrated at Abbottabad by 18 October 1947. They were to be moved in civil buses which had been Commandeered for this task. A separate area 16 km outside Abbottabad was earmarked for the the lashkars.

The broad outline of the operational plan was for six lashkars to advance along the main road from Muzaffarabad to Srinagar via Domel, Uri and Baramula, with the specific task of capturing the Srinagar aerodrome, and subsequently advance to the Banihal Pass. Two lashkars were to advance from the Haji Pir Pass direct on to Gulmarg, thereby securing the right flank of the main force advancing from Muzaffarabad. A similar force of two lashkars was to advance from Tithwal through the Nastachhun Pass for capturing Sopore, Handwara and Bandipur. Another force of ten lashkars was to operate in the Poonch, Bhimbar and Rawalkot area with the intention of capturing Poonch and Rajauri and then advancing to Jammu. D-day for Operation Gulmarg was fixed as 22 October 1947, on which date the various lashkars were to cross into J&K territory. The 7 Infantry Division of the Pakistan Army was to concentrate in area Murree-Abbottabad by last light on 21 October, and was ordered to be ready to move immediately into J&K to back up the tribal lashkars and consolidate their hold on the Kashmir Valley. One Infantry Brigade was also held in readiness at Sialkot to move on to Jammu.

Sequence of Events

The sequence of events can be divided into the following phases.

August–October 1947

The partition of India was accompanied by mass migration across the new border and considerable violence. In August 1947, open revolt broke out in Poonch and the first Muslim militia was raised. Attacks on police stations and army garrisons became more frequent, and the Azad Kashmir (Free Kashmir) Government was formed on 24 October of that year.

In early September, attacks from Pakistani territory commenced. Pathan groups of several hundred men raided Hindu and Sikh villages along the border, then fled back to Pakistan when government forces responded. The Pakistan Army supported the raiders with arms, ammunition, communications equipment and transport, and its patrols entered Kashmiri territory on several occasions. The Pakistani authorities feigned ignorance of the incidents and of the role of the army, and, at the same time, accused the Kashmiri government of atrocities against the Muslim population. By the middle of October, the situation was ripe for a general offensive. The incidents were becoming more serious along the 300 km long border, and they were occurring in many locations at unpredictable times. The state forces could not protect every village and every vulnerable point; they could only react to the attacks, but could not prevent them. Their forces gradually became fragmented and they became incapable of concerted action.

Late October 1947

The general offensive commenced on two fronts on October 22, 1947. Six Pathan lashkars (6,000 men) broke into the Kashmir Valley from the direction of Garhi Habibullah and attacked Muzaffarabad. The Muslims serving in the Kashmiri state forces mutinied, killed their non-Muslim fellow soldiers and joined the Pathans or the local militias. The attackers destroyed a State Forces Battalion, but met with stiff resistance near Uri: the State Forces withstood their attacks for a while, then destroyed the bridge over the Uri River and withdrew towards Baramulla. However, the lashkars were warlike tribal militias, not disciplined, regular forces. Their weakness—lack of discipline—became apparent in the operations around Uri. For disciplined, well-trained and well-led troops the destroyed bridge over the Uri River would have been a challenge, but not an obstacle to success: crossing the river without vehicles was no problem, and the distance between Uri and Srinagar was around 102 km. However, the lashkars refused to give up their vehicles (which they needed more for carrying their plunder, than for transporting personnel), and thus they delayed the advance for nearly four days and they were also delayed due to the engagement with the State Forces troops. As a result of this delay, they reached Baramulla (50 km from Srinagar) only on 26 October. Once they seized the town, the only force between them and Srinagar was a roadblock manned by fifty men of the State Forces, 5 km East of Baramulla. The situation and the lashkars' lack of discipline resulted in them indulging in looting and massacre. These delays gave the Maharaja time to make up his mind and appeal to India for assistance. The Indian government was ready to provide it, but only on the condition that Kashmir accedes to India. The Instrument of Accession was signed on 26 October 1947 and accepted by Lord Mountbatten, the Viceroy, on 27 October; Indian forces entered the conflict the next day.

On the other front, the militias attacking in the Jammu region were also met with stiff resistance, and they achieved their objectives only after some serious fighting. They seized border towns like Bagh, surrounded Poonch and cut-off the Poonch-Jammu Road; but, by the time they reached Jammu, Indian forces were already on the move. Jammu remained in Indian hands and subsequently served as the base of Indian operations in the South.

Soon after the attacks commenced on 24 October, the Azad Kashmir government was formed under the leadership of Mohamed Ibrahim. Henceforth, two governments existed in the state, each claiming full jurisdiction over the entire territory. The operations in the South (in the Jammu region) were useful because they distracted the defender's attention and forced him to split his forces. But the key to Kashmir was the Kashmir Valley, and the key of the Valley was Srinagar—thus, seizing the city was the most important goal of the invasion.[9]

The Indian rescue effort had to overcome challenges from the outset. The closest point on the Indian border was more than 480 kms away from Srinagar. Dealing with the refugees and upholding law and order were issues for the troops in East Punjab. As a result, air travel was the only option. Even worse, Srinagar's airport was not suitable for receiving fully loaded transport planes. However, that was the only choice, therefore it had to be made. Operation Jak was the name of the rescue effort. 1 SIKH, which was then stationed in Gurgaon and was commanded by Lt Col D R Rai, was the first Battalion to enter the area. Four Dakota aircraft were used to transport the troops, and they departed from Safdarjung Airport in Delhi at 0500 hour on 27 October and arrived in Srinagar at 0830 hour that same day.[10] On 27 October, the initial hostilities commenced. After learning that the enemy had reached the outskirts of Baramulla, he promptly dispatched his first Company on arrival at Srinagar to the area to bolster the Dogra soldiers of the J&K State Forces' defensive posture. On 28

October, Lt Col Rai was the first Indian officer to be killed at Baramulla during the war to free Jammu and Kashmir from the raiders, who numbered four thousand. He was the first person to receive the Maha Vir Chakra, which was given to him posthumously. The advance of the army had protected Srinagar. The threat to Srinagar was eliminated with the recapture of the Uri area on 13 November 1947. The attackers had taken control of a huge area of land close to the Pakistani border. In truth, the raiders' lust and covetousness had hindered their progress. The attackers had also left a path of rape, robbery, and plunder. The Battle of Badgam, the battle of Shalateng, the capture and recapture of Jhangar, the Battle of Naushara, the Advance to Tithawal, the Relief in Punch, and the Fight of Chhamb to Tithwal were some of the key engagements that took place in Jammu and Kashmir.

The Battle of Badgam

Three Companies of 4 KUMAON were stationed in the Badgam region on November 3 to conduct patrols. At around 1430 Hours, shots were fired at Major Somnath Sharma's D Company from nearby houses in Badgam. He was the first awardee of the Param Vir Chakra. Unexpectedly, a tribal lashkar of 700 infiltrators headed upon Badgam from Gulmarg. He rallied his Company to fight boldly under heavy fire and a seven to one disadvantage. The position held by the Company had already been overrun by the time a relief Company from the 1 KUMAON arrived in Badgam. However, the 200 casualties that the tribe infiltrators sustained stopped them from moving forward.

The Fall of Jhangar and Recapture of Jhangar

On 24 December 1947, the enemy conquered Jhangar. It significantly benefited the adversary. Therefore, recapturing Jhangar was essential to Indian strategy. To regain control of Jhangar, Operation Vijay was started. By 05 March, both Kaman Gosha Gala and Ambli Dhar had been liberated from the enemy. Now was the right time to launch the last attack on Jhangar. Two phases were planned for the completion of Operation Vijay. 19 Independent Infantry Brigade, made up of 1 RAJPUT, 4 DOGRA, 1 KUMAON, and ancillary forces, was tasked with securing Points 3327 and 3283 in the initial phase. The 50 Para Brigade Group commanded by Brig Usman, made up of the 3 (Para) MARATHA LI, the 3 (Para) RAJPUT, the 1 PATIALA, and other units, was tasked with securing Points 2701, Jhangar, 3399, and 3374 in Phase two. The operation also included the use of armour. Pir Thil, which the enemy held, was one of the crucial strategic locations. 3 MARATHA LI was dispatched on offensive reconnaissance on 15 March. The Pir Thil Nakka had been taken by 17

March, clearing the way for the last assault on Jhangar. On 18 March, the offensive got under way. The 50 Para Brigade, the 3 MARATHA LI, and the 1 PATIALA concentrated at this feature after the 3 (Para) RAJPUT took Point 3477 on that day.

Naushera Victory - The fight of Naushera, which took place on February 6, 1948, was important and cleared the path for the eventual recapture of Jhangar. Operation Satyanas was given to Lt Col R G Naidu, CO of 2 JAT, to lead in removing the enemy from the vicinity of Beri Pattan. On January 23, the army entered Tung, and the following morning they crossed the Thandapaniwali Tawi. Early on 25 January, as they moved forward to attack Siot and Point 2502, they came under heavy enemy fire and were forced to retreat, but not before inflicting significant casualties—an estimated 100 dead and wounded—on the enemy.

Battle of Tithwal- A fierce and protracted combat that took place in the conflict of 1947–1948 was the Battle of Tithwal. Initial border crossings by Pashtun tribal militia resulted in the vital Indian settlement of Tithwal being taken. Their main objective was to seize the Richhmar Gali, which was controlled by the Indian Army, and Nastachun Pass, which was located East of Tithwal. On 13 October, 1948, the Pakistani Army launched a huge attack in an attempt to seize the stations held by Indian troops. The attack, however, was utterly unsuccessful and resulted in terrible deaths due to the Indian troops' unwavering courage and valour. The Indian Army's unwavering zeal and tenacity contributed to India's success in keeping the position of Tithwal. 1 SIKH, 1 MADRAS, and 6 RAJ RIF were the involved Battalions. In order to attack and seize an enemy-occupied hill feature at Tithwal on July 18, 1948, CHM Piru Singh of the 6 RAJ RIF was given the mission. He received the Param Vir Chakra for performing the operation with the utmost bravery, unwavering gallantry, and supreme sacrifice (Posthumous).

Central Kashmir Valley is divided from Gilgit and Baltistan to the North and North-West by the Burzil Mountains, which are a component of the Great Himala-yan Nanga Parbat range. The historic caravan route connecting Srinagar and Gilgit crosses these mountains at a height of 4,000 metres through the Burzil Pass. This Western most region of the Ladakh province was originally ruled by the Dogras up until the early 20th century. Maharaja Hari Singh then leased it to the British, who used it as a defensive high-altitude buffer between British India and the Russian Empire as the "Great Game" played out in the area.The Sectors of Gurais, Skardu, Dras and Kargil, as well as Leh, were part of the Northern Front of the Kashmir Campaign. During the period of November 1947 to August 1948, the enemy made significant gains in the area. They were encouraged by the early success in the South and by the radical narrative that the tribal laskhars were heavily involved in planning a coup in Gilgit on 31 October 1947. The force was commanded by a British Commander by the name of Major Brown and was supplemented by substantial portions of the Gilgit Scouts, a Regiment with a local Shia Muslim Majority, and a portion of the J&K State Forces.[11] This was only one of many alleged occasions in which British officers serving in the Pakistani Army actively supported the raiders and then the regular Pakistan Army during the conflict's later phases.[12] The Indian forces' bravery in holding their posts despite all odds was equally impressive. In particular, the Skardu siege was significant. The actual soul of a regular Indian soldier was first revealed in Skardu. Lt Col Sher Jung Thapa and his soldiers from the 6 J&K Infantry were tasked with defending Skardu after Gilgit was captured by the enemy in November 1947. On 03 December, the forces arrived at Skardu and took up position inside a fort. Lt Col Thapa defended his picket against a 600-man adversary who was armed with modern rifles, 2" and 3" mortars, and was led by experienced fighters with a total strength of roughly 285 soldiers. On 11 February 1948, the enemy launched an offensive. From that day until 13 August 1948, when Skardu ultimately fell to the enemy after resisting for six months against insurmountable odds, it was a tale of defiance, bravery, and tenacity. At its lowest point, the Ladakh Valley is located at a height of about 10,000 feet. Mountains range in height from 17,000 to 25,000 feet, while settlements are scattered between 12,000 and 15,000 feet above sea level. Skardu to Leh is around a 360 km drive, as is the trip from Srinagar to Leh through the Zoji La Pass.[13] Therefore, from a tactical standpoint, the Indian Army and the raiders were in a race to Leh. Forty brave Lahaulis from the 2 DOGRA, which had arrived to support 161 Infantry Brigade, were led by Captain Prithi Chand and Captain Kushal Chand, and they left Srinagar in the middle of February 1948 to attempt to breach the 16,000-foot-high Zoji La Pass.

As the raiders proceeded across Dras and Kargil to attack Leh at the beginning of May, the Kashmir Infantry troops of the Kargil garrison and the small Leh garrison managed to organise defences ahead of the town to thwart their repeated assaults. Even with well-planned defences, the situation became unstable by the third week of May, and Leh could only be rescued by receiving reinforcements from the air. On 24 May 1948, Air Commodore Meher Singh and Major General Thimayya touched down in Leh on a historic day for Indian military Aviation. This accomplishment served as a practice run for later missions that involved four and six aircraft landing in Leh over the course of the following two weeks to induct a Company of the 2/4 GORKHA RIFLES. One of the four pilots who received the Maha Vir Chakra for their daring transport flying achievements and motivational leadership was Air Commodore Meher Singh. Men from the 2/8 GORKHA RIFLES were then enlisted. Reports of the massacre of Buddhist monks in Kargil by the Gilgit Scouts and Pakistan Frontier Rifles surfaced in the summer of 1948 when the raiders reinforced their hold on the regions near Kargil and Dras.The lama of Ganskar Padam monastery was shot dead and the Rangdom Gompa, the second largest monastery in Ladakh, was desecrated and razed to the ground. General Thimayya devised an audacious operation that involved the covert movement of Stuart light tanks of the 7th Light Cavalry regiment from Jammu to Srinagar in the middle of October 1948.[14] This was done in response to the frustration of the 77 Para Brigade's infantry assaults to retake Zoji La Pass in August and September 1948. These tanks were taken apart in Srinagar and moved to Baltal, which is located roughly 80 kms away. They received commendable assistance from two Companies of Engineers from the Madras Engineering Group (MEG) under the leadership of Major Thangaraju, who not only made it possible for the tanks to travel from Jammu to Srinagar across flimsy wooden bridges, but also built tracks from Baltal to Zoji La Pass that were friendly to tanks while enduring enemy fire for the final few yards of the road. The unit led by Lt Col Rajinder Singh Sparrow acclimatised for a few days while the track was being constructed before shocking the enemy in subfreezing conditions. On 01 November 1948, Pakistani raiders were driven out of Zoji La Pass after being taken by surprise over the course of the following two weeks by a combined arms assault by tanks and fighter aircraft. After fierce hand-to-hand combat, the Indian Army took back Kargil and Dras.

January 1949: Ceasefire

After protracted negotiations, both countries agreed to a cease-fire. The terms of the cease-fire, laid out in a UN Commission resolution on 13 August 1948, were adopted by the commission on 05 January 1949. This required Pakistan to withdraw its forces, both regular and irregular, while allowing India to maintain minimal forces within the state to preserve law and order. The belligerents retained their positions: the Ceasefire Line (CFL) of January 1949—later the Line of Control (LOC). The two countries fought twice more for the possession of Kashmir, in 1965 and 1999.

The War's Balance Sheet

Casualties

The war caused many casualties to Indian Armed Forces personnel, State Forces as well as civilians. As far as the Indian armed forces are concerned: they lost 1,500 dead and 3,500 were wounded. There is no reliable data on the Pakistani losses; due to the nature of the Pakistani forces in this conflict, there could have been no reliable record keeping. The Kashmiri civilian population sustained the heaviest losses.

Land Forces

On both sides, the Infantry played the dominant role. This was due to three principal factors: the terrain, the inventory, and the nature of the enemy. The rugged terrain, especially that outside the Kashmir Valley, restricted vehicle movement to a few bad roads. Most off-road movement had to be carried out on foot, with the equipment either man-packed or on mules. Also, the equipment available in the belligerents' inventories was nowhere near the scale of contemporary European (much less American) forces: Brigade-scale operations were routinely supported by a few mountain howitzers and mortars, even for the better equipped Indian forces. In any case, artillery was of limited utility against the Pathans who appeared unexpectedly as ghosts among the rocks, and disappeared just as quickly. The Pathan and Azad militias occasionally deployed a few mortars and, in the last months of the conflict, Pakistani Artillery also appeared, but also on a very limited scale.

Artillery did play a significant role in the defence of Poonch: in the early phase of the siege the IAF flew in a light mountain battery, which kept the besiegers' mortars away from the emergency airstrip. In larger engagements—such as the Battle of Shalateng, the recapture of Baramulla, and the relief of Poonch—Artillery again played a significant role. The number and calibre of the available guns, however, limited the effectiveness of their fire. The Pakistani planners had counted on quick successes and did not expect the instantaneous reaction of the Indian armed forces; consequently, they failed to prepare the militias to fight against Armoured forces, and to provide them with anti-tank weapons. As a result, Armoured formations could play a decisive role on three occasions—the Battle of Shalateng, the relief of Poonch, and in the Zoji La. This was despite the fact that the forces were very small in every case, and their equipment—consisting of Daimler Armoured cars and M5 Stuart light tanks—were already obsolescent in 1947–48.

The experience gained in the war had a great influence on the development of Indian tactics in later Indo-Pakistani wars.

Use of Air Forces

From the very first day of the conflict to the last, the IAF was in complete control of the skies. As soon as the first Indian ground forces secured the Srinagar airfield, Spitfire and Tempest fighters were flown in and commenced air operations, even though there was hardly any aviation fuel available locally.[15] Control of the skies guaranteed air supply to remote garrisons as long as an airfield was available. In addition to maintaining air supremacy, the fighters were also used for reconnaissance and for ground support to land forces, for example, prior to the Battle of Shalateng, although due to the extreme dispersal of the Pakistani forces these functions were not nearly as useful as they would have been in more conventional theatre.

Indian control of the skies hampered Pakistani air reconnaissance and concentration of forces, and on the rare occasions when the belligerents' aircraft met in the air, the Indians prevailed. The Air Transport Squadron (No 12) played a particularly prominent role in the conflict. Its pilots flew in nearly impossible weather conditions, undertook missions that promised certain death—they landed on airfields under enemy fire and lit only by the torches of local citizens. Since the Squadron's lift capacity (eight C47 Dakota aircraft) was not sufficient to support for any length of time the forces deployed in Kashmir, the Air Force leased some 30 civilian airliners. The Indians also tried to compensate for their lack of bombers by using large explosive devices rolled out of the doors of C47 transports. These did little or no damage, hardly any to the enemy, at any rate, but they served as a morale booster to the Indian forces. Bomber Squadrons were organised late in 1948 (using refurbished American B17 bombers), but these came too late to play a role in the war. The PAF did not see participation in the conflict, partly for political reasons, in order to maintain the deniability of the country's involvement in Kashmir, and perhaps partly to husband a scarce, but very valuable resource.

Militias

The employment of militias proved to be advantageous for Pakistan. They could be deployed in offensive operations when the combat readiness of the regular forces was still very low. Also, the militias were quite expendable. Playing the roles of 'freedom fighting forces spontaneously organised by the local population', and 'volunteers helping their Muslim brothers suffering under Hindu oppression', the militias also served to conceal Pakistan's role or provide an element of plausible deniability. To independent observers, the Indians and the soldiers on the ground, it was obvious that Pakistan was orchestrating the events, but 'obvious' was not sufficient reason to start an international conflict. Since they had no doctrinal foundations and had little experience in the employment of irregular forces, the Pakistani officers directing the operations had unrealistic expectations about the endurance, discipline and combat readiness of the militias, and had to improvise when the latter failed to perform as expected. Although the lashkars' lack of discipline deprived Pakistan of success in the first operation (and thereby deprived it of outright victory), Pakistan still managed to seize the strategically significant one-third of J&K's territory.

1962 Sino-Indian Conflict

Introduction

The People's Republic of China (China) annexed Tibet in 1950–51 and with that an independent India acquired a new neighbour. The two countries also shared a 4,000 km long land border which was neither delineated nor mutually defined. India was quick to recognise Chinese sovereignty over Tibet and hoped that the two countries would have friendly relations. The 'Agreement on Trade and Intercourse between the Tibet Region of China and India', commonly known as the Panchsheel Agreement, signed on 29 April 1954, was the high point of friendly relations and gave rise to the slogan *Hindi-Chini, Bhai-Bhai.* Through this Agreement, India also gave up the special rights and privileges in Tibet which it had inherited from British India without negotiating anything substantial in return. There was no reference to the unsettled boundary. India presumed that the absence of the same meant Chinese acceptance of India's perception of the boundary. That this was a fallacy as was to be proved soon after.

It did not take long for the first Chinese incursion into Barahoti in Uttar Pradesh (now Uttarakhand), which occurred in June 1954. From then on, there were hundreds of incursions leading to the conflict in 1962. More than a thousand memoranda, notes and letters were exchanged between the two governments over the next 10 years. These have been published by the Government of India in a series of white papers.[16] Gradually, these diplomatic exchanges became shriller and accusatory in nature.

The first bloodshed occurred at Longju in erstwhile North East Frontier Agency or NEFA (now Arunachal Pradesh) on 25 August 1959. While the fallout of this incident was still being resolved, another, more serious, incident took place on 20/21 October 1959 in the area of Kongka Pass in Ladakh. An Indian Police (now the Central Reserve Police Force or CRPF) patrol was ambushed by the Chinese border guards in which 10 Indian policemen were killed and nine were taken prisoner. The net result of these incidents was that the defence of India's Northern borders—until then the responsibility of Indian Police under the Ministry of Home Affairs and Assam Rifles under the Ministry of External Affairs—was handed over to the Indian Army in 1959.

Nehru's Forward Policy and Mao's Armed Co-existence

At the beginning of 1960, Prime Minister Jawaharlal Nehru decided to make one more effort to resolve the boundary dispute through talks. On 05 February 1960, he invited Chinese Premier Zhou Enlai to visit New Delhi to explore avenues that might lead to a peaceful settlement. The Nehru-Zhou talks were held in New Delhi from 19–25 April 1960, but were unsuccessful. After the failure of these talks, China started to establish additional posts on Indian territory, inside their 'Claim Line'. In order to check this unrelenting forward movement by Chinese troops, Nehru issued orders on 02 November 1961 for certain measures to be adopted—and that came to be known as the 'Forward Policy'. In essence, it involved the establishment of forward posts, close to the Chinese posts previously established, to prevent any further encroachment into Indian territory. The Chinese responded by establishing more of their own posts, at times encircling the Indian posts. Mao defined this policy as 'armed co-existence'. Thus, Indian and Chinese posts virtually came to be interlocked with each other, especially in the Ladakh region.

End of Diplomacy

By the end of 1961, Chinese had concluded that their objective to prevent any further Indian advances without bloodshed was not being met. They began to consider whether a sudden blow might force India to the negotiating table.[17] On 26 July 1962, the Government of India offered to send a ministerial level delegation to Beijing to discuss, without preconditions, all bilateral problems and disputes. In a meeting with the Indian Charge d'Affaires, PK Banerjee on 04 August 1962, Zhou Enlai responded that China was willing to hold talks but only on Chinese terms. By early September, Beijing was warning New Delhi that if India played with fire, it would be consumed by fire.[18]

The Spark

In early June 1962, India had established an Assam Rifles post called 'Dhola' in the area of Bridge III on the Southern bank of Namka Chu. Chinese reacted on 08 September and surrounded the Indian post, warning the troops to vacate the area as that was Chinese territory. For 12 days, the troops of both sides remained eye ball to eye ball in confrontation but there was no firing by either side. However, an armed clash took place on 21 September 1962 on the Namka Chu resulting in casualties on both sides. Thereafter, the events moved fast. On the Indian side, 7th Infantry Brigade moved forward from Tawang to Namka Chu with orders to evict the Chinese from Thagla Ridge. On the Chinese side, the attacking troops were already on the move to their assembly areas. The stage was now set for the events that were to unfold with a full-scale Chinese offensive on 20 October 1962.

Chinese War Aim and Grand Strategy

The overall aim set by the Central Military Commission (CMC) for the People's Liberation Army (PLA) was to inflict a crushing military defeat on Indian troops deployed on the border. While the real strategic aim of the Chinese lay in the Western Sector, the main military effort was to be directed in the Eastern Sector, specifically against the Kameng Frontier Division because the terrain here facilitated employment of large forces.

Further, the operations in the Western Sector were directed at securing the 1960 Claim Line but the aim set for the PLA forces in the Kameng Frontier Division was to annihilate the Indian forces deployed there. Marshal Liu Bocheng, a seasoned PLA Commander who had successfully fought the Japanese and the Kuomintang Nationalist Army, was assigned the responsibility to formulate military strategy and approve operational plans for the campaign.[19]

Western Sector: War in Ladakh

Soon after their annexation of Xinjiang in November 1949 and Tibet in 1950–51, the Chinese set about developing a road to connect Xinjiang with Tibet. This road, called Highway 215, was announced as having been completed in September 1957 and cut across about 160 km of Indian territory on the Aksai Chin plateau. The construction of the highway in this remote and inaccessible region of India took New Delhi by surprise.[20]

The Chinese soon began to establish posts to provide security to the above highway. In turn, India too established posts to stake claim to its rightful border and to prevent the Chinese from further encroaching upon Indian territory. This policy brought the two forces in eye ball to eye ball confrontation, which finally led to the armed conflict in October 1962.

Indian Dispositions on the Eve of the War

India had deployed the 114 Infantry Brigade comprising six Battalions from North to South, namely, 14 J&K Militia, 5 JAT, 1/8 Gorkha Rifles (GR), 13 KUMAON, 1 JAT, and 7 J&K Militia for the defence of Ladakh. A large proportion of the Indian troop strength was distributed over 70 posts across a wide geographical area, aimed at showing the Indian flag.

China Prepares for the Onslaught

China had started active preparations for the attack from about July of 1962. Specific instructions were issued by the CMC to avoid any premature commencement of hostilities while responding to Indian actions. The overall Command and control were to be exercised by the Xinjiang Military Command through a forward HQ at Kangshiwar (South of Kunlun Mountain range). The whole area of operations was divided into four defence areas, from North to South as under:

1. Tianwendian Defence Area.
2. Heweitan Defence Area.
3. Kongka Pass Defence Area.
4. Ali Defence Area (part of Tibet Region).

Chinese troops in the area of operations consisted of the 2nd Infantry Regiment which was deployed North of Pangong Tso, and the Ali Detachment (a Regiment sized force) which was deployed South of Pangong Tso and in the Indus Valley. Prior to the operations, Xinjiang Military Command inducted additional troops: two Infantry Battalions, a Cavalry Regiment and other combat support elements from the 4th Infantry Division based in Xinjiang.[21] Thus, the total troops amounted to roughly a Division strength but these were strong in terms of reconnaissance, Artillery and engineer elements. The attacking troops were primarily based on two Infantry Battalions from the 4th Infantry Division, which were recycled time and again after rest and reorganisation.

The Chinese Plan

Broadly, the Chinese planned to eliminate all the 43 Indian Posts which they perceived to be intrusions across their 1960 Claim Line in Ladakh. However, priority was to be given to the two Northern defence areas of 'Tianwendian Defence Area' (Daulat Beg Oldi [DBO] Sub-Sector) and 'Heweitan Defence Area' (Galwan River Valley Sub-Sector). D Day was scheduled for 20 October 1962. The following two objectives were selected for the initial attacks on that day:

1. Point 5270, a commanding hill top in the DBO Sub-Sector which was held by a Company less a Platoon of 14 J&K Militia with a strength of 62 All Ranks.
2. Galwan Post was considered as the most dangerous position held by the Indian Army in the 'Heweitan Defence Area' because it cut off rearward communication of three Chinese posts. It was held by a Company of 5 JAT with a strength of 68 All Ranks.

Opening Attacks: 20 October 1962

The Chinese built up a numerical superiority of about 10:1 and fire power superiority of 7:1 before launching any Major attack. They also blocked any route of withdrawal available to the defenders. As they had been in a state of armed co-existence with the Indian posts for a long time, they had intimate knowledge of the Indian strength and dispositions. The attacks commenced at first light with intense artillery bombardment for about 30 minutes and the battle was over in two to three hours. Indian troops suffered heavy casualties; for instance, at Point 5270, 14 J&K Militia suffered

42 killed and 20 wounded/taken prisoners of war (POW). Similarly, at the Galwan post, 5 JAT suffered 36 killed and 32 wounded/taken POW.

By 24 October, all the forward posts established in the Chip Chap and Nacho Chu River Valleys were either captured or withdrawn. DBO was also abandoned. Similarly, in the Galwan Valley, the Chinese had managed to remove all the six Indian posts established on the Northern and Southern banks of Galwan River in about 72 hours. Some of these Posts were withdrawn even without being attacked as these were neither, tactically viable nor, logistically sustainable.[22]

Battles on the Pangong Tso: 21–23 October 1962

The next area of interest for the Chinese was the Pangong Tso, which was under Indian control right up to the Khurnak Fort. Here, Chinese were operating on a very slender margin of superiority as far as the strength of attacking troops was concerned. Hence, for subsequent operations they created ad-hoc Task Forces, especially in the area of Pangong Tso.

There were two Indian positions (Sirijap I and II) on the Northern bank of Pangong Tso held by a Company less a Platoon of 1/8 GORKHA RIFLES and together they formed the Sirijap Complex. These two positions were not mutually supporting and were face to face with two Chinese posts. As no uncommitted troops were available, Chinese organised a Task Force of 117 personnel drawn from various detachments defending this area for carrying out this task. The Sirijap Complex was attacked and captured on 21 October after stiff resistance by Indian troops.

1/8 GORKHA RIFLES had also established three posts—Youla 1,2 and 3—on the Southern bank of Pangong Tso with a total strength of a Company. Chinese considered these posts to be about 20 km inside their Claim Line and planned to remove them. The Indian troops located at Youla Complex had seen the battles that raged on the northern bank opposite them on 21 October and would have anticipated Chinese action against them at any moment. They were isolated, dominated by Chinese posts and their route of withdrawal was also cut off. It is not difficult to visualise the hopeless position that they would have felt themselves in. Under the above circumstances, the Indian troops were ordered to withdraw during the night of 21/22 October and move to a high ground North of Gurung Hill which was also held by 1/8 GORKHA RIFLES. However, they were intercepted during the withdrawal and got involved in a running fight, suffering many casualties.[23] Thus ended the battles on the Northern and Southern banks of Pangong Tso.

Operations in the Indus Valley: 26–28 October 1962

Chinese now turned their attention to the Indus Valley Sector, which lies to the South of Chushul. The Indus River Valley is flanked by low hills to the East with several passes leading to the Tibetan Plateau. Chinese were apparently concerned by a threat emerging from the Indian forces along the Indus Valley approach. Hence, their next set of operations were directed to eliminate such a possibility while also securing their Claim Line in this Sector. 7 J&K Militia was responsible for defence of the Indus Valley Sub-Sector. On 22 October, the Xinjiang Military Command issued orders for all the troops of 4th Infantry Division, which had launched Major attacks in the north to start moving South to Rituzong in the Ali Defence Area and be ready for the next phase of battle by 26 October.

The troops had to move about 500 km over rough and frozen tracks. It took them three days and two nights of continuous movement. As India had decided not to use the IAF, the PLA was able to move over open and barren terrain of Ladakh, even during day, with impunity.

The attacking troops were divided into two groups, each of about a Battalion group, and a pincer movement was planned. One group was to advance on the northern flank and cut off the route of withdrawal of the Indian forces. The second group, which was the heavier force, was to advance on the Southern flank and launch the main attack along Shiquan River Valley and attempt to surround Indian forces in an area between Zhamagere-Kariguo and annihilate them.

The main attack was launched during the night of 27/28 October 1962. Since the Southern outflanking move was delayed, the Chinese did not quite succeed in closing the trap and Indian troops were able to withdraw during the night of 27/28 October in fairly good order. However, by the end of the day on 28 October, the Chinese troops had achieved their objectives and had occupied the Kailash Range that dominated the Eastern bank of the Indus River. The attacking troops were now ordered to withdraw to Area Rituzong and await further orders.

There was a lull in fighting in the Western Sector from 29 October to 17 November 1962. On the Indian side, this period was utilised to organise the defence of Leh and to strengthen the defensive posture in the Chushul Sub-Sector. The 3 Himalyan Division was raised on 26 October at Leh. HQ 114 Infantry Brigade was moved from Leh to Chushul on 27 October and took over the responsibility for Chushul and Phobrang Sub-Sectors. HQ 70 Infantry Brigade was inducted into Ladakh on 25 October and took over the responsibility for the Indus Valley Sub-Sector. 163 Infantry Brigade was inducted for defence of Leh. Two troops of AMX-13 light tanks of 20 LANCERS were air lifted from Ambala Cantt to Chushul on 24–25 October by AN-12 aircraft of 44 Squadron, IAF, which was a Major Aviation feat.[24]

Second Chinese Offensive: 18–21 November 1962

The Chinese opened their second offensive on 18 November with the aim of securing the Spangur Gap. They identified two objectives: Gurung Hill, which constituted the

Northern Shoulder of the Spangur Gap, and the Rezang La Complex in the South. Gurung Hill was held by two companies of 1/8 GORKHA RIFLES, while Rezang La was held by a Company of 13 KUMAON.

Rezang La was given greater importance of the two objectives as it dominated the Chinese posts and their rear areas to a considerable distance. For the attack on Rezang La, they organised the two Infantry Battalions of the 4 Infantry Division into two Task Forces, each comprising two Companies, along with the 3rd Cavalry Regiment less two Companies in reserve. Gurung Hill was to be attacked by an ad-hoc Task Force of about a Battalion strength with troops drawn from the Ali Detachment, 3rd Cavalry Regiment, and an engineer platoon.

Both the attacks commenced soon after first light on 18 November with an intense artillery bombardment. The attacks were stalled time and again, and Chinese had to commit their reserves. As the telephone line to the Battalion HQ was cut and the radio set was destroyed in the initial stages, no reinforcements could reach the Indian troops there. For C Company, 13 KUMAON it was a fight to the finish. The guns fell silent around 2200 hours on 18 November. Chinese accounts indicate that out of a total strength of 141 Indian troops, 136 were killed including the Company Commander Major Shaitan Singh, who was awarded the Param Vir Chakra posthumously, and five wounded men were taken POW. The Chinese suffered 21 killed and 98 wounded.

As regards Gurung Hill, only a portion of it could be captured by the Chinese by last light on 18 November. They attacked again on 19 November but did not succeed in dislodging the Gorkhas. Their attack was poorly planned, coordinated and executed. The Gorkhas were also supported by a troop of AMX-13 tanks by indirect fire. The Gorkhas suffered about 50 killed, while the Chinese suffered 81 casualties (killed and wounded).

Keeping the overall situation in view, it was decided to withdraw troops from the Kailash Range and to redeploy them on mountains West of Chushul. Thus, despite the fact that some of the defensive positions were still holding out, a withdrawal was ordered on the night of 19/20 November 1962 and with that the whole of the Kailash Range passed into Chinese hands. The Chinese made no attempt to follow the withdrawing Indians, nor did they try to capture the Chushul airfield.[25]

The unilateral ceasefire declared by the Chinese came into effect from the midnight of 21/22 November 1962 and there was no further fighting in this Sector. However, Chinese did not carry out any unilateral withdrawal in Ladakh and have maintained their Claim Line since then.

Eastern Sector: Kameng Frontier Division

During the official level talks in 1960, the Chinese had raised a dispute about the exact alignment of the McMahon Line in the area of Thagla Ridge. By early

September 1962, they had occupied the Thagla Ridge in some strength. Around mid-September, in a meeting held in the Ministry of Defence (MoD) in New Delhi, chaired by then Defence Minister VK Krishna Menon, a decision was taken to throw the Chinese out from Thagla Ridge. This decision set into motion a chain of events which saw the 7th Infantry Brigade commanded by Brigadier JP Dalvi strung along Namka Chu by the end of September 1962. This was the situation when Lt Gen B M Kaul, the newly appointed General Officer Commanding (GOC) of the freshly raised IV Corps arrived on the scene on 05 October and put into fast gear actions aimed at evicting the Chinese from Thagla Ridge.

The Trigger

Lt Gen Kaul ordered 2 RAJPUT to move to Yumstola (16,000 ft) on the Thagla Ridge, to sit behind the Chinese. However, after strong remonstrations by the Commanding Officers (COs), the Brigade Commander, and the GOC of 4 Infantry Division, who were all present on the scene, the order was changed to send a Company strength patrol of 9 PUNJAB under Maj Mahander Singh Chaudhry to occupy Tseng-Jong, a herder's hut half way to the top of the Thagla Ridge in order to ascertain Chinese reaction to our crossing of the Namka Chu.

The 9 PUNJAB patrol of about 50 men reached Tseng-Jong before dusk on 9 October and hurriedly deployed as best as they could. The next morning at 0500 Hours Indian time, they were attacked by a Battalion of the PLA. The patrol lacked fire support and soon ran out of ammunition. Maj Chaudhry was wounded but continued to lead his men with great determination and courage. They managed to repulse the first attack but were eventually overwhelmed by sheer numbers. The Punjabis suffered six dead, including one officer and 11 wounded. The Chinese admitted to have suffered 11 killed and 22 wounded. However, on this day the Chinese allowed the Indians to withdraw and even take away their wounded without interference. They even cremated our dead. All this was watched in amazement by the Indian troops deployed on the Namka Chu and Commanders, including the Corps Commander, who were present there.[26]

Shortly thereafter, the GOC left for Delhi; before leaving he ordered 7 Infantry Brigade to continue to hold their positions on the South Bank of Namka Chu and ensure the security of the crossings at all costs. The irony was that the Indian troops deployed on the Namka Chu could see the Chinese preparations opposite them on the dominating slopes of Thagla Ridge but were constrained from taking action until further directions from New Delhi.

On 12 October, Prime Minister Nehru, at Chennai airport while on his way to Colombo, told reporters that the Indian Army had been told 'to throw the Chinese out from the Indian territory'.[27] This, coupled with the incident of 10 October at Tseng-Jong, gave the Chinese the perfect excuse that they had been waiting for to launch a massive military operation to teach India a lesson, while terming their aggression as a 'Counter Attack in Self Defence'.

Battle of Namka Chu: 20–21 October 1962

The Indian 7 Infantry Brigade commanded by Brig JP Dalvi of 4 Infantry Division was deployed on the Namka Chu in a linear fashion, strung over 25 km from Tsangle in the West to Drakung Samba Bridge in the East and dominated by Chinese troops on the Thagla Ridge. As there was no road beyond Tawang, the maintenance of the Brigade was undertaken by porters or mules from the Logistics Base at Lumpu and by air at a Dropping Zone (DZ) at Tsangdhar, which was not entirely suitable for air drops and was in full view of the enemy. It needs to be noted here that being a river valley, Namka Chu was tactically unsound as a defensive position.

For the battle of Namka Chu, the Chinese had concentrated approximately 10,300 troops comprising Force 419 (a Divisional sized force), two Battalions ex 11 Infantry Division and an Infantry Regiment of border troops with enhanced complement of Artillery and Engineers. They struck in the early hours of 20 October on the unsuspecting and ill-prepared 7 Infantry Brigade in a kind of double envelopment manoeuvre with the main thrust being delivered from the left flank of the Indian troops deployed on the Namka Chu. The Chinese had infiltrated through Indian positions during the night as there were large gaps. They had thus occupied higher ground behind Indian forces and were attacking downhill. The Indian defenders were forced to turn around and face the attack. The units fought bravely but the result was a foregone conclusion. By the morning of 21 October, the battle of Namka Chu was over and the 7 Infantry Brigade had ceased to be an effective force.

Fall of Tawang: 22–24 October 1962

Buoyed by the success on the Namka Chu, the Chinese High Command ordered their forces to continue the attack for the capture of Tawang. With the 7 Infantry Brigade having been moved forward to Namka Chu, the defence of Tawang was now the responsibility of the Commander, 4 Artillery Brigade with troops from 1 SIKH, 4 GARHWAL RIFLES and an Artillery Regiment—a most unusual arrangement to defend vital ground. The Chinese commenced their advance to Tawang at first light on 23 October, and by last light the same day Tawang had been surrounded and came under attack from many directions. As Tawang had been vacated by the Indian troops during the night of 22/23 October, there was no coordinated resistance from the defenders and Tawang was occupied by the Chinese by first light on 24 October. The Chinese now controlled all areas North of Tawang Chu in the Kameng Frontier Division.

Battle of Se La and Bomdi La: 18–20 November 1962

After the fall of Tawang, it was decided to develop Se La and Bomdi La into strong defensive positions. Se La was to be held by 62 Infantry Brigade, comprising five Battalions supported by a field Regiment and a troop of heavy mortars. Bomdi La was to be defended by 48 Infantry Brigade having three Battalions supported by a battery of field guns. HQ 4 Infantry Division and other administrative elements were located in the valley at Dirang Dzong. In addition, two companies ex 62 Infantry Brigade and one Company ex 48 Infantry Brigade were also located at Dirang Dzong for protection of the Divisional HQ. The 67 Infantry Brigade located at Missamari was available to reinforce 4 Infantry Division Defended Sector in case of an eventuality.

After the fall of Tawang, Lt Gen Harbaksh Singh took over as GOC 4 Corps for a brief period. He assumed command of the Corps on the evening of 25 October and proceeded the next day for reconnaissance and planning for the battle ahead. There was a lull in fighting after 24 October. Hence, on 29 October 1962, Lt Gen Kaul flew back to Tezpur and re-assumed Command of the Corps.

The Chinese, on the other hand, were busy developing a road from their forward base at Le to Tawang and concentrating forces for the next phase of operations. They had managed to concentrate by 15 November 1962, a force of three Divisions—Force 419, 11 and 55 Infantry Divisions—and other combat support elements to undertake further operations. While 55 Infantry Division was to advance along Axis Tawang–Se La, Force 419 was to advance from the west through the narrow corridor between Se La and the Indo-Bhutanese border, assist in the capture of Se La from the South, while simultaneously capturing Dirang Dzong in concert with the troops of 11 Infantry Division who were advancing from the East in a wide outflanking move. The attack was to be launched on 18 November, simultaneously in the Western and Eastern Sectors.

It was the advance of 11 Infantry Division that was the most audacious part of the Chinese offensive, and which unhinged the defenders completely. They commenced their advance on 10 November and carried out a wide outflanking move from the East along the Bailley Trail.[28] The Division moved on manpack basis, each soldier carrying about 30 kg of provisions in addition to his personal weapon and ammunition. They were provided about 1,000 porters recruited locally. The Division marched approximately 160 km over six days and seven nights, and secured Thembang (North of Bomdi La) by last light on 17 November. During the night of 17/18 November, they seized a vital bridge on the road to Dirang Dzong–Bomdi La and thus cut off HQ 4 Infantry Division from the South.

Thus by the morning of 18 November, the troops of Indian 4 Infantry Division had been split into three isolated pockets at Se La, Dirang Dzong and Bomdi La. Further, the Divisional HQ itself was cut off from the North and South; it was thus rendered incapable of exercising Command and control because its own security was threatened. This was to have a disastrous effect on subsequent conduct of the battle. In fact, the battle was lost before it was even joined (emphasis by author).

The Se La Brigade was ordered to withdraw without a fight and fall back on Bomdi La. The Division HQ itself was in the process of withdrawing and Bomdi La fell without a fight by early hours of 19 November. The Chinese went in pursuit of the withdrawing Indian troops:a large number were killed or taken POW, and a few made their way back through Bhutan after marching for many days without food and water. There were many acts of bravery and heroism but these contributed little to the final outcome. Chaku in the foothills was captured by the Chinese by the morning of 20 November.

By this time, the HQ of the Indian 4 Infantry Division had moved to Tezpur and the Division had ceased to exist as an effective fighting force. They had suffered about 5,100 casualties (killed, wounded and captured). Whatever troops could be mustered were deployed South of Brahmputra river. As per Chinese accounts, they had suffered 225 killed (27 officers and 198 men) and 477 wounded (46 officers and 431 men).[29] The PLA General HQ issued orders on 20 November for a unilateral ceasefire and withdrawal (from NEFA only), which was to take effect from the midnight of 21/22 November. The war was over.

It would be worth mentioning that the Chinese operational plan for the battle of Se La–Bomdi La can be compared with their plan for the battle of Chosin Reservoir from 27 November–9 December 1950 during the Korean War of 1950-53.[30] However, the outcome of that battle was markedly different. The US 1st Marine Division not only survived as a fighting force but, through the use of air and fire power, inflicted such attrition on the Chinese IX Army Group that they even disappeared from the Korean battlefield for three months.

Eastern Sector: Lohit Frontier Division (Battle of Walong)

Walong is located about 30 km from the Tibetan border (McMahon Line) and, in 1962, was approximately 200 km from the road-head at Teju involving a march of 14 stages over a goat track. Walong also had an advance landing ground (ALG) which was only fit for small aircraft—Otters and Caribous—to operate. While the main Chinese offensive in NEFA was directed against the Kameng Frontier Division, a subsidiary offensive was launched in the Lohit Frontier Division. Here again, the Chinese aim was to annihilate the Indian troops deployed in the Walong Sector and, in the process, to advance up to their Claim Line. Traditionally, it was the Assam Rifles which manned the border posts in this Sector. However, due to the increase in Chinese incursions, 6 KUMAON was inducted into this area in March 1962. The overall responsibility for the defence of the whole of NEFA, a frontage of nearly 1,100 km, was that of 4 Infantry Division. By 20 October, the Chinese had built up an Infantry Regiment plus a reinforced Battalion opposite the Walong Sector at Rima.

Preliminary Operations: 22–24 October 1962

At about midnight on 22 Oct, the Chinese launched an attack by a Battalion on Kibithoo held by a Company of 6 KUMAON. The Chinese were able to ultimately breakthrough by sheer weight of numbers. 6 KUMAON withdrew to occupy a defensive position at Walong, leaving behind a screen position at Ash Hill. Chinese struck again at the screen position in the early hours of 23 October. The screen put up a determined fight and was ordered to withdraw to the main defences after it had served its purpose. By the morning of 24 October, the Chinese had contacted the main defences at Walong.[31] By this time, 4 SIKH had occupied a defended area at Walong along with two Companies of 2/8 GORKHA RIFLES who were in the process of being inducted. Hereafter, there was a lull in the battle for some time, except for patrol clashes.

Reorganisation by India: 25–31October 1962

As a sequel to the fall of Tawang, a new formation 2 Infantry Division was raised at Teju under the Command of Maj Gen MS Pathania. The newly raised Division was assigned the responsibility for the whole of NEFA, less the Kameng Sector. As a result of the reorganisation, 11 Infantry Brigade under Brig NC Rawlley assumed responsibility for the Walong Sector by 31 October. During the same period, 2/8 GORKHA RIFLES which was in the process of being inducted was ordered to be replaced by 3/3 GORKHA RIFLES. It will subsequently be seen that too many changes in the Order of Battle of the Brigade were being carried out in the face of the enemy, which is extremely hazardous under the best of circumstances. This had a disastrous effect on the conduct of subsequent operations.

Build-up by China: 25 October–13 November 1962

Subsequent to the induction of additional troops by India, on 29 October, the Chinese ordered the move of 130 Infantry Division located in Sichuan Province for the main offensive in the Walong Sector. This involved a move of nearly 1,800 km to the road head at Shugden (approximately 90 km north of Rima). The concentration of this

Division was completed in 10 days which was a great logistics feat. All preparations for the main offensive were completed by 13 November, which was to commence on 18 November. In the event, it was advanced to 16 November.

6 KUMAON Attack on 14 November 1962: Prelude to the Main Battle

As part of consolidation and extension of the Firm Base, Chinese had secured Yellow Pimple and Green Pimple by the end of October 1962, thus posing a threat to the Walong defences from the western flank. By about 10 November, it became clear to Brig Rawlley that the enemy's build up for attack from the western flank was nearing completion. He came to the conclusion that it was essential to wrest the areas of Tri-junction, Yellow Pimple and Green Pimple from the Chinese control, in order to provide security to Walong defences from the West which was the vulnerable flank. Accordingly, he decided to pull out 6 KUMAON from the defences and concentrate them for an attack to secure these areas. However, this weakened the main defences of Walong.

6 KUMAON commenced their attack on the morning of 14 November. They managed to secure the Tri-junction and then proceeded to secure Yellow Pimple. The Chinese had by now firmed up on the Yellow Pimple and 6 KUMAON casualties began to mount. 4 DOGRA who were in the process of being inducted were also fed into the attack piecemeal. 6 KUMAON had managed to reach within 50 m of the Yellow Pimple by last light on 14 November, but the attack got stalled there due to very heavy casualties and the stiff resistance by the Chinese. At about 0100 Hours on 15 November, the Chinese counter attacked with a Regiment plus under intense artillery bombardment. By first light 15 November, 6 KUMAON, which had been fighting continuously for nearly 24 hours, was pushed back to near the top of the Tri-junction. Thus, ended the brave but ill-timed attack by 6 KUMAON. In the process, the defences of Walong had been laid bare and two companies of 4 DOGRA, the only reserve available to the Brigade had also been used up. It seems that the Brigade Commander at that point of time was unaware that the Chinese had managed to concentrate another Division for the main offensive. This would also point to an intelligence failure at the operational level.

The Main Battle: 16 November 1962

In order to exploit the success of their counter attack, the Chinese higher Command decided to advance D Day for the main offensive from 18 November to 16 November. The offensive by a Division plus a Regiment commenced on 16 November morning on both flanks of Walong defences with the main effort on the western flank. Already denuded and weakened, by about 1100 Hours, the 11 Infantry Brigade Defended Sector had crumbled and the situation became untenable. At that point of time, the Brigade Commander in consultation with the Corps Commander (Lt Gen Kaul) who had been in Walong since 15 November, and had seen the situation first hand, took a decision to withdraw.[32] The orders for withdrawal were issued and it commenced at about 1400 Hours on 16 November. Due to breakdown in communications, some of the sub-units could not receive these orders and continued to fight till the end. The Brigade, though badly battered, managed to withdraw to the next main position at Hayuliang. The Chinese followed up closely as far as Chingwinty but did not succeed in annihilating the Brigade. Thus, ended the battle of Walong.

Eastern Sector: Operations in Subansiri and Siang Frontier Divisions

The Central Sector of NEFA was of secondary importance for the Chinese from an operational point of view. Their aim was to tie down maximum troops in this area by launching small forces and, in the process, also capture some territory to stake their territorial claims. They assembled an ad-hoc force of about three Battalions by milking troops from Shannan Sub-Area, Linzhi Sub-Area and the Lhasa Area. The overall command was to be exercised by the Political Commissar of the Tibet Military Command. The main attack was to be launched on 18 November in coordination with operations in the Kameng Frontier Division. On the Indian side, 5 Infantry Brigade of 4 Infantry Division with its HQ at North Lakhimpur was responsible for defence of the rest of NEFA less Kameng Frontier Division.[33]

Subansiri Frontier Division

In October 1962, the defence of Subansiri Frontier Division was bifurcated into two Sub-Sectors—Lower and Upper Subansiri. Lower Subansiri was the responsibility of 9 Assam Rifles and Upper Subansiri that of 2 JAK RIF with its HQ at Daporijo. On 22 October, 5 Infantry Brigade, which till then had been under 4 Infantry Division, was placed directly under Command of the newly raised IV Corps. On the same day, 2 JAK RIF and other troops at Daporijo were ordered to move and redeploy at Taliha by 24 October, while the war had already started on 20 October.

The Chinese commenced their operations in this Sector on 23 October with an attack by a Battalion group against the border posts of Asaphila, Sagamla, Tamala and Potrang. All the border posts were ordered to withdraw to Taliha under the orders of HQ IV Corps issued through the HQ 5 Infantry Brigade. Chinese now started preparing for the main offensive which was set to commence on 18 November.

During this period, there was some reorganisation carried out by the Indian side with the raising of HQ 2 Infantry Division and the induction of 192 Infantry Brigade. Another Battalion, 1/4 GORKHA RIFLES was inducted and the Brigade was ordered to occupy a cohesive Brigade defended Sector. Alas, these measures came a bit too late as the Chinese struck on 18 November.

The Chinese Battalion commenced their advance on 18 November with Limeking as their objective. Their advance was slow due to Indian resistance and the difficult terrain; they made contact with the main defences at Limeking on 21 November. The Indian troops at Limeking had already been ordered to withdraw during the night of 20/21 November to Daporijo. Thus, Chinese were able to secure Limeking by the morning of 21 November without a fight. Thereafter, they continued their advance towards Daporijo till last light on 21 November, at which time they received orders to stop and return to Limeking.[34] There was no further fighting in this Sector.

Siang Sector

This Sector was also the responsibility of HQ 5 Infantry Brigade. The troops allotted were 2/8 GORKHA RIFLES, 2 MADRAS and 11 ASSAM RIFLES supported by 70 Heavy Mortar Battery. The above troops were maintained by Kalinga Airways with ALGs at Along, Menchuka and Tuting.

Chinese had mustered an adhoc force of about 1,650 troops from their line of communication troops. They commenced their probing attacks on 21 October and continued to progress gradually. They had planned a pincer movement towards Tuting and Gelling but were unable to execute the same due to poor planning and ad-hoc nature of the force. By the end of October, Chinese had captured areas up to Lamang, Manigong and Gelling.

On the Indian side, the situation was reviewed after the raising of HQ 2 Infantry Division. The responsibility for defence of this Sector now passed from HQ 5 Infantry Brigade to HQ 192 Infantry Brigade, which was effective only by about 13 November. One of its Battalions, 2/8 GORKHA RIFLES was in the process of moving piecemeal by air from Walong where they had been in contact with the enemy. On the eve of the battle the Brigade Sector was in the process of reorganisation and could hardly be expected to fight a cohesive defensive battle.

Chinese commenced their main offensive on 16 November with a Battalion heading for Tuting and another Battalion going for Menchuka. On the Indian side, there was confusion as 2/8 GORKHA RIFLES were still being inducted into Menchuka. There were orders and counter orders. Menchuka was vacated on the night of 18/19 November and the Chinese occupied it by the morning of 19 November. Thereafter, the Chinese occupied Gelling on 21 November. On 22 November, while closing up with Tuting, they learnt that it had already been vacated. However, since China had declared a unilateral ceasefire with effect from midnight 21 November, further operations were halted and they were ordered to fall back to Limeking and Menchuka, and await further orders.[35] Tuting was re-occupied by the Assam Rifles on 25 November and there was no further fighting in this Sector.

Air Aspects

No account of the 1962 Sino-Indian Conflict can be complete without touching upon the air aspects. It is well known that India did not use its Air Force in an offensive role during the conflict. The reasons for the same are to be found in the political domain. The decision might have been influenced by an exaggerated and incorrect assessment given by the Intelligence Bureau (IB) to the political and military leadership about the Chinese air capabilities and the threat that they could pose to Indian cities in the hinterland.

There were three factual errors in the assessment given by the IB. Firstly, the Chinese did not have any night fighters in 1962 as MIG-19 P with night fighting capability were inducted into the PLA Air Force (AF) many years later. Secondly, India did have night interception capability with its two Squadrons of Vampire night fighters. Thirdly, as far as MIG-21s were concerned, post conflict reports indicate that the Chinese did not have these aircraft in 1962 but got them from erstwhile Soviet Union much later.[36]

Post-conflict intelligence also indicated that there were no Chinese combat aircraft deployed in Tibet in 1962. Hence, the PLA AF did not pose any threat to India as it was neither allocated for this operation, nor deployed during the operations. The IAF, if committed into action, would have had practically a free run in the tactical battle area.

In the overall assessment, the use of IAF for offensive operations was likely to have made a tremendous difference to the final outcome, especially in Ladakh. Then there is also the psychological effect on own troops when they see their own aircraft above them.

Indian POWs in Chinese Custody

By the end of the war, there were more than 3,900 Indian officers and men in Chinese custody. Thus, Chinese held all the cards as far as repatriation of the POWs was concerned. The handing over of seriously wounded POWs commenced on 5 December 1962 at Bomdi La and the repatriation of all the prisoners was completed by 25 May 1963. As there was no formal declaration of war between India and China, the Chinese termed the captured Indian army personnel as 'captives' and not 'prisoners of war'.[37] The Indian POWs in Chinese custody did not receive any official visit by ICRC officials throughout their stay.

The repatriation of POWs was generally handled between the ICRC, the Indian Red Cross (IRC) and the Chinese Red Cross (CRC). Even though diplomatic ties between the two countries were not severed entirely, there were very few direct interactions between the two governments on the subject of repatriation of the POWs. Probably, the Indian Prime Minister felt betrayed and he expected the Non-Aligned countries to act on India's behalf. However, China on its part was insistent on negotiating directly with Delhi. This impasse certainly hampered early repatriation of the POWs.[38]

The Chinese also tried to derive propaganda value from their treatment of officer prisoners by taking them on a conducted tour of various cities to showcase the progress made by Communist China and even tried to parade them in Tiananmen Square on 01 May 1963, but Brig Dalvi refused in no uncertain terms and the Chinese had to drop the idea. While the men were handed over at various points at the border, 27 Indian officers were handed over by the CRC to the IRC at Kunming, the capital city of Yunnan on 04 May 1963 and flown to Dum Dum airport in Calcutta (now Kolkata).[39]

Conclusion

In retrospect, one may say that the war was the result of differing geopolitical perceptions on both sides. The Indian political leadership of the post-Independence period was keen to have friendly relations with Communist China. They also presumed that the border between the two neighbours was a settled matter through treaties negotiated in the past. They were proved wrong on both counts as China had differing priorities and perceptions. The Chinese believed that the border was unsettled and required fresh negotiations. The friendly relationship (till 1954) turned into frostiness gradually due to repeated Chinese incursions across the boundary. This was especially the case after the Tibetan rebellion of 1959 and the escape of Dalai Lama to India. The state of armed co-existence which came about between the two armies could result in open hostilities at any moment.

Notwithstanding the signals emerging to the contrary (from China), India still continued to believe that it was unlikely to initiate any large-scale military action. On the other hand, China had been actively contemplating and preparing for such an eventuality since 1960, if not earlier. India just failed to recognise the ground realties and continued to neglect defence preparedness. There was over reliance on diplomacy which had run its course by mid-1962. As a result, India was taken by complete surprise and the Indian Army was hustled into a war for which it was not prepared, organised, trained or equipped.

Notes

1. Hau Khan Sum, Ravichandran Moorthy, Guido Benny, 'The Genesis of Kashmir Dispute', *Asian Social Science*, Vol. 9, No. 11, 2013, p. 7.
2. P Dawson, *The Peacekeepers of Kashmir: The UN Military Observer Group in India and Pakistan*, London: C. Hurst & Co., 1994.
3. Sumit Ganguly, *The Crisis in Kashmir: Portents of War, Hopes of Peace*, Cambridge: Cambridge University Press, 1997.
4. Dawson, *The Peacekeepers of Kashmir*, n. 2.
5. 'Independence and Partition, 1947', National Army Museum, UK, at www.nam.ac.uk/explore/independence-and-partition-1947.
6. Maj KC Praval, 'Parting of the Ways', in *Indian Army After Independence*, Delhi: Lancer Publishers, 2013.
7. Peter Kiss, 'The First Indo-Pakistani War, 1947-48', unpublished draft paper, n.d., *Academia.edu*, p. 6.
8. Sajid Ali, 'How, on this day 72 years ago, Jammu & Kashmir agreed to become a part of India', *The Print*, 26 October 2019, at https://theprint.in/past-forward/how-on-this-day-72-years-ago-jammu-kashmir-agreed-to-become-a-part-of-india/311724/.
9. For a detailed description, see LP Sen, *Slender Was the Thread: Kashmir Confrontation 1947-48*, Hyderabad: Orient Longman, 1969, pp. 78–100.
10. At 3,300 m altitude, this was the world's highest airstrip at the time and it was doubtful that the C47 Dakotas of the IAF would be able to land and take off at such altitude. To dispel these doubts, the first C47 landed piloted by Colonel Mehar Singh, Commander of air operations. Maj Gen Thimayya, the Commander of the Srinagar Division sat in the co-pilot's seat (24 May 1948).
11. Subsequently, the J&K Division became the 26th Infantry Division, Srinagar Division became the 19th Infantry Division and the J&K Force became 5 Corps.
12. Muhammad Akbar Khan, *Raiders in Kashmir*, Lahore: Jang Publishers, 1970, pp. 82–92.
13. The Zoji La is a narrow, 3 km long corridor at an altitude of 3,600 m above sea level, squeezed on either side by mountains of over 5,000 m.
14. Maj Gen Thimayya was a firm believer in leading from the front: in the attack on the pass, he was directing operations from the lead tank's turret.
15. Sufficient fuel stocks were eventually built up. Initially, however, the transport aircraft landing at Srinagar airfield had their tanks drained until they had only sufficient fuel left to return to base.
16. Claude Arpi, *Tibet: When the Gods Spoke—India Tibet Relations 1947-62*, Part 3, Delhi: Vij Books, 2019, p. 16.
17. Henry Kissinger, *On China*, London: Penguin, 2011, p. 189.
18. John W Garver, 'China's Decision for War with India in 1962', in Alastair Ian Johnston and Robert S Ross (eds), *New Directions in the Study of China's Foreign Policy*, Stanford: Stanford University Press, 2006, pp. 86–130.
19. *A History of the Counter Attack War in Self Defence Along the Sino-Indian Border*, Beijing: Military Science Publications, 1994, Chapter 4, Section 2. An English translated version

of the original book in Mandarin is available with the Centre for Military History and Conflict Studies (CMHCS, formerly the Centre for Armed Forces Historical Research [CAFHR] at the USI of India (archives).

20. Government of India, Ministry of External Affairs, *White Paper I* (1954–59), p. 26.
21. For details see Major Gen PJS Sandhu (ed.), *A View from the Other Side of the Hill*, USI Study, Delhi: Vij Books, 2015, pp. 46–51.
22. Ibid., pp. 52–54.
23. Ibid., pp. 55–58.
24. Ibid., pp. 59–62.
25. Ibid., pp. 63–67.
26. Brig JP Dalvi, *Himalayan Blunder: The Curtain-Raiser to the Sino-Indian War of 1962*, Bombay: Thacker & Co. Ltd., 1969, pp. 72–74.
27. Maj Gen DK Palit, *War in High Himalaya: The Indian Army in Crisis, 1962*, London: Hurst and Company, 1991, pp. 195–200.
28. The Bailey's Trail dates back to the historic route taken by Lt Col FM Bailey and Captain HT Morshead while on a reconnaissance mission in 1913–14, prior to the Shimla Conference where the McMahon Line delineating the boundary between Tibet and British India was drawn.
29. Sandhu (ed.), *A View from the Other Side of the Hill*, n. 21, p. 89.
30. For a detailed comparison see Major General PJS Sandhu (Retd), '1962—Battle of Se La and Bomdi La', *USI Journal*, Volume CXLI, No. 586, October-December 2011, pp. 585–589.
31. Brig NC Rawlley's Papers, held with the CMHCS in the USI Archives.
32. Ibid.
33. Sandhu (ed.), *A View from the Other Side of the Hill*, n. 21, p. 109.
34. Ibid., pp. 110–111.
35. Ibid., pp. 111–115.
36. BN Mullik, *My Years with Nehru: The Chinese Betrayal*, Bombay: Allied Publishers, 1971, p. 350.
37. Claude Arpi, *The End of an Era: India Exits Tibet, India-Tibet Relations 1947-62*, Part 4, Delhi: Vij Books, 2020, p. 530.
38. Ibid., p. 531.
39. Ibid., p. 557.

Additional Sources

SN Prasad and Dharam Pal, *Operations In Jammu and Kashmir 1947-1948*, New Delhi: Ministry of Defence, Government of India, n.d.

Sanjay Dikshit, 'The Original Himalayan Blunder: How India Lost Gilgit-Baltistan', Indifacts.org, 2015, at https://indiafacts.org/the-original-himalayan-blunder-how-india-lost-gilgit-baltistan/.

'22 October 1947: The Darkest Day in the History of Jammu & Kashmir', *European Foundation for South Asian Studies,* 16 October 2020.

Ram Chander Sharma, 'Mirpur Massacre of 1947', *iKashmir.net,* April 2011, at https://ikashmir.net/massacres/mirpur.html.

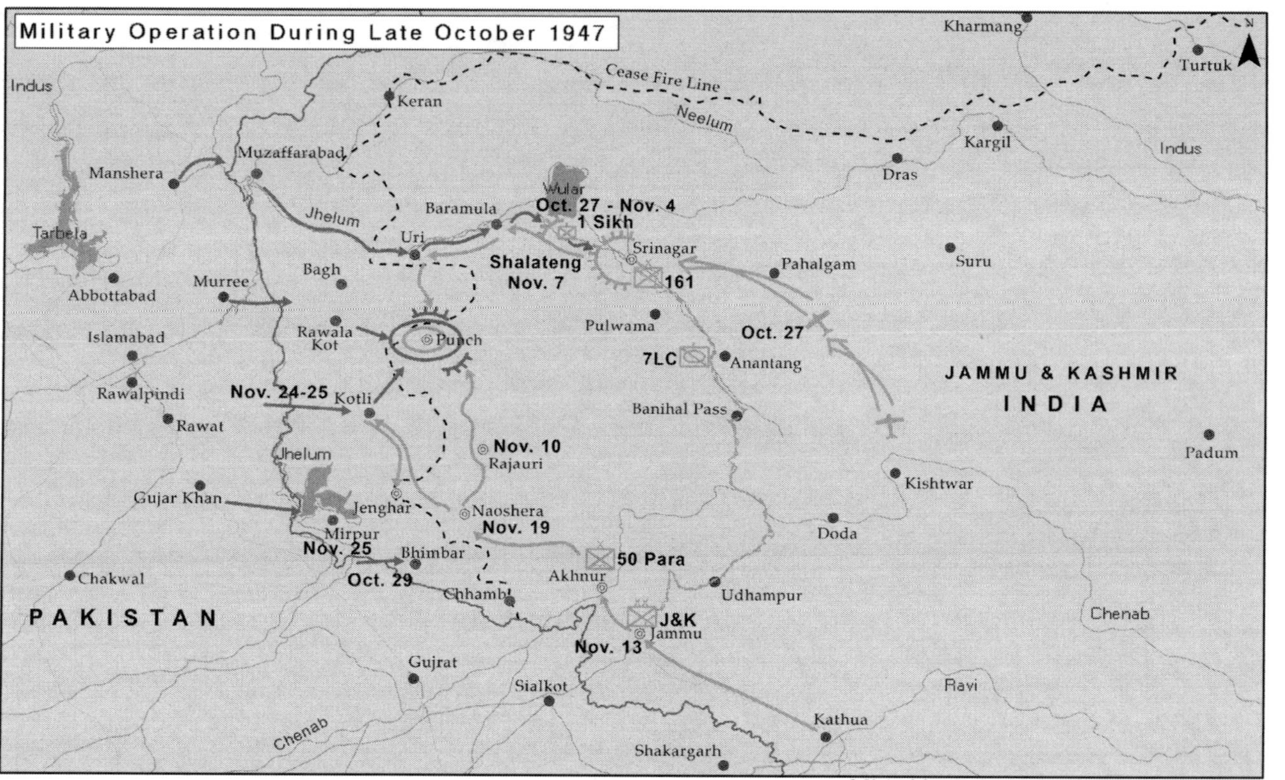

Map 1 1947–48, Kashmir Conflict

Stuart Tanks of 7 Light Cavalry advance through Zoji La, 1948
Source: USI, CMHCS.

Indian troops marching through Zoji La
Source: 1/5 GORKHA RIFLES.

Maj Gen KS Thimayya, DSO, GOC, 19 Infantry Division with Sub Harka Bahadur Rana, MC and Jem Lal Bahadur Pun, VrC of 1/5 GORKHA RIFLES, Kargil, 1948

Source: 1/5 GR.

A supply convoy winds its way through Fatu La, J&K, 1947–48
Source: USI, CMHCS.

Troops of 15 PUNJAB (1 Patiala) piqueting the heights beyond Zoji La
Source: USI, CMHCS.

Maj Gen Thimayya, DSO, GOC 19 Infantry Division with senior Commanders before the assault on Zoji La
Source: USI, CMHCS.

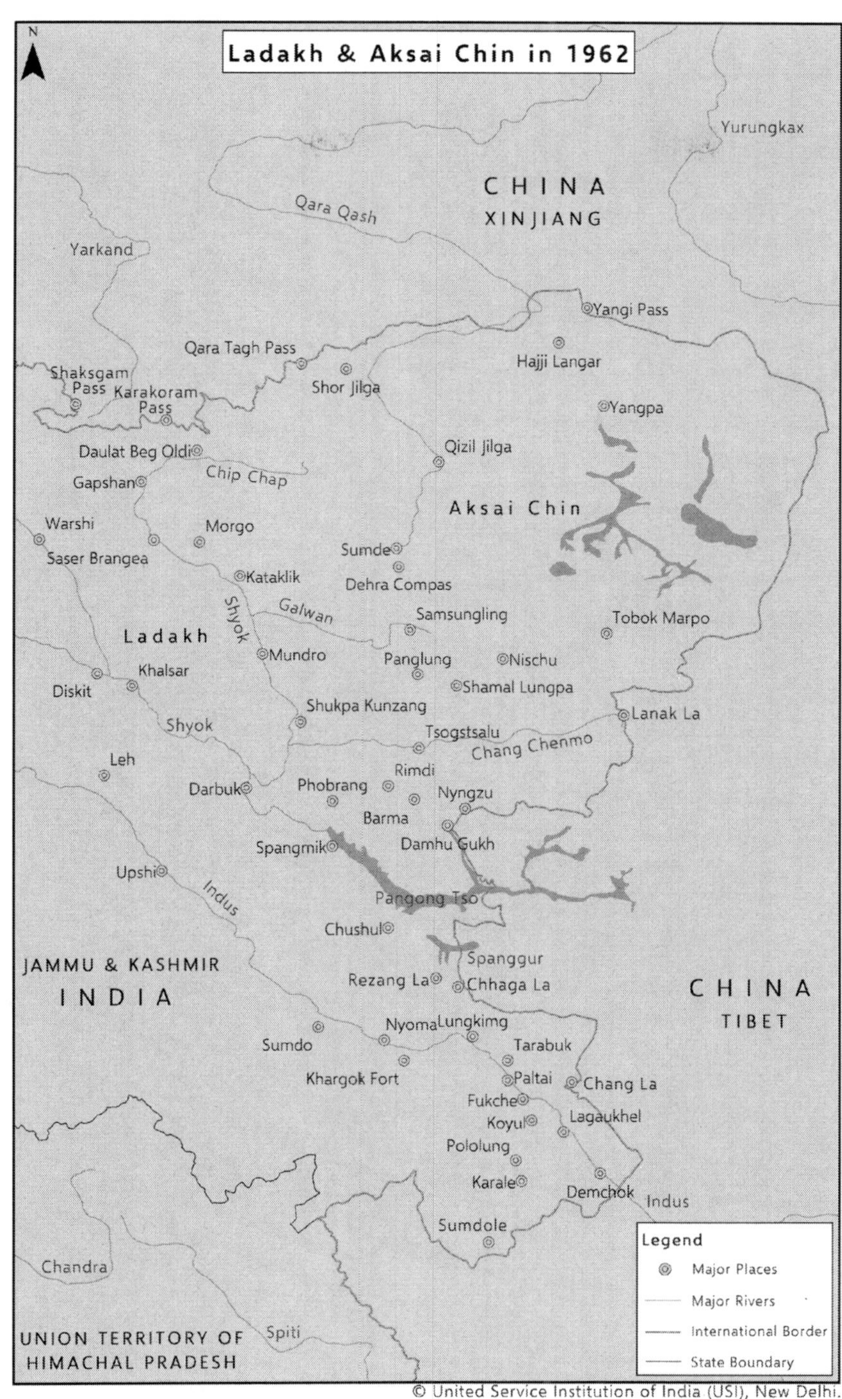

Map 2 1962: Aksai Chin

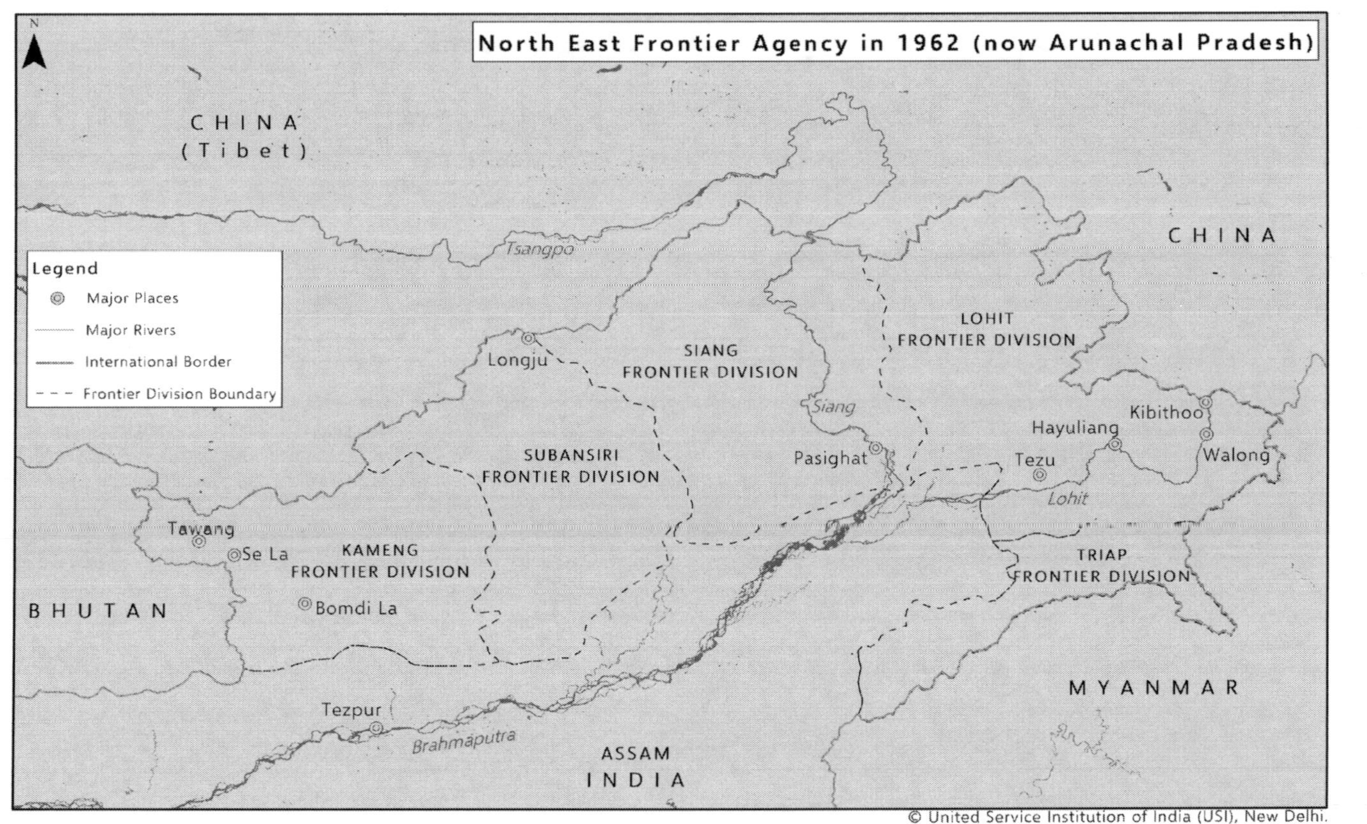

Map 3 1962: North East Frontier Agency

25 pounder gun in action
Source: MoD, DPR.

Indian troops which moved to high-altitude defences in 1962 were poorly equipped to repulse the Chinese offensive
Source: MoD, DPR.

AMX-13 tanks of 20m Lancers operating in the Chushul area, October 1962
Source: MoD, DPR.

Soldiers patrolling at a post near Tso Pangong Lake, 1963
Source: MoD, DPR.

The Sino-Indian Conflict of 1962 shook India's belief in the 'impregnable' Himalayan barrier and led to far reaching changes in defence preparedness and policy
Source: USI, CMHCS.

Gorkha Memorial at Chushul
Source: MoD, DPR.

Rezangla Memorial Plaque

Brigadier T K Theograj with his 'O' Group after the tank battle in Khem-Karan Sector
From Left: Lt Col Arun Vaidya; Commandant Deccan Horse, Maj Reggie Christan; Brigade Major, Lt Col PC Mehta; Commandant 8 CAV, Lt Col Salim Caleb, Commandant 3 CAV; Brigadier TK Theograj, Commader 2 (I) Armd Bde; and a FAC

4

Post-Independence Wars II

India-Pakistan Wars, 1965 and 1971

TEAM USI

1965 India–Pakistan War[1]

Background

In 1965, India was picking itself up from the fallout of the 1962 war; it was heavily dependent on dwindling US imports to battle an acute famine; and it was undergoing a political transition in the aftermath of Pandit Nehru's death. Not only did Rawalpindi perceive India to be weak after the defeat of 1962, but an additional driver was the concern that the Americans were supplying India with light arms for troops on the Eastern front, especially after the Nehru–Kennedy understanding post-1962. The Soviets, Czechs and the Romanians had offered to send India heavy machinery, including tanks, as they found common ground with India after having fallen out with China since the Sino-Soviet split. On its part, Pakistan had also been consolidating its special friendship with China.

The then Pakistani Army Chief General Mohammad Musa's book, *My Version*, provides a detailed account of the planning process. Musa says that 'the Kashmir

Cell'—a highly secretive group put together by the Pakistani Army in early 1964, which reported directly to the President—had by now concluded that 'it was time for Pakistan to take some overt action for reviving the Kashmir issue and "defreezing", what from Pakistan's point of view was a dishearteningly quiet and stable situation in Kashmir.'[2] With these calculations, Pakistan prepared a four-phased strategy for a war with India:

1. A probing encounter in some place of Pakistan's choosing;
2. An all-out disguised invasion of Kashmir by the Pakistani Army for 'guerrilla warfare' camouflaged as a revolt by the local population;
3. A full-scale assault by the Pakistani Army in the Chhamb Sector in Kashmir to cut off the Indian supply line in J&K; and
4. A massive lightening Armoured attack to capture Amritsar and as much of other Indian territory as possible, to be exchanged eventually for Kashmir.

To test the status of Indian capabilities, in April 1965, Pakistan first launched a limited offensive in the Rann of Kutch, while simultaneously planning for a large-scale infiltration in Kashmir, namely, 'Operation Gibraltar'.

The Rann of Kutch Incident: The Smokescreen

Terrain

The Rann of Kutch is a salt waste stretching West to East, North of Kutch. It separates Kutch from Sind (Pakistan) in the North. This area is divided into two parts: the Great Rann to the North of Kutch, about 250 km from East to West and 125 km from North to South; and the Little Rann to the South-East and South of Kutch. It is generally flooded from June to October by the sea waters pushed into it by the South-West monsoon, turning it into a salt lake. In other seasons, it is a desert, flat, firm and bare except for a few islands, sprinkled with scanty herbage. When the monsoon abates, the waters recede, leaving behind a morass. In Northern Rann, there are few villages with sparse population, having little contact with the rest of the region. Even the area around Bhuj, the main town of Kutch, is barren, with oppressive heat and forbidding dust most of the year. In 1965, in terms of connectivity, there was a road from Bhuj to Khavda in Kutch, near the border of the Rann. Northward from Khavda, a track led to Diplo (in Pakistan) across the Rann. The Northern portion of the Rann was easily accessible from the side of Sind (Pakistan). There was also a road along the border on the Pakistani side, which was motorable during the dry season.

Historical Background

The British annexed Sind in 1843. This necessitated determination of boundary between Sind, the British territory, and Kutch. As there was no immediate urgency, the border remained undemarcated, though some effort in this direction was initiated by planting pillars. During the Partition in 1947, Sind went to Pakistan by virtue of its Muslim majority, whereas Kutch, with its predominantly Hindu population, remained in India. Even before the Partition, the Sind authorities had been disputing the rights of the Kutch government over the entire Rann. In 1938, they had laid claim over half of it. On 14 July 1948, Pakistan wrote to India that the Sind–Kutch 'boundary was still in dispute and must be settled'.[3] On 10 August 1949, India cited evidence to prove that there was no dispute in this regard. In a note of 09 April 1956, Pakistan put forth the argument:

> It has been emphasised that the Rann is dead sea. According to the international practice also seas are divided equally between the states situated on either side of it. The same principle appears to have been followed while settling the dispute over the little Rann between the Princely states of Morvi and Kutch. The Pakistani claim to the Northern portion of the Rann upto Dharamsala is, therefore, supported not only by possession and exercise of authority, but also by international practice and precedent.[4]

They also cited maps and letters of the British province of Sind to prove that they had never ceased to claim rights over portions of the Rann. India, in turn, pointed out that the Survey of India maps issued during the British period marked the entire Rann as part of Kutch. The exchange of notes notwithstanding, Pakistan's intrusions into the Rann and military movements near the border started as early as 1949. To contain this, Indian authorities in Kutch also demanded the strengthening of patrol arrangements.

By the end of 1955, Pakistan had built a motor track leading to Gulmamad Talavadi, a small depression in the Rann, and reports said that contingents of Sind Reserve Police (SRP) (about 50 in each) had been stationed at Vingi and Baliari or Jat Tarai, opposite Chhad Bet area. Men of the Sind Reserve Police (SRP) were reported to be patrolling Bet area and instigating Pakistani cattle owners not to pay the grazing fees to the Indian authorities. India lodged a protest with the Government of Pakistan on 12 January 1956, but it did not have any effect. On 17 February 1956, an Indian police patrol found that Pakistani armed personnel had intruded up to Gulmamad Talavadi and taken up position there. They fired some shots in retaliation. Against this background, Pakistan decided on Chhad Bet area for a probing encounter.

The Intrusion

In January–February 1965, trouble started in Kanjarkot area. Kanjarkot was a Fort in ruins, about 1.5 km South of the Pakistan border on the North-Western fringe of the Rann of Kutch. The area South of Kanjarkot was a flat plain and the area to the North consisted of a series of parallel sand dunes. Communications in the area favoured Pakistanis rather than the Indians. The Indian administrative base at Bhuj was about 177 km South of the border; the Bhuj–Khavda road was liable to breaches during rains; and the desert track ran from Khavda to the border. Meanwhile, the position was quite different on the Pakistani side. Badin, a sizeable town, was only 30 km from the border. It had a large airfield, capable of handling all types of fighter and transport aircraft. There was also a road running from Badin to Maro, and further East to Nagar Parkar. Thus, the maintenance of the border posts was much easier for the Pakistanis than the Indians.

Pakistan started building up forces in the Kanjarkot area from about the third week of January 1965. On 10 February, this was reported by a routine Indian patrol. Pakistan deployed one company of Indus Rangers at Kanjarkot, 400 Indus Rangers at Rahim-Ki-Bazar and one wing of Indus Rangers along the border. Two Battalions of Indus Rangers were kept in reserve at Hyderabad (Sind) and Chhor. Against this, the Indians had five Companies of State Reserve Police: two at Vigokot; one at Karim Shahi; and two at Chhad Bet. However, this force was not adequate to dislodge the Pakistani encroachment.

On 21 February 1965, the Maharashtra and Gujarat Area Commander, Maj Gen PC Gupta, issued Operation Instruction No. 1 (Operation Kabadi) to Brig SSM Pahalajani, Commander 31 Infantry Brigade Group, to capture Kanjarkot. Headquarters 31 Infantry Brigade Group reached Bhuj on 27 February. The troops of 17 RAJ RIF were already in Bhuj. A Parachute Battalion was also placed at 24 hours' notice for move to the area. Pakistan retaliated by ordering Maj Gen Tikka Khan, Commander 8 Infantry Division, to assume operational command of the Indus Rangers and to take measures for effective retaliation. He, in turn, alerted 51 Infantry Brigade Group to move forward, if necessary. The Pakistanis reinforced the posts at Rahim-Ki-Bazar and Kanjarkot to Company strength, and also deployed mortars and machine guns around Kanjarkot. On 13 March, India's 2 Central Reserve Police (CRP) Battalion established Sardar Post, 4,600 m to the South-West of Kanjarkot. This effectively blocked the Pakistani route of ingress. The location was a featureless mudflat with some scrub-covered area around.

Desert Hawk-I

To forestall a likely attack on Kanjarkot by the Indian forces, a pre-emptive operation by 51 Infantry Brigade, code-named 'Operation Desert Hawk', was formulated by

Pakistan's 8 Infantry Division. The Commander of the 51 Infantry Brigade decided to attack Sardar Post with two battalions and the attack was launched on 09 April 1965 at 0100 Hours. After facing the first Pakistan attack boldly, many CRP personnel withdrew to Vigokot. At 1600 Hours, the Pakistan artillery fired shells of coloured smoke, which prompted the rest of the CRP personnel to leave Sardar Post. Soon afterwards, Brig Pahalajani took over the command from Lt Col K Sundarji who had been officiating as the Commander in his absence and asked 1 MAHAR to withdraw from Sardar Post.

In February 1965, the area of Kanjarkot (Rann of Kutch) had been seized by a company of Pakistan's Indus Rangers. Surprised by the move, India assigned the responsibility for removing this encroachment to 31 Infantry Brigade Group. Pakistan retaliated by moving in their 8 Infantry Division under Maj Gen Tikka Khan, and also inducting armour into the area. There were series of land battles between the two forces in March–April 1965, with Pakistan capturing Biar Bet on 27 April 1965.

In May 1965, Pakistani troops, bolstered by their success in Kutch, regularly violated the ceasefire along the Jammu and Kashmir border. The road to Leh was frequently targeted by them from their positions at Point 13,260 and Black Rocks. Gen J N Chaudhuri and the Western Army Commander Lt Gen Harbaksh Singh decided to get proactive in the Kargil Sector. Brigadier V K Ghai tasked the 4 RAJPUT for capturing Point 13,260 and Peaks 1 and 2 of the Black Rocks feature; it was decided to launch the offensive on the night of 16 May.

Walking in single file, the Indian troops managed to reach within 90meters of the Pakistani bunker but faced heavy mortar attack on being spotted. The Rajputs, however, shot back and captured the peaks.

The heights captured by the Indians had to be returned on 30 June after the United Nations assured the safety of the Srinagar-Leh road. The assurance did not hold for long as the Pakistanis started firing again from Point 13,260, which had been returned to them in June.

The Army then decided that the heights had to be recaptured, and this time the task was assigned to 17 PUNJAB. The Commanding Officer of the unit was asked to be prepared to capture Point 13,260 complex along with Black Rock peaks and Saddle features.

They noticed that the Pakistanis were patrolling the complex only in the daytime. The unit was asked to capture the features by early morning of 15 August. The operation commenced at midnight on 14 August and complete radio silence was maintained to prevent detection. Three Platoons under Major Balwant Singh managed to reach the three features and captured the heights without suffering a single casualty.

However, due to the intervention of Prime Minister Harold Wilson of the United Kingdom (UK), a ceasefire came into effect on 01 July 1965 and both sides agreed to restore status quo as on 01 January 1965. Though the Kutch affair ended visibly on a peaceful note, in reality it was only a prelude to another effort by Pakistan to annex J&K, which was to unfold later.

Operation Ablaze (India)

Operation Ablaze is an important interlude between the operations in the Rann of Kutch and Operation Gibraltar by Pakistan, leading to a full-scale war. This operation included the measures taken by the Indian Army along the Western border, in May–June 1965, following Pakistan's attack in the Rann of Kutch. All the formations in Punjab, mainly under 11 Corps, were ordered to move and deploy in their battle locations. It appeared that India was ready for offensive operations across the international border in Punjab if the situation in the Rann of Kutch escalated further. Following the ceasefire in the Rann of Kutch, Operation Ablaze was called off and troops were ordered to return to their peace locations.

Operation Gibraltar (Pakistan)

Even before the ceasefire took effect in the Rann of Kutch, Pakistan had been planning much bigger things in J&K commencing in May 1965.

Operation Gibraltar was conceptualised with the objective of creating large-scale disturbances in J&K. The plan was to send Pakistani soldiers and Razakars into J&K disguised as guerrillas. The first phase was to create a shock wave by launching raids on selected targets, thereby preparing the ground for a civil uprising due to the chaos and consternation that would be caused in the state. The second was the fusion of the civil uprising with the infiltration operation. This would compel India to take major political and military steps to tackle the situation, presenting a picture to the world that a problem exists in Kashmir. The armed fighters were meant to tie down Indian forces in a protracted guerrilla war in a manner similar to the war in Vietnam. Maj Gen Akhtar Malik, GOC 12 Infantry Division, in charge of the overall operation, felt that Operation Gibraltar would not succeed as a stand-alone operation. Accordingly, he combined it with Operation Grand Slam, which was the plan for an armoured thrust across the ceasefire line (CFL), with a view to capture Akhnoor, thereby threatening the line of supplies from India to Srinagar. The plan, in principle, was accepted by Field Marshal Ayub Khan in May 1965. He was convinced that military action was required to resolve the Kashmir issue. The operation was planned in the beginning of August.

Pakistan commenced infiltration of the Gibraltar Force in small groups across the CFL in J&K between 1 August and 5 August 1965. The areas covered were as follows: right from Kargil in the North to Chhamb in the South. Once inside the Valley, they were to mingle unnoticed among the crowds celebrating the festival of Pir Dastgir Sahib on 08 August 1965. Then, they were to engineer an armed uprising and in the process, capture the radio station, Srinagar airfield and some vital installations. Following this, a 'Revolutionary Council' was to proclaim itself as the lawful government and broadcast an appeal for recognition and assistance from all countries, especially Pakistan. This was to be the signal for the Pakistan Army to move in for the kill.

Lt Gen Harbaksh Singh, the Western Army Commander, read the infiltration campaign correctly. He analysed that apart from eliminating the infiltrators, there was a need to undertake offensive operations at Haji Pir and across the Kishanganga to counter the infiltration. In the ensuing operations, the Indian Army captured critical areas in Haji Pir, the Kishanganga Bulge and Kargil, which helped to contain the infiltration and enhanced the morale of troops in the ensuing operations against Pakistan which commenced on 1 September.

Operation Gibraltar came to naught mainly for two reasons. First, the internal conditions in the Valley were not ripe for an insurrection of the kind that Pakistan had hoped to incite. Second, the quick and firm response by India took Pakistan by surprise and thwarted their well-laid-out plans. The operation lost its sting as Pakistan's ensuing Operation Grand Slam was delayed to 01 September, by which time most of the infiltrators were killed or exfiltrated. India achieved its objectives by capturing areas which dominated the infiltration routes, thereby causing the termination of the entire process.

The War: Chhamb–Jaurian Sector

Indian offensive operations in Pakistan-occupied Kashmir provoked Pakistan to move into Chhamb and Jaurian. Pakistan launched Operation Grand Slam on 1 September 1965. It was launched across the Southern-most portion of the CFL and was aimed at Akhnoor, thus isolating Indian positions in Naushera, Rajauri and Poonch. Thereafter, an armoured thrust could be developed towards Jammu, the capture of which would have severed all land communications to J&K. This would place Pakistan in a position to dictate terms to India. The surprise offensive made good progress initially, but lost its momentum by 03 September 1965. In this battle the ation of Maj Bhaskar Roy of 20 LANCERS with his Squadron of AMX-13 tanks stood out. The Indian Air Force (IAF) played a major role in blunting the Pakistani offensive. The situation in this Sector was stabilised by about 10 September and Pakistan remained in control of the areas up to and including Jaurian.

Indian Counter-offensives

As mentioned earlier, the Pakistani offensive in Chhamb–Jaurian Sector took the Indians by surprise. India decided to conduct an offensive across the international border against Lahore and Sialkot to relieve the pressure on this Sector. The 'go-ahead' for an all-out military response had been given by the Emergency Committee of the Cabinet, chaired by Prime Minister Lal Bahadur Shastri, on 03 September 1965.

Indian 11 Corps Offensive (Operation Riddle)

The main aim of the offensive was to secure the line of Ichhogil Canal, thus posing a threat to Lahore. The offensives commenced at 0500 Hours on 6 September 1965. 15 Infantry Division advanced along Amritsar–Lahore axis; 7 Infantry Division advanced along Khalra–Barki axis; and 4 Mountain Division advanced on Khemkaran–Kasur axis. However, a major portion of 4 Mountain Division was also required to occupy defences in Khemkaran area to counter an expected offensive by Pakistani Armoured Division in the area.

The Indian offensives, due to the surprise factor, made good progress initially. Along the Grand Trunk Road axis, 3 JAT, under 15 Infantry Division, crossed the Ichhogil Canal at Dograi and reached Batapore on the outskirts of Lahore. However, this initial success of 3 JAT under Lt Col Desmond Hayde was not exploited and by about the end of day one, the Indian offensive had lost its momentum. Though Ichhogil canal was breached at a few points, no crossings could be secured and held. The situation became particularly grave in the 4 Mountain Division Sector where the enemy launched its counter-offensive by 1 Armoured Division on 08 September towards Jandiala Guru, Beas Bridge and Harike. 4 Mountain Division had to occupy a hastily prepared Division-defended Sector in area Asal Uttar in the face of this powerful offensive. The defended Sector had approximately three-and-a-half Battalions of Infantry (18 RAJ RIF, 1/9 GORKHA RIFLES less two Companies, 4 GRENADIERS and 9 JAK RIF), along with units of 2 (Independent) Armoured Brigade (3 CAVALRY, 8 CAVALRY less a Squadron and 9 HORSE) and artillery support. Fierce battles raged on 08–09 September, in which Indian forces repelled repeated attacks by Pakistan's armour and Infantry. More importantly, personal intervention by the Army Commander, Lt Gen Harbaksh Singh, ensured that there were no withdrawals; Indian troops held firm and the situation was stabilised by 10 September with heavy losses to Pakistan armour. The area later became the graveyard of Pakistani armour. By the time of ceasefire, Indian forces were on the home bank (Eastern) of Ichhogil Canal, while Pakistan remained in control of a small enclave in the Khemkaran Sector. After the launch of

Indian 1 Corps in the Sialkot Sector, Pakistan was forced to pull out and divert an Armoured Brigade from this Sector to Sialkot Sector to stabilise the situation there.

Indian 1 Corps Offensive in Sialkot Sector (Operation Nepal)

As part of the overall strategy, India decided to launch its main counter-offensive by the newly raised 1 Corps in the Sialkot Sector in order to relieve pressure in the Chhamb Sector, as also to degrade Pakistan's fighting potential. The offensive was launched on the night of 07–08 September 1965 on a frontage from Suchetgarh in the West to Degh Nadi in the East. The Corps was commanded by Lt Gen PO Dunn and had 1 Armoured Division, 6 Mountain Division, 14 Infantry Division and 26 Infantry Division also advanced towards Sialkot with tanks of 18 Cavalry under Lt Col Hari reaching short of Sialkot.

1 Corps was tasked to secure areas of Bhagowal–Phillaurah–Chawinda–Cross Roads (Badiana) with a view to advance towards the Marala Ravi Link (MRL) Canal and eventually, to the line of Dhalliwali–Wuhilam–Daska–Mandhali. The Corps offensive was opposed by Pakistan's 1 Corps comprising 6 Armoured Division and 15 Infantry Division. Initially, the area into which Indian 1 Corps was launched was the area of responsibility of Pakistan's 15 Infantry Division, with its HQ in Sialkot. However, as the operations progressed, the responsibility to counter the Indian offensive was given to Pakistan's 6 Armoured Division, with 24 Infantry Brigade of 15 Infantry Division placed under its command. So, it was a contest between the Indian 1 Corps, which was on the offensive, and the Pakistani 6 Armoured Division with attached troops, who were defending. The battles were fought in general area of Bhagowal–Badiana–Pasrur–Zafarwal.

Indian 1 Corps offensive had achieved complete surprise but after initial success, operations came to a near standstill and there was no major operational activity on 9 and 10 September. This gave adequate time to Pakistan's 6 Armoured Division to organise its defences. The 1 Armoured Division of India commenced its attack on Phillaurah at first light on 10 September from an unexpected direction. It was a well-coordinated attack between armour, lorried Infantry and artillery. The high points of the battle were the manoeuvres by 4 HORSE and 17 HORSE, who were operating on both flanks of Phillaurah. They manoeuvred to draw out enemy armour (11 Cavalry) deployed at Phillaurah. In the tank versus tank battles that ensued that morning, Pakistan lost 28 tanks. After the capture of Phillaurah, there was a lull in the battle on 12 and 13 September, till Indian 1 Corps renewed its offensive for capture of Chawinda on 14 September. Two attempts were made (the first one by 1 Armoured Division and the second one by 6 Mountain Division), but both were a failure. There was lack of coordination between armour and Infantry, and air support had not been planned. By now, Pakistan had also moved an Armoured Brigade from Khemkaran into this Sector and the forces, especially armour, were almost evenly matched. The formations came out of these battles badly battered and there followed a stalemate which lasted for the rest of the war.

Operations in Barmer Sector (Desert Sector)

In order to contain the Pakistani offensive in Chhamb Sector as also pre-empt any Pakistani offensive in the Desert Sector, India launched a limited offensive by 30 Infantry Brigade of 11 Infantry Division on axis Barmer–Hyderabad (Sind). By the time of the ceasefire, India had captured 390 sq km of Pakistani territory in this Sector, while Pakistan held on to the Indian border post at Munabao.

War in the Air

On the eve of the war, Pakistan Air Force (PAF) consisted of about 17 Squadrons having a total of 260 aircraft of all types approximately. As against this, the IAF had an overall strength of 26 Squadrons, with a total holding of about 460 combat aircraft of all types. A few of these Squadrons had also to be deployed in the East. The Indian edge in numbers was more than offset by Pakistan's qualitative superiority. Thus, the two Air Forces in the West were almost evenly matched.

As the war opened with a strong ground offensive by Pakistan in the Chhamb Sector on 1 September 1965, the IAF swung into action in support of the Army almost immediately and continued to do so day after day, thus playing a major role in blunting the Pakistani offensive. As a reaction to the Pakistani offensive in the Chhamb Sector, India launched its counter-offensive by 11 Corps in Lahore Sector on 6 September 1965. In accordance with their war plans, PAF responded by a pre-emptive strike on Indian air bases at Pathankot, Adampur, Halwara and Amritsar, commencing at 1740 Hours (time on target).

From 7 September onwards, the air war intensified and both the Air Forces were carrying out air operations in support of ground forces, including counter air, air interdiction and air defence. The IAF carried out a number of attacks against Pakistani air bases, railway yards, logistics installations, radar sites and even a train carrying tanks. A number of search and destroy and tactical reconnaissance missions were also flown by the IAF. However, neither side could establish a favourable air situation over the battle area. Thus, overall, neither side could claim air superiority.

War at Sea

There were no naval battles fought during 1965. The Indian Navy was no doubt larger and stronger, but it had a huge coastline and many island territories to defend.

India had only one fleet and at the time of the commencement of hostilities, the fleet was operating off the East coast in the Bay of Bengal. The fleet was able to reach Bombay only by about 8–9 September 1965.

During the night of 07–08 September, some Pakistani naval ships, disguised as merchant ships, carried out bombing of the minor port of Dwarka but with little damage as most of the shells landed on the beach.

Casualties and Territory Captured

The total number of casualties suffered by the Indian Armed Forces during the Indo-Pak War of 1965 and in the subsequent ceasefire violations amounted to 2,862 killed and 8,617 wounded.[5] According to the Defence Minister of Pakistan, 1,033 Pakistanis were killed during the war. The Indian official sources, however, state that about 5,800 Pakistanis were killed. In the war, India captured approximately 1,920 sq km of Pakistani territory. Pakistan, on the other hand, occupied 540 sq km of Indian territory.

Ceasefire and Tashkent Accord

It was not a comfortable situation for the US and the UK that Pakistan, an ally of the US and a member of both South East Asia Treaty Organization (SEATO) and Central Treaty Organization (CENTO), decided to join hands with China against India. In the communist bloc, differences between China and the Soviet Union had also emerged. It did not welcome the growth of China's influence in South Asia, particularly at the cost of non-aligned India where it had significant economic and political stakes. Hence, persistent efforts were being made by Moscow, Washington, London and UN Security Council for immediate cessation of hostilities.

On 04 September 1965, the Security Council adopted a resolution calling for an immediate ceasefire in Kashmir. When neither India nor Pakistan responded to this, the Security Council requested UN Secretary-General to visit both the countries in an effort to bring about a ceasefire. As a result, U. Thant visited Pakistan on 09 September and left for Delhi on 12 September 1965, but without any positive outcome.

Meanwhile, China, showing solidarity with Pakistan, issued a warning note to India on 08 September 1965 that blamed the Indian government of expansionist action against it and said that India must dismantle all aggressive military structures it had illegally built on China–Sikkim boundary or else bear the responsibility for all consequences. China issued another ultimatum to India on 16 September and reiterated its support to Pakistan on Kashmir.

On 19 September, China issued another note to India, reiterating its allegations and putting off the time limit set in its note of 16 September to 'before midnight of 22 Sep 1965'. The superpowers and other members of the Security Council were keenly watching China. They wanted India and Pakistan to accept a ceasefire proposal before China's second ultimatum expired on 22 September. On 20 September, the Security Council adopted a resolution calling upon India and Pakistan to accept a ceasefire on Wednesday, 22 September 1965, at 0700 Hours GMT (1230 Hours IST). The ceasefire was accepted by both the countries and it became effective with effect from 0330 Hours (IST) on 23 September 1965.

Soviet Premier Alexei Kosygin, through his earlier letter of 17 September, had invited the Prime Minister of India and President of Pakistan to hold peace talks in Tashkent, to which both sides eventually agreed. Before going to Tashkent, India made it clear that Kashmir could not be made an issue for discussion, while Pakistan said that it would not sign a 'no war pact' unless Kashmir problem was resolved. However, the Soviet Premier persuaded them to agree to a joint declaration. The agreement was signed at 1630 Hours on 10 January 1966.[6]

The Tashkent Agreement satisfied the leaders of both the countries to some extent. India's takeaway from Tashkent was that the conference did not make any reference to Kashmir and Pakistan was happy that it got back from India the territories that it had lost to India during the war, especially the Haji Pir Pass.

Assessment of the War

The 1965 war was a continuation of the 1947–48 war launched by Pakistan for the annexation of J&K. Pakistan had not given up its dream of annexing the complete state of J&K by any means and was constantly planning for the same.

The next opportunity that came Pakistan's way was the Sino-Indian War of 1962, which was a setback for India. However, Pakistan was restrained from taking advantage of the situation by the Western powers. In the middle of the crisis, India appealed for Western help, especially from the US and the UK. Both the countries readily agreed to help provided India and Pakistan could resolve the Kashmir dispute. Six rounds of talks were held between December 1962 and May 1963, but failed to produce any results. It was a win-win situation for Pakistan. From then on, India faced a two-front scenario. It also emboldened Pakistan to plan its next move for annexation of J&K, which unfolded in the form of Operation Gibraltar commencing on 5 August 1965.

There was a change in political leadership in India following the passing away of Pandit Nehru on 27 May 1964. In Pakistan's perception, India had a weak political leadership and the Indian Army was still recovering from the 1962 debacle. Pakistan, on the other hand, had a new friend in China, which was India's enemy. In addition, Pakistan's armed forces had developed a degree of renewed confidence with newly inducted American arms and equipment, which was further reinforced by the outcome of the confrontation in the Rann of Kutch. Thus, Pakistan considered this to be the appropriate time to decide the issue of J&K by force of arms. This, then, was Pakistan's calculation and thinking which set the stage for the 22-day war that followed.

In the Rann of Kutch episode, India's response left a lot to be desired. When Pakistan Army crossed the international border, the Indian reaction need not have remained confined to the Rann of Kutch alone. Military prudence lies in avoiding headlong collision and adopting a strategy of 'indirect approach'. Even a limited reaction in the neighbouring desert Sector would have produced the desired results and sent a strong signal to Pakistan, that is, not to take India for granted. Also, not using own Air Force in offensive role when the adversary has crossed the international border does not make strategic sense, especially after a similar experience in 1962 against the Chinese.

Soon after the ceasefire in the Rann of Kutch, based on the assurances by the UN Secretary-General of Pakistan's good behaviour, India called off Operation Ablaze, returned the territories captured in J&K and moved its Army formations to their peace locations. Pakistan, meantime, was giving finishing touches to the launch of Operation Gibraltar. Two aspects stand out: at the politico-diplomatic level, India was gullible; and it did not obtain enough intelligence about Pakistan's intentions and capabilities.

War erupted in all its fury on 01 September 1965. It is ironic that prior to the 1962 war, most of the Indian Army was deployed on the Western border with Pakistan. So, in the war with China, troops from the plains of Punjab and the deserts of Rajasthan had to be moved straight to the Himalayas to face the Chinese. Now, the reverse happened. Mountain Divisions from the Northern borders with China had to be moved post-haste to the plains of Punjab and J&K to face Pakistani armour; for example, 4th, 6th and the 23rd Mountain Divisions. There was no comprehensive defence plan taking into account a threat from China and Pakistan, both proven adversaries at that time.[7]

On the Western Sector, once Pakistan had played its hand in Chhamb–Jaurian Sector, Indian reaction was swift and decisive. The Army was given a free hand to launch its offensives across the international border, as it deemed necessary. However, close air support of ground operations had not been planned and coordinated; hence, the same was not forthcoming to the desired extent. This was not due to any inhibition on the part of the IAF, but due to lack of joint planning and coordination. However, when the crisis had developed on 01 September in Chhamb Sector, the IAF, in spite of no prior warning, responded magnificently and was not found wanting.

The main Indian counter-offensives had been launched in Punjab (Lahore Sector) and in J&K (Sialkot Sector). Indian formations in Punjab, which had to move from their peace locations straight into attack, without going into concentration areas where 'marrying up' could take place, were at a great disadvantage. As armour and Infantry coordination was poor, initial success on the Ichhogil Canal could not be exploited. The 4 Mountain Division offensive ran headlong into a Pakistani offensive by 1 Armoured Division. As a result, a serious crisis developed on 4 Mountain Division front in the Khemkaran Sector on 08 September. Had it not been for the tenacity and cool courage displayed by the Western Army Commander, Lt Gen Harbaksh Singh, to stay put and fight, the results could have been disastrous.

The main Indian punch was delivered by 1 Corps in the Sialkot Sector. Though complete strategic surprise was achieved, the Corps was not able to make much progress after initial successes. Pakistani defences in the area of operations were quite thin. However, there was complete inactivity by Indian 1 Corps on 09 and 10 September for almost 48 Hours, which gave Pakistan time to rehash its defensive plans and by 10 September, Pakistan's 6 Armoured Division had set itself up for a mobile defence.

In hindsight, instead of getting involved in clearing strong points like Phillaurah/Chawinda, Indian 1 Corps could have isolated these and projected the Armoured Division in the area of Badiana–Chawinda–Pasrur. Also, contacting the MRL Canal (in accordance with the mission assigned) in an early time frame would have denied freedom of movement to the Pakistani forces. The Infantry Divisions, with their integral Armoured Regiments, could have cleared the axis of maintenance. In the event, as time passed, Pakistan was able to build up its strength by pulling in forces from Chhamb Sector and moving an additional Armoured Brigade from its 1 Armoured Division in the Khemkaran Sector. Thus, by about 12 September, there was near parity of forces, especially armour. The initial advantage of the attacker and the momentum of attack had both been lost. There was no cohesive plan for a Corps battle, with each Division fighting its own battle. Instead of a battle of manoeuvre which should have found the Corps leaning on the MRL Canal, it got involved in a battle of attrition for the capture of Chawinda, in which it did not succeed till the very end.

At an operational level, the Pakistani attempts to break through the Indian defences at Asal Uttar on 08–09 September and the Indian attacks for the capture of Chawinda, on 14 September and, again, on 18–19 September, were a mirror image of each other. Both were failures, though for different reasons. The Pakistan Army tried to break through Indian positions at Asal Uttar employing 1 Armoured Division and suffered very heavy tank casualties. Meanwhile, the Indian 1 Corps tried to capture Chawinda, a strongly held position, employing 1 Armoured Division under Maj Gen Rajinder Singh Sparrow, MVC and a Mountain Division, but separately without proper coordination, resulting in heavy attrition to the attacking troops. Both sides (in both cases) knew that they were defending the most politically sensitive territory; the ramifications of a breakthrough by the enemy were serious; and there were no further reserves available to restore an adverse situation. At the end of it, both sides had suffered so much attrition that they were unable to mount any fresh major offensive operations.

After the 1962 war, India had undertaken a large-scale expansion of its armed forces, but the emphasis was on the Chinese border. The capabilities required for the Western front, including the Navy and the Air Force, were still neglected. The result was that when the 1965 war came, India's mountain Divisions were fighting in the plains and the tank fleet, except for four regiments of Centurions and two regiments of AMX-13 light tanks, consisted of obsolete Shermans which were no match for Patton M-47/48s. The Air Force, which could have played a major role in the plains and deserts, was superior in numbers but was at a disadvantage qualitatively. Indian Navy, in spite of remonstrations by the Chief of Naval Staff, was not given any offensive task, just like the Air Force in 1962. In retrospect, one can say that in war, a nation ought to bring to bear all its military strength in a synergised manner and more so, in a short duration war.

There was generally a policy of drift towards the security of the CFL and the international border in J&K. Hence, security threats were not seen in advance and the armed forces had to react only after a threat had manifested itself. The Rann of Kutch episode and Operation Gibraltar are prime examples.

If a country goes to war, it is important that the politico-military objectives are well defined and once defined, these must be pursued vigorously. In 1965, neither of the above happened. We simply reacted to the situations created by Pakistan. Having gone to war, we accepted a ceasefire without achieving any worthwhile politico-military objectives. If the Rann of Kutch had been taken as a warning, a number of measures to upgrade our military capability could have been taken in the ensuing months. For instance, we could have raised a few more Infantry Divisions for the Western front.

Lastly and most importantly, should India have accepted the ceasefire when it did? It has been argued that Indian stocks of all types of ammunition had run extremely low, hence there was no alternative but to accept the ceasefire. Post-conflict enquiries have revealed that in overall terms, only about 14–20 per cent of the Indian Army's ammunition stocks had been used up; and large dumps of unused ammunition were lying in Sectors where fighting had not been intensive. On the other hand, in Pakistan, nearly 80 per cent of ammunition stocks had actually been expended. It may be conjectured that it was in India's interest to continue the war. However, hindsight and an objective assessment would indicate that India was fighting a war that was thrust upon it; furthermore, it was unable to create a favourable diplomatic environment internationally to prolong fighting, unlike the situation in 1971.

However, it can be said without hesitation that the Indian soldiers (sailors and airmen included) had, once again, given their best in service of the nation. The soldiers were brave, resolute and steadfast in battle, and units sought to achieve their missions relentlessly against heavy odds. The nation too rallied and stood behind its soldiers in a magnificent manner. In the final analysis, the outcome of the war is a tribute to the Indian soldier.

1971 India–Pakistan War

Background

The 1971 war was a manifestation of domestic political estrangement between the two halves of the Pakistani state. With little beyond a common religious belief and a deep distrust of India to bind them, these two halves slipped towards civil war as discontent in the Eastern part (now Bangladesh) grew into an autonomy movement in the late 1960s. The breaking point came in March 1971 when the Bengalis (the ethnic group which constituted the vast majority of East Pakistan's population) were denied the fruits of their victory in the December 1970 elections. The principal East Pakistani party, the Awami League, had won the majority of seats in the country's parliament, but the politically dominant West Pakistani leadership—particularly the ambitious head of Pakistan People's Party, Zulfikar Ali Bhutto—had no desire to relinquish supremacy, and thus stalled on convening the National Assembly. The law-and-order situation deteriorated and the tensions between the two sides reached unbearable levels. Last-minute attempts at negotiations floundered on the irreconcilable differences between Awami Party leader, Sheikh Mujibur Rahman, on the one side, and the military government of West Pakistan under General Agha Mohammed Yahya Khan on the other.

The Pakistan Army, overwhelmingly drawn from West Pakistan, indulged in harsh repression in a misguided effort to control the situation through military force. Under a plan called 'Operation Searchlight', West Pakistani troops endeavoured to disarm Bengali elements of the armed forces, paramilitary and police, while arresting hundreds of suspected separatists. Predictably, the Bengalis retaliated and open rebellion broke out in the East. The rebels proclaimed the independence of 'Bangladesh' on 26 March 1971. By early April, a provisional government had come into existence at 'Mujibnagar' in India. The level of violence increased during the spring and summer of 1971, as a result of which hundreds of thousands of refugees began to pour into India, including thousands of former East Pakistani regular soldiers and paramilitary troops. The Pakistan Army managed to re-establish a degree of control over most of the cities and towns in the East by the end of May, but no viable political solution was forthcoming from Islamabad to exploit this momentary military success. As a result, the rebellion, or civil war as some participants termed it, slowly grew in intensity and scope in the monsoon months, between May and October.

The civil conflict in East Pakistan presented a major challenge to Indian policy, particularly the enormous burden imposed by millions of refugees who had arrived by midsummer. Beyond the strain on finances and social services, India was deeply concerned about the leftist elements within the Bengali separatist movement. Naxalites had conducted an especially vicious militant campaign in Eastern India in the late 1960s and New Delhi had no desire to see that insurgency reignited by Bengali radicals, or see East Pakistan established as an independent state under the auspices of leftist extremists. At the same time, the government had to contend with widespread sympathy for the Bengalis and the resultant outcry for intervention from opposition politicians and the public at large. Many Indians advocated exploiting Pakistan's predicament, including K Subrahmanyam, a leading commentator and Director of the Institute of Defence Studies and Analyses, who urged military action to take advantage of what he called 'an opportunity the like of which will never come again'.[8] Though other important Indian writers promoted restraint, Subrahmanyam's statements received wide publicity in Pakistan, deepening animosity and leaving a lasting impression.

Domestic pressure notwithstanding, the initial Indian reaction was relatively cautious. Indian Border Security Force (BSF) troops began providing low-level assistance to Bengali rebels (the Mukti Bahini or Liberation Force) in early April in the form of safe havens, training and limited arms. However, New Delhi chose not to recognise the provisional government of Bangladesh (declared on 17 April 1971), and it also did not authorise direct military action across the border. In a meeting on 29 April, Prime Minister Indira Gandhi apparently considered ordering a military advance, but Foreign Minister Swaran Singh counselled restraint and recommended holding military intervention in reserve in case 'interim measures did not resolve the East Pakistan crisis' diplomatically. Similarly, Gen SHFJ Manekshaw, the Chief of the Army Staff and also the Chairman of the Joint Chiefs of Staff Committee, advised Mrs Indira Gandhi that India's armed forces would need some time to prepare for the conflict. Moreover, the imminent arrival of the monsoon would prevent major operations until November at the earliest. Prime Minister Indira Gandhi agreed to a delay, but ordered Gen Sam Manekshaw to plan for war as a policy option for the future.

The Indian leadership, thus, seems to have hoped for a resolution short of open war in the intervening period, as long as the refugees departed and stability returned to the East either through a resolution that gave power to a moderate Awami League regime within the Pakistani state or through the creation of an independent Bangladesh. From spring onwards, however, India began to prepare, both diplomatically and militarily, for the possibility of an armed contest: securing international support; increasing assistance to the Mukti Bahini; and boosting military readiness. During the summer and fall, Pakistan also placed its military on a war footing, transferring significant forces to the East (9th and 16th Infantry Divisions as well as several thousand paramilitary and police) and raising new units in the West to take their places (17th and 33rd Infantry Divisions). However, the counter-insurgency campaign did not go well for Pakistan. As the months passed, the Mukti Bahini improved with Indian assistance, while the Pakistani security forces, isolated amidst a hostile population, struggled with physical and mental exhaustion. Though relatively secure within their cantonments, they were unable to quell the unrest within East Pakistan; collect reliable intelligence; or execute unrealistic orders to 'seal' the long, twisting border with India in what one commander characterised as an exercise in 'quixotic dreaming'.

The Eastern Command's successes were local and transitory. The civil war became a cruel and seemingly endless cycle of raids, ambushes, bombings, sabotage, assassinations and shellings. Pakistan could not eradicate the guerrillas, and the Mukti Bahini by themselves lacked the strength and coordination to force a Pakistani withdrawal. Brutality was commonplace on both sides and the death toll climbed to thousands. By November 1971, the Indian Army and paramilitary troops were regularly providing artillery support to the Mukti Bahini and, towards the end of the month, the Army had even made several small incursions into East Pakistan. Cross-border raids and artillery exchanges by both sides became common. Ultimately, in the evening of 03 December 1971, Pakistan, whose strategy for defence of the East called for offensive in the West, launched its Air Force against several targets in Western India. That night, the Pakistan Army opened an offensive all along the Western front, from Poonch in Kashmir to Longewala in the Rajasthan desert.

India had been preparing for Pakistan to make the first move and had drafted its plans accordingly. Its principal focus was in the East, where it was hoped that a well-conceived offensive would crush Pakistani resistance quickly and result in the conclusive establishment of Bangladesh as an independent country. India's Eastern Command overran East Pakistan in two weeks.

Despite often spirited resistance, the Pakistani defenders were faced with an impossible strategic situation. Their Commander, Lt Gen AAK Niazi, signed an instrument of surrender at 1630 Hours on 16 December 1971 and a ceasefire went into effect on both fronts at 2000 Hours the following day, leaving some 90,000 Pakistani prisoners of war and civilian detainees in Indian hands. In the West, the two armies sparred indecisively, each side's small advances being balanced by the other side's gains. The only exception was the dramatic drive by India's 11th InfantryDivision into the sandy wastes of Pakistan's Sindh province, which netted India approximately 4,500 sq km of Pakistani territory, albeit barren desert. Pakistan's military debacle led to a political upheaval that ended with Zulfikar Ali Bhutto coming to power as the truncated country's new leader. After prolonged wrangling and some additional skirmishing,

Bhutto and Gandhi signed the Simla Accord on 03 July 1972. Innumerable details remained unresolved, however, and the two sides did not come to an agreement on the redefinition of the CFL, from thenceforth to be called the Line of Control (LOC), in Kashmir until December 1972. The first exchange of prisoners also took place that month, but the last of them, held hostage to bitter political machinations, did not return home until April 1974.

Strategies and Forces

The Indian strategy in 1971 gave primacy to operations in East Pakistan. For decision makers in New Delhi, the aim of the war was to create conditions that would allow the refugees to return and would leave an Awami League government in power in Dacca. Early Indian plans thus focused on support to the Mukti Bahini and diplomatic efforts to bring about a political resolution to the crisis. By autumn, however, when it became clear that neither diplomacy nor insurgency would suffice to achieve India's objectives, preparations for a military invasion of East Pakistan were accelerated, including seizure of enclaves along the frontier. The focus on the East dictated that the war in the West would be a defensive holding action. No ground was to be lost, especially in Kashmir, and offensive operations were authorised where feasible to gain advantages for use at the negotiating table or to pre-empt a Pakistani advance, but the war would be won or lost in the East.

Prime Minister Gandhi rejected suggestions that the conflict be prolonged to permit the conquest of major areas in West Pakistan or the destruction of the Pakistan Army. The time element was also key to Indian planning. Based on the assumption that only a few weeks would be available before foreign pressure brought the war to a halt, Indian plans stressed the need for a quick invasion that could deliver decisive results before the international community could intervene in any significant manner. Finally, the Indian military was to ensure the security of the border with China.

Although the political leadership was confident that Beijing would not intervene with armed force, the Indian commanders had to include China in their planning. Indeed, one reason operations were delayed until November/December was to allow winter snow to close the passes leading from Tibet into India. Pakistan's strategy was almost the exact opposite of India's. Recognising the near impossibility of successfully holding its Eastern half against a determined Indian onslaught, Pakistani strategy was predicated on the conviction that the East would have to be defended in the West. In practical terms, this axiom meant that Pakistan would launch a major offensive into India from the West at the start of any conflict. By threatening vital Indian assets, such as Kashmir and the Punjab, Pakistani planners hoped to draw Indian forces away from the East and gain enough time for outside powers to restrain New Delhi. In the meantime, Pakistan's Eastern Command, isolated and effectively surrounded, would have to hold on as best it could. Pakistan also hoped for a short war. First, because of the difficulty in defending the East for any extended period of time against a determined foe; and second, because the military services, especially the Army, were desperately short of replacement equipment and reserve manpower necessary for a lengthy conflict. Contrary to India's fairly realistic appraisal of the likelihood of international intervention, many Pakistani officers hopefully assumed that China, and possibly others, would play an active combat role if the situation escalated to war.

The forces available to the two sides to execute their strategies were among the largest in the world at the time. India's Army of 833,800 men could field 14 Infantry Divisions, 10 Mountain Divisions, two Parachute Brigades, as well as an Armoured Division and four Independent Armoured Brigades. Key items of combat equipment included more than 1,450 tanks and 3,000 artillery pieces.[9] Beyond first-line troops, India enjoyed a considerable advantage in reserves of personnel and equipment over Pakistan; it thus had a substantial ability to endure losses and to continue a conflict longer than its adversary.

At 365,000 men, the Pakistan Army was about half the size of its Indian counterpart, but was nonetheless a formidable force with two Armoured Divisions, 13 Infantry Divisions and three independent Armoured Brigades with approximately 850 tanks and 800 guns. Two of these Infantry Divisions (the 17th and 33rd), however, were still being organised and suffered from numerous difficulties attendant upon construction of military formations. Three Divisions were in East Pakistan, the original garrison (14th Infantry Division) having been joined in March/April by the 9th and 16th Infantry Divisions (albeit minus much of their equipment). Lt Gen Niazi organised two additional Infantry Divisions in the East (the 36th and 39th Infantry Divisions), but these were Divisions in name only—a futile attempt to make the Eastern Command appear more powerful than it was. In fact, each was hardly more than brigade strength, lacking staff, supporting arms and equipment of every sort. It is noteworthy that both armies relied heavily on foot-mobile Infantry Divisions, having only limited capability to conduct mechanised warfare despite the large overall size of the ground forces. Both sides supplemented their regular troops with extraordinarily large paramilitary establishments (some 280,000 in Pakistan's case, for example), but, as with regular units, India had a significant numerical advantage in paramilitary forces.

Pakistan also attempted to form a considerable body of hastily assembled militia and home guard units for rear area duties and counter-insurgency missions, especially in East Pakistan. The results, however, were disappointing and many of these units in both Wings proved unreliable, unless backed by regulars. The air arms of both countries were commensurately large. The IAF, with some 625 combat aircraft and over 450 transport and support planes. outnumbered the 273 fighters and bombers in the PAF. Moreover, the IAF had improved in quality since its controversial showing during the 1965 war. The Indian Navy had also grown since 1965. By 1971, it was not only one of the few navies in the world to feature an aircraft carrier (*INS Vikrant*) in its order of battle but also included 21 other major surface combatants, four submarines and a number of patrol boats that would play an interesting role in the war. Pakistan's Navy also had four submarines, but its surface fleet counted only eight major combatants and a few patrol boats.

Although India enjoyed a significant quantitative superiority in numbers of soldiers and equipment, the two militaries were fairly equal in qualitative categories, such as maintenance, logistics, training and leadership, as they entered the war. With respect to command and control, however, Pakistan suffered from serious problems. On taking over as President and Chief Martial Law Administrator in early 1969, Gen Yahya Khan had retained his previous position as Commander in Chief of the Army. He thus placed himself at the pinnacle of a tangled bureaucratic structure, with responsibility for domestic and foreign policy as well as Army issues and the operational direction of all three services in combat. The burden proved too great. Furthermore, he exacerbated this confused situation by filling the staff of the martial law administration with military officers (mostly Army) and appointing serving officers to key positions in the country's governmental structure. The requirements of administering the martial law regime not only distracted the armed forces from their primary missions but also created an atmosphere in which lines of command and authority were blurred and uncertain, slowing reaction time and fostering confusion. Joint operations among the three services—ground, air and sea—were another weak point for Pakistan's command and control system. In the words of the official post-war analysis, 'there was an utter lack of joint planning by the three services', so that the Pakistanis were not able to generate the synergy inherent in multi-service operations on a consistent basis.[10]

Pakistan's command problems were compounded by poor communications between the different HQ in the Eastern and Western Wings. While Lt Gen Niazi created misleading impressions by submitting rosy appreciations of the deteriorating situation in the East, his superiors in Rawalpindi did not always keep him apprised of plans at the national level. Senior officers in Dacca 'had no prior knowledge of the start of the war, nor of the developments on the ground and in the air' on 03 December 1971.[11] Similarly, the Commander in Chief of the Pakistan Navy and other senior officials apparently only learned of the attack on India from news broadcasts. The Indian Army, IAF and Indian Navy also experienced problems in coordinating their actions, especially in the West, but the overall level of joint cooperation was much higher. In the Eastern theatre in particular, the three Services worked together quite effectively, largely as a result of the senior leaders' personalities and professionalism. Nonetheless, as an Indian Division Commander during the war has observed: 'there were flaws which might have caused serious danger under other circumstances.[12]

The Eastern Front

East Pakistan presented an extraordinarily challenging theatre of operations for both sides. Marshes, rice paddies and innumerable small lakes and watercourses made movement difficult, effectively prohibiting major military operations during the monsoon (approximately May to late September). The region's transportation infrastructure was very weak in 1971, with few all-weather roads capable of accepting heavy military traffic and even fewer railroads. Moreover, the larger rivers broke the country into four principal zones: North-West, South-West, Central and East. These Sectors were connected by only two railroad bridges: the Hardinge Bridge across the Padma (Ganges) linking the South-West and the North-West; and a bridge at Ashuganj across the Meghna River to tie the East and central zones together. With the exception of these two bridges, neither of which was decked for vehicular traffic, movement across the Padma, Jamuna and Meghna could only be accomplished by water or by air.

For Pakistan's planners, the situation in the East was enormously daunting. Lt Gen Niazi's Eastern Command was surrounded on its three land sides by the numerically superior Indian Army; its sea flank was dominated by the Indian Navy; and its limited air cover was unlikely to endure beyond the first few days of action. No substantial reinforcements could be expected once the war began. Moreover, movement, security and intelligence collection inside East Pakistan were badly hampered by the activities of the Mukti Bahini. Guerrilla actions, insufficient logistical support and the pervading sense of isolation also contributed to the psychological exhaustion of the Pakistani troops and commanders. Describing the mental state of the troops, a Division commander commented that their 'minds were clogged by an incomprehensible conflict'.[13] Similarly, a Brigade Commander in 14 Infantry Division recorded that 03 December found his men already 'very near exhaustion' and burdened by 'terrible fatigue and sleeplessness'.[14] Further, growing distrust of their Bengali comrades-in-arms exacerbated the anxiety and uncertainty among the West Pakistani soldiers.

The forces available were inadequate to cope with these pressing external and internal threats. Lt Gen Niazi had only three regular Infantry Divisions in Eastern Command, two of which lacked their full complement of artillery, vehicles and signals equipment. Only one Armoured Regiment (29 Cavalry) was on hand and its tanks were mostly World War II vintage American M24 Chaffees, supplemented by a handful of Russian PT-76s captured from India during the 1965 war. Two additional 'ad hoc' Division HQ (36th and 39th) and several Brigades were created during the autumn of 1971 in an effort to deceive Indian intelligence, but these were cobbled together hastily from existing resources and did little to improve command and control. The problems experienced by these units led one Pakistani commentator to describe the 36th Division as 'a hoax..a patchwork of a formation put on crutches.'[15]

The other Services were equally threadbare. The PAF presence was limited to one Squadron (No 14) consisting of 16 Sabre VIs and three RT-33s. The Pakistan Navy in the East was capable of some riverine operations, but with only four patrol craft and some two dozen improvised or confiscated river vessels, it could hardly challenge the Indian Navy, especially in the absence of air cover. Curiously, Niazi did not have formal authority over the air and Navy components of the force in East Pakistan; they were simply expected to cooperate with him in his guise as Commander, Eastern Command. Under such circumstances, it is perhaps not surprising that one Pakistani General later commented, 'the defeat in East Pakistan was inevitable'.[16]

Lt Gen Niazi's plans for the defence of the East were formulated in July 1971 and approved by Army HQ the following month. The primary aim was to prevent the Mukti Bahini and the Indians from seizing a parcel of East Pakistan from which an independent state of Bangladesh could be declared. Associated with this strategic aim was the key assumption that India would not launch a full-scale attack in the East, but would limit its actions to steadily increasing support for the Mukti Bahini. Niazi's general concept, therefore, called for a 'forward posture of defense' along the borders to prevent incursions, with the Army falling back to so-called 'strong points' and 'fortresses' if necessary.[17] Thus, if the Indians invaded, the Army would supposedly fall back slowly and endeavour to hold out in these fortresses as long as possible to allow the offensive in the West to take effect.

There were several serious flaws in this concept. First, the cordon defence along the frontier was brittle because there were insufficient troops to defend the entire border while trying to prosecute the counter-insurgency war. Second, the Pakistani Eastern Command had practically no reserves, making the strong point defence a questionable proposition. Moreover, with limited mobility and faced with a hostile population in difficult riverine terrain, there was, at best, small likelihood that the forward Pakistani troops would be able to withdraw to the fortresses intact. Niazi compounded the withdrawal problem by decreeing that no unit could pull back until it had suffered atleast 75 per cent casualties. Third, no regular troops were left to defend Dacca, even though the planners recognised that the capital was the nerve centre of East Pakistan with enormous symbolic importance. One Pakistani veteran, summarising the problem concisely, stated: 'Pakistan fought the war in East Pakistan with a troop deployment designed for internal security operations.'[18] The most curious aspect of the plan, however, was Niazi's desire—with which the Army General HQ initially concurred—to launch offensive operations into India at several points. A subsequent Pakistani commentator regarded this proposal as 'sheer folly'.[19]

Across the border was India's Eastern Command, under Lt Gen Jagjit Singh Aurora. The orders issued to Lt Gen Aurora instructed him to destroy the bulk of the

Pakistani forces in the East and to occupy most of East Pakistan. These two objectives seem to have been allotted equal priority by the Army HQ, and Aurora addressed them by preparing plans to seize territory up to the lines of the major rivers through offensives in the South-Western, North-Western and Eastern Sectors. One Corps was allotted to each of these Sectors: 2 Corps in the South-West; 33 Corps in the North-West; and 4 Corps in the East. Indian offensive operations in the East were to begin in the first week of December, and New Delhi was thus both pleased and relieved when the Pakistani air strikes on the afternoon of 03 December (and ground attacks that night) came in advance of the planned operations. Notably absent from the Indian plans was any formal reference to Dacca. Army planners thought it would be impossible to secure the city within the time frame of a short war. As a result, the best approach to the East Pakistani capital, the central or Northern Sector, was initially assigned only one regular brigade under an ad hoc HQ called 101 Communications Zone Area. Nonetheless, several senior Indian generals certainly had their eyes on the city.

Verbal coordination between Maj Gen Gurbax Singh Gill, GOC 101 Communications Zone, and the Chief of Staff at Eastern Command, Maj Gen JFR Jacob, led to an outline plan for a possible advance on Dacca, including a parachute drop at Tangail in Battalion strength. Likewise, Lt Gen Sagat Singh, GOC 4 Corps, clearly intended to head for Dacca if the opportunity arose, even though this was not part of his written orders. More than Dacca, the possibility that Pakistani forces would escape by sea had been on Gen Manekshaw's mind in New Delhi. The Indian Navy, however, promised to deny Pakistan the use of Chittagong and Chalna Ports, reducing his concern about this eventuality. Manekshaw would later come to worry about the potential for an overland withdrawal into Burma.

With six full Divisions (plus parts of 6th Mountain Division), four additional Brigades and the equivalent of three Armoured Regiments, India's Eastern Command decidedly outnumbered Lt Gen Niazi's defenders. Several additional Brigades and the HQ of 6 Mountain Division would be added to this imposing force as the war progressed and the likelihood of Chinese intervention diminished. Although the Mountain Divisions composing Eastern Command had few vehicles, a Squadron of approximately 12 operational Mi-4 helicopters was available to enhance mobility and there were sufficient transport aircraft to airdrop up to a Battalion of 50 Para Brigade at any one time. In combat aircraft, the IAF contributed 11 fighter Squadrons and one Squadron of Canberra bombers to the offensive in the East. The Indian Navy's principal surface combatant, the aircraft carrier *INS Vikrant*, with her task force, would seal the coast and support inland operations with air strikes and naval gunfire.

The various Mukti Bahini groups multiplied the strength of India's armed forces. Some of these groups had been formed from men with experience in the Pakistan Army, or with various Pakistani paramilitary organisations. During most of the rebellion, the Mukti Bahini guerrillas operated in geographically defined 'Sectors'. As open war approached, however, some of these troops were assembled into three brigade-sized groupings called 'forces'. Designated 'Zulu', 'Kilo' and 'Sierra', according to the initials of their commanders, they provided a total of eight Infantry Battalions (East Bengal Regiment) and three artillery batteries under the overall command of India's 4 Corps. These 'forces' were capable of limited conventional operations in cooperation with the Indian Army, and were closely intermingled with Indian units during the actual fighting. Although some Battalions were attached to Indian brigades individually, Sierra Force and Kilo Force essentially functioned as subordinate brigades under Indian Divisions for much of the war. Other Bangladeshi groups constituted 'Freedom Fighters', who operated deep within East Pakistan as guerrillas and political cadres. Although the Freedom Fighters seldom inflicted heavy losses on the Pakistani regulars, they represented a ubiquitous menace, constantly harassing their opponents with ambushes, raids, sabotage and propaganda. Their activities exhausted the Pakistani troops while creating an enervating sense of constant uncertainty and danger. They also supplied Indian authorities with invaluable intelligence information. By November 1971, some 100,000 Bengalis could claim membership in these varied elements of the Mukti Bahini, and half of them were already operating inside East Pakistan.

South-West Sector

Cut up with innumerable water obstacles, the South-Western corner of East Pakistan offered many advantages to the defender. The Pakistani force assigned to this Sector, however, was inadequate to its mission. With only nine regular Infantry Battalions, the 9 Infantry Division could hardly cover its assigned terrain. Of its two brigades, 107 Infantry Brigade had to protect the immense frontier from Satkhira to Kotchandpur, while 57 Infantry Brigade held the Sector from the latter town North to the Padma. Moreover, 9th Division's Commander, Maj Gen MH Ansari, proved incapable of providing the determined, imaginative leadership necessary to compensate for his formation's numerical inferiority. An additional formation, the ad hoc 314 Brigade of paramilitary troops, was initially formed at Khulna, but moved to Dacca by boat on approximately 7 December 1971.

On the Indian side, the newly raised 2 Corps consisted of the 4 Mountain Division and the 9 Infantry Division (the only Infantry Division in the East, it had more motor vehicles and heavier artillery than its mountain counterparts); the Corps was later reinforced by 50 (Independent) Para Brigade (minus one Battalion). Under Lt Gen Tapishwar Narain (Tappy) Raina, MVC, the twenty Infantry Battalions of 2 Corps were to take Khulna, Jessore, Goalundo Ghat, Faridpur, and the Hardinge Bridge. Convinced that Khulna was one of the keys to East Pakistan, Gen Manekshaw placed special stress on its capture. Dacca was not mentioned, except in some contingency plans for crossing the Padma (Ganges) at Faridpur and Goalundo Ghat. Thus, paying little attention to possible operations against the chief city of East Pakistan, Raina planned to advance on two axes, with 4th Division in the North towards Jhenida and the 9 Infantry Division aiming for Jessore on the Southern approach. Operations by Indian troops and Mukti Bahini in late November had secured a sizable enclave between Boyra and Jessore. An Indian success at Garibpur on 21/22 November 1971 was particularly significant, as it allowed 9 Infantry Division to gain considerable ground towards Jessore and resulted in the virtual destruction of the lone Pakistani Armoured Squadron in the area.[20]

The action at Garibpur, however, also alerted the Pakistanis to the 9 Division's proposed line of advance. As a result, once the full-scale conflict broke out, the Division quickly became embroiled in a tough and costly slogging match on 04 and 05 December 1971. This fight took its toll on the Pakistanis too, and the exhausted 107 Infantry Brigade abandoned Jessore on the night of 06/07 December, withdrawing South to Khulna in considerable confusion. The Pakistani Division HQ and other remnants fled East towards the Madhumati River. A Pakistani officer recalled: 'The front here had crumbled completely...Withdrawal quickly turned into a rout.'[21] Riding into Jessore in the dawn hours of 07 December, he noted, 'It looked like a ghost town, except for sleepy dogs and chickens, not a soul stirred. Doors were wide open, all kinds of personal belongings littered the roads...It looked like the end of East Pakistan.' The Indians occupied Jessore later that day, but Maj Gen Dalbir Singh, GOC 9 Infantry Division, allowed himself to be distracted by Khulna and turned his entire Division towards an objective that was supposed to be taken by a Brigade. The town held out stoutly for the remainder of the war in the face of repeated attacks.

The Indian Navy was also involved in the fighting around Khulna. A small task group of one Indian Navy patrol boat and two Mukti Bahini boats, called 'Force Alpha', steamed towards Khulna from Chalna on 09/10 December 1971. Pakistani fire and tragically accurate air strikes by IAF fighters disabled two of the boats and forced the other to withdraw without contributing much to the advance. The 9th Division's reserve force, 50 (Independent) Para Brigade, engaged in a brief skirmish at Khajura, North of Jessore, on 08 December, before being pulled out the next day for transfer to the Western front. A planned two-Company airborne attack by 8 Para near Jhenida was called off as being unnecessary. The 'Red Eagles', Indian 4 Mountain Division, launched a well-conducted attack North and East from its positions around Jibannagar, skillfully bypassing or overwhelming resistance to enter Jhenida on 07 December.

Like the 9 Infantry Division, however, the leadership of 4 Mountain Division was distracted by a flank objective. In this case, when a hasty attempt to capture Kushtia and the Hardinge Bridge miscarried, the senior commanders overreacted and diverted the entire Division to the North. Although the Indian advance helped urge Pakistan's 57 Infantry Brigade in its retreat across the Ganges, by the time 4 Mountain Division had returned to the Magura area (14 December), it was too late to participate in the drive for Dacca. The Division made a fine crossing of the Madhumati (albeit against light resistance) and took the surrender of the broken remnants of the Pakistani 9th Division at Faridpur on 16 December 1971. Indian Army and BSF troops from the Bengal Area, under Maj Gen P Chowdry, made limited gains on the Satkhira axis.

North-West Sector

Somewhat drier than the other operational areas in East Pakistan, the North-West Sector offered better terrain for mechanised forces and the possibility of fairly rapid movement. Consequently, both sides allotted the bulk of their Armoured Units to this Sector (the Pakistani 29 Cavalry; Indian 63 Cavalry and 69 Armoured Regiments, as well as 20 MARATHA LI in SKOT Armoured Personnel Carriers) and tanks played an important role in the success of India's 340 Mountain Brigade. Pakistan's 16 Infantry Division had the task to defend the North-West, but its Commander, Maj Gen Nazir Hussain Shah, dissipated his strength by creating ad hoc commands and haphazardly mixing troops from various units. The result was a reduction in cohesion and morale.

On the Indian side, 33 Corps, under Lt Gen M L Thapan, controlled the 6th and 20th Mountain Divisions and the 71 Mountain Brigade. However, while fighting the war to the South, the Corps also had to look North and retained command of the 17 and 27 Mountain Divisions on the Tibetan frontier. Furthermore, Thapan could not commit 6 Mountain Division without permission from New Delhi as it was to be held ready to move to the Bhutanese border in case China intervened in the war. As elsewhere along the border, Indian forces in support of the Mukti Bahini made significant inroads into East Pakistan prior to 03 December. Most notable was Brig Pran Nath Kathpalia's 71 Mountain Brigade, which had pushed to the outskirts of Thakurgaon by the eve of war. Efforts to capture the heavily fortified border village of Hilli, however, failed repeatedly in a struggle that raged off and on from 24 November to 11 December 1971. Resolutely defended by Pakistani 4 Frontier Force, Hilli blocked the proposed advance of 20 Division across the narrow 'waist' of this Sector.

After suffering heavy losses in front of Hilli, the Division solved this problem by swinging around to the North and unleashing 340 Infantry Brigade under Brig Joginder Singh Bakshi. Bakshi moved swiftly to control the main North–South road, unhinging the defence of Hilli, splitting Pakistani 16 Infantry Division and opening the way to Bogra, a town he effectively controlled by the war's end. The Pakistani

Division, despite continued resistance by isolated units, had ceased to exist as a coherent combat formation. Indicative of the chaotic situation, Gen Shah and the Commander of 205 Infantry Brigade, Brig Tajammul Hussain Malik, were almost captured when Indian forces ambushed their convoy on 07 December 1971.

On the other hand, a last-minute Indian move North by the 66 and 202 Mountain Brigades to capture Rangpur proved unsuccessful. In secondary actions, 9 Mountain Brigade secured most of the area North of the Tista River and an ad hoc command of Indian BSF and Mukti Bahini, under Brig Prem Singh, pushed out of Malda to capture Nawabganj in the extreme South-Eastern corner of the Sector. Despite Bakshi's performance and the generally successful advance of 71 Mountain Brigade, much of 33 Corps' offensive power was allowed to lie idle far too long and Pakistani troops still held the major towns of the Sector—Rangpur, Saidpur, Dinajpur, Nator, Rajshahi—when the ceasefire was announced. Likewise, the ceasefire intervened before the Indians could implement a hastily conceived plan to transfer 340 Infantry Brigade, a tank Squadron and an artillery battery across the Jamuna via the Phulchari ferry to take part in the advance on Dacca. With the exception of this Squadron, all armour was preparing to transfer to the West by the end of the war.

Northern and Eastern Sectors

The crucial Indian offensive actions were those undertaken in the Northern and Eastern Sectors. As elsewhere, the innumerable water obstacles and poor infrastructure here presented daunting challenges to manoeuvre and logistics, but the 101 Communications Zone in the North and 4 Corps in the East overcame these hurdles to cut through the defenders and isolate Dacca, leaving Niazi little choice but surrender. The combat in these two Sectors generally falls into two phases. In the first phase, from 03 December to 09 December 1971, Indian and Bangladeshi troops broke through the crust of the Pakistani defences in a series of border battles and established themselves on the banks of the major rivers in each area.

The second phase, from 10 December to 16 December 1971, was a race to Dacca against increasingly fragmented and dispirited resistance, with the lead Indian elements finally coming to a halt within miles of the city just before the ceasefire. In the North, India's 101 Communications Zone, an administrative HQ forced into service as a combat command, spent three weeks—from 14 November to 04 December—battering itself against the stubborn resistance of a small Pakistani border post at Kamalpur. When the outnumbered band of Pakistani defenders (from 31 Baloch) finally ran out of food and ammunition, the road to the South was open and 95 Brigade pushed on to Jamalpur. The reduction of this well-defended town consumed several more days, but by the 11 December 1971, it was in Indian hands; and 31 Baloch, half of the regular Pakistani force in this

Sector, was no longer an effective fighting force. The same day, Indian troops of 'FJ Sector' entered Mymensingh unopposed. The stage was set for the drive on Dacca.

In the East, Indian 4 Corps, with all eight East Bengal Regiment Battalions, had made small gains in the last weeks of November. An enclave South of Akaura served as a springboard for the 57 Mountain Division, which advanced along the rail line to Ashuganj. In see-saw fighting that featured several successful Pakistani counter-attacks, 27 Infantry Brigade of the Pakistani 14 Infantry Division fell back across the Meghna and destroyed part of the rail bridge, blocking immediate passage of the river. Lt Gen Sagat Singh, however, saw Dacca as 'the final answer' and decided 'to go beyond [his] assigned task'.[22] In an impressive display of improvisation, 4 Corps began crossing the broad Meghna on 09 December 1971, in a hastily assembled helicopter lift operation, supplemented by every variety of local water craft.[23] Pakistan's 14 Infantry Division was no longer a hindrance as its 27 Mountain Brigade had retired to Bhairab Bazar and its other two Brigades (202 and 313) were isolated at Sylhet. Further South, the Indian 23 Mountain Division also reached the Meghna on 09 December, seizing both Daudkandi and Chandpur against light resistance. The isolated Pakistani force at Laksham capitulated the same day, leaving only the garrison of Mayanmati to offer organised resistance East of the Meghna. Pakistan 39 Infantry Division had disintegrated.

A sense of imminent victory drove the Indians and as the 57 Mountain Division painfully built up its strength West of the river, 23 Mountain Division—having shed the 83 Mountain Brigade and 'Kilo Force' to push towards Chittagong—prepared to make its own improvised crossing. In another colourful, tenuous helicopter and boat operation, 301 Mountain Brigade landed at Baidya Bazar on 14 December 1971 and closed on the Lakhya the following day. 'Like the Mughal Army of yore,' recalled the Brigade Commander, 'we marched Northwards helped and surrounded by civilians.'[24] India's 57 Mountain Division was also advancing: 311 Mountain Brigade and 'Sierra Force' were threatening Demra; and 73rd Mountain Brigade had reached the Balu, East of Tungi. Lt Gen Sagat Singh's decision to 'go beyond his assigned task' had paid off. The Indians were also approaching Dacca from the North-West, hindered more by severe logistics constraints than by the near non-existent Pakistani opposition. Indeed, the Pakistan Army's 93rd Infantry Brigade, over the protest of its commander, had been withdrawn towards Dacca in a desperate attempt to shield the unprotected capital against the Indian troops advancing rapidly from the East and the North-East.

The Indian airborne drop of 2 PARA at Tangail on 11 December 1971 accentuated the menace to Dacca. Although 2 PARA's appearance made only a marginal contribution to the tactical battle, it helped to unnerve Niazi and others in Eastern Command HQ, already anxious because of the lack of regular combat troops in the capital. Predations of the local Mukti Bahini under Qadir 'Tiger' Siddiqi compounded

Pakistan's woes, disrupting movements and depleting morale. The Indian paratroopers joined hands with the 95 Mountain Brigade on 12 December 1971 and, with the 167 Mountain Brigade hastening up from Jamalpur, soon reached and crossed the Turag. By 15 December, the Pakistani situation around Dacca was hopeless: the lone brigade of the 36th Infantry Division was broken; the newly arrived 314 Infantry Brigade was little more than a paper organisation; the 14th Infantry Division was sitting demoralised and useless at Bhairab Bazar; and the 39 Infantry Division had ceased to exist. On the morning of 16 December 1971, Maj Gen Mohammed Jamshed Khan drove out of Dacca to arrange the ceasefire.

Sylhet Sector

The Sylhet area, surrounded on three sides by Indian territory, was painfully vulnerable to attack. With only two weak Brigades (202 and 313 Infantry Brigade of 14 Infantry Division) to cover the long, twisting border, the prospects for a successful defence were dim. As in other areas, there were not enough troops for the task at hand: 'motley detachments of East Pakistan Rifles, Mujahids, Razakars, and Civil Armed Forces (from West Pakistan) were thrown in to support totally inadequate regular Pakistan Army units to fight in penny packets over vastly extended distances.'[25] The newly raised 202 Infantry Brigade, for example, had to cover some 61 miles of the frontier with only one regular Battalion (31 PUNJAB), some paramilitary troops and five guns.[26] India's 8th Mountain Division and the three Bangladesh Battalions of 'Z Force' exacerbated the Pakistani defensive problem by leading the Pakistani Generals to believe that the principal advance would come from the North and East between Jaintiapur and Karimganj. As a result, most of 202 Infantry Brigade was deployed along the arc between these two localities and the two regular Battalions of Pakistani 313 Infantry Brigade were in no position to repel 8 Mountain Division's two-brigade attack when the Indians struck from an unexpected direction.

Despite a costly setback at Dhalai (also known as Dhullai), the Indians had secured significant terrain before 03 December 1971, especially in the Karimganj salient and between Shamshernagar and Kalaura. The Indian 59 Mountain Brigade, which had cleared the Karimganj area, shifted South to Dharmanagar and constituted the Northern arm of the 8th Mountain Division attack, while the 81 Mountain Brigade pushed from Shamshernagar towards Maulvi Bazar on the Southern axis. Pakistan's 313 Brigade offered spirited resistance but, badly reduced by the earlier fighting, it could not hold on for long. By 07 December 1971, Indian troops in the South were advancing on Fenchuganj and had reached the defences outside Maulvi Bazar. Operations seemed to be progressing satisfactorily and the Corps commander, having learned that Sylhet was weakly held and fearing that Pakistani troops would slip South to reinforce the defences around Dacca, jumped 4/5 GORKHA RIFLES to Sylhet by helicopter. Expecting that 'Echo Sector' would effect a quick link up with the Gorkhas, he simultaneously withdrew the rest of the 59 Mountain Brigade to Kailashahar to prepare to reinforce 57 Mountain Division. The Gorkha Battalion established a foothold against near non-existent resistance, but Brig M Wadke's 'Echo Sector' was held up just South of Jaintiapur and Lt Gen Sagat Singh had to send the 59th Brigade hurrying back up to Fenchuganj. The Gorkhas, thus, found themselves in trouble.

By 14 December 1971, however, the Brigade had reached the Southern side of Sylhet and established contact with the Gorkhas. The same day, 81 Mountain Brigade troops and 9 GUARDS of 59 Mountain Brigade captured Sylhet railroad station from the South-West. From the North-East, 5/5 GORKHA RIFLES were within two miles of Sylhet by 15 December, along the Jaintiapur road. The town was also under pressure by 1 East Bengal Rifles commanded by Maj Ziaur Rahman, a future President of Bangladesh. Finally, 87 BSF was approaching from the East. While the Indians were advancing, the Pakistanis suffered from command problems. Through a series of confused decisions, 313 Infantry Brigade withdrew towards Sylhet to be encircled, instead of withdrawing towards Ashuganj where it might have helped slow the Indian advance. As a result, both Pakistani brigades remained trapped in this remote town until they surrendered on 16 December 1971.

Chittagong Sector

This remote Sector was remarkable for two reasons: the extensive operations by India's Special Frontier Force (SFF); and for the only amphibious operation of the war. Although Gen Manekshaw initially placed great emphasis on Chittagong as a possible ingress port for Pakistani reinforcements or escape route for a Pakistani evacuation, the only Indian conventional unit dedicated to this area in early planning was 'Kilo Force', a mix of Indian regular and paramilitary troops supported by Mukti Bahini. This force captured Feni and pushed down the coast towards Chittagong, reaching Sitakund by 12 December. Here, it was joined by 83 Mountain Brigade which had been diverted South from 23 Mountain Division after the fall of Laksham. The two brigades had advanced as far as Faujdahat by 15 December 1971 and accepted the surrender of the Chittagong garrison the next day.

The Pakistani 91st and 97th Infantry Brigades played almost no substantial role in the fighting. Operating from four bases in India—Marpara, Demagiri, Bornapansuri and Jarulchari—the SFF conducted successful offensive operations in the central area of the Chittagong Hill Tracts against Pakistani troops and anti-Indian Mizo tribal guerrillas supported by Pakistan. Its most spectacular accomplishments were the destruction of the Dohazari Bridge over the Sangu River and the capture of Rangamati. Thoroughly pleased with this little victory, the SFF commander, Brig SS Uban, transferred his HQ from Demagiri to Rangamati. Though peripheral to the battles taking place further North, Uban and his men displayed determination and resourcefulness in achieving considerable success in a challenging campaign with minimal logistical support. Uban's men attacked the Dohazari Bridge because Manekshaw was apprehensive that Pakistani troops would escape South into Burma along the old 'Arakan Road'.

This concern also motivated Manekshaw to order an amphibious assault South of Cox's Bazar towards the end of the war under a plan named Operation Beaver. With almost no planning or reconnaissance, 1/3 GORKHA RIFLES and some other troops from Bengal Area Command were loaded aboard two Navy landing craft as 'Romeo Force' and dispatched across the Bay of Bengal. Predictably, the attempt to land on 14 December failed. A handful of Gorkhas got ashore, but two men drowned when they disembarked in water that was around 7–9 feet deep. Nonetheless, a platoon eventually landed and sent out a patrol that made its way North to Cox's Bazar and confirmed that there were no Pakistanis in the vicinity. The ceasefire came into effect before the bulk of the men could get ashore, which they did at Cox's Bazar from 16 December to 18 December 1971 using local lighters.

The Western Front

The long Western frontier was far more varied than the border in the East. Both ends of the line were desolate. In the extreme North, the CFL in Kashmir traversed a barren, nearly uninhabited land of snow-covered peaks stretching to 23,000 feet in altitude, before shifting to cold, rugged and heavily forested mountains further South. Altitudes gradually decreased along the Southern reaches of the CFL, but the terrain remained broken and difficult until the final foothills disappeared into the lush plains of the Punjab. The Punjab, densely populated and cultivated on both sides of this border, had a relatively robust transportation infrastructure and offered some opportunities for mechanised forces. However, its cities and villages could serve as ready-made strong points for a defender and its numerous watercourses, large and small, represented significant impediments to rapid movement. The land grew increasingly arid and the infrastructure less sturdy South of the Punjab as the border passed through the great Thar Desert and ended in seasonal salt marshes barely above sea level at the Southern extreme.

Pakistani Forces and Plans

Adhering to its grand strategy of defending the East by offensive action in the West, Pakistan retained the bulk of its forces on this lengthy and often difficult frontier. As compared with three underequipped regular Divisions and two ad hoc 'hoax' Divisions in the East, the Army held 10 Infantry Divisions in the West, along with both Armoured Divisions and three independent Armoured Brigades. Unlike the

East, the tank fleet in the West included relatively modern types, such as American M-48s and Chinese T-59s, along with a number of slightly older but still serviceable American M-47s and some World War II-era models—American M-4 tanks and M-36 tank destroyers, as well as one regiment of Soviet T-34s. A large body of paramilitary and militia units (Razakars) supported the regular Army but, as in the East, many of the militiamen proved unreliable. Cumbersome command and control arrangements within the Army hampered effective utilisation of these large forces. Although there were three Corps HQ to serve as an intermediate level of command between General HQ and the combat manoeuvre Divisions, atleast three Divisions and possibly some separate brigades came under direct control of Army HQ in Rawalpindi.

Poor cooperation among the three services compounded the Pakistan Army's problems. The PAF in the West totalled 12 Squadrons. Of these, half were sturdy but outdated F-86/Sabre VI fighters and the remainder were a mix of Chinese, French and American airframes: F-6s, Mirage IIIs, F-104s and B-57s.[27] The F-104 and B-57 Squadrons, however, stood at about half of their authorised strength. In addition, Pakistan would use some of its American C-130 transports as bombers during the course of the conflict. All of the Pakistan Navy's major combatants were located in the West and were based out of the Karachi area. These included a cruiser, five destroyers and three frigates. Also available were two gunboats, seven minesweepers and an oiler. Most important, however, were the three submarines left in the West after *PNS Ghazi* had sailed for the Bay of Bengal.

Pakistan's plan in the West called for the beginning of offensive operations five or six days after an Indian attack in the East. These, however, were 'preliminary operations', essentially distractions, designed 'to fix the enemy and to divert his attention'[28] away from the intended site of the main attack. They would thus come in the North, with advances on Poonch and Chhamb. A small probe South-East of Shakargarh by 1 Corps was included to provoke a reaction by Indian Armoured Reserves. The aggressive impression created by these drives would be reinforced by moving the 7th Infantry Division, a key reserve formation, from its cantonments near Peshawar Eastwards to assembly areas, from which it could support either of the Northern attacks. In the meantime, the true offensive was to be prepared by 2 Corps. With one Armoured and two Infantry Divisions (including the rapidly shifted 7 Infantry Division), 2 Corps would strike into India from the Bahawalnagar area approximately three days after the secondary attacks (and thus some eight or nine days after the Indian invasion of the East). It was hoped that most of India's Armoured Reserves would have become entangled in Pakistan's defences in the Shakargarh salient during this three-day interval between the diversionary attacks and the main effort.

The PAF was apprised of the Army's plan and may have kept as many as four Squadrons in reserve to support the grand offensive. In central and Southern Punjab,

Pakistan's 4 Corps was to conduct several small operations to seize vulnerable enclaves along the twisting border. In the far South, the Army's Chief of Staff, 'somewhat peremptorily and without due process of staff study',[29] instructed 18 Infantry Division to launch a push towards Ramgarh on the road to Jaisalmer. This would lead to a minor disaster when the war began.

Indian Forces and Plans

Despite its concentration on the Eastern front and its nagging worries about the Chinese border, India's forces in the West still outnumbered Pakistan's in almost every category. In addition to its lone Armoured Division, India had 13 Infantry Divisions, four independent Armoured Brigades, and three unattached Infantry Brigades on its Western border with Pakistan. A host of Territorial Army (reserves) and paramilitary BSF Battalions provided critical support both on the border and in the rear areas. Additional ground units were already being transferred from the East to the West when the war ended. The Indian Armoured Corps was even more variegated than Pakistan's with British (Centurions), French (AMX-13s), Russian (T-54/55s and PT-76s) and domestic (Vijayantas) models, complicating ammunition, repair parts and training requirements. The Indian Army command structure, however, was superior to that of its adversary. Joint service cooperation, though by no means ideal, was better on the Indian side, and the Army's Western and Southern Commands represented a well-understood echelon of command between the Corps HQ and the Chief of the Army Staff in New Delhi.

The IAF enjoyed a considerable numerical advantage in the West with some 24 Combat Squadrons on hand when all-out war began on 03 December 1971. Nearly half of these Squadrons were composed of relatively modern Soviet aircraft (Su-7s and MiG-21s), with the remainder being a mixture of compact Gnats, British Hawker Hunters, indigenous HF-24 Maruts, aging French Mysteres and Canberra bombers. This formidable force was quickly reinforced by units from the East as the war there turned increasingly in India's favour. Beyond these fighters and bombers, India, like Pakistan, used some transports (a Squadron of An-12s) in the bomber role during the war. The Indian Navy presence in the Arabian Sea included a cruiser, a destroyer, eight frigates, two patrol vessels and two submarines. There were also eight Osa-class patrol boats that would play a significant role in the conflict.

India's strategy in the West was primarily defensive but, as with Pakistan, Indian planning incorporated a number of small strikes to seize vulnerable salients along the CFL and the border. Two larger offensives were also planned. One was to drive into the Shakargarh salient to unhinge any Pakistani attempt to thrust North between Jammu and Pathankot; an attack in the Chhamb/Sialkot area would support this effort. The other major advance was to take place in the desert along the rail line towards Naya Chor. A smaller push in the direction of Rahimyar Khan may also have been considered, but India never made 'the long and careful preparations required' to cut Pakistan in half along its narrow line of communications between Karachi and Lahore.[30] In addition, the Army staff developed a contingency plan to launch 1 Armoured Division across the border if Pakistan's reserves were committed to the Shakargarh area.[31] The lack of reliable intelligence concerning the locations of Pakistan's reserve formations, especially the two Armoured Divisions and the 7th Infantry Division, hampered Indian planning prior to the conflict and introduced a measure of caution during the war.

As with the Army, the primary missions of the Air Force and the Navy were defensive in nature. Both services, however, also included major offensive tasks in their portfolios. For the IAF, 'support to the Army and Navy, including gaining and maintaining a favorable air situation over the tactical area'[32] was the top priority after defence of the homeland, but Air Force commanders also planned a counter-air campaign against Pakistani bases and radars. The Navy was responsible for defending the country's long Western and Southern coastline, but was to act offensively as quickly as possible either to lock the Pakistan Navy in Karachi or to draw it out and destroy it. Additionally, the Navy was tasked with interdicting Pakistani commercial shipping.

Turtok Sector

The Turtok area features some of the most difficult terrain in the world; with arid, rocky slopes climbing steeply up to heights of 18,000–23,000 ft, it is almost completely devoid of vegetation. Even the Shyok River valley rests at approximately 9,000 ft. Sub-zero winter temperatures and a near-total absence of motorable tracks exacerbated the effects of the altitude, making military operations extraordinarily challenging. Pakistan defended this desolate Northern end of the Kashmir CFL (loosely from Kel to Turtok) with six Battalions (called 'wings') of paramilitary troops belonging to the Frontier Corps. These units reported to the Director General of the Frontier Corps in Gilgit, who, in turn, reported directly to Army HQ. The Turtok Sector itself was held by two or three Companies of Karakoram and Gilgit Scouts recruited from mountain peoples on the Pakistan side of the CFL.

The Indian troops in the area consisted of three Companies of semi-regular Ladakh Scouts and 500 hastily raised local militia called Nubra Guards. In both cases, the Indian troops were hardy men, locals who were atleast somewhat inured to its extreme conditions. They operated under the command of the 3rd Infantry Division with its HQ at Leh; the Division was also responsible for the boundary with China to the East. The Ladakh Scouts were well-trained and well-led, but the 'Nubra Guards' had only received two weeks of instruction in basic weapons handling when the war began. The Pakistani Scouts, on the other hand, were not as well prepared as their foes in training or equipment.[33]

The Commandant of the Ladakh Scouts was a local officer, Maj Chewang Rinchen MVC, who had won India's second highest combat gallantry award in the first Indo-Pak conflict in Kashmir in 1948, but had become infamous for being 'in constant trouble because he found military discipline irksome'.[34] He was an energetic and resourceful Commander who knew his men and the terrain. Under Rinchen's leadership, the Indian forces attacked on the night of 08 December and quickly captured several Pakistani posts. One of the skirmishes centred on possession of a position at nearly 20,000 ft. Rinchen rapidly exploited his success, frequently using night attacks. By the time the ceasefire was announced, his men had overcome terrain, climate and enemy resistance to reach Thang. Logistical problems precluded further advances, but Rinchen's superiors had every reason to be pleased with his performance under appalling conditions. Indian losses illustrate the physical challenges of the region: although only three men were wounded by enemy action, Rinchen's force suffered 45 cases of frostbite during this two-week period. He was awarded his second Maha Vir Chakra for these operations.

Kargil Sector

As with the Turtok Sector, the high-altitude 'moonscape' around Kargil presented both sides with enormous challenges. In this Sector, India had a specific and important military objective: to clear Pakistani troops from the heights that dominated the Dras–Kargil–Leh road. This road, which was open only from May to September, served as the main supply line for the civilian population as well as the military garrison in remote Ladakh. (It continues to perform this function today, hence the Indian sensitivity to the Pakistani incursion in 1999.) Pushing across the 'windswept and inhospitable heights' against several Companies of Karakoram Scouts, five Battalions of Brig ML Whig's 121 (Independent) Infantry Brigade Group successfully secured about 110 sq km North of Kargil between 7 and 17 December.[35] However, the brigade failed to reach its principal objective, the tiny village of Olthingthang near the confluence of the Shingo and Indus Rivers. Contending with fierce weather as well as the enemy, the Indians losses were as follows: 55 killed; 195 wounded; and 'an inordinately high toll' of 517 cases of frostbite, more than 300 of these were from a single Battalion. India claimed Pakistani casualties of 114 killed and 32 prisoners of war. Brig ML Whig was awarded the Maha Vir Chakra.

Tangdhar and Uri Sectors

The forbidding peaks of the Zanskar Range block precipitation and make Ladakh a high desert, but to the South and West of these crags Kashmir is green and lush from heavy annual rainfall. Though not so high as Ladakh, the thickly wooded slopes of Kashmir are rugged and pose a significant obstacle to military movement.

Furthermore, in 1971, neither side planned major offensive operations in the Tangdhar and Uri Sectors. Pakistan's 12th Division, with six Infantry brigades, was responsible for almost the entire North–South face of Kashmir, a distance of some 186 miles. Although twice as large as a normal Division, the men were spread thinly on the ground to cover this enormous zone. The Division Commander, Maj Gen Akbar Khan, had to economise even more to scrape together enough men for a strike towards Poonch further South.[36] India's 19 Infantry Division was not as desperately short on manpower, but uncertainty regarding the location of Pakistan's 7th Infantry Division made Indian Commanders chary of committing their own reserves. As a result, this area only witnessed a few small Indian advances as the 19 Infantry Division attempted to secure several tactically advantageous features.

Despite snow, rough terrain and Pakistani defences, the Indian 104 Infantry Brigade made tactical gains on the Southern front of the Tangdhar salient, especially in the area of the Tutmari Galli where 9 SIKH performed well. This Indian pressure forced Maj Gen Akbar Khan to transfer a Battalion from the Poonch area to the Tangdhar/Lipa Sector on 09 December, thus reducing the capacity of 12 Infantry Division to conduct offensive operations. A second Battalion was detached from 12 Infantry Division's reserve on 16 December to reinforce the defenders. A tiny enclave in the Tutmari Galli area was still in Pakistani hands when the ceasefire was announced. This situation occasioned renewed skirmishing in May 1972, when Indian troops launched an abortive attempt to capture it before the final peace agreement was signed. The Indian 161Infantry Brigade's efforts to seize two small areas on the Southern flank of the Uri salient failed to achieve their objectives. Pakistani defenders repulsed 8 SIKH and 7 SIKH LI on the night of 04/05 December 1971 and action settled to desultory skirmishing for the remainder of the war.Minor skirmishes continued in this Sector for several days even after the ceasefire.[37] North-East of Tangdhar, Indian paramilitary BSF troops gained some terrain (Northern Gallies Sector), pushing Pakistani paramilitary outposts back towards the Kishanganga (or Neelam) River.

Poonch Sector

The region in and around the town of Poonch is also rugged and heavily forested. Pakistan included a thrust against Poonch in its overall offensive plan, in part to distract Indian attention from the main attack to be launched by 2 Corps, and in part to exploit the apparent vulnerability of the Poonch salient. India, however, noticed a Pakistani build-up opposite the salient during November and moved the 33 Infantry Brigade of 39 Infantry Division into the Sector to support 25 Infantry Division's 93 Infantry Brigade. Strong Indian reserves were thus already on hand and prepared when the war broke out. On 03 December 1971, Pakistan's 12 Infantry Division took advantage of the terrain and vegetation to infiltrate two Battalions (9 and 16

Azad Kashmir) as part of a two-Brigade attack across the Northern face of the Poonch salient.

Although the two Battalions succeeded in threading their way past the Indian outpost line, the Indian defences along the CFL held firm and reinforcements from 33 Mountain Brigade soon counter-attacked, forcing the infiltrators to withdraw. A cohesive defence, well-directed at the brigade level and enjoying excellent artillery support, succeeded in repelling the attackers, despite the danger posed to resupply and morale by the two infiltrating Pakistani Battalions. By 07 December, the Pakistani troops had returned to their side of the CFL. Heavy casualties among the attacking Pakistani troops, failure to capture a significant portion of the outer Indian defences and the Indian advances further North in the Lipa area were the major factors in convincing the 12 Infantry Division Commander to call off the Poonch offensive.[38] India struck back on the night of 10/11 December 1971, taking a promontory above the Poonch River opposite Kahuta in a well-conducted assault by 21 PUNJAB and 9 RAJ RIF. Further South at Daruchian, however, a similar night attack by 14 GRENADIERS was thrown back, with heavy losses, on 13/14 December (158 Indian casualties).

Chhamb and Jammu Sectors

Pakistan made its most significant advances in the Chhamb Sector, revisiting a battlefield from the 1965 war to threaten one of India's key overland links to Kashmir and to deprive India of a launching pad for potential offensive operations. Pressing forward on the night of 03/40 December 1971, the Pakistani 23 Infantry Division, reinforced with the artillery assets of 17 Infantry Division and three additional manoeuvre brigades, pushed back the forward Brigade (the 191 Infantry Brigade under Brig RK Jasbir Singh) of India's 10 Infantry Division.[39]

The Indian forces, initially postured to assume the offensive, had been hastily realigned for a defensive mission after the Indian Army's senior leaders suddenly changed their plans at a meeting on the evening of 01 December 1971. The Division was thus ill prepared when the Pakistanis attacked. After three days of heavy fighting which saw, among other things, the capture of two batteries of 216 Medium Regiment by infiltrating Pakistani Infantry, the 191 Infantry Brigade withdrew behind the river on 06 December.[40] The tenacious defence by 5 SIKH was key in delaying the Pakistani advance. The Indian 68 Infantry Brigade hastily took up the defence of the Munnawar Tawi line as the broken 191 Infantry Brigade pulled back to the West. Fortunately for the Indians, 23 Division's mission was only to secure the line of the river, so the Pakistanis did not seize the opportunity to pursue during this moment of Indian vulnerability.[41] On the Division Commander's initiative, however, Pakistan's 23 Infantry

Division soon returned to the attack and, by the morning of 10 December, had established a shallow bridgehead across the Manawar Tawi. This proved to be the limit of the 23 Infantry Division's advance. The accidental death of the energetic Division Commander in a helicopter crash on 09 December robbed the attack of its impetus and the lodgement on the Indian side of the river was evacuated during the following day (11 December). The Sector remained quiet for the remainder of the war and Pakistan retained the area West of the Munnawar Tawi in the peace settlement.[42]

South-East of Chhamb, Indian 26 Infantry Division scored a success by capturing a narrow salient known as 'the Chicken's Neck' (or Phuklian salient to the Pakistanis) in a quick two-day operation against light resistance (06–07 December 1971). The Division also evicted small Pakistani groups that had occupied two Indian border posts. To the frustration of its aggressive Commander, Maj Gen ZC (Zoru) Bakshi, the 26 Infantry Division was restricted to these minor offensive actions and a pre-war plan to push for Sialkot was cancelled: 'After the Pakistani thrust at Chhamb, Headquarters was in a flap and they took away one of my Brigades and told me not to attack.'[43] Bakshi's missing Brigade (the 168 Infantry Brigade) ended up with a defensive mission under an ad hoc HQ called 'X-ray Sector', with 323 Infantry Brigade of 39 Infantry Division. 'X-ray Sector', thus, became the right flank unit of 1 Corps, protecting the area from the Degh Nadi to the left flank of the 26 Infantry Division.

Shakargarh Salient

India planned its major Western front offensive action for the Shakargarh Bulge area. With three Infantry Divisions and two Armoured Brigades, Indian 1 Corps was to push into the salient from the North and East to shield vulnerable parts of India, tie down Pakistani mechanised forces and seize as much territory as possible with an eye towards peace negotiations. Pakistan's 1 Corps, charged with the defence of the Shakargarh Bulge, had the 15 Infantry Division on the left around Sialkot, the 8th Infantry Division on the right East of the Degh Nadi and the 8th Armoured Brigade in support of both forward Divisions. Also belonging to 1 Corps but held in the rear was Pakistan's so-called 'Army Reserve North', consisting of the 6 Armoured Division and the 17 Infantry Division.

Opening on 05 December 1971, the Indian attack fell on Pakistan's 8th Infantry Division but quickly ran into trouble. In the view of many Indian commentators, poor coordination and excessive caution retarded progress, so that the most successful Indian formation (the 54 Infantry Division) only managed a small advance of approximately 8 miles in two weeks of operations.[44] Moreover, the Indians spent most of these two weeks negotiating minefields and nudging back the 8 Infantry Division's covering troops (a capably commanded ad hoc grouping called 'Changez Force') and only ran up against the main defences as the war was ending.[45] On the other hand, repeated counter-attacks conducted by Pakistan's 8 (Independent) Armoured Brigade near Jarpal and Barapind, North-East of Zafarwal, from 15 December to 17 December, were repulsed with heavy losses by Indian 54 Infantry Division (notably POONA HORSE and HODSONS HORSE of 16 (Independent) Armoured Brigade).

In a fruitless assault in the dawn hours of 17 December 1971, the last day of the war, 35 Frontier Force alone lost 57 men, with 73 wounded. Pakistani tank losses during the two-day struggle were also high: 40–50 tanks from the two attacking regiments (13 Lancers and 31 Cavalry) of 8 Armoured Brigade.[46] The failure and cost of these assaults led one Pakistani General to comment that 'the few counterattacks which 8 Infantry Division tried during the war were most noticeable by their lack of planning.' In the end, India occupied a substantial piece of Pakistani territory, but failed to penetrate its main defences or engage its mechanised reserves.[47] These Pakistani reserves, however, remained well back from the front line and played only a marginal role in the conflict: while the 6th Armoured Division waited for orders near Pasrur, 17 Infantry Division found itself reduced to little more than a lone manoeuvre brigade as major detachments were sent off to the 23 Infantry Division on the left and 4 Corps on the right.

Northern Punjab Sector

Unlike 1965 and despite a heavy concentration of forces on both sides, this part of Punjab did not see major action by either Army. On the Pakistani side, 4 Corps was to stay on the defensive, attempting to cover an immense Sector with inadequate resources until ordered to support the main offensive. When Army HQ decided to launch this main offensive, 4 Corps was to attack towards Ajnala in the North as a feint, while seizing Hussainiwala, cutting the road between Ferozepur and Jalalabad, capturing Sulaimanke and establishing a lodgement on the Indian side of the border, South of Bahawalnagar, for 2 Corps to exploit. Given the paucity of forces assigned to 4 Corps, the feasibility of these manifold operations must be questioned. In the event, little happened in this Sector.

In Northern Punjab between Amritsar and Lahore, India's reinforced 15 Infantry Division of 11 Corps captured Pakistani enclaves along the Ravi River at Dera Baba Nanak (usually called Jassar in Pakistani accounts) and Burj. Pakistan occupied an Indian enclave at Kassowal (also known as the Dharam enclave), South-West of Dera Baba Nanak, and made shallow inroads at several points opposite Lahore, most notably near Khalra in the Indian 7th Infantry Division zone. A number of minor border posts were also exchanged along the Ravi, but neither side engaged in anything beyond these local offensive operations.[48] On 10 December, Pakistani 4 Corps deposited a quantity of unserviceable bridging equipment in the 88 Brigade Sector as a ruse to support the impression that a major attack would indeed be launched across the Ravi near Maqboolpur.[49] There is no indication, however, that the Indians either noticed or gave much heed to this deception.

Central Punjab Sector

Concerned about the possibility of a Pakistani thrust emanating from Bahawalnagar, India initially kept a significant reserve in this area: the 14 Infantry Division and 1 Armoured Division. After the first few days of the war, however, 14 Infantry Division found itself committed to the border in several locations and was thus no longer available as a true reserve. India's lone Armoured Division, on the other hand, remained in this area throughout the conflict, but took no active part in the fighting. As in Northern Punjab, this area was the scene of several dramatic struggles for small Enclaves along a major river, the Sutlej. The 48 Infantry Brigade of India's 7 Infantry Division cleared a protrusion known as the Sehjra Bulge on 05/06 December and 35 Infantry Brigade of 14 Infantry Division occupied a fairly large enclave near Mamdot just prior to the ceasefire. Pakistan's 106 Infantry Brigade, however, succeeded in overwhelming stout resistance by Indian 15 PUNJAB to take a significant piece of ground near Hussainiwala, thereby controlling a key dam and threatening the important border town of Ferozepur. Further South, the Indian 116 Infantry Brigade (also 14 Infantry Division) captured thirteen Pakistani border posts in its zone along the Sutlej.

Fazilka Sector

As at Hussainiwala, Pakistan achieved surprise against the Indian defenders West of Fazilka across the border from the Sulaimanke Headworks where Pakistan occupied Beriwala Bridge, but repeated and costly counter-attacks by a Squadron of 18 Cavalry and 4 JAT prevented any expansion. Fortunately for India, indecision on the part of Pakistan's high command kept its potentially powerful 2 Corps from executing a planned offensive against India's 'Foxtrot Sector' (or simply 'F Sector'). This area was intended to be the zone of attack for Pakistan's 2 Corps in the grand offensive to relieve pressure on East Pakistan and exploit presumed Indian weakness in the West.[50]

The Pakistani plan, called 'Changez Khan', was approved in September 1971. It called for 105th Infantry Brigade and 25th Infantry Brigade to come under 2 Corps as it drove East from the vicinity of Bahawalnagar to cross the international border before turning to the North-East to push for Bhatinda and Ludhiana. Once 2 Corps had secured its objectives, 4 Corps was to advance East from its positions along the Ravi. In addition to reserving several Squadrons to support the planned attack, the PAF had also positioned mobile radar and pre-stocked forward airfields in the proposed battle area.[51] Army HQ issued the order for 2 Corps to shift to its forward assembly areas on 14 December and major elements of the 1st Armoured Division began to move the following day, while the 7th Infantry Division was also concentrating South of the Sutlej, its officers hoping for 'an end to the agony of suspense'.[52]

By this time, however, the other major component of 2 Corps, namely, 33 Infantry Division, had already been detached from the reserve. Army HQ had responded to Indian advances elsewhere by breaking up 33 Infantry Division to reinforce 1 Corps in the North and 18 Infantry Division in the South. As a consequence, the 2 Corps offensive was deprived of approximately one-third of its striking power before it had even begun. At 1845 Hours on 16 December 1971, new instructions arrived from Army HQ 'freezing all movements' until further notice. Nine trains carrying the 1st Armoured Division were laboriously unloaded, the equipment was dispersed, and 2 Corps, with its constituent pieces on both sides of the Sutlej, settled in to await orders. Had the operation proceeded according to schedule, the Corps probably could have opened its attack in the early morning hours of 17 December 1971, but the 'freeze' order meant that it was still on the Pakistan side of the border when the ceasefire went into effect at 2000 Hours on 17 December.[53]

Although it is doubtful that 2 Corps could have achieved its optimistic operational goals, nothing in Pakistan's conduct of the war in the West has generated more controversy among subsequent commentators than the failure to launch the 2 Corps counter-offensive. The details of the delay in beginning the attack and the issuance of the 'freeze' order are unclear, but most writers point to confusion and vacillation prevalent within the high command.[54] One source contends that the lack of adequate PAF support was a major contributing factor; he avers that the Commander in Chief of the Air Force retracted previous promises of assistance a few days before the operation was to begin.[55] There was no significant action South of Fazilka, although Indian 4 PARA supported by B Squadron 18 Cavalry of the 51 (Independent)Para Brigade conducted a costly assault to evict an intruding Pakistani platoon from a nameless sand dune near the village of Nagi several days after the ceasefire (26/27 December 1971). This action cost 4 PARA, 21 killed and 60 wounded.

Jaisalmer Sector

The great desert that sweeps across the Southern portion of India–Pakistan border presents a formidable obstacle to operations by major military formations. In addition to climatic extremes and lack of water, road and rail connections are scarce and vehicular movement is generally restricted to the area's few tracks. Nonetheless, both sides committed significant forces to this barren region and planned advances across the border. Pakistani Army HQ had allotted this enormous zone to a single Division, supported by some paramilitary and irregular troops. This formation—18 Infantry

Division, had two Brigades opposite Jaisalmer and one in the Southern portion of its Sector near Naya Chor. On the Indian side of the border, Lt Gen Gopal Gurunath Bewoor's Southern Command, with two regular Infantry Divisions and two Sector HQ, was responsible for the area.

In the Jaisalmer Sector, both sides planned to take the offensive. Although Pakistan's 18 Infantry Division had neither the training, the equipment, nor the logistical support necessary to sustain a major advance, it was expected to capture Ramgarh and press on to neutralise the airfield at Jaisalmer. Unfortunately for 18 Division, no proper coordination was arranged with the PAF.[56] The Pakistani 51and 206 Infantry Brigades, reinforced by two tank Regiments (22 and 38 Cavalry), duly headed for the Western face of the Jaisalmer Bulge on 03 December 1971. The Indian 12 Infantry Division, methodically preparing its own offensive, was caught by surprise when the Pakistanis appeared around Longewala. Pakistani indecision and staunch resistance by the Indian Army's 23 PUNJAB, however, stalled the attack and provided an opportunity for the IAF to come to the assistance of 23 PUNJAB. With no opposition in the air to trouble them, marauding IAF Hunters from Jaisalmer wreaked havoc on the vulnerable Pakistani tank columns strung out in the open desert. By 07 December 1971, the attacking Pakistani brigades were in full retreat having suffered heavy losses, including at least 20 tanks and more than 100 other vehicles destroyed or abandoned.[57]

India's 12 Infantry Division did not pursue very far ('mercifully', wrote Pakistani Maj Gen Fazal Muqeem Khan) and, other than the capture of Islamgarh on 04 December, 12 Infantry Division spent the remainder of the war screening its Sector.[58] Pakistan's leadership, alarmed by the serious reverse at Longewala, sent a Brigade of 33 Infantry Division to reinforce 18 Infantry Division in this Sector, while the Division HQ, artillery and 60 Infantry Brigade hurried South to take control of the Naya Chor Sector.[59] North of Jaisalmer was India's Bikaner Sector, also known as 'K or 'Kilo Sector'. In this desolate landscape, 13 GRENADIERS, a camel Battalion, supported by two BSF Battalions, occupied a number of Pakistani border posts.

Barmer Sector

With only one Brigade of regulars in this area—55 Infantry Brigade of 18 Infantry Division—Pakistani offensive operations were out of the question. India's 11 Infantry Division, however, struck across the desert on the evening of 04 December 1971 in an effort to reach the 'green belt' along the Indus near Hyderabad. While a camel-mounted Battalion—17 Grenadiers—shielded the Division's Northern flank, two Brigades—the 85 and 330 Infantry Brigades pushed for Naya Chor astride the rail line and 31 Infantry Brigade advanced on Chachra. Facing little resistance at first, the Indians quickly achieved major territorial gains and constructed a link between the Indian and

Pakistani railroads (Munabao to Khokhrapar) to support further operations. Despite the rail connection, logistical problems and prolonged hesitation brought the Division's progress to a halt before it reached Naya Chor on its Northern axis of advance. This was also the Sector in which 10 PARA under Lt Col K Bhawani Singh advanced seventy kilometres deepe into enemy territory.

Persistent air attacks by the PAF increased the difficulty of supplying 11 Infantry Division's forward elements.[60] By the time the advance resumed, the Pakistani troops had been reinforced by the 60 Infantry Brigade from the 33 Infantry Division. Moreover, 33 Infantry Division had taken responsibility for the Sector, assuming command of 55 Infantry Brigade in the process. Thus bolstered, the Pakistanis easily repelled 11 Infantry Division's renewed attempts to push forward.[61] On the Southern axis, Chachra fell to 31 Infantry Brigade after a brief fight, but a Battalion probing towards Umarkot—18 MADRAS—found itself unsupported and was forced back by a Pakistani counter-attack. The ceasefire precluded further Indian advances, but 11 Infantry Division had seized almost 3,000 sq miles of Pakistani territory, more than any other formation on the Western front. Moreover, anxiety following 18 Infantry Division's failure at Longewala and the Indian drive on Naya Chor caused Pakistan's high command to deplete 2 Corps by sending 33 Infantry Division South with two of its Brigades. As mentioned earlier, this move, combined with the detachment of 33 Infantry Division's other Brigade to 1 Corps, effectively diminished 2 Corps' offensive power by one-third, thus reducing the threat it could pose to India in the Ferozepur–Fazilka area. On the other hand, Lt Gen Bewoor was in the process of shifting the 322 Infantry Brigade of 12 Infantry Division to reinforce 11 Infantry Division almost at the same time as the Pakistani moves were taking place.

Kutch Sector

The Rann of Kutch, an inhospitable salt waste, separates India and Pakistan at the Southern extremes of their border. Although no regular troops were available on the Indian side at the start of hostilities in this Sector, two BSF Battalions succeeded in making considerable advances against light opposition from Pakistani Rangers. Thanks to their efforts, by 17 December 1971, India controlled two large islands of elevated desert above the salt flats—Chhad Bet and the area South of Virawah.[62] The Indian 10 PARA Commando Battalion conducted successful raids as far as Islamkot in this Sector. In all, Southern Command ended the war in occupation of a significant chunk of Pakistani territory, albeit unproductive desert, and had distracted key elements of

Pakistan's strategic reserve. It had not, however, reached Pakistan's 'green belt' along the Indus, as had been hoped by some Indian planners at the war's beginning.

Notes

1. This section has been adapted from the official history of the 1965 India-Pakistan War. See BC Chakravorty, *History of the Indo-Pak War, 1965*, New Delhi: History Division, Ministry of Defence, 1992 at https://www.bharat-rakshak.com/Army/history/1965war/275-war-history-1965.html.
2. Gen Mohammad Musa HJ, *My Version: India Pakistan War 1965*, Peace Publications, 2018.
3. Chakravorty, *History of the Indo-Pak War, 1965*, n. 1, Chapter 2, p. 17.
4. Ibid.
5. Lt Gen Harbakhsh Singh, VrC, *In the Line of Duty*, New Delhi: Lancer Publishers and Distributors, 2000, pp. 239–41.
6. For a detailed description see Maj Gen PJS Sandhu, '1965 Indo-Pak War – A Critical Appraisal', *Journal of the United Service Institution of India*, Vol. CXLV, No. 601, July-September 2015.
7. Ibid.
8. Richard Sisson and Leo E Rose, *War and Secession: Pakistan, India, and the Creation of Bangladesh*, Berkeley: University of California Press, 1990, pp. 149–50. Subrahmanyam was quoted in Sisson and Rose, pp. 149–50. His opinions appeared in several Indian newspapers starting on 31 March and 5 April; some remarks were then reported in the *Times* (London) in July. Sisson and Rose offer a thorough discussion of the facts surrounding Subrahmanyam's statements, citing the incident as another example of 'The tendency in both India and Pakistan to look for "worst case" interpretations of each other's behavior.' Also see SN Prasad, *The India-Pakistan War of 1971: A History*, Delhi: Natraj Publishers, 2019, p. 110, and Maj Gen Sukhwant Singh, *The Liberation of Bangladesh*, New Delhi: Vikas, 1981, pp. 93–99. To support the contention that India sought to break up Pakistan, Pakistani commentators often cite the so-called 'Agartala conspiracy', a case of alleged sedition involving Sheikh Mujib and named for the Indian city of Agartala where he is said to have met with Indian agents during 1966.
9. *HRC Report Supplement*, Part III, Chapter VIII; Lt Gen M Attiqur Rahman, *Back to the Pavilion*, Karachi: Cowasjee, 1990, p. 241; Maj Mumtaz Hussain Shah, 'The Battle of Sylhet Fortress', *Defence Journal*, January 1999; Brig Saadullah Khan, *East Pakistan to Bangladesh*, Lahore: Lahore Law Times Publications, 1975, pp. 142, 182.
10. *HRC Report*, Part IV, Chapters IV, V, and XI; Pakistan Navy Historical Section, *Story of the Pakistan Navy* (Islamabad, 1991, p. 320; Mansoor Shah, *The Gold Bird: Pakistan and Its Air Force—Observations of a Pilot*, Karachi: Oxford University Press, 2002, p. 242.

11. Maj Gen Rao Farman Ali Khan, *How Pakistan Got Divided*, Lahore: Jang, 1992, pp. 119–20. Brig AR Siddiqi remarked that 'back in Rawalpindi none appeared to be in command', adding that there was an atmosphere of 'forced optimism' at headquarters. See AR Siddiqi, '1971 Curtain-Raiser', *Pakistan Army Journal*, December 1977.
12. Maj Gen Lachhman Singh Lehl, *Victory in Bangladesh*, Dehra Dun: Natraj, 1991, pp. 55, 64–65, 289, 298. Similar comments are in Air Marshal CV Gole, 'Air Operations in the Western Sector During 1971 Indo-Pak War', *The Journal of the United Services Institution of India*, July-September 1990; also Lt Gen EA Vas, *Fools and Infantrymen: One View of History, 1923–1993*, Meerut: Kartikeya, 1995, p. 224. For an incisively critical view, see Lt Gen VR Raghavan's commentary in *The Telegraph*, dated 28 November 2000. More favourable analyses are in Gen KV Krishna Rao, *Prepare or Perish*, New Delhi: Lancer, 1991, p. 249; Admiral JG Nadkarni, 'When the Gods Smiled on India', *Rediff.com*, 4 December 2002; Maj Gen Rajendra Nath, *Military Leadership in India*, New Delhi: Lancer, 1990, p. 475; Maj Gen Joginder Singh, *Behind the Scene*, New Delhi: Lancer: 1993, p. 247.
13. Maj Gen Shaukat Riza, *The Pakistan Army 1966-71*, Dehra Dun: Natraj, 1977, p. 110. Gen Riza commanded the 9 Infantry Division in East Pakistan in early 1971.
14. Khan, *East Pakistan to Bangladesh*, n. 9, p. 110. Siddiqi, '1971 Curtain-Raiser', and 'The War of Self-Attrition'. See also the eminently readable and insightful account by the then-commander of 26 Frontier Force in the NorthWestern Sector, Maj Gen Hakeem Arshad Qureshi, *The 1971 Indo-Pak War: A Soldier's Narrative*, Karachi: Oxford University Press, 2002, pp. 17–21, 76, 101: 'Not a day passed when a firefight or an explosion did not take place.'
15. Lt Gen Kamal Matinuddin, *Tragedy of Errors*, Lahore: Wajidalis, 1994, p. 415.
16. Maj Gen Rahim Khan, Commander of 39 Division in 1971, Interview in *The Herald*, September 2000.
17. John H Gill, *An Atlas of the 1971 India–Pakistan War: The Creation of Bangladesh*, National Defense University, Near East South Asia Center for Strategic Studies, 2003, p. 17.
18. Lt Gen Ali Kuli Khan, interview in *Defence Journal*, December 2001.
19. Lt Gen Kamal Matinuddin, *Tragedy of Errors*, Lahore: Wajidalis, 1994, pp. 342–43, 347–50.
20. Ten of the Squadron's 12 tanks were captured or destroyed. In addition to the basic sources, see, Col Anil Shorey, 'The Unique Battle of Garibpur', *Sainik Samachar*, 16–30 April 2002. Not all of the Indian probes prospered: Pakistani Lt Gen Imtiaz Waraich, for example, narrates a successful defence by his Battalion, 21 Punjab, in 'Remembering Our Warriors'", *Defence Journal*, October 2001.
21. Lt Col Muhammad Mehboob Qadir, 'Echoes from the Event Horizon', *Pakistan Army Journal*, March 1991.
22. Lt Gen Sagat Singh's notes cited in Cdr Suresh D Sinha, *Sailing and Soldiering in Defence of India*, New Delhi: Chanakya, 1990, p. 167.
23. The destruction of the rail bridge actually did little to slow the Indian advance as IV Corps did not have adequate material to lay decking for vehicular traffic. For this and

other details of engineering support to IV Corps as well as vivid scenes from the drive to the Meghna, see Brig Jagdev Singh, *The Dismemberment of Pakistan*, New Delhi: Lancer, 1988, pp. 147–66.

24. Brig HS Sodhi, *'Operation Windfall': Emergence of Bangladesh*, New Delhi: Allied, 1980, p. 280.
25. Col Iqbal M Shafi, letter to the editor, *Defence Journal*, February 1999.
26. Maj Mumtaz Hussain Shah, 'The Battle of Sylhet Fortress', *Defence Journal*, January 1999.
27. To augment its limited aviation assets, the Pakistan Army commandeered aircraft from flying clubs and other civilian associations, gave them a hasty coat of desert camouflage paint, and stenciled them with military markings. See John Fricker, 'The Tree-top Warriors', *Air Enthusiast*, October 1972, published on the web by the Pakistan Military Consortium at www.pakdef.info.
28. Maj Gen Fazal Muqeem Khan, *Pakistan's Crisis in Leadership*, New Delhi: Alpha & Alpha, 1973, p. 114.
29. Ibid., p. 115.
30. SN Prasad (ed.), *History of Indo-Pak War, 1971*, New Delhi: Government of India, 1992, p. 298.
31. Maj Gen Sukhwant Singh, *Defence of the Western Border*, New Delhi: Lancer, 1998, p. 12.
32. Prasad, *History of Ind-Pak War 1971*, p. 298.
33. *HRC Report*, Part IV, Chapter VIII.
34. Singh, *Defence of the Western Border*, n. 31, p. 26.
35. Ibid., p. 28.
36. Owing to the lack of troops, only one regular company (C/2 Frontier Force) was available in the Tangdhar area at the start of the conflict and some portions of the Lipa valley were defended by ad hoc collections of regulars, paramilitary men and local levies. See Maj Gen Fazal Muqeem Khan, *History of the 2nd Battalion (Guides) Frontier Force Regiment*, Rawalpindi: The Army Press, 1996, pp. 123–26.
37. Col RD Palsokar, *History of the SIKH Light Infantry*, Fategarh: The Sikh Light Infantry, 1997, pp. 304–309. The commander of 8 Sikh was relieved of command as a result of this action. Also see Maj Gen Jagjit Singh, *With Honour and Glory*, New Delhi: Lancer, 2001, p. 79. Some Indian authors are quite critical of the entire enterprise; see Singh, *Defence of the Western Border*, n. 30, pp. 41–44; Col MN Gulati, *Pakistan's Downfall in Kashmir*, New Delhi: Manas, 2001, pp. 261–62.
38. Brig Asif Haroon, *Kashmir Battles of 1948-1965-1971 and Ongoing Freedom Struggle*, Lahore: Takhleeqat, 1995, pp. 155–59. Pakistan's 12 Division reportedly held an exercise in September/October to prepare for the assault on Poonch; See Gulati, *Pakistan's Downfall in Kashmir*, n. 37, p. 264.
39. 23 Division's artillery practiced some innovative deception techniques such as deploying guns well forward of doctrinal norms to avoid counterbattery fire and using a few heavy guns from the Artillery School to simulate the presence of Corps artillery support. See interview with the Divisional artillery commander (and 111 Brigade Commander from 5 December), Maj Gen Naseerullah Khan Babar in *Defence Journal*, April 2001.
40. Singh, *With Honour and Glory*, n. 37, p. 75–90.

41. According to the *HRC Report*, Part IV, Chapter VIII, 23 Division had accomplished its mission by gaining the line of the river. The Division commander, however, decided to press across after reforming his troops.
42. Additional sources on the fight for Chhamb include: Brig Safdar Ali, 'Chhamb--A Battle Won Twice', *Pakistan Army Journal*, September 1992; Maj Agha Humayun Amin, 'The Battle of Chhamb 1971', *Defence Journal*, September 1999; Brig Shamin Yasin Manto, 'Remembering Our Warriors]' (interview), *Defence Journal*, February 2002; Lt Col Ahmad Saeed, *The Battle of Chhamb 1971*, Rawalpindi: Army Education Press, 1973; Lt Gen RK Jasbir Singh, 'Battle of Chhamb: Indo-Pak War 1971', *Journal of the United Services Institution of India*, July-September 1990; Maj Gen Prem K Khanna and Pushpindar Singh Chopra, *Portrait of Courage: Century of the 5th Battalion, The Sikh Regiment*, New Delhi: Military Studies Convention, 2001, pp. 193–232. Manto avers that the Division's attempts to cross the Manawar Tawi were undertaken without sufficient preparation: '*The effort to achieve speed actually turned into haste*' (emphasis in original).
43. Quoted in 'Defending the West', from *1971 India-Pakistan War: Remembering a Liberation War*, at www.bharatrakshak.com.
44. Brig Harinder Singh Sodhi, *Top Brass: A Critical Appraisal of the Indian Military Leadership*, Noida: Trishul, 1993. Sodhi calls the advance 'pathetic', averring that it demonstrated 'pedestrian thinking' (pp. 130, 147). Likewise, Jagjit Singh, *With Honour and Glory*, n. 36, pp. 92–93, 104; Maj Gen Kuldip Singh Bajwa, *The Falcon in My Name: A Soldier's Diary*, New Delhi: South Asia Publications, 2000, pp. 200–14; Lal, pp. 237–40; Sukhwant Singh, *Defence of the Western Border*, n. 30, pp. 106–9; Lt Col JR Saigal, *Pakistan Splits: The Birth of Bangladesh*, New Delhi: Manas, 2000, pp. 155–68.
45. Sources for the Changez Force: Lt Col Asif Duraiz Akhtar, 'My Memories of War: The Battle of Tola', *Pakistan Army Journal*, June 1988; Col MY Effendi, 'Smouldering Embers of Ten December Days'," *Pakistan Army Journal*, Winter 1994; Brig Nasir Ahmed Khan, 'Covering Troops Battle', *Pakistan Army Journal*, September 1984. Some Indian participants aver that the Pakistani minefields were much overrated by the Indians and should have been crossed with greater expedition; see Bajwa, pp. 206, 212; Saigal, pp. 65–76.
46. Maj Agha Humayun Amin, 'Battle of Barapind-Jarpal 16 Dec 1971', *Defence Journal*, October 1999; *HRC Report*, Part IV, Chapter VIII; Lt Gen Hanut Singh, *'Fakhr-e-Hind': The Story of the Poona HORSE*, Dehra Dun: Agrim, 1993, pp. 259–90; also Anil Bhat, 'Taken by the Gathering Storm', *Sainik Samachar*, 16–28 February 1997. The other regiment of 8 Armoured Brigade, 27 Cavalry, played only a limited role in the fighting. The engagement is variously known as the 'Battle of Barapind-Jarpal' and the 'Battle of Basantar'.
47. Many Indian writers (notably Sukhwant Singh, HS Sodhi, and KC Praval) are very critical of the performance of Indian I Corps in the Shakargarh fighting. Colonel Ranjit Sengupta, on the other hand, points out that the Corps did succeed in protecting a vulnerable segment of India's border with Pakistan; see 'Battlefield Management and Logistics: Shakargarh 1971', *Indian Defence Review*, April 1994.

48. For two views of one of these engagements, see Lt Col Ghulam Qadir, 'The Maqboolpur Enclave Encounter', *Pakistan Army Journal*, September 1982; and 'Attack on Pak Fatehpur Post (8 Sikh LI),' *Sainik Samachar*, 26 May 1991.
49. *HRC Report*, Part IV, Chapter VIII.
50. Major General Ghulam Umar, then Secretary of the National Security Council, has since disparaged this plan: 'We always chanted that the defense of the East lies in the West. It was a bogus theory.' Quoted in Muntassir Mamoon, *The Vanquished Generals and the Liberation War of Bangladesh*, Somoy Prakashan, 2000, p. 92.
51. Shah, *The Golden Bird*, n. 10, 2002, p. 256.
52. Lt Gen Jahan Dad Khan, *Pakistan Leadership Challenges*, Karachi: Oxford University Press, 1999, p. 121; Arif, p. 124.
53. The bulk of this narrative and the quote from the Army orders are taken from *HRC Report*, Part IV, Chapter VIII. Lt Gen Candeth, Army commander of India's Western Command, opined that a Pakistani attack between Jammu and Gurdaspur during October would have stood a good chance of success as Indian I Corps was not in position there until late in the month. A recent Pakistani commentator suggests that the time to attack was late November after the Indian incursions into East Pakistan that resulted in the engagements around Garibpur and other locales: Lt Col Mukhtar Ahmad Gilani, "Lost Opportunity—A Military Analysis 1971," *Defence Journal*, January 2003.
54. Among others, see Gul Hassan Khan, pp. 329–39; Jahan Dad Khan, p. 121; Pakistan Air Force, pp. 467–74; Gilani, 'Lost Opportunity' (citing interviews with Gul Hassan Khan); Maj Agha Humayun Amin, 'The Anatomy of Indo-Pak Wars: A Strategic and Operational Analysis', *Defence Journal*, August 2001; Maj Agha Humayun Amin, 'The Western Theatre in 1971: A Strategic and Operational Analysis,' *Defence Journal*, February 2002; Brig AR Siddiqi, 'The War of Self-Attrition'; and 'National Defence and Security: A Reappraisal', *The Nation*, 8 January 1990.
55. Maj Gen Aboobaker Osman Mitha, *Fallacies & Realities: An Analysis of Lt Gen Gul Hassan's 'Memoirs'*, Lahore: 99 Maktaba Fikr-o-Danish, 1994, pp. 66–67.
56. There is disagreement over who ordered the attack on Jaisalmer. Gul Hassan Khan and other Pakistani writers state that the operation was a favourite project of the Chief of the Army Staff, General Abdul Hamid Khan, and that the attack was arranged at the last minute despite the strenuous objections of 18 Division's commander, Maj Gen BM Mustafa. Furthermore, they claim that the PAF was not apprised of the scheme. Brig ZA Khan (commander of 38 Cavalry at the time), however, claims that the push to Jaisalmer was planned in October and that the Chief of the Air Staff knew of the plan weeks before the war, atleast in outline form. See his autobiography *The Way It Was*, Karachi: Ahbab, 1998, and an interview 'Remembering Our Warriors: Brig (Retd) Zahir Alam Khan', *Defence Journal*, April 2002. Khan also writes that the plan to take Jaisalmer was abandoned just prior to the attack. Another veteran, however, questions many of the details in ZA Khan's accounts: Lt Col HK Afridi, 'Letter to the Editor', *Defence Journal*, February 1999. Similarly, Mansoor Shah makes a convincing case that general contingency plans to support the Army in Sindh/Rajasthan did exist, but that the Army did not call on the PAF until the disaster at Longewala was in progress (Shah, *The Golden Bird*, n. 10, pp. 257–63).

57. The defeat of the Pakistani attack on Longewala has drawn the attention of numerous Indian writers. In addition to the standard war histories, see Air Marshal MS Bawa, 'Saga of Longewala', *Indian Air Force Journal*, 1997, at www.bharat-rakshak.com/IAF/History; Brig VP Dev, 'The Desert War—1971', *Indian Defence Review*, January 1994; James Hattar, 'Taking on the Enemy at Longewala', *The Tribune*, 16 December 2000; Virendra Verma, *Hunting Hunters: Battle of Longewala December 1971*, Dehra Dun: Youth Education Publications, 1992; Lt Col Jai Singh, *Tanot Longewala and Other Battles of the Rajasthan Desert 1965 & 1971*, Dehra Dun: Palit & Palit, 1973; Wg Cdr Kukke Suresh, 'Battle of Longewala',at www.bharat-rakshak.com/IAF/History.
58. Fazal Muqeem Khan, p. 212. Among other things, 12 Division cited inadequate artillery and armour support; see Jagjit Singh, *With Honour and Glory*, n. 37, pp. 118–19.
59. The inclusion of the Divisional artillery is from V. Longer, *Red Coats to Olive Green*, Bombay: Allied Publishers, 1974, p. 497.
60. Mansoor Shah, pp. 264–65, 284–85; Pakistan Air Force, p. 464; Prasad, pp. 399–400; Singh, *Defence of the Western Border*, n. 31, pp. 215–42.
61. Singh, *Western Border*, pp. 176–245, is very critical of Indian operations in Rajasthan. Also see Maj Agha Humayun Amin, 'Remembering Our Warriors: Brig Muhammad Taj', *Defence Journal*, September 2002.
62. The BSF advances began on 13 December. Some limited information is in 'Kutch during the 1971 Indo-Pak War,' www.kutchinfo.com.

Additional Sources

SN Prasad and UP Thapliyal (ed.), *The India–Pakistan War of 1965: A History.*, New Delhi: Ministry of Defence, 2011.

RD Pradhan, *1965 War—The Inside Story: Defence Minister's Diary of the India–Pakistan War*, New Delhi: Atlantic Publishers and Distributors, 2007.

PK Chakravorty and Gurmeet Kanwal, 'Operation Gibraltar: An Uprising that Never Was', *Journal of Defence Studies*, Vol. 9, No. 3, July–September 2015, pp. 33–52.

Shruti Pandalai, 'Recounting 1965: War, Diplomacy and Great Games in the Subcontinent', *Journal of Defence Studies*, Vol. 9, No. 3, July–September 2015, pp. 7–32.

Rahul K. Bhonsle, 'Indian Army's Continuity and Transformation: Through the Prism of the Battle of Dograi', *Journal of Defence Studies*, Vol. 9, No. 3, July–September 2015, pp. 75–94.

Maj Gen Kuldip Bajwa, *India–Pakistan War 1971: Military Triumph and Political Failure*, New Delhi: Har-Anand Publications, 2012.

Col Anil Shorey, *Pakistan's Failed Gamble: The Battle of Laungewala*, New Delhi: Manas, 2004.

Lt Gen JFR Jacob, *Surrender at Dacca: Birth of a Nation*, New Delhi: Manohar, 2011.

Srinath Raghavan, *1971: A Global History of the Creation of Bangladesh*, New Delhi: Orient Blackswan, 2015.

PVS Jagan Mohan and Samir Chopra, *Eagles Over Bangladesh: The Indian Air Force in the 1971 Liberation War*, New Delhi: Harper Collins, 2013.

Sarmila Bose, *Dead Reckoning: Memories of the 1971 Bangladesh War*, Gurgaon: Hachette India, 2016.

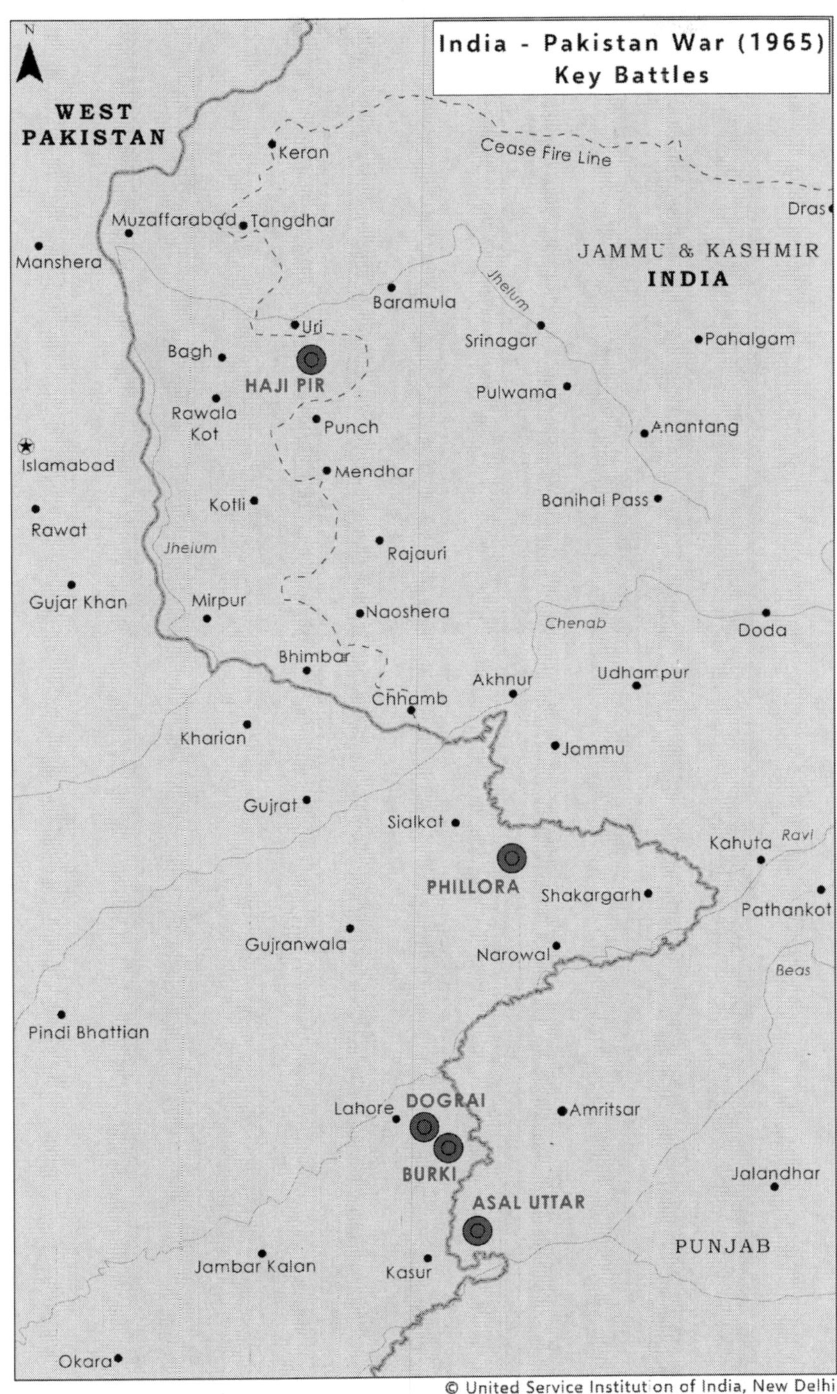

Map 1 1965 India-Pakistan War

Howitzer guns of Uri facing Haji Pir Pass, 1965

Army jawans patrolling in Kashmir Valley, 1965

Centurion tanks in action, Lahore Sector

Captured tank, Forward Area, Lahore Sector, 1965

PM Lal Bahadur Shastri visits Forward Areas, Punjab, 1965

Arrival of POWs from Kashmir, 11 August 1965

National Flag being hoisted at Khem Karan, 1965

Captured Pakistani Patton tank brought to New Delhi station, 1965

Captured Pakistani arms on show at Parliament House

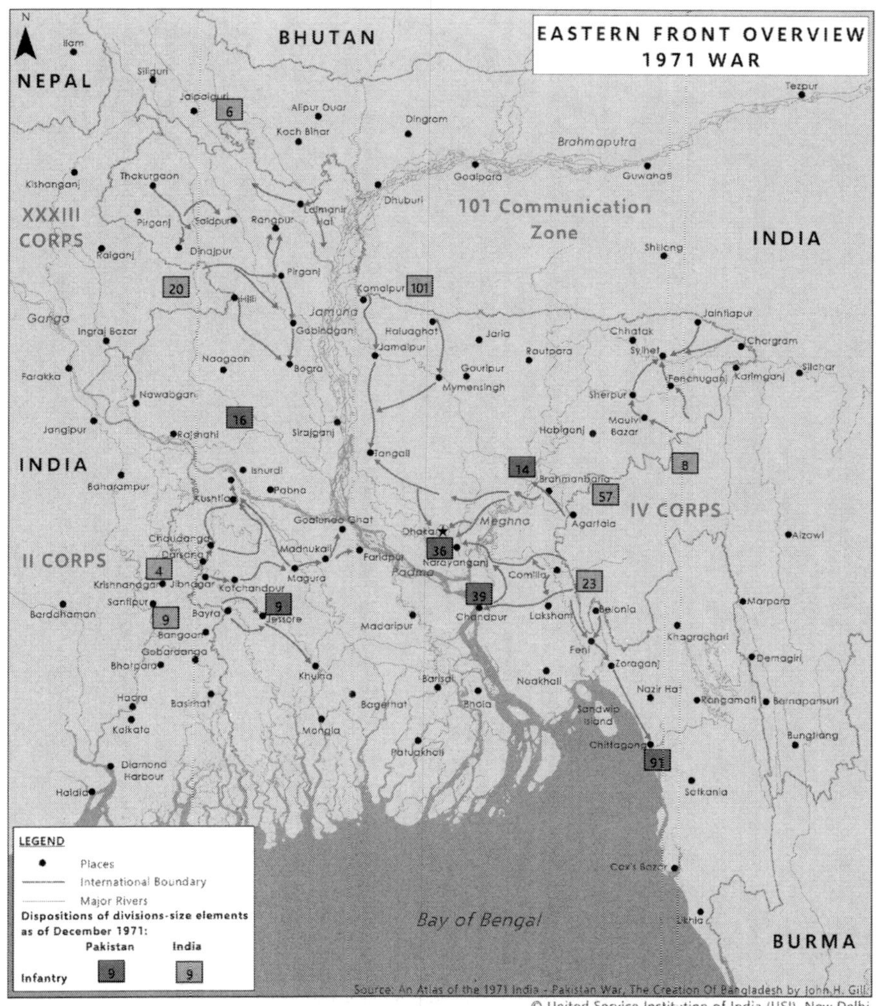

Map 2 1971 Eastern Front

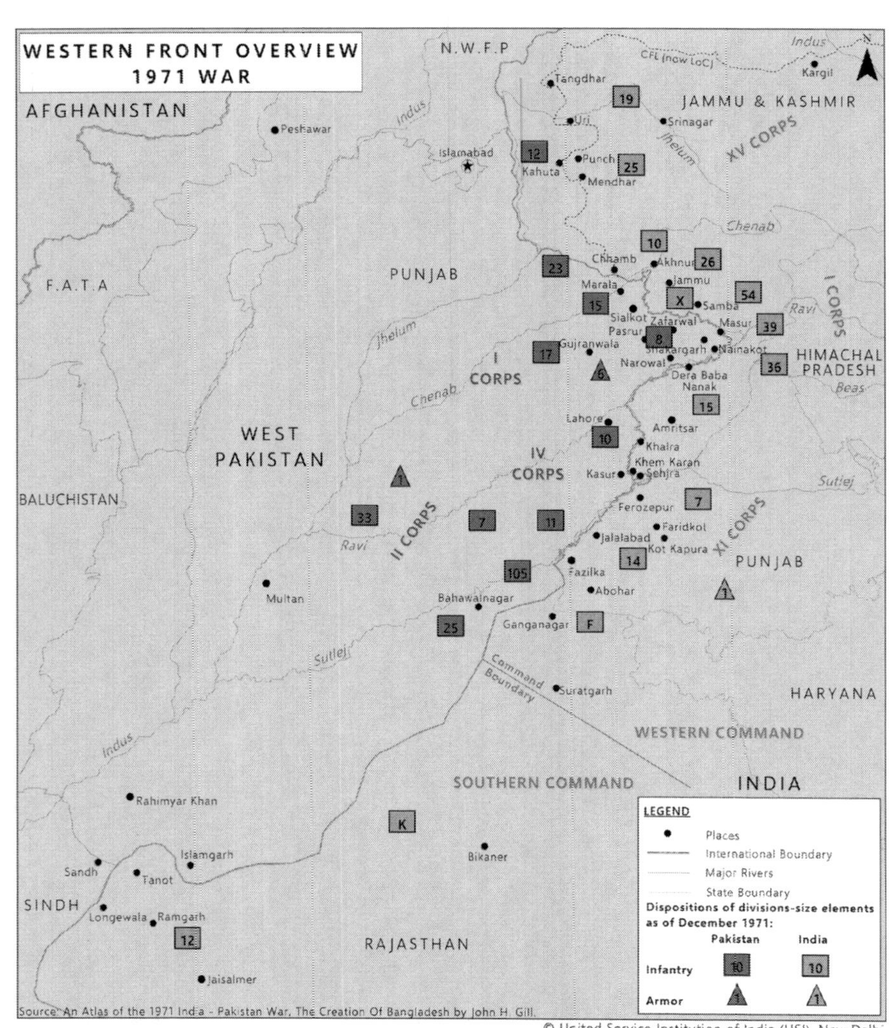

© United Service Institution of India (USI), New Delhi.

Map 3 1971 Western Front

Camel patrol (Grenadiers) in the Thar Desert
Source: MoD, DPR.

Destroyed tank of Pakistan's 22 Cavalry, Longewala, December 1971
Source: MoD, DPR.

Prime Minister Indira Gandhi being briefed on the Western Front, 1971
Source: MoD, DPR.

Gen Manekshaw, COAS, addressing 16 MADRAS

Indian Troops, CEC TIVITER, Shakargarh Area, 1971

Withdrawal of Sikh troops and armaments, Shakargarh

Captured tanks and guns, Chamb sector

Lt Gen Sagat Singh, Maj Gen RD Hira, Lt Gen AAK Niazi, and Maj Gen JFR Jacob proceeding for the surrender ceremony at Dacca, December 1971
Source: MoD, DPR.

Lt Gen AAK Niazi signs the Instrument of Surrender, Dacca, 16 December 1971. Lt Gen JS Aurora sits to his right

Source: MoD, DPR.

The PAKISTAN Eastern Command agree to surrender all PAKISTAN Armed Forces in BANGLA DESH to Lieutenant-General JAGJIT SINGH AURORA, General Officer Commanding in Chief of the Indian and BANGLA DESH forces in the Eastern Theatre. This surrender includes all PAKISTAN land, air and naval forces as also all para-military forces and civil armed forces. These forces will lay down their arms and surrender at the places where they are currently located to the nearest regular troops under the command of Lieutenant-General JAGJIT SINGH AURORA.

The PAKISTAN Eastern Command shall come under the orders of Lieutenant-General JAGJIT SINGH AURORA as soon as this instrument has been signed. Disobedience of orders will be regarded as a breach of the surrender terms and will be dealt with in accordance with the accepted laws and usages of war. The decision of Lieutenant-General JAGJIT SINGH AURORA will be final, should any doubt arise as to the meaning or interpretation of the surrender terms.

Lieutenant-General JAGJIT SINGH AURORA gives a solemn assurance that personnel who surrender shall be treated with dignity and respect that soldiers are entitled to in accordance with the provisions of the GENEVA Convention and guarantees the safety and well-being of all PAKISTAN military and para-military forces who surrender. Protection will be provided to foreign nationals, ethnic minorities and personnel of WEST PAKISTAN origin by the forces under the command of Lieutenant-General JAGJIT SINGH AURORA.

Jagjit Singh

(JAGJIT SINGH AURORA)
Lieutenant-General
General Officer Commanding in Chief
Indian and BANGLA DESH Forces in the
Eastern Theatre

16 December 1971.

AAK Niazi Lt.

(AMIR ABDULLAH KHAN NIAZI)
Lieutenant-General
Martial Law Administrator Zone
Commander Eastern Command (PAK)

16 December 1971.

Instrument of Surrender, 1971
Source: USI, CMHCS.

COAS's first visit to Dacca, 26 December 1971

Jessore, 1 January 1972

Farewell at Dacca

Sheikh Mujibur Rahman takes the salute at Dacca, March 1972. On the extreme left is Lt Gen JS Aurora
Source: MoD, DPR.

5

Indian Army and Operations Other than War, 1948–1999

NEHA KOHLI AND MAJ GEN VK SINGH*(RETD)

The primary task of the Indian Army is the defence of India's borders and in keeping with this, it has fought four major wars with its Northern and Western neighbours, China and Pakistan in 1962 and 1947–48, 1965 and 1971, respectively. These have been discussed in great detail in the previous chapter. However, in the course of the past 75 years, the Army has undertaken the conduct of many operations that can be termed as 'operations other than war'. This chapter looks at some key operations short of war, in which the Indian Army played a stellar role. These operations cover both domestic as well as extra-territorial domains and provide an overview of the Indian Army's role in the post-independence era. These operations are listed chronologically, beginning with Operation Polo in 1948 till the most recent one, Kargil, in 1999.

Operation Polo 1948

Background

When India gained independence from the British in 1947, the various princely states were given the option of joining either of the two new nations of India or Pakistan.

*The segment titled 'Sikkim: Skirmish at Nathu La 1967' has been authored by Maj Gen VK Singh (Retd). Research for the rest of the chapter was conducted by Ms Jharna Sonowal, Researcher and Archivist at CMHCS, USI of India.

Many acceded to India, while others to Pakistan. Hyderabad, which was India's largest princely state ruled by the Nizam, Mir Osman Ali, declined to join either country at the time. The Government of India had a great interest in Hyderabad as the Nizam's sprawling domains were located at the very centre of India.[1] It had a majority Hindu population and the capital city of Hyderabad was a major transportation and communication hub.

Hyderabad's refusal to join either India or Pakistan upon independence led the Government of India to offer a 'Standstill Agreement' to the Nizam, which was signed in November 1947 by Governor General Lord Mountbatten and the Nizam Mir Osman Ali Khan. The agreement assured that the status quo would be maintained without any military action. However, by 1948, while the other princely states had acceded to India, Hyderabad had not done so. Moreover, Hyderabad violated the terms of the agreement. 'The Nizam appointed an agent in Pakistan and also gave a loan of 20 Crore Rupees to Pakistan secretly.[2] The Razakars, which were 'a private militia aligned to the seventh Nizam, Mir Osman Ali Khan, were headed by Qasim Razvi…[and] reportedly committed atrocities on Congress supporters, Communists and other people who wanted an end to Nizam's rule or favoured a merger with India. Between 1946 and 1948, Razvi controlled a force numbering anywhere between 50,000 to 2 lakh men.'[3] The Razakars were apparently against the signing of the Standstill Agreement while envoys from Hyderabad accused India of attempts to economically isolate the state.

In 1948, the decision was taken to move the armed forces into Hyderabad to make it accede to the Indian Union. Home Minister Sardar Vallabh Bhai Patel, who was also the Minister in charge for the accession of the princely states, took the decision to annex Hyderabad. 'Operation Polo' was a military operation, by which Hyderabad was to be annexed into the Indian Union. 'Though termed a "Police Action", the Army played a stellar role in quelling internal strife in the State and restoring law and order.'[4]

The Indian Troops marched into Hyderabad in the early hours of 13 September 1948.[5] 1 Armoured Division, under the command of Maj Gen JN Chaudhuri (later Chief of Army Staff) delivered the main thrust against Hyderabad, with the objective of reaching Hyderabad city as quickly as possible. The plan consisted of two thrusts, one from Vijayawada in the East and the other from Sholapur in the West:

1. Maj Gen AA Rudra led the attack from Vijayawada which comprised the 2/5 GORKHA RIFLESs, one Squadron of the 17th (Poona) HORSE, and Troops from the 19th Field Battery along with engineering and ancillary units. The Vijaywada attack was to accomplish the following tasks: a) Launching the Eastern Striking Force into Hyderabad territory, so that it could advance to Suriapet and, if necessary up to Chityal;

b) Protecting the line of communication behind the Eastern Striking Force; and
c). Safeguarding the Gannavaram airfield and the strategic railway bridges at Vijayawada and Rajahmundry, together with the rail-line from Rajahmundry to Tenali.[6]

2. The attack from Sholapur was led by Maj Gen Chaudhari. For this purpose, 1 Armoured Division was to be composed of 1 Armoured Brigade and 9 Infantry Brigade, along with the usual Divisional complement of Artillery, Engineers, Signals, etc. The Armoured units were 17 HORSE, 3 Cavalry, and one Troop of 18 Cavalry. The Artillery component included 1 Field Regiment of 25 pounder self-propelled guns, 34 Anti-Tank Regiment and 9 Para Field Regiment.[7] The Sholapur attack was composed of four task forces:

a) Strike Force comprising a mix of fast-moving infantry, cavalry and light Artillery;
b) Smash Force consisting of predominantly Armoured units and Artillery;
c) Kilo Force composed of infantry and engineering units; and
d) Vir Force which comprised infantry, anti-tank and engineering units.

The Indian Army was to be given air support by the Indian Air Force (IAF) which undertook the air operations, the plans for which were chalked out as early as June 1948.

Ground Operations

From commencement on 13 September till completion on 17 September 1948, Operation Polo lasted for a total of five days. On 13 September, Indian forces entered the state early in the morning. The very first battle was fought at Naldurg Fort on the Sholapur-Secunderabad Highway. It was located between a defending force of the 1st Hyderabad Infantry and an attacking force of 7 Infantry Brigade, which managed to secure a vital bridge on the Bori River intact. This was followed by an assault by 2 SIKH on the Hyderabadi positions at Naldurg. The Smash Force moved into the town of Jalkot, paving the way for the Strike Force units under Lieutenant Colonel Ram Singh to pass through. By the evening, the forward Troops of Strike Force were at Umarga, 1 Armoured Brigade was at Yenegur, 7 Infantry Brigade was near Jalkot, and 9 Infantry Brigade was at a point 6 km South-East of Tuljapur.[8] At dawn, when they reached Tuljapur, they encountered resistance from a unit of the 1st Hyderabad Infantry and about 200 Razakars who fought for two hours before surrendering.

The forces led by Maj Gen AA Rudra in the East, met with fierce resistance from two Armoured car cavalry units of the Hyderabad State Forces, namely, the 2nd and 4th Hyderabad Lancers. However, the forces managed to reach the town of Kodar and reached Mungala by the afternoon.

On the second day, the Strike Force under Lieutenant Colonel (Lt Col) Ram Singh remained in the lead. The Smash Force moved just behind the Strike Force, ready to take and destroy any major enemy opposition.[9] The forces that were at Umarga proceeded to the town of Rajeshwar and secured it by the afternoon with the help of airstrikes that were called in from the Squadrons of Tempests. Meanwhile, assault forces from the East came under heavy firing by the 1st Lancers and 5th Infantry. At the same time, the 3/11 GORKHA RIFLES and a Squadron of 8th Cavalry attacked Osmanabad and took the town after combat with Razakars. Further, the city of Aurangabad was captured by a force under the command of Maj Gen DS Brar. Six columns of infantry and cavalry attacked the city, resulting in the surrender of the civil administration.

On day three, 3/11 GORKHA RIFLES left a Company to occupy the town of Jalna and the remaining force moved to Latur. The Strike Force surrounded the town of Humnabad and the Smash Force entered it, where a few Razakars resisted the forces. The Smash Force left Humnabad in the hands of 9 Infantry Brigade and began its advance on the subsidiary road to Bidar. Most of the Hyderabadi defences were cleared by airstrikes at the town of Suryapet. The Razakars resisted the 2/5 GORKHA RIFLES that occupied the town. Another incident occurred at Narketpally where a Razakar unit was decimated by the Indian forces.

On day four, the Strike Force under Lt Col Ram Singh was directed to capture the road junction to the West of Zahirabad, then advancing to Bidar Road. Smash Force followed closely behind the Strike Force, which was to continue down the main road to capture Zahirabad and go on to Sadaseopet. On reaching the junction of the Bidar Road with the Sholapur-Hyderabad City Highway, the forces encountered gunfire from ambush positions. The bulk of the force moved on, leaving some of the units to handle the ambush. They reached 15 km beyond Zahirabad by nightfall in spite of hit-and-miss resistance along the way. Most of the resistance was from Razakar units who ambushed the Indians as they passed through urban areas. The Razakars were able to use the terrain to their advantage until the Indian Army brought in their 75 mm guns. The Army wanted to use minimum force and cause the least destruction of life or property in Hyderabad state, but it was found necessary to allow the tanks to use their main guns of 75 mm at Zahirabad.[10] Maj Gen El Syed Ahmed Edroos, the Commander of the Hyderabad forces, was called upon to surrender and avoid needless losses and human suffering.

On 17 September 1948, the Strike Force headed to enter Bidar. Smash Force along with 2/1 GORKHA RIFLES were ordered to capture Sadaseopat. 7 Infantry Brigade was to pass through 9 Infantry Brigade to clear up the major village of Digwal, East of Zahirabad.[11] In the morning, a Squadron of 3 Cavalry took up the advance, which was joined by the 1 Armoured Brigade Group that reached Sadaseopet at noon. The forces led by the 1st Armoured Brigade were at the town of Chityal, while another column took over the town of Hingoli. The Main HQ 1 Armoured Division and HQ 9 Infantry Brigade settled down near Zahirabad, while HQ 7 Infantry Brigade was in the village of Digwal.

As the Indian forces moved closer towards Hyderabad, on 17 September, Hyderabad Radio announced an offer of surrender by the Hyderabad State Forces. At 1600 Hours on 18 September, Maj Gen JN Chaudhuri accepted the surrender of Maj Gen El Edroos at a simple ceremony and was appointed 'Military Governor' of Hyderabad.[12]

Formal Accession

On 18 October 1948, a new Military Government of Hyderabad including two Hyderabad members was appointed. Maj Gen JN Chaudhuri, who led Operation Polo, remained in charge of the state's armed forces and police, and as Military Governor till December 1949. The Chief Civil Administrator, SD Bakhle, was placed in charge of Home and Judicial Affairs as well as Supply and Railway. The Additional Chief Civil Administrator, DR Pradhan, received the charge of Finance, Revenue, Commerce and Industry. Nawab Zain Yar Jung took over Public Works, Labour and Rural Reconstruction and Raja Dhoondi Raj was to look after Education, Customs and Excise, and Relief and Rehabilitation.

On 29 October 1948, the future of Hyderabad State was discussed by Sardar Vallabh Bhai Patel along with VP Menon and Maj Gen Chaudhuri. Prime Minister Jawaharlal Nehru visited Hyderabad and addressed a meeting of nearly 50,000 people on 25 December 1948, in which he stressed on the ending of feudal conditions and the carrying out of agrarian reforms in the state.

In a Farman dated 24 November 1949, the Nizam declared: 'Whereas in the rest of India…in political, economic and other fields, it is desirable that…between the State and the Union of India…I declare and direct that the Constitution of India… shall be the Constitution of Hyderabad.'[13] The Nizam's acceptance of the Indian Constitution thus formalised Hyderabad's accession to the Indian Union.

Operation Vijay 1961

Background

The state of Goa became part of the Indian Union in 1961, a decade and a half after independence. Prior to that, it was a Portuguese colony beginning 1510 when Alfonso de Albuquerque gained control of Goa from Sultan Adil Shah of Bijapur. Under Portuguese rule as the Estado da India along with the territories of Daman and Diu and Dadra and Nagar Haveli, Goa was one of the last of colonial possessions in the Indian subcontinent to become part of independent India. The story of how Goa became part of the Union of India is the story of Operation Vijay, an armed, military operation involving all the three Services—the Indian Air Force (IAF), the Indian Navy, and the Indian Army.

The beginnings of nationalist stirrings in Goa date to the third decade of the twentieth century when the Goa Congress Committee was formed by Tristão de Bragança Cunha in 1928. In 1938, the Goa Congress Committee was made an affiliate of the Indian National Congress that was spearheading the nationalist movement in India. On 18 June 1946, a large-scale civil disobedience movement against Portuguese rule was organised by Dr Ram Manohar Lohia and Tristão de Bragança Cunha, among others. The Goa liberation movement took a sharp turn when civilians started to boycott government offices and the Portuguese government took every possible step to quell the Satyagraha movement. After India gained independence in 1947, Goa remained in Portuguese hands. The Government of India approached the Portuguese in 1950 to begin negotiations on the status of Portuguese colonies in India, but the stand taken by the latter was that Portuguese possessions on the subcontinent were part of the territory of Portugal. The next few years saw diplomatic endeavouring on New Delhi's part with the issuance of multiple aide-de-memoires to the Portuguese government, without much success. With waning chances for negotiations, in 1953, India thus closed its Legation in Lisbon and the door to a diplomatic solution to the issue appeared to have closed. 'In July 1954, volunteers of the "Free Goa Movement" took possession of the Portuguese enclaves of Dadra and Nagar Haveli.'[14] This further added to tensions between New Delhi and Lisbon.

By the end of the decade, it became evident that there were no diplomatic solutions to the issue and the Indian government increasingly warmed up to the idea that it might need to use force to resolve the issue. Accordingly, plans were drawn up for a possible military operation to handle the Goa issue in November 1961. In November 1961, 'the Portuguese contingent based at Anjadip island, off the coast of Canacona, fired at the Indian merchant ship *Sabarmati* in a display of its maritime supremacy in the region. Subsequently, the Portuguese garrisons resorted to indiscriminate firing on Indian fishing boats off Karwar (in present-day Karnataka) and South Goa.'[15] This provided the spark to move forward on military front. The incidents had precipitated matters to the point where India found no other option than to liberate Goa from the Portuguese by force.

Before the official commencement of hostilities on ground on 11 December 1961, the Indian Navy initiated Operation Chutney to re-establish the position of India in sea territory near Goa and retaliate against the Portuguese Naval forces.[16] The operation once again established the Indian Naval presence in area near Goa's territorial waters. Later, along with Goa the other Portuguese territory of Daman and Diu were also liberated and joined the Indian Union on 19 December 1961.

Daman and Diu

The advance on the enclave of Daman was conducted by the 1 MARATHA LI under the command of Lt Col SJS Bhonsle in a pre-dawn operation on 18 December 1961. 1 MARATHA LI launched an operation under the cover of darkness and planned to overrun the airfield with stealth. The IAF struck using Mystere fighters against enemy mortar positions and guns inside Moti Daman Fort. At 0430 Hours, Indian Artillery began to bombard Damao Grande. By the evening, the Indians had secured most of the colony, except the airfield and Damao Pequeno. The IAF launched six successive attacks, but the enemy still refused to surrender. The Indian forces then followed up with ground assault on the airfield which was eventually overrun.

Diu was a tiny island, off the coast of Gujarat, held by approximately 500 Portuguese soldiers, supported by Artillery and the Patrol Boat *Vega*. While the main defences were based in the Diu Fort, the Portuguese had covered the crossings with Artillery, mortars and machine guns. India, on the other hand, had the advantage of air support and naval gunfire.

It was decided that the Indian forces would cross the creek exploiting darkness and launch silent attacks. Diu was attacked on 18 December from the North West along Kob Forte by two Companies of 20 RAJPUT and a Company of 4 MADRAS. They attempted initial crossings but proved unsuccessful. It was 4 MADRAS that made the first attack on a police border post at 0130 Hours on 18 December at Gogol. At 0200hours another attempt was made by 4 MADRAS which was repulsed. Although India had advantage of air support and naval gunfire, it could not be exploited at night time. Fresh air attacks were made at dawn on 18 December, with the aim of destroying Diu's fortifications which faced the mainland.

Goa

D-Day for Goa was set for 18 December 1961, which was planned in two phases.[17]

Phase I:

(a) Advance of 50 Para Brigade Group under Brigadier Sagat Singh along Dodamarg – Sanquelim – Usgao – Piliem.
   (i) Secure Bicholim and Usgao bridges with a view to advancing on Ponda.
   (ii) Secure Mapusa.

(b) Advance of 63 Infantry Brigade Group under Brigadier Kalwant Singh Dhillon along Mollem – Ponda and Mollem – Collem – Ponda, to capture Ponda.

Phase II:
This phase involved orders for the capture of Panjim and Marmagoa.

Hostilities at Goa operations commenced on 17 December 1961 with the capture of the border town Maulinguem. Brig Sagat Singh's 50 Para Brigade Group planned an unconventional and bold operation which captured Doddu Morogu by 1 PARA on 17 December. A unit of Indian Troops were sent to attack and occupy the town of Maulinguem. At 0400 Hours, the Indian assault commenced with Artillery bombardment on Portuguese positions South of Maulinguem, launched on the basis of the false intelligence that the Portuguese had stationed heavy battle tanks in the area. They occupied Maulinguem in the North-East, killing two Portuguese soldiers.

A deceptive thrust, in Company strength, was to be made from the South along the Majali-Canacona-Margao axis. Despite the 50 (Independent) Para Brigade being charged with merely assisting the main thrust conducted by the 17th Infantry, its units moved rapidly across minefields, roadblocks and four riverine obstacles to reach Panaji at the fastest. Lt Col Sucha Singh's 2 PARA, which led the 50 Para Brigade along Bacholim-Ponda axis, secured Bicholim. At 0440 hours, Portuguese forces destroyed the bridge at Bicholim, followed by the destruction of the bridges at Chapora in Colvale and at Assonora.

On the morning of 18 December, the 50 (Independent) Para Brigade of the Indian Army moved into Goa in three columns. The Western column, the main thrust of the attack comprised 2 SIKH LI as well as an Armoured Troops, which crossed the border at 0630 Hours and advanced on Tivim. At 0530 Hours, Portuguese Troops left their barracks at Ponda in Central Goa and marched towards the town of Usgao, in the direction of the advancing Eastern column of the 2 PARA, which had under command tanks of the Indian 7th Light Cavalry commanded by Maj Dalip Singh Jind. By 0900 hours, Indian Troops had already covered half the distance to the town of Ponda. By 1000 Hours, Portuguese forces of the 1st EREC, faced with the advancing 2 SIKH LI by Lt Col RB Nanda advanced to Mapusa via Assonora, capturing Mapusa. By 1745 Hours, the forces of the 1st EREC and the 9th Cazadores Company of the Portuguese Battlegroup North had completed their ferry crossing of the Mandovi River to Panaji, just minutes ahead of the arrival of the Indian Armoured forces. On 18 December, they reached the general line Betim-Piligao in the North and Banastarim-Ponda in the East.

The same night, Maj Shivdev Singh Sidhu with a force of the 7 Light Cavalry decided to take Fort Aguada and obtain its surrender, after receiving information that a number of supporters of the Indian Republic were held prisoners there. On the Mollem Axis, Lt Col JD Bobb's 3 SIKH led the advance of 63 Infantry Brigade under Brigadier Kalwant Singh Dhillon. The advance was to be on two routes named the Yellow Axis and the Green Axis. The Yellow Axis was from Mollem to Collem track and then to Ponda. However, the Portuguese defenders of the fort had not yet received orders to surrender and responded by opening fire on the Indian forces, and Maj Sidhu and Capt Vinod Sehgal were killed in the firefight.

The order for Indian forces to cross the Mandovi River was received on the morning of 19 December, upon which two Rifle Companies of the 2 SIKH LI advanced on Panaji at 0730 Hours and secured the town without facing any resistance. The right column, consisting of the 2 BIHAR Battalion, and the left column, consisting of the 3 SIKH, linked up at the border town of Mollem and then advanced by separate routes on Ponda.

Phase II of the D-Day Plan was to capture Panjim and Marmagoa subsequently.

In Action

Although the battle on Anjadip was in progress, the Indian Army and the IAF began closing in on Goa. Offensive action commenced with four IAF Canberra bombers strafing the Dabolim airfield on 18 December. A three-pronged advance was made by the Army into Goa—from the North (Karwar), South (Sawantwadi), and the South-West (Belgaum). The seaward approach was controlled by the Indian Navy frigates, *Betwa*, *Beas* and *Cauvery*. These ships patrolled entrances to the ports of Marmagao and Panjim.

Operation Vijay was planned as an Army operation with the IAF and the Indian Navy providing air and naval support. Maj Gen KP Candeth, who was commanding the 17th Infantry Division, at the time had 50 Parachute Brigade placed under him. The Navy organised four Task Forces in order to accomplish the tasks that were being assigned: Surface Action Group (INS *Mysore*, *Trishul*, *Betwa*, *Beas* and *Cauvery*), Carrier Task Group (INS *Vikrant*, *Delhi*, *Kuthar*, *Kirpan*, *Khukri* and *RAJPUT*), Minesweeping Group (INS *Karwar*, *Kakinada*, *Cannanore* and *Bimilipatan*), and Support Group (INS *Dharini*). On the other hand, the air plans were kept flexible.

By the evening of 18 December 1961, most of Goa had been overrun by advancing Indian forces. Operation Vijay had ended in a success in less than 40 hours. About 4,668 people were taken prisoner by the Indian forces, which included both military and civilian personnel, Portuguese, Africans and Goans. The official Portuguese surrender was conducted in a formal ceremony at 2030 Hours on 19 December 1961 with the signing of the Instrument of Surrender by the last Portuguese Governor-General, Antonio Vassalo e Silva. Upon the surrender of the Portuguese Governor General, Goa, Daman and Diu were declared a federally administered Union Territory placed directly under the President of India, and Maj Gen Candeth was appointed as the military governor. Thus, 451 years of Portuguese rule in India came to an end and the Indian armed forces restored Goa and other Portuguese territories to India.

Sikkim: Skirmish at Nathu La 1967

Background

The Nathu La pass lies on the Old Silk Route between Tibet and India. In 1904, Major Francis Younghusband, serving as the British Commissioner to Tibet, led a successful mission through Nathu La to capture Lhasa. This led to the setting up of trading posts at Gyantse and Gartok in Tibet, and gave the British control of the surrounding Chumbi Valley. The following year, China and Great Britain ratified an agreement approving trade between Sikkim and Tibet. In 1947, Sikkim became an Indian protectorate. After China took control of Tibet in 1950 and suppressed a Tibetan uprising in 1959, refugees entered Sikkim through Nathu La. During the 1962 Sino-Indian War, Nathu La witnessed skirmishes between soldiers of the two countries. Shortly thereafter, the pass was sealed and was closed for trade. Five years later, Nathu La was the scene of a 'border skirmish' between Indian and China, which resulted in heavy casualties to both sides. Significantly, it was the first instance when the Chinese got a 'bloody nose' from the Indians.

Post 1962, India raised seven Mountain Divisions to defend her Northern borders against further Chinese threat. Of these, approximately two Divisions were deployed to guard the border between Sikkim and the Chumbi Valley in the Tibet Autonomous Region. 17 Mountain Division covered the approach to Gangtok from Yatung in the Chumbi Valley via the Nathu La pass, while 27 Mountain Division covered the route to East Sikkim via Jelep La. At Nathu La, the Chinese held the Northern shoulder of the pass, while the Indians held the Southern shoulder. From 1963 onwards, there were minor scuffles between Indian and Chinese Troops. Since the border was not demarcated, patrols sometimes crossed the border inadvertently, leading to clashes, which were frequently reported in the press.

During the Indo-Pak War of 1965, China gave an ultimatum and demanded that India withdrew her posts at Nathu La and Jelep La. According to HQ 33 Corps, the main defences of 17 Mountain Division were at Changgu, while Nathu La was only an observation post. In the adjoining Sector, manned by 27 Mountain Division, Jelep La was also considered an observation post, with the main defences located at Lungthu. In case of hostilities, the Divisional Commanders had been given the authority to vacate the posts, and fall back on the main defences. Accordingly, orders were issued by Corps HQ to both Divisions to vacate Nathu La and Jelep La.

Maj Gen Sagat Singh, GOC 17 Mountain Division, disagreed with the views of the Corps HQ as both Nathu La and Jelep La were passes on the watershed—the natural boundary—and vacating them would give the Chinese the tactical advantage of observation and fire into India, while denying the same to our own Troops. These passes also provided the only means of ingress through the Chumbi Valley. Sagat also reasoned that the discretion to vacate the posts lay with the Divisional Commander, and he was not obliged to do so, based on instructions from Corps HQ.

As a result of orders issued by Corps HQ, 27 Mountain Division vacated Jelep La, which the Chinese promptly occupied. However, Maj Gen Sagat Singh refused to vacate Nathu La, and when the Chinese became belligerent and opened fire, he responded with guns and mortars, though there was a restriction imposed by Corps on the use of Artillery. Lieutenant General (later General) G G Bewoor, the Corps Commander, was extremely annoyed, and tried to speak to Sagat to ask him to explain his actions. But Sagat was not in his HQ, and was with the forward Troops. So it was his GSO 1, Lieut. Colonel Lakhpat Singh, who bore the brunt of the Corps Commander's wrath.

Chinese loudspeakers at Nathu La warned the Indians that if they did not withdraw, they would suffer as they did in 1962. However, Gen Sagat concluded that the Chinese were bluffing. They made threatening postures, such as advancing in large numbers, but on reaching the border, always stopped, and withdrew. They also did not use any Artillery, for covering fire, which they would have certainly done if they were serious about capturing any Indian positions. Indian Artillery observation posts on Camel's Back and Sebu La overlooked into the Yatung valley for several kilometres, and could bring down accurate fire on the enemy, an advantage that the Chinese did not have. It would have been a tactical blunder to vacate Nathu La and gift it to the enemy. Ultimately, his fortitude saved the day for India, and his stand was vindicated two years later, when there was a show down there.

Lead-up to the Skirmish

Vexed by their failure to occupy Nathu La in 1965, the Chinese continued to put pressure on the Indians. In December 1965, the Chinese fired on a patrol of 17 Assam Rifles, in North Sikkim, at a height of 16,000 feet, killing two men. They made regular propaganda broadcasts from loudspeakers at Nathu La, a form of psychological warfare in which the Chinese were adept. Maj Gen Sagat had similar loud speakers installed on our own side and tape recorded messages, in Mandarin, which were broadcast daily. Throughout 1966, and early 1967, Chinese propaganda, intimidation and attempted incursions into Indian territory continued. The border was not marked, and there were several vantage points on the crest line which both sides thought belonged to them. Patrols which walked along the border often clashed, resulting in tension, and sometimes even casualties.[18]

In the first week of August 1967, the border out posts (BOPs) at Nathu La were occupied by 2 GRENADIERS, relieving 18 RAJPUT. Lt Col Rai Singh was then commanding 2 GRENADIERS. Maj Bishan Singh took over as 'Tiger Nathu La', as the Company Commander holding the pass was generally known, with Capt PS Dagar as his second-in-command. The deployment at Nathu La comprised a Platoon each on Camel's Back, South Shoulder, Centre Bump and Sebu La. The Battalion headquarters was at Gole Ghar, while the Battalion 3-inch mortars were just above Sherathang, which also had the administrative base and forward aid post. 18 RAJPUT took over the BOP at Yakla where they had a Platoon plus. The BOP's at Cho La were occupied by a Company of 10 Jammu & Kashmir (J&K) Rifles.

Even while 2 GRENADIERS was in the process of taking over the defences at Nathu La, Chinese activities increased. They were noticed repairing their bunkers on North Shoulder and making preparations to construct new ones. On 13 August, the observation post at Sebu La reported that the Chinese had arrived on the crest line and dug trenches on the Indian side of the international border. When challenged, they filled up the trenches and withdrew. The same day, they added eight more loud speakers to the already existing 21 speakers on South Shoulder. Due to this the volume of their propaganda increased and could now be heard at Changgu.

In 1967, the Divisional Commander—Maj Gen Sagat Singh—discussed the problem with the Corps Commander, Lt Gen JS Aurora, and suggested that the border at Nathu La should be clearly marked to prevent such incidents. He offered to walk along the crest line to test the Chinese resolve; if they did not object, the line along which he walked could be taken to be acceptable to them. This was agreed to, and Gen Sagat, accompanied by an escort, began walking along the crest. The Chinese Commander also walked alongside, accompanied by a photographer, who kept taking pictures. The 'walk' ended peacefully.

Maj Gen Sagat then obtained the concurrence of the Corps Commander to mark the crest line, ordering a double wire fence to be erected, from Nathu La towards the North and South Shoulders. 2 GRENADIERS was ordered to lay a three-strand wire fence along the border from Nathu La towards the North Shoulder. However, as soon as work began on the fence on 20 August 1967, the Chinese asked the Indians to stop. One strand of wire was laid that day, and two more were added over the next two days. This led to an escalation in Chinese activity. On 23 August, at about 1400 Hours, Major Bishan Singh reported that about 75 Chinese in battle dress carrying Rifles fitted with bayonets were advancing towards Nathu La. They advanced slowly in an extended line and stopped on reaching the border. At 1430 Hours they started shouting slogans which the Political Commissar read out from a red book, repeated by the rest of the Troops. The Indian Troops were 'stand to', watching and waiting. The Chinese withdrew after standing on the border for around an hour.

On 01 September 1967, the Corps Commander and the Divisional Commander visited Nathu La. Despite poor visibility, they went to Centre Bump first and then to South Shoulder. Thereafter, they walked along the border to Four Poles area, where they crossed the border and went a few steps inside. At once, the Chinese Political Commissar came running up to them, shouting 'Chini, Chini', indicating that they have crossed the border into China. The two officers immediately withdrew, but the Chinese kept on grumbling. Soon a photographer came and took photographs of their footsteps across the border.

The next morning Maj Gen Sagat went to Nathu La again and directed that the border from Right OP to Camels Back must be patrolled. A patrol of two officers, one JCO, and 15 Other Ranks (OR) was immediately sent out under Maj Bishan Singh. As soon as the patrol reached the U Bump near Tekri, the Chinese surrounded them. Major Bishan Singh tried to explain to the Chinese officer that they had not crossed the border and that, in fact, it was the Chinese who were within Indian territory. However, the Chinese did not budge.

On 04 September, Maj Gen Sagat Singh again went to Nathu La and directed that the wire fence be converted into a Cat Wire Type 1 obstacle, using concertina coils. The task was allotted to 2 GRENADIERS and a Platoon of 70 Field Company Engineers under Maj Cheema was allotted to assist them. Work commenced on 5 September at 0500 Hours, but the Chinese objected. There was an argument between Lt. Col Rai Singh and the Chinese Political Commissar over the alignment of the border and the work was stopped at 0800 Hours. However, work on Chinese defences on North and South Shoulder continued. During the night the Chinese came up to the Bump and cut off one shoulder so that if water was poured on the other shoulder it would flow into China. The next morning when our men went to straighten out some wire, a few Chinese came running up to the border with a bucket of water and poured it on the Bump indicating the watershed.

On 07 September, the work started again on laying the wire. This time around 100 Chinese came to the fence and there was hand-to-hand fighting between the Troops. Realising that they were unequal to the Jats, the Chinese withdrew and began pelting stones, the Indians responding in the same manner. The fighting delayed progress in the laying of the wire. Two Indian soldiers were wounded and the Chinese suffered a few casualties. Things were relatively quiet on 08 and 09 September 1967, but the Chinese continued work on their defences.

On the night of 10 September 1967, Maj Gen Sagat Singh held a conference at HQ 112 Mountain Brigade in Changgu, where he personally briefed everyone on how the operation for laying the wire was to be carried out on 11 September. Additional resources in men and material were moved for this purpose. One Company of 18 RAJPUT was brought in to reinforce the defences. An ad hoc force of 90 men was organised into a protection party to charge the Chinese positions if they opened fire. Maj Bishan Singh was in charge of the work with Captain PS Dagar as his assistant. Apart from the Platoon of 70 Field Company, a pioneer Platoon was to assist in the construction of the fence.[19]

The Events of 11 September 1967

Work on the fencing commenced at about 0600 hours on 11 September 1967. The Chinese immediately came up to the fence, and tried to stop its progress. There was a lot of shouting and the Indian Troops refused to back down and started fighting with the Chinese. There was a heated discussion between the Chinese Commander, who was accompanied by the Political Commissar, and Lt Col Rai Singh. Foreseeing this eventuality, Maj Gen Sagat told Rai Singh not to expose himself but remain in his bunker where the Brigade Commander, Brig MMS Bakshi, was also present. However, this was not heeded and Rai Singh came out in the open with an escort to stand face-to-face with the Chinese officers. As the arguments became more heated, tempers rose, with both sides standing their ground. There was a scuffle during which the political commissar fell down and broke his spectacles.

At about 0745 hours, the Chinese started withdrawing to their bunkers. The strength of Chinese opposing the Indian Troops working on the fence gradually reduced. The loudspeakers on the Chinese side started blaring a speech of Mao Tse Tung in Hindi. The volume of the loudspeakers shielded the commotion of the hand-to-hand fight along the fence. Then there was a loud whistle, after which the guns of the Chinese on the North and South Shoulders opened fire on Indian Troops with medium machine guns. The Indian Troops laying the fence, who were in the open, bore the initial brunt of the firing. Lt Col Rai Singh was hit by a Chinese bullet, and fell down.

Seeing their CO fall, the Grenadiers, led by Capt PS Dagar came out of their trenches and attacked the Chinese post. The Company of 18 RAJPUT, under Maj Harbhajan Singh, and the Sappers and Pioneers working on the fence had been caught in the open, and suffered heavy casualties from the Chinese firing. Realising that the only way to neutralise the Chinese fire was a physical assault, Harbhajan led his men in a charge on the Chinese position. Several of the Indian Troops were mowed down by Chinese machine guns, but those who reached the Chinese bunkers used their bayonets and accounted for many of the enemy. Both Harbhajan and Dagar lost their lives in the action, for which they were awarded the MVC and VrC, respectively. Soon after this, Chinese Artillery also started firing on Indian positions.

By about 0930 hours, Chinese fire intensified and gradually the Brigade headquarters started getting out of touch with the Troops at North and South Shoulders. By 0945 hours, there was no contact with anyone on the shoulders even on the Artillery network. All the lines were down as was the B1 wireless link to the pass. The Brigade signal officer, Second Lieutenant. NC Gupta was with the Brigade Commander at the Central Bump. This was a Platoon location overlooking the entire pass including North and South Shoulders, H Section, etc. It was around 400 m behind the border and an excellent vantage point. Gupta tried to enter the Battalion net and the Company net but failed. There was no response on any of the almost dozen frequencies of the Battalion in use that day for various nets.

Around this time from the vantage position at Central Bump, the Brigade Commander saw over a dozen Troops running down the slopes of South Shoulder towards Sherathang. He also observed that some of them had shed their helmets, packs and even Rifles as they ran down. He asked Gupta to call South Shoulder but there was no response. They tried to observe the area of South Shoulder but could see no movement. By this time, the shelling on the South Shoulder had also increased.

Under the circumstances there was no other option for the Brigade Commander but to send someone to South Shoulder to restore communications. Gupta had a line party and spare radio sets with him. It was decided that a radio set be sent to South

Shoulder. The linemen with Gupta were new to Nathula and had never gone to South Shoulder. Havildar Bhakuni, the Commander's rover operator had gone there many times. But sending him would have left the Commander without communications. Seeing the gravity of the situation and the shelling the Commander told Gupta to go himself with a radio set.

The distance to South Shoulder was about 500 meters. The route was open at places and involved going down around 300 meters and then up around 200 meters. Gupta reached South Shoulder at around 1000 Hours. He found the post totally abandoned. He informed the Brigade Commander, who asked him to look around for wounded if any and remain at the post and keep him in picture. From the bunkers on South Shoulder Gupta could see the Chinese in their bunker. By this time intermittent fog had started setting in. He informed the Brigade Commander that he could see a few dead soldiers in the area ahead of our defences close to the fence and resorted to intermittent firing from his carbine to indicate that the post was still occupied. Soon, he found an LMG in its bunker which he used it to try and depict our presence on the post.

At around 1100 hours, the Brigade Commander informed Gupta that reinforcements were on their way but would take atleast three hours to reach and that he must hold on till then. A little later he asked Gupta to go around 100 m down South Shoulder where he had spotted a few soldiers sitting behind a huge rock. After firing a few salvos of LMG, Gupta went down. He found six soldiers of 2 GRENADIERS comprising 2/Lt Attar Singh (fresh from IMA), one Havildar and four Jawans, who then accompanied Gupta back to the South Shoulder.

By 1200 Hours, the fog had intensified. As he was watching from one of the bunkers, Gupta saw one of the dead moving next to the fence, barely 10 m from the Chinese bunker. Taking advantage of the fog he went ahead to try and recover him. It was Maj Bishan Singh, 'Tiger Nathula', who had been badly injured in the initial firing. Gupta managed to lift him and drag him into our defences with the help of the men of 2 GRENADIERS and once inside made him speak to the Brigade Commander. After having been briefed by Bishan Singh, the Brigade Commander asked Gupta to evacuate him using the four jawans. He ordered Gupta, Attar Singh and the Havildar to remain at the post. Ten minutes later the Brigade Commander asked Gupta to return to the area of Bumps leaving the radio set with 2/Lt Attar Singh.[20]

Assessment

The skirmish developed into a full-scale battle, lasting five days. Maj Gen Sagat Singh had asked for some medium guns which were moved up to Kyangnosa La, at a height of over 10,000 ft. The Artillery observation posts proved their worth in bringing down effective fire on the Chinese. Because of lack of observation, and the steep incline West of Nathu La, most Chinese shells fell behind the forward defences, and did not harm the Indians. During the first day's action, some Troops of 2 GRENADIERS, who were occupying the South Shoulder, vacated their positions. The position was re-occupied and the Troops pushed back into their trenches. The Brigade signal officer, 2/Lt NC Gupta played an important role in this operation, for which he was awarded a Sena Medal.

The Indian casualties in the action were just over 200, with 65 dead and 145 wounded. The Chinese are estimated to have suffered about 300 casualties. Though the action taken by Maj Gen Sagat Singh in marking the border with a wire fence had the approval of higher authorities, the large number of casualties suffered by both sides created a furore. Perhaps the casualties to Indian Troops would have been minimal if they had remained in their defences and not exposed themselves by coming out of their trenches and rushing at the Chinese post. This happened on the spur of the moment, because seeing their CO fall, the Troops lost their cool, and rushed forward under the orders of a young officer, who lost his life in the action. The Chinese had already announced that it was the Indians who started the conflict, and the large number of Indian bodies and wounded Indian soldiers in their possession, seemed to support their claim. However, Gen Sagat was not perturbed. For the last two years, the Chinese had been instigating him, and had killed several Indian soldiers. The spectre of the Chinese attack of 1962 had haunted India. The events at Nathu La in 1967, where the Chinese got a bloody nose for the first time since 1962, broke the myth of their invincibility.

Operation Meghdoot, 1984

Background

Located in the Eastern Karakoram range in the Himalayas, the Siachen Glacier has the distinction of being the world's highest battlefield. Since 1987, India has had complete control over the heights and passes on the glacier.

The origin of the dispute lies in the differing interpretations by both sides of the alignment of the undemarcated portion of the Line of Control (LOC) established by the Simla Agreement signed on 02 July 1972.The LOC itself is a modification of the Cease Fire Line (CFL) demarcated by the Karachi Agreement finalised on 27 July 1949 after the 1947–48 Kashmir war.[21] Both these agreements indicated point NJ9842 as the end of the Northern line. The Baltoro and Siachen glaciers, divided by the Saltoro ridge, lie North of this line. NJ9842 is located at the lower edge of the Saltoro ridge and the Indian interpretation was that the logical extension of the line would lie along its crest.[22] Pakistan's claims, however, took the LOC from NJ9842 North-East to the Karakoram Pass. Thus, the boundary was not clearly demarcated and differing perceptions laid the ground for potential conflict. This region became more significant in the geopolitical calculations of Pakistan once it gave access to China to the Shaksgam Valley in 1963. Further, the glacier is the source for the Nubra River that eventually feeds the Indus river, which is the major water source that irrigates the Punjab plains in Pakistan.

Throughout the 1970s, a number of mountaineering expeditions were mounted from the Pakistan side, many of which included foreign participants. These crossed the Saltoro ridge and the Siachen glacier. The 1974 edition of the US Defence Mapping Agency's operational navigation chart was the first to show an Air Defence Information Zone (ADIZ) separating India and Pakistan in the Karakoram region. The line marking the separation was drawn straight from NJ 9842 to the Karakoram Pass.[23] It is impossible to have a straight line boundary in the Mountains as these are either formed along the watersheds of Mountains or along rivers, and the ADIZ was along neither.[24]

In January 1978, Indian authorities became aware of implications of the line joining NJ9842 to the Karakoram Pass and Pakistan-sponsored Mountaineering expeditions. The first response was to send a strong military Mountaineers' expedition to climb a series of peaks on either side of the Siachen glacier.[25] Colonel Narinder 'Bull' Kumar of the Indian Army led an expedition to Teram Kangri, along with medical officer Captain AVS Gupta. The IAF provided valuable support to this expedition through logistic support and supply of fresh rations. Kumar's expedition was a success and also revealed evidence of other expeditions having entered the Siachen area from the West. Kumar alerted Lt Gen ML Chibber about the Siachen Mountaineering expeditions from Pakistan and 'recommended that to ensure the Pakistanis do not intrude into Siachen, India should establish a post in the area which could be manned during the summer.'[26]

Bilafond La had been used as a traditional pass, much for climbing from the West. From the North to South, there were four important passes on the Saltoro Ridge: Sia La, Bilafond La, Gyong La and Chulung La. Sia La and Bilafond La were at altitudes in excess of 20,000 ft and 18,000 ft, respectively. In 1983, two Indian Army patrols were sent into the area, a move which saw protests from Pakistan. In January 1984, an attack was launched by Pakistan to drive off the Indian Army from Bilafond La, but it was repelled. In February 1985 another attempt was made to occupy the height overlooking Sia La; this attempt too met with failure. The next major effort to change the situation on the ground took place in 1987, when the Pakistani Special Services Group (SSG) occupied a position overlooking the Bilafond La area in March-April.[27]

Under the leadership of Lt Gen ML Chibber, Maj Gen Shiv Sharma and Lt Gen PN Hoon, the Indian Army learned of the plan by the Pakistan Army to seize Sia La and Bilafond La on the glacier. The 26 Sector which was commanded by Brig

Vijay Channa was given the task of occupying the Saltoro Ridge. Brig Channa was tasked to launch the Operation between 10–30 April, when he supposedly chose 13 April, considering it to be a lucky day on the occasion of Vaisakhi Day. The military decided to deploy Troops from the Northern Ladakh region as well as some paramilitary forces to the glacier area. The operation by the Indian Army, planned to control the Siachen glacier was executed phase-wise. 4 KUMAON, supported by a Company of Ladakh Scouts under Major VS Salaria were in turn tasked to occupy the Siachen Glacier Complex. Before undertaking the task, the Troops carried out rigorous training for several weeks, which included ice craft, snow craft, survival, physical fitness and mental robustness. The first Troops to be heli-dropped as part of the Zorawar Task Force were commanded by Major (later Colonel) RS Sandhu, VrC of 4 KUMAON. The first wave was under Captain (later Lieutenant General) Sanjay Kulkarni, who landed on the Glacier on 13 April 1984, and hoisted the Indian tricolour on Bilafond La four days later as they could not move ahead initially due to a severe snowstorm.

Commencement of the Operation

Operation Meghdoot commenced with the airlift of Indian Army soldiers by the IAF. The IAF used IL-76, AN-12, AN-32 planes and MI-17, MI-8 helicopters to transport stores and Troops and to airdrop supplies to high altitude airfields. From there Mi-17, Mi-8 and HAL Chetak helicopters carried provisions and personnel to the East of the hitherto unscaled peaks. It was at 0530 Hours on 13 April that the first Chetak helicopter carrying Capt Sanjay Kulkarni of 4 KUMAON and one soldier took off from the base camp, followed by 17 such sorties by noon. Further, 29 soldiers were heli-dropped at Bilafond La. Soon, the weather packed up and the Platoon was cut off from the headquarters. The contact was established after three days, when five Cheetah and two Mi-8 helicopters flew a record 32 sorties on April 17 to Sia La.

'That same day', according to Sushant Singh, 'a Pakistani helicopter flew overhead to see Indian soldiers already deployed at the glacier.'[29] This move highlighted the gravity of the situation and a force named Burzil Force was raised by the Pakistan SSG to conduct Operation Ababeel. Several days later, elements of the force were sighted in Bilafond La. On 22 April, two Pakistani jet aircraft had flown over the Indian position. On 25 April, Burzil Forces, comprising the SSG and the Northern LI (NLI), started the firefight with small arms and machine guns.[30] Thus, military conflict between India and Pakistan began for control of the glacier.

Pakistan responded sharply after being denied the two major passes. Forced attempts were made and getting hold of the next higher place became an operational aim. The Pakistani Army strove to secure any place on Saltoro range, but the inevitable Indian response denied them any foothold on Soltoro. Defending every part of the ridge became a political necessity. The Saltoro experience proved a turning point as it forced the Indian Army to experiment and innovate in all aspects of combat. With the defence of the whole of Saltoro becoming a military responsibility, a doctrine to achieve the desired ends became essential. Lt Gen Chibber wrote in an official note:

> The two main passes were sealed off. The enemy was taken completely by surprise and an area of approximately 3,300 sq km, illegally shown as part of PoK on the maps published by Pak and USA, was now under our control. The enemy had been preempted in their attempt to occupy the area claimed by them.

The Siachen glacier continues to be occupied by the Indian Army till date. India and Pakistan have held 13 rounds of negotiations in order to find a solution to the Siachen dispute.[31] The first round of talks were held in 1986 and the last round took place in 2012. The situation on Siachen has been at an impasse since. Operation Meghdoot was a major victory for the Indian military. Both India and Pakistan maintain a permanent military presence on the glacier.

Battle for Bana Post

In 1987, military operations on the Saltoro ridge reached higher thresholds in terms of both size and intensity.[32] The Pakistan Amy was by then jostling for a foothold on the ridgeline, aiming to secure a position on or near the Bilafond La Pass, which was the main gateway to the Siachen glacier. The strategically important Siachen area had been infiltrated by Pakistani forces, who had captured an important position: this was called Quaid Post, named after Quaid-e-Azam Muhammad Ali Jinnah. The post was located at a height of 6,500 m on the highest peak in the Siachen Glacier area.

Pakistan's establishment of the Quaid Post on this peak threatened Indian movement on the Western Siachen Glacier. The Quaid Post had been occupied by Pakistan's SSG in late March or early April of 1987.[33] An Indian Army patrol was sent to assault the post on 24 May 1987, but it was fired upon by the SSG which was occupying the post. The Army then planned yet another operation, which was conducted in June 1987, to capture the post and evict the Pakistanis from there.

The Task Force launched multiple unsuccessful attacks on the Pakistani Troops stationed at the post. On the night of 25 June 1987, a team led by Naib Subedar (now Honarary Captain) Bana Singh of 8 Jammu and Kashmir LI (JAK LI) moved forward to attack the post. They managed to capture it successfully by 26 June 1987. For his role in capturing this strategically significant post, Bana Singh was awarded the Param Vir Chakra (PVC). The Quaid Post was renamed 'Bana Post'.

The actions of the Indian Army ensured that Pakistan had no further presence on the Siachen Glacier.

In September 1987, Pakistan launched a major attack to capture the areas around Bilafond La.[34] The attack failed due to insufficient understanding of the impact of terrain on military operations. This attack ended up as a major defeat for Pakistan, with nearly a hundred soldiers killed on the glacier near the pass.[35]

Chumik Glacier

The Chumik Glacier is one of the many that flow West from the Saltoro.[36] The ridgeline in the area is closer to the Siachen and is a difficult part of Saltoro, whose ridgeline cannot be easily scaled either by Pakistan or by India.

After Pakistan's failed attempt in April 1987 to gain a foothold on the Saltoro ridgeline, another attempt was made in March 1989 on the Chumik glacier, 3 km East of Giari. Routine aerial reconnaissance in April 1989 revealed that Pakistan had established a post on the ridge in the Chumik glacier Sector. The glacier was difficult to spot and so it gave an opportunity to the Pakistan Army to open Artillery fire on part of helicopter supply routes used by the Indian posts. The post on the ridge was unapproachable from the Indian side other than by helicopter and, at the same time, the Artillery fire had to be neutralised. The Indian Army conducted Operation Ibex, which set out to seize the Pakistani post overlooking the Chumik Glacier. Although the operation was unsuccessful at dislodging Pakistani Troops from their positions, the Indian Army under Brig RK Nanavatty launched an Artillery attack on Kauser Base—the Pakistani logistical node in Chumik—and successfully destroyed it. The destruction of Kauser Base induced the Pakistani Troops to vacate the Chumik posts, thus concluding Operation Ibex successfully. 'In May 1989', as the Indian Army 'had succeeded in neutralising the supply base supporting the [Pakistani] soldiers on the peak, the post was vacated.[37]

Operation Pawan: Indian Peace Keeping Force, 1987

Background

Sri Lanka is an island nation in the Indian Ocean, separated from the Asian mainland via the Palk Strait and the Gulf of Mannar, thus sharing a maritime border with India. Its Northern part is roughly contiguous to the state of Tamil Nadu in peninsular India. A British colony like India, Sri Lanka gained independence from British rule in 1948. As with much of South Asia, Sri Lanka too is a multi-cultural and multi-ethnic society. There are three main ethnic groups in the country: the majority Sinhala (largely Buddhist), Sri Lankan Tamils (mainly Hindus), and Sri Lankan Muslims. During the colonial period, the British moved Tamils from the

Indian mainland to work on Sri Lankan tea plantations. A sizeable population of these Tamils was located in the Northern part of the country.

The origins of the conflict in Sri Lanka can be traced to the time of independence. During British rule, the Tamils made better use of available educational facilities and by the time Sri Lanka became an independent Dominion in 1947, the Tamils dominated in the white and blue-collar jobs.[38] With the end of British rule in Sri Lanka, the government was formed by the majority Sinhalese and steps taken to correct 'their perception of imbalance between the two communities. Sinhalese was declared as the official language, Buddhism the pre-eminent religion and rules were promulgated that made it difficult for Tamils to get admission in institutes for higher learning.'[39] While the Sri Lankan Tamil Congress was part of the post-independence government, such policies led to resentment among the Tamils; over the years the grievance of the Tamils against the majority Sinhala increased, and with little opportunity for political resolution, it soon turned into a demand for secession.

Power in Sri Lanka has been traditionally shared by two principal parties: the Sri Lanka Freedom Party (SLFP) and the United National Party (UNP). Until 1977, each party had been in power for about 15 years. In the 1970s, Tamil parties came together to form the Tamil United Liberation Front (TULF)[40], which articulated the demand for a separate state of Tamil Eelam in the Northern and Eastern areas of the country and which would give the Tamils greater say in the country's federal system. The TULF fought in the 1977 general elections and won 18 seats out of the 24 seats in which it contested. However, there were also other Tamil groups in the fray which were impatient with the political process. The cry for creation of Tamil Eelam saw the emergence of various militant groups like Tamil Eelam Liberation Front (TELF), later renamed Tamil Eelam Liberation Organisation (TELO), Liberation Tigers of Tamil Eelam (LTTE), Eelam Revolutionary Organisation of Students (EROS), People's Liberation Organisation of Tamil Eelam (PLOTE), and the Eelam People's Revolutionary Liberation Front (EPRLF).[41] The LTTE, originally called the Tamil New Tigers, was formed in 1972 in Jaffna by a group of ten students among whom was Vellupillai Prabhakaran.[42] It had emerged as a leading rebel faction with an aim to carve a Tamil homeland in Northern and Eastern Sri Lanka. The LTTE was banned by the Sri Lankan Government in 1978; despite this, it continued to grow in strength. On 23 July 1983, it carried out its first major terrorist act by ambushing a Sri Lankan Army patrol killing 15. In reprisal, the Sri Lankan Army went on a rampage in Colombo (Black July Riots) attacking Tamils, and the rioting spread to other parts of Sri Lanka with an estimated 3,000–6,000 Tamils killed.[43] As refugees reached Tamil Nadu the impact of political discord in Sri Lanka was felt in India. It is around this time that India also set about trying to resolve the conflict using diplomatic means.[44]

In January 1987, the LTTE, by this time the primary militant group in the country, announced that it was taking over the administration of Jaffna. The Sri Lankan government reacted by imposing an economic blockade of the Jaffna Peninsula, resulting in economic hardship; and refugees again moved out to India. In June of that year, Sri Lanka 'launched an offensive to regain control of Jaffna [using] air and Artillery power. There were reports of heavy civilian casualties that led to an adverse reaction in Tamil Nadu', which put pressure on the Government of India to take some action.[45] On 04 June 1987, the IAF launched Operation Poomalai and air-dropped supplies over Jaffna, following an unsuccessful naval operation to provide supplies via sea.

This foreshadowed the possibility of further Indian action and thus the Government of Sri Lanka, under President JR Jayawardene offered to hold talks with the Government of India. The negotiations resulted in the signing of the Sri-Lankan Accord in Colombo on 29 July 1987. JN Dixit, India's High Commissioner to Sri Lanka from 1985 to 1989, played a major role in drafting the Indo-Sri Lankan Accord in 1987, and the subsequent induction of the Indian Peace Keeping Force (IPKF) to implement it.[46] The Indo-Sri Lankan Accord stipulated that the Sri Lankan government would give the nation's provinces more autonomy and power, while withdrawing its military. The Tamil rebels, on the other hand, were to surrender their arms. The Accord did not talk of an Indian peacekeeping force but did say that India would assist in the implementation of this accord.[47]

After the Accord was signed, President Jayawardene requested then Indian Prime Minister Rajiv Gandhi for armed assistance to help implement it and to maintain law and order as the Sri Lankan Army was to be confined to barracks as per the agreement. Thus, the 54 Infantry Division, which was to form the IPKF began induction into Sri Lanka.

The IPKF's initial tasks were defined thus: separate the two warring groups, that is, the Sri Lankan armed forces and the LTTE and ensure the cease-fire; take over the weapons and munitions handed over by the LTTE and other militant groups; ensure the dismantling of all camps established by the Sri Lankan Forces after May 1987; and aid the local population in returning to their homes and provide a sense of security.

Operation Pawan

Operation Pawan was an operation by the IPKF to take control of Jaffna from the LTTE, better known as the Tamil Tigers. The initial task was to separate the Sri Lankan Armed Forces and the LTTE and ensure ceasefire, take over weapons and munitions, ensure dismantling of camps, and aid in the safe return of the local Tamil population. Maj Gen Harkirat Singh, who was commanding the Secunderabad-based 54 Infantry Division became the first Commander of the IPKF based at Palali.[48] It was originally assumed that the IPKF would carry out peacekeeping activities as done in United Nations (UN) Peacekeeping missions. However, the IPKF ultimately ended up undertaking a 'peace enforcement' in Sri Lanka, which it was inadequately prepared and equipped for.

Troop movements for military operations in Sri Lanka by the Indian Army began on 30 July 1987 under Lt Gen Depinder Singh, who was designated Overall Force Commander (OFC) as he was then General Officer Commanding in Chief, Southern Command, close to Sri Lanka. Maj Gen Harkirat Singh commanded the 54 Infantry Division, which was located at Secunderbad with its Unit spread in South India. The Division was ordered to move minus heavy weapons. The Division had to distribute its units around the Northern and Eastern Provinces. Only the 91 Infantry Brigade went to Jaffna Sector, while 76 Infantry Brigade and 47 Infantry Brigade occupied the Trincomalee Sector, the former at the port city of Trincomalee and the latter at Vavuniya in the interior.[49] The Indian forces available at the commencement of operations were:[50]

1. Jaffna Sector: 54 Infantry Division with two Infantry Brigades, a Squadron of Armour, light Artillery Regiment less one Battery, one Mechanised Company and a Parachute Commando Battalion. Three additional Infantry Brigades were under induction, the first to arrive between 10-12 October, the second by 15 October, and the third by 18 October 1987.
2. Trincomalee Sector: 36 Infantry Division with a Brigade each at Vavuniya, Batticaloa and Trincomalee. The Division also had an Armoured Regiment less one Squadron, an Artillery Regiment and two Companies of Mechanised Infantry.

Soon after its intervention in Sri Lanka and especially after the confrontation with the LTTE, the IPKF received a substantial commitment from the IAF, mainly transport and helicopter Squadrons under the command of Gp Capt MP Premi.[51] The Indian Navy regularly rotated naval vessels through Sri Lanka waters, mostly smaller vessels such as patrol boats.

On 9 October 1987, the Chief of Army Staff, General K Sundarji launched Operation Pawan, which was expected to neutralise the operational capability of LTTE in and around Jaffna. The mission was to capture Jaffna first. The opening moves of Operation Pawan took place with a heliborne assault on Jaffna University, which was the headquarters of the LTTE. The attack was led by a detachment of the Indian Para forces on the night of 11/12 October.

On 11 October, the 18 Infantry Brigade's 12 GRENADIERS, who were advancing to Navatkulli, were ambushed seven times in the move up to Navatkuli, while 4 MAHAR established contact with Kopai North. The 91 Infantry's Brigades 5 MAHAR contacted Chunnakam and 8 MAHAR, in a wide loop to the West, contacted Navanthurai. The seaborne landing had to be aborted and 1 MARATHA

LI attempted some forays from the Jaffna Fort. The HQ 72 Infantry Brigade, 4/5 GORKHA RIFLES (FF) and 13 SIKH LI, less two Companies, arrived in Palali between 11 and 12 October 1987.

On 12/13 October 1987, 4 MAHAR of 18 Infantry Brigade cleared Kopai North and contacted Kopai South where it came under intense fire from three directions. The Fourth Rifle Company that was moving behind helped with extra ammunition and supplies. 12 GRENADIERS that was advancing Navatkuli could advance only 3 km to its West. 4/5 GORKHA RIFLES (FF) of 72 Infantry Brigade advanced to, and contacted Pond Crossing, with the 13 SIKH LI, still deficient of two rifle Companies. one Platoon also joined 4/5 GORKHA RIFLES(FF). 5 MADRAS of 91 Infantry Brigade secured Chunnakam and 8 MAHAR was ordered to assist 5 MADRAS that wheeled towards North East and secured Udiliv.[52]

The heliborne operation in Jaffna was planned to raid a house in Kokuvil where the LTTE leadership was believed to be staying. The operation was launched on the night of 11/12 October 1987. The plan was to first land a para commando team to secure the landing zone, which was to be followed by landing a Company of 13 SIKH LI that would take over and secure the helipad. Between 0100 and 0230 Hours, 12 October 1987, 103 Para Commandos and 30 personnel of 13 SIKH LI were heli-lifted.[53] The helidrop ended in a catastrophe when the LTTE intercepted the radio transmission of the commando force. The helicopters came under intense anti-aircraft firing that forced them to abandon the mission halfway through. Out of the total 17, the commandos lost two of their members and while 13 SIKH LI lost 29 out of 30 men.

Army HQ then inducted more Troops into the Jaffna Peninsula. On 15 October 1987, 41 Infantry Brigade was inducted and arrived in Palali, where it was tasked to advance to Jaffna on 17 October. The 115 Infantry Brigade was inducted on 18 October and was ordered to outflank the main Jaffna defence on 19 October. After two weeks of bitter fighting, the IPKF wrested control of Jaffna and other major cities from the LTTE, but operations were to continue well into November, with major operations coming to an end with the fall of Jaffna Fort on 28 November 1987.[54]

The IPKF suffered a considerable number of casualties during the operation. The seizure of Jaffna, while successfully ejecting the LTTE and weakening it, did not destroy it. Rather, a new war began in which the LTTE cadre broke up into small groups and began fighting a guerrilla war.

By March 1988, two more Divisions were inducted and the deployment was as follows:

1. Jaffna Peninsula: 54 Infantry Division
2. Vavuniya and Manar: 4 Infantry Division

3. Trincomalee: 36 Infantry Division
4. Batticaloa and Amparai: 57 Mountain Division

In 1988, the IPKF conducted four major operations in the Northern Province and two in the Eastern Province of Sri Lanka. Additional reinforcements arrived from India: the 4 Infantry Division, 57 Mountain Division, and the 55 (Independent) Mechanised Infantry Brigade.[55] The IPKF now effectively moved towards undertaking counterinsurgency operations in Sri Lanka and continued to do so throughout 1988. It was in one such operation that Major Ramaswamy Parmeswaram of the Mahar Regiment was awarded the PVC posthumously.

Operation Vajra took place in February-March 1988, which used four Brigades to sweep the North. The LTTE lost valuable base camps in this, but their leader escaped. Operation Virat Trishul took place in March 1988, which was a follow-up designed to neutralise the remaining enemy hideouts. Operation Checkmate took place in May-August 1988, which was focused on trapping the LTTE in the jungles around Mullaitivu on the East coast and Vavuniya. Operation Toofan took place in June 1989, which was another attempt to subdue LTTE field strongholds. Operations Tulip Bloom and Sword Edge were similar sweeps in the East.[56]

Sri Lankan Politics and IPKF Withdrawal

Sri Lanka's political crisis required political solutions rather than purely military ones. Keeping this in mind, elections were held in keeping with the Indo-Sri Lanka Accord in November 1988. The Eelam People's Revolutionary Liberation Front (EPRLF) emerged as the largest party in these elections and its leader, Annamalai Varadaraja Perumal, became the Chief Minister of the North-Eastern Province on 10 December 1988. Subsequently the IPKF provided security for the successful conduct of the Presidential elections in December 1988 and Parliamentary elections in February 1989. However, the Sri Lankan government showed little inclination to devolve the necessary powers and to give the requisite administrative support to the North-Eastern Council. The new President, Ranasinghe Premadasa, was opposed to the Accord and worked to undermine it. He began negotiations with the LTTE and encouraged it to act against the Indian Army as well as the NorthEast Provincial Council.

Premadasa further demanded that the IPKF withdraw from Sri Lanka and return to India as the Sri Lankan government no longer required its presence. This demand was rejected but the IPKF's staying on in Sri Lanka would not produce any results without the cooperation of the government. Additionally, Opposition parties at the Centre in India as well as all political parties in Tamil Nadu were increasingly clamouring for the IPKF's pull out.

The Sri Lankan Government declared a surprise cease-fire and the LTTE in July 1989 ended all offensives. In the talks between the governments of India and Sri

Lanka, held on 12 September 1989, it was agreed that IPKF would be de-inducted from Sri Lanka by 31 March 1990 and in this event, the last Indian Troops embarked on their voyage home on 24 March 1990.[57] In all, the IPKF lost 1,155 men in Sri Lanka between 1987, when it moved into Sri Lanka, and 1990, when it withdrew from the country.[58]

Assessment

An assessment of the IPKF must recall the context in which was deployed in Sri Lanka. The choice before the Government of India in June 1987 was difficult: the Sri Lankan offensive into Jaffna was affecting the local Tamil population detrimentally, causing destruction, economic hardship and loss of life. The situation in Sri Lanka was leading to a domestic fallout in neighbouring Tamil Nadu and people of the state as well as local political parties were clamouring for action. The Indo-Sri Lanka Accord might have succeeded if all parties to it were sincere about implementing it. India's mistake was in not realising that neither the Sri Lankan Government nor the LTTE were serious about making the Accord work. When it began to unravel India was faced with a choice to either withdraw and leave Sri Lanka and the Tamils to their own fate or undertake military action to make the LTTE agree to work within the Accord. The choice of the latter by India led to the induction of the IPKF into Sri Lanka. The events in Jaffna in 1987 highlighted the underpreparedness of the Army in urban warfare, particularly fighting guerrillas in an urban environment. There was also lack of intelligence on the LTTE's capabilities despite the fact that 'the 54 Infantry Division had been in close contact with the LTTE for a few months and should have been able to judge their potential and their methods.'[59] As the IPKF got further enmeshed in Sri Lanka, Troops were being rushed in from India and being pushed into battle almost immediately with little or no time to orient themselves or learn lessons from what had occurred.

Maldives: Operation Cactus 1998

Maldives is an island nation in the Indian Ocean, composed entirely of about 1,190 low-lying coral islands, grouped in 26 atolls sprawled over nearly 90,000 sq km. Its Northern tip is located about 600 km South of the Indian landmass. In 1988, the country had a police force called National Security Service (NSS) but no armed forces.

Operation Cactus was a military operation undertaken by the Indian Armed Forces in 1988 in response to an attempted coup in Maldives by a group led by Abdullah Luthufi, in order to overthrow the government of President Maumoon

Abdul Gayoom. Luthufi was a Maldivian businessman and Gayoom's political rival. The group was aided by armed mercenaries of the People's Liberation Organisation of Tamil Eelam (PLOTE), a Sri Lankan Tamil secessionist organisation. Maldives had seen earlier coup attempts in 1980 and 1983 as well; however, it is coup attempt of 1988 that saw the involvement of the Indian Army.

On the dawn of 03 November 1988, an armed party consisting of approximately 80 Sri Lankan Tamil militants from PLOTE, operating as mercenaries for Luthifi had launched a seaborne attack on the capital, Male. By 0700 hours, they were in control of most of Male, including the Presidential Palace; President Gayoom, however, managed to escape. On failing to secure the President, the mercenaries resorted to taking hostages from among key government functionaries. The NSS Headquarters was also under siege. At 0830 hours, the Indian High Commissioner in Sri Lanka, JN Dixit, received a call from his counterpart in Maldives, who informed him that some armed men had attacked and taken over Male.[60] President Gayoom's request for armed assistance was also conveyed to New Delhi.

India accepted President Gayoom's request swiftly. The Service Headquarters were warned and contingency planning commenced immediately and warning orders were issued to the Troops and aircraft likely to be deployed.[61] It must be remembered that this was in the midst of the Indian involvement in Sri Lanka via the IPKF.

Given the urgency of the situation, the Indian officials swiftly put together a plan of action. An airborne operation was considered best suitable. Thus, Air Marshal Denzil Keelor was called up and asked to prepare an IAF team for the Maldives.[62] It was agreed that for the operation, soldiers would be sent out from the Parachute Regiments; the Troops were trained for landing in hostile terrain, being self-reliant and taking quick, effective action in tough conditions. The 50 (Independent) Parachute Brigade (popularly known as the Para Brigade), commanded by Brig Farukh Bulsara, located at Agra, was the only one of its kind in India.[63] As per Bulsara's initial plan, a Company Group with Battalion HQ was to airland at the Hulule airport, provided the airfield was in safe hands.

A truncated Company of 60–65 men would jump from the IL-76 aircraft, if the need arose. Another IL-76 would airlift a Company group with a skeleton Tactical HQ.[64] After reviewing and refining several times before the aircrafts got airborne, it was decided to airland 6 PARA and 411 PARA Field Engineers.

Government clearance for the operation was received at 1215 Hours and the first two IL-76 Aircraft, with elements of the 6 PARA and the 17 Parachute Field Regiment, took off from Agra between 1556 hours and 1558 hours. They flew non-stop over 2,000 km. Of the Para Brigade's Battalions, 6 PARA was designated to lead the operation as the other Batallions were scattered far and wide; 7 PARA had been designated for deployment in the NorthEast; and 3 PARA was commited elsewhere.[65]

The very first information that came in suggested that Hulule airfield was under control of the NSS. However, the Indian Troops were prepared for an airborne assault to capture the airfield if need arose.

The first two aircrafts that landed, discharged 316 troops and one RCL Jeep. In the process, while some Troops secured the airfield for the purpose of further landing, one of the parties immediately crossed over to Male and by 0235 hours on 04 November 1988, it had reached the vicinity of President Gayoom's residence and ensured his safety. Indian Army paratroopers reached Hulhule within a mere nine hours since the appeal from President Gayoom was received. By 0430 hours, the Presidential Palace was secured and Male was freed, followed by the surrender of attackers during the morning of 05 November 1988. Frigates of the Indian Navy intercepted the hijacked freighter in which the mercenary force had escaped, off the Sri Lankan coast.

Though there was limited fighting in Operation Cactus. what remains commendable is the speed and the efficiency with which the Indian Armed Forces reacted and carried out the operation. It was also demonstrative of India's willingness and ability to aid a neighbouring country. The successful execution of Operation Cactus was instrumental in averting a political crisis in India's immediate neighbourhood. The operation also strengthened Indo-Maldivian relations as a result of the successful restoration of the President Gayoom's government.

The Indian Troops deployed in Operation Cactus were de-inducted between 05-12 November 1988. A small contingent stayed behind at the request of the Maldivian Government to provide security in the immediate aftermath of the attempted coup and to further train the National Security Service, and returned to India on the completion of their tasks.[66]

Operation Vijay: Kargil 1999

Background

The Jammu and Kashmir (J&K) region has had political and cultural connections with the Indian heartland for millennia. The state which acceded to India on October 26 1947, had five main regions: Kashmir, Jammu, Ladakh, Pakistan Occupied Kashmir and the Northern areas.[67] Of a total area of 2,22,236 sq km, 78,114 sq km is under Pakistan's occupation; of this, 5,180 sq km in the Shaksgam Valley was ceded by it to China in 1963 as part of a boundary settlement. Approximately 33,555 sq km in Ladakh (Aksai Chin) remains under Chinese occupation. Before 2019, J&K broadly consisted of three regions: Jammu, Kashmir Valley and the Ladakh region. Kargil is the second largest town of Ladakh after Leh, and lies at the junction of the Suru and Shingo Rivers in the Kargil district. It is roughly 200 km from Srinagar in the Kashmir Valley, located to the NorthWest of Zoji La with National Highway 1A from Srinagar to Leh passing through it.

In 1999, the Kargil Sector was subdivided into the Dras, Kaksar, Channigund and Batalik sub-Sectors. Kargil was the Headquarters of 121 (Independent) Infantry Brigade, responsible for the Kargil Sector, that extends 168 km along the Line of Control (LOC), stretching from Kaobal Gali in the West (near Zoji La) to Chorbat La in the East (on the Ladakh range).[68] The basic deployment of the 121 Infantry Brigade was: one Infantry Battalion at Dras, two Infantry Battalions and a Border Security Force (BSF) Battalion covering Kargil, and one Infantry Battalion at Batalik astride the Indus.[69] The Brigade came under 3 Infantry Division based at Leh in Ladakh.

Build-up to the Crisis

The Kargil crisis had several layers of significance for both Pakistan and India, though these were very different for the two countries.[70] The LOC owes its existence to the Karachi Agreement of 27 July 1949, a consequence of the first India-Pakistan Conflict over Kashmir. The Karachi Agreement was signed by the Indian and Pakistan military Commanders as well as by representatives of the United Nations Commission for India and Pakistan (UNCIP).[71] Although both India and Pakistan had celebrated 50 years of independence in August 1997, an increase of Artillery exchanges in the Kargil Sector was seen from the beginning of the year followed by heavy exchanges in 1998, especially in the aftermath of the nuclear tests.

Kargil had not been immune to the rising militancy in J&K in the 1990s, although the intensity here was less as compared to the Valley. In 1990, two militants were killed and one militant was captured in the West of Kaobal Gali. In November 1993, 27 militants were killed in Mashkoh Valley by 2/5 GORKHA RIFLES. In June 1997, four militants were killed at Kaobal Gali by 9 RAJ RIF. Also, in 1997, Tashi Namghyal of Garkhun village had reported the presence of unarmed Pakistani personnel in Yaldor, in the Batalik Sector,[72] which led to the establishment of a patrol base in Yaldor in the same year.

The conflict in 1999 was initiated when, as part of Operation Badr, Pakistani Army soldiers infiltrated into the Indian side of the LoC disguised as Kashmiri militants and covertly captured the vacated winter Posts of the Indian Army. The aim was to cut the link between Kashmir and Ladakh, to isolate Indian Army Troops on the Siachen Glacier, and force India to negotiate a settlement of the Kashmir dispute.[73]

Intrusions and Response

The first indication of Pakistani intrusions into the area was reported and communicated to HQ 3 Division, which, in turn, passed on the information to 15 Corps and Northern Command. Then, on 03 May 1999, a similar intrusion was sighted. A group of three shepherds belonging to the village of Garkhun, located just above Indus River and Garkhun Barnala Junction, saw a group of armed men in Pathan attire digging bunkers in the area of Banju. This activity was reported to 3 PUNJAB, leading to the launch of a series of patrols. Immediate action was taken by the HQ 3 Infantry Division and two Battalions that moved from Siachen were positioned in the Batalik Sector by 10 May 1999. HQ 70 Infantry Brigade, that had just moved to Dras was diverted to Batalik to take control of operations in this Sector.[74] The detection of intrusion in Batalik region increased the alertness in other Sectors as well.

After the initial detection of intrusion, the Indian Army's response was rapid. The 'situation report' initiated by HQ 15 Corps on May 11 1999 shows that a comprehensive set of action had been initiated in the Yaldor Sector to establish contact with the intruders in order to fix the extent of the intrusion and contain it.[75]

On 04 and 06 May 1999, 3 PUNJAB launched two patrols in the Batalik Sector to investigate the reported intrusion. It was confirmed on 07 May and one Company each of 10 Garhwal Rifles (GARH RIF) and 16 GRENADIERS was immediately moved to contain the intrusion. On 08 May, HQ 70 Infantry Brigade which was taking over at Dras was moved and made responsible for the Batalik Sector. Soon thereafter, two Battalions, 1/11 GORKHA RIFLES and 12 JAK LI, that had just been de-inducted from Siachen and were readily available, were moved on 9 May and were in position in the Batalik Sector by 10 May.[76]

Enemy intrusion was detected in the Dras and Mashkoh Sectors on 12 May 1999 by a patrol of Ladakh Scouts, and in the Mashkoh Sector by Army Aviation Corps helicopters on 14 May. The Battalion which had been moved from Valley on 09 May 1999 soon after the detections in the Batalik Sector, was diverted to Dras and employed from 12 May onwards to contain the intrusion in that area. 8 SIKH and 28 Rashtriya Rifles (RR) Battalions were moved in on 14 May 1999.[77]

On 14 May, enemy intrusion was detected in Kaksar Sector by a patrol of 4 JAT in the area of Pt 5299 South West Spur, commonly known as Bajrang Post. Initially, one Company of 28 RR was released to contain the intrusion and, subsequently, on 21 May 1999, 14 JAK RIF moved for deployment in the Kaksar Sector.[78]

During the last week of April 1999, seven Pakistani helicopters were seen flying with underslung loads in Turtok. A patrol from 12 JAT sent to monitor activity along the Line of Control (LOC) was ambushed on 06 May. Subsequent patrols sent on 16 May and 19 May confirmed that the enemy had occupied the ridge line along and across the LOC at five locations. 11 RAJ RIF and 9 MAHAR were tasked to occupy defences and the enemy was subsequently evicted by physical assault.[79]

Once the enemy intrusion in Kargil and Turtok were established, five units of Ladakh Scouts were moved to reinforce the Chorbat La Sector. They occupied defences along the LOC during the period 18–31 May, and foiled all enemy attempts to intrude into the area. By 17 May 1999, it was confirmed that the armed intruders had occupied heights and were assessed to be about 200–250 in number in the Batalik Sector, between 80–100 in the Kaksar Sector, between 60–80 in the Dras Sector, and around 200–250 in the Mushkoh Sector.

All troops in J&K were placed on a state of high alert by the HQ Northern Command on 12 May. Initially, heavy firing and a number of casualties were witnessed in the attempt to clear the enemy position. On 22 May, the Indian Navy's Western and Eastern fleets met up in the North Arabian Sea and began aggressive patrols. They prepared to blockade the Pakistani ports in order to cut off supply routes under Operation Talwar, which was the naval operation carried out by the Navy during the Kargil War of 1999. It was one of the three operations carried out by the Indian Armed Forces during the conflict, the other two being Operation Safed Sagar by the IAF and Operation Vijay by the Army.

Operation Vijay

The first priority of Operation Vijay was to recapture peaks that were in the immediate vicinity of National Highway (NH) 1. This resulted in Indian Troops first targeting the Tiger Hill and Tololing complex in Dras, which dominated the Srinagar-Leh route.[80] Operation Vijay was a joint Infantry-Artillery endeavour to evict regular Pakistani soldiers of the Northern LI (NLI) who had intruded across the LoC into Indian territory and had occupied un-held Mountain peaks at high-altitude and ridgelines. After many unsuccessful attempts to regain Tololing, the 18 GRENADIERS reached a point about 30 meters below the Pakistani position on 10 June.

The 2 RAJ RIF used this firm base on 12 June to launch the assault on Tololing. The attack commenced at 2300 Hours followed by securing of Point 4590 by early hours of 13 June 1999. The 18 GRENADIERS further pushed through 12 RAJ RIF to secure position 3 km ahead of Point 4590, which was to be used for attacking Point 5140, the highest feature of Tololing Complex. A concerted multi-directional attack was launched on 19 June 1999 by 18 GARH RIF, 13 JAK RIF and 1 NAGA, and the position was captured by 0335 hours on 20 June.

While the Tololing area was cleared, the point 4075 complex NorthWest of Dras that dominated some 20 km of NH 1A remained. The task of capturing this feature was given to 79 Mountain Brigade ; the attack commenced on the night of 4 July, followed by the capture of the objective by 17 JAT by 0500 hours on 5 July.

Ground Troops were supported by the IAF from 11–25 May and tried to contain the threat, judge the positions of the enemy dispositions, and carried out several preparatory actions. On 26 May 1999, the IAF came into picture. A series of special operations, limited attacks and patrols were launched to gain information. Identifications revealed enemy Brigades each in the Batalik and Kargil-Dras-Mushkoh

Sectors. Each Brigade initially comprised two Battalions of the Pakistan Army's NLI, two Companies of the SSG, and about 600-700 Frontier Corps Troops. These were supported by some 15 Artillery units and had the usual engineer, signal and administrative units.[81]

The IAF was tasked to act jointly with ground Troops during Operation Safed Sagar.[82] On 27 May 1999, the IAF lost a MiG-27 strike aircraft piloted by Flight Lieutenant (Fl Lt) Nachiketa, which it attributed to an engine failure, and a MiG-21 fighter piloted by Squadron Leader (Sqn Ldr) Ajay Ahuja, which was shot down by the Pakistani Army, both over the Batalik Sector. One Indian Mi-8 helicopter was also lost to Stinger surface to air missiles (SAMs). French-made Mirage 2000 jets of the IAF were tasked to drop laser-guided bombs to destroy well-entrenched positions of the Pakistani forces[83] and flew their first sortie on 30 May 1999.[84]

Assessment of the Kargil Conflict

Following the outbreak of armed fighting, Pakistan sought American help in de-escalating the conflict. Following the Washington Accord of 04 July 1999, most of the fighting came to a gradual halt, but some Pakistani forces remained in positions on the Indian side of the LOC. The Indian Army launched its final attacks in the last week of July in coordination with relentless attacks by the IAF, both by day and night. Once the Drass Sub-Sector had been cleared of Pakistani forces, the fighting ceased on 26 July 1999. This day has since been marked as Kargil Vijay Diwas in India.

The Pakistani establishment was compelled to negotiate a face saving withdrawal from the residual areas on the Indian side of the LOC, thereby restoring its sanctity, as was established in July 1972 in the Simla Agreement. The Pakistan Army withdrew from Kargil due, in part, to the pressure from Washington as the US adopted a unilateral approach which clearly articulated that Pakistan must withdraw from Kargil.

The Kargil conflict ended with numerous casualties on both sides. Around 527 officers and men of the Indian Armed Forces laid down their lives in Kargil to protect the integrity of the country and 453 were killed on the Pakistan side. Soon after the conflict, the Government of India set up an inquiry committee to examine its causes and to analyse perceived Indian intelligence failures. The Kargil Review Committee (KRC) report flagged numerous flaws on multiple levels of intelligence collection, operational strategies, and procedural sharing of data. The Committee was initially given a period of three months to submit the report but its deadline was extended to 15 December 1999.

The Committee's report surmised that a Kargil-type situation could perhaps have been avoided had the Indian Army followed a policy of Siachenisation to plug unheld gaps along the 168 km stretch from Kaobal Gali to Chorbat La.[85] The findings of the KRC highlighted grave deficiencies in India's security management system. The

Table 5.1 Chronology of the Kargil War

MAY 1999	JUNE 1999	JULY 1999
• **03 MAY 1999-** Shepherds report Intruders sighted for the first time at Banju Headquarters, 70 Infantry Brigade arrives at Dras.	• **01 JUNE 1999-** Headquarters 8 Mountain Division completes take over. Start of the military build-up.	• **01 JULY 1999-** 70 Mountain Brigade captures Point 5000.
• **05 MAY 1999-** Captain Saurabh Kalia Patrol sent out to examine the suspicion of intrusion, the war commences.	• **03 JUNE 1999-** 8 Mountain Division assumes responsibility for the part of the Kargil Theatre west of Thasgam.	• **03 JULY 1999-** (a) 70 Mountain Brigade captures Point 5287. (b) End of 8 SIKH siege of Tiger Hill.
• **06 MAY 1999-** NH 1A opened to traffic.	• **12 JUNE 1999-** (a) Ongoing talks between Indian and Pakistani Foreign Ministers deadlocked. (b) 50 (I) Parachute Brigade arrives in Gumri from Army reserve and comes under command of 8 Mountain Division.	• **4 JULY 1999-** (a) 192 Brigade captures Tiger Hill (b) Nawaz Sharif, in Washington, urged by Clinton to start talking with India.
• **16 MAY 1999-** 56 Mountain Brigade takes over Dras-Mushkoh Sector.	• **13 JUNE 1999-** 56 Mountain Brigade takes Tololing and Point 4590.	• **05 JULY 1999-** 79 Mountain Brigade takes Point 4875 complex. By now, virtually the whole of Mushkoh and Dras were clear of enemy.
• **18 MAY 1999-** The Capture of Points 4295 and 4460	• **14 JUNE 1999-** They take 'Hump'.	• **12 -18 JULY 1999-** Cease-fire to allow safe withdrawal of Pakistan Troops across LoC. • (They reneged and the war was resumed)
• **21 MAY 1999-** 8 SIKH start siege of Tiger Hill	• **15 JUNE 1999-** United States President Bill Clinton urges Prime Minister Nawaz Sharif to withdraw.	• **24 JULY 1999-** 192 Mountain Brigade takes Zulu Spur Complex
• **23 MAY 1999-** Chief of Army Staff (COAS) visits Kargil sector and lays down the priorities and doctrine for the conduct of operation.	• **20 JUNE 1999-** 56 Mountain Brigade takes Point 5140.	• **26 JULY 1999-** Kargil War officially ends
• **24 MAY 1999-** 79 Mountain Brigade takes over Mushkoh Sub-Sector.		

(*Continued*)

Table 5.1 *(Continued)*

MAY 1999	JUNE 1999	JULY 1999
• **25 MAY 1999-** Operation Vijay Launched. • **26 MAY 1999-** Indian Air Force begins Air Operations in support of 15 Corps.	• **23 JUNE 1999-** (a) General Zinni, Commanding General United States Central Command visits Pakistan to urge Nawaz Sharif to withdraw. (b) The G-8 Nations call for an end to the intrusion.	

Source: Amarinder Singh, *A Ridge Too Far: War in the Kargil Heights, 1999,* Patiala: Motibagh Palace, 2001, pp. 100–101.

Committee strongly felt that the Kargil experience, the continuing proxy war [with Pakistan], and the prevailing nuclearised security environment justified a thorough review of the National Security System in its entirety.[86]

Table 5.1 below gives a detailed chronology of the events at Kargil in 1999.

Notes

1. Srinath Raghavan, *War and Peace in Modern India,* Ranikhet: Permanent Black, 2010, p. 65.
2. Maj Gen (Retd) LS Lehl, PVSM, VrC, 'Army of the Republic: Phase of Consolidation', in Maj Gen (Retd) Ian Cardozo, AVSM, SM (ed.), *The Indian Army: A Brief History,* New Delhi: USI, 2007, p. 75.
3. Rahul Devulapalli, 'Tracing Razakar Legacy: When Razvi's Granddaughter Visited Hyderabad', *The Week,* 30 September 2021, at https://www.theweek.in/leisure/society/2021/09/30/tracing-razakar-legacy-when-razvis-granddaughter-visited-hyderabad.html.
4. See https://indianArmy.nic.in/Site/FormTemplete/frmTempSimple.aspx?MnId=nmnz/S66ueKkrJc8PBO1kw==&ParentID=z2xdy5FtH8G+oZz4hw/CKg==
5. RNP Singh, *Sardar Patel—Unifier of Modern India,* New Delhi: Vitasta, 2018, p. 151.
6. SN Prasad, *Operation Polo—The Police Action against Hyderabad, 1948,* Delhi: Ministry of Defence, 1972, pp. 74–75.
7. Ibid., p. 44.
8. Ibid., pp. 56–57.
9. Ibid., p. 58.
10. Ibid., p. 65.
11. Ibid., p. 67.

12. Lehl, 'A Nation Divided and the 1947 Indo-Pak War', n. 2, p. 76.
13. Prasad, *Operation Polo: The Police Action against Hyderabad*, n. 6, p. 115.
14. Lehl, 'Army of the Republic: Phase of Consolidation', n. 2, p. 88.
15. 'From Op Chutney to Op Vijay, How Goa was Liberated in 40 Hours', *Telangana Today*, 19 December 2021, at https://telanganatoday.com/from-op-chutney-to-op-vijay-how-goa-was-liberated-in-40-hours.
16. Newton Sequeira, 'When the Navy's Operation Chutney Evicted Portugal from Anjadiv', *The Times of India*, 19 December 2020, at http://timesofindia.indiatimes.com/articleshow/79805877.cms?utm_source=contentofinterest&utm_medium=text&utm_campaign=cppst.
17. Lehl, 'Army of the Republic: Phase of Consolidation', n. 2, p. 89.
18. Maj Gen VK Singh, *Leadership in the Indian Army: Biographies of Twelve Soldiers*, New Delhi: Sage, 2005, pp. 309–10.
19. Col RD Palsokar, *The GRENADIERS: A Tradition of Valour*, Jabalpur: GRENADIERS Regimental Centre, 1980, p. 363.
20. From the diary of Second Lieutenant NC Gupta.
21. Maj Gen (Retd) VK Singh, 'Times of Trial', in Maj Gen Ian Cardozo, AVSM, SM (ed.), *The Indian Army: A Brief History*, New Delhi: USI), 2007, p. 165.
22. Ibid.
23. VR Raghavan, *Siachen: Conflict Without End*, New Delhi, Penguin Books, 2002, p. 33.
24. Ibid.
25. Ibid., p. 47.
26. Sushant Singh, 'Operation Meghdoot: 34 Years Ago, How India Won Siachen', *The Indian Express*, 13 April 2018, at https://indianexpress.com/article/explained/operation-meghdoot-34-years-ago-how-india-won-siachen-5135429/.
27. Singh, 'Times of Trial, n. 21, p. 165.
28. Singh, 'Operation Meghdoot: 34 Years Ago, How India Won Siachen', n. 26.
29. Ibid.
30. Raghavan, *Siachen: Conflict Without End*, n. 23, p. 55.
31. Ibid., p. 125.
32. Ibid., p. 87.
33. Ibid., p. 89.
34. Ibid., p. 93.
35. Ibid.
36. Ibid., p. 95.
37. Javed Hussain, 'The Fight for Siachen', *The Express Tribune*, 22 April 2012, at https://tribune.com.pk/story/368394/the-fight-for-siachen.
38. Singh, 'Times of Trial', n. 21, p. 171.
39. Ibid.
40. Lt Gen Depinder Singh, *Indian Peacekeeping Force in Sri Lanka 1987-1989*, New Delhi, Natraj Publishers, 2001, p. 14.
41. Ibid., pp. 14–15.
42. Singh, 'Times of Trial', n. 21, p. 170.

43. Ibid.
44. Ibid.
45. Ibid., p. 172.
46. See 'India's Vietnam – The IPKF in Sri Lanka: 10 Years On', at https://m.rediff.com/news/2000/mar/24lanka.htm.
47. Singh, 'Times of Trial', n. 21, p. 171.
48. Sushant Singh, *Mission Overseas, Daring Operations by the Indian Military*, New Delhi: Juggernaut Books, 2017, p. 85.
49. Lt Gen Depinder Singh (Retd), *The IPKF in Sri Lanka* Delhi: Trishul Publications, p. 41.
50. Singh, 'Times of Trial', n. 21, p. 172.
51. See http://www.bharat-rakshak.com/IAF/History/1987IPKF/Pushpindar01.html.
52. Singh, *Indian Peacekeeping Force in Sri Lanka 1987-1989*, n. 40, p. 89.
53. Singh, 'Times of Trial', n. 21, p. 173.
54. Dagmar Hellman-Rajanayagam, 'The Tamil Militants—Before the Accord and After', *Pacific Affairs*, Winter 1988–1989, pp. 603–619.
55. Rajesh Kadian, *India's Sri Lanka Fiasco*, Delhi: Vision Books Pvt. Ltd., 1990, p. 117.
56. SD Muni, *Pangs of Proximity: India and Sri Lanka's Ethnic Crisis*, New Delhi: SAGE Publications Pvt. Ltd., 1993, pp. 138–140.
57. Singh, 'Times of Trial', n. 21, p. 175.
58. Singh, *Mission Overseas*, n. 48, p. 148.
59. Singh, 'Times of Trial', n. 21, p. 175.
60. Ibid., p. 178.
61. Ibid.
62. Singh, *Mission Overseas*, n. 48, p. 23.
63. Ibid., p. 27
64. Ashok K Chordia, *Operation Cactus: Anatomy of One of India's Most Daring Military Operations*, New Delhi: KW Publishers, 2018, p. 83.
65. Ibid., p. 34.
66. Singh, 'Times of Trial', n. 21, p. 179.
67. *From Surprise to Reckoning: Kargil Review Committee Report*, New Delhi: Sage, 2000, p. 37.
68. Maj Gen Ashok Kalyan Verma, *Kargil: Blood on the Snow*, New Delhi: Manohar, 2002, p. 85.
69. Singh, 'Times of Trial', n. 21, p. 180.
70. Ashley J Tellis, C. Christine Fair, and, Jamison Jo Medby, *Limited Conflicts Under the Nuclear Umbrella: Indian and Pakistani Lessons from the Kargil Crisis*, Santa Monica: RAND Corporation, 2001, p. 5.
71. *From Surprise to Reckoning*, n. 67, p. 47.
72. Ibid., p. 90.
73. Vijay Oberoi, 'India's Wars since Independence: A Concise History', *Journal of the United Service Institution of India*, Vol. CL, No. 622, October-December 2020, at https://usiofindia.org/publication/usi-journal/indias-wars-since-independence-a-concise-history/.

74. Singh, 'Times of Trial', n. 21, p. 180.
75. *From Surprise to Reckoning*, n. 67, p. 104.
76. Verma, *Kargil: Blood on the Snow*, n. 68. p. 96.
77. Ibid.
78. Ibid.
79. Ibid.
80. Adekeya Adebajo and Chandra Lekha Sriram (eds), *Managing Armed Conflicts in the 21st Century*, London: Frank Cass, pp. 192–193.
81. Singh, 'Times of Trial', n. 21, p. 181.
82. See https://indianAir Force.nic.in.
83. See https://www.globalsecurity.org/military/world/war/kargil-99.htm.
84. See https://web.archive.org/web/20110807084357/http://www.bharat-rakshak.com/IAF/History/Kargil/PCamp.html.
85. *From Surprise to Reckoning*, n. 67, p. 250.
86. Ibid., p. 253.

Field Marshal KM Cariappa, OBE
Source: USI of India.

Field Marshal SHFJ Manekshaw, MC
Source: USI of India.

General KS Thimayya, DSO

Indian Prisoners of War released by the Chinese pay homage to their motherland upon their return to India.
Source: MoD, DPR

Indian troops landing in Goa in 1961 after the liberation to reinforce the initial columns and secure the territory
Source: USI of India.

Indian troops welcomed in Goa, 1961
Source: MoD, DPR.

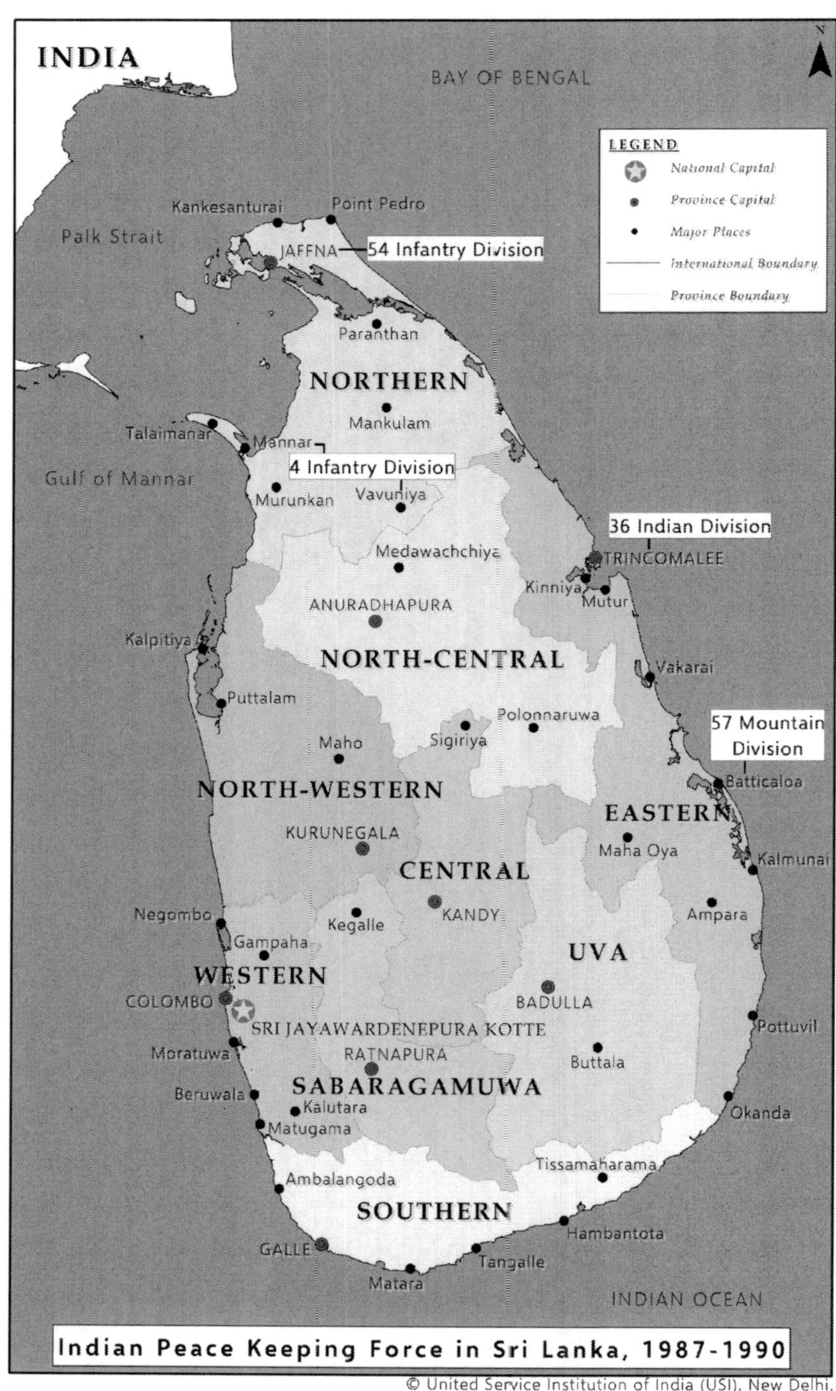

Map 1 Indian Peace Keeping Force in Sri Lanka. 1987–90

A BMP during Operation Pawan in Sri Lanka
Source: Army HQ.

A Jonga based Detachment in Sri Lanka
Source: Army HQ.

A Mortar Platoon training in the desert during Operation Parakram 2001
Source: Army HQ.

Tanks executing a manoeuvre during Operation Parakram, 2001
Source: Capt Suresh Sharma.

A soldier of 8 MARATHA LI on Saltoro Ridge, 1985
Source: Army HQ.

View of a Post in the Siachen Region
Source: Army HQ.

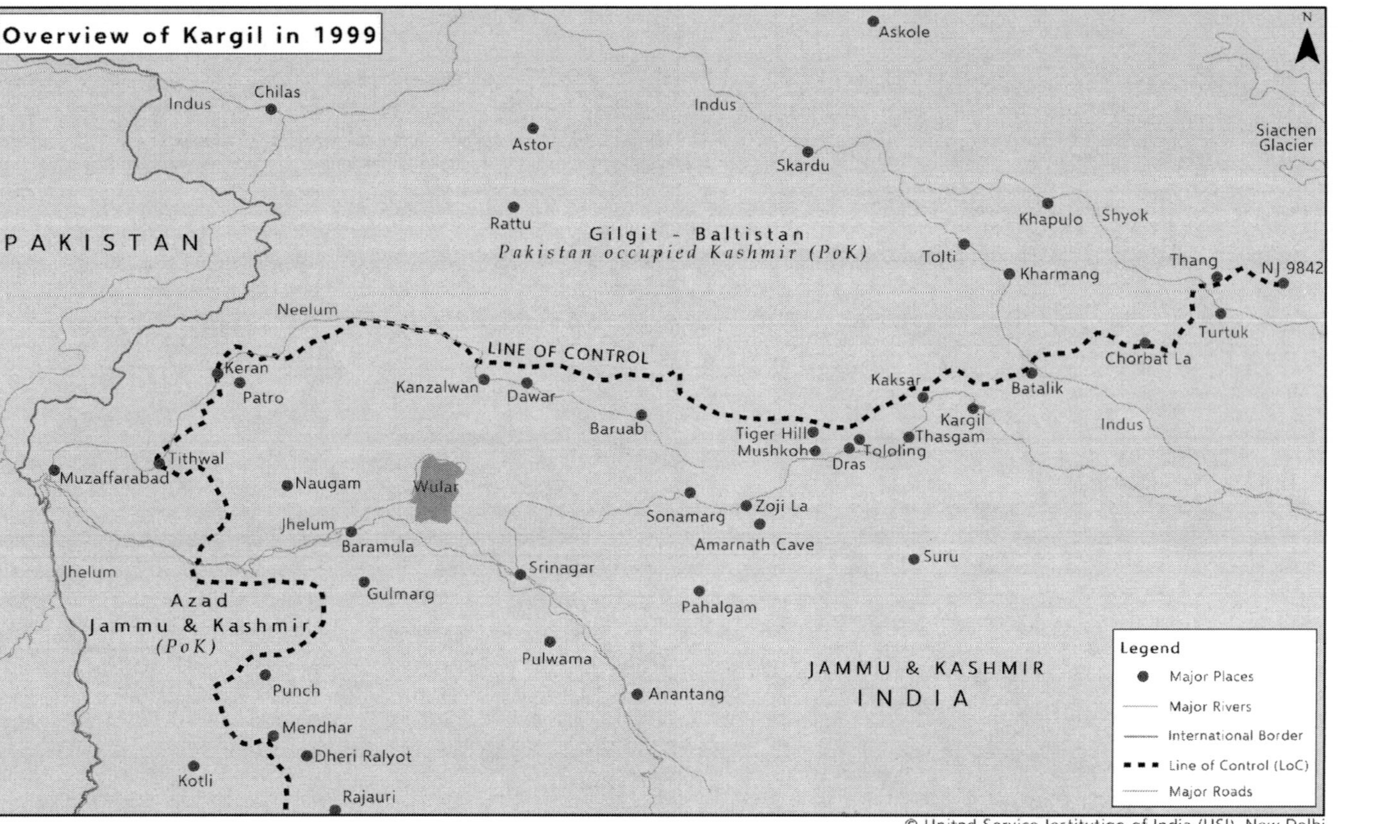

Map 2 Kargil 1999

Infantry soldiers going for assault during Kargil, 1999
Source: MoD, DPR.

Army Aviation Cheetah Helicopters during Operation Vijay, Kargil 1999
Source: MoD, DPR.

Soldiers holding Indian Tricolour atop one of the recaptured Peaks
Source: MoD, DPR.

Gen VP Malik, PVSM, AVSM, then COAS during one of his visits to Batalik during Operation Vijay, Commander 70 Infantry Brigade Brigadeer Devender Singh, SM VSM is standing behind him.
Source: MoD, DPR.

Repatriated POWs handed over to Northern Command, Neutral Nations Repatriation Commission, Korea 1951–53
Source: USI of India.

Captured Katangese Staghound, UN Peacekeeping Mission in Congo

Dental check up of a civilian in a remote village in Lebanon
Source: USI of India.

Patrolling the Temporary Security Zone (TSZ), during the UN mission in Ethiopia and Eritrea (UNMEE)

Bash on Regardless. Jawans ford a water obstacle.
Source: Army HQ

Road clearing party takes position during CI operations

Arjun Tanks carrying out joint manouver with the Air Force in the Deserts of Rajasthan.
Photo: Angad Singh

Sudan Block, National Defence Academy, Khadakwasla, Pune
Source: MoD, DPR.

Indian Military Academy, Dehradun

Chetwode Motto, Indian Military Academy, Dehradun

6

Low-Intensity Conflicts and Counter-terrorism

Col Vivek Chadha (Retd)

The Indian Army has the unique distinction of being involved in fighting low-intensity conflicts for most of its pre- and post-independence history. This involvement can be debated on the basis of definitions and descriptions of conflicts ranging from frontier warfare to counter-insurgency. However, the fact remains that insurrections of the type faced in Afghanistan, North-West Frontier Province (NWFP) and north-east India provided the Army with early years of experience and expertise, which became the foundation for fighting what is now termed in some quarters as 'low-intensity conflicts' or 'sub-conventional warfare'.[1] Within the wider ambit of the term, it has also been referred to as counter-insurgency and counter-terrorism.[2]

The post-independence deployment in Nagaland of the Indian Army to fight an insurgency provided as much an opportunity to learn as it did to unlearn previous battle procedures. Unlike the past when the pre-independence Indian Army fought rebellious regions in the country's periphery, independent India was now attempting to bring alienated citizens of the country back into the mainstream, despite some of them taking up arms.

Though the outbreak of counter-insurgency in Nagaland marked the commencement of low-intensity conflicts in post-independence India, the contagion did not remain restricted to this region. In fact, Nagaland emerged as the mother insurgency for the North-East and continues to remain the oldest continuous violent armed struggle anywhere in the country.[3]

Since then, India has experienced similar violent uprisings in Jammu and Kashmir (J&K), Punjab, areas affected by left-wing extremism (LWE), as also Islamic terrorism within the hinterland, in most cases with support from Pakistan. In addition, the nature and scope of terrorism has undergone change, with the line dividing low and medium intensity—that was more distinct in the past—merging. This is because states like Pakistan have started pursuing their strategic objectives largely through the low-intensity route rather than war, as was the case earlier.[4]

It is a challenge to delve into a detailed historical analysis of low-intensity conflicts in India and its multiple facets in a single chapter. Keeping this constraint in view, an attempt will be made to provide an overview of experiences of the Indian Army in counter-insurgency and counter-terrorism operations. As some readers would possibly be aware of this historical survey, the more important specific aspects of this experience will be highlighted. The chapter, therefore, will provide a broad-based perspective of the Army's role over the decades, and simultaneously focus more closely on issues which defined and made this contribution distinct when compared with experiences elsewhere across the world.

A Historical Perspective

The experience of the Indian Army with low-intensity conflicts, which includes a wide variety of more specific violent experiences to include terrorism, insurgency, local uprisings and skirmishes, emerges from the state's involvement prior to India's independence. The British Indian Army was involved in expeditionary operations not only beyond the subcontinent but also within it. These experiences in Afghanistan and north-east India, to name a few, led to its encapsulated documentation. In some cases, it became a part of the training curriculum for officers who were trained to operate in these areas. While these experiences may not be directly related to post-independence operations undertaken by the Indian government and more specifically, the Indian Army, the importance of the same deserves to be underlined to highlight the contrast and shift that became evident after India's independence.

The British War Office, General Staff, published *Field Service Regulations, Part I*, in 1909, dealing with operations. Similar to more recent manuals for the armed forces, the regulations provided an introduction to fundamentals, like the fighting troops, intercommunication and orders, movement by land and sea and different types of quarters. It also highlighted operational aspects, like protective duties, information, battles, siege operations and night operations. In addition, and of greater relevance to this chapter, the regulations included a chapter on 'Warfare against an Uncivilized Enemy'.[5] The approach to operations becomes evident from not only the title of the chapter but, subsequently, from the manner in which the countries concerned are referred to. A footnote on the very first page of the chapter refers to the relevance of transport and convoys to operations in these areas and in doing so, describes the region as an 'uncivilized country'.[6]

This description does not come as a surprise. It is reinforced by more specific tactics to deal with the 'enemy'. This includes: 'in dealing with independent fanatical tribes, an advance against a sacred town or shrine may have the same effect' (end of organised resistance); and 'If no such objective is available, the enemy may be brought to oppose the advance by a movement against his wells or sources of supply.' The manual goes on to further suggest: 'Should the enemy refuse to make any organized resistance, the occupation of his country, the seizure of his flocks and supplies, and the destruction of his villages and crops may be necessary to obtain his submission.'[7]

This prescribed manual indicates the nature of tactics taught and followed in low-intensity operations by the Indian Army in undivided India, to control the peripheral areas of the country and beyond. The nature of punitive measures undertaken, use of force and the parameters that guided its employment created a foundational understanding within the rank and file of the Army about handling such uprisings.

These operations were followed by Indian Army's overseas deployment during World War II. It was during this phase, after a nearly two decades pause, that some Indian officers and men were exposed to the challenges of conventional operations. They acquitted themselves well and the Indian Army emerged amongst the highest decorated forces in the world. With the end of the war in 1945 and independence soon thereafter in 1947, the nascent Army of an independent India emerged with an indelible impact of both these phases. The political leadership of the country understood the paradigm shift that the Army was required to deal with while being employed to suppress violence and unrest within the country. This became evident when the Army was called out in aid of civil authorities to fight Naga insurgents in 1955.

The induction of the Army into its first major counter-insurgency campaign was accompanied by a guideline both from the then Prime Minister, Jawaharlal Nehru, and the Chief of the Army Staff: 'Nehru reminded the Army that the Nagas were fellow-countrymen who had to be won over, not suppressed.'[8] The Chief, through an order of the day, provided a more detailed perspective on how the Army was expected to conduct itself and the approach towards the insurgents:

> You must remember that all the people of the area in which you are operating are fellow Indians...Some of these people are misguided and have taken to arms against their own people, and are disrupting the peace of this area...You are not there to fight the people in the area, but to protect them...You must do everything possible to win their confidence and respect and to help them feel that they belong to India.[9]

These words were as appropriate then as they are in the present context. Also, these words are not only relevant to India but also in any area where security forces are deployed to fight terrorism and insurgency. In many ways, this remains the essence of the approach to fighting counter-insurgency in India. Therefore, it does not come as a surprise that the evolving nature of India's counter-insurgency doctrine captured this well, as will be seen later in the chapter.

Post-independence Employment

Nagaland

As mentioned earlier, the first major involvement of the Indian Army in countering insurgency began in Nagaland. The gauntlet was thrown by Angami Zapu Phizo when he declared independence on 14 August 1947, a day prior to India gaining independence. This, however, did not stop negotiations between the Naga National Council (NNC), which Phizo headed, and representatives of the government, including Nehru. By 1953, during a visit by Nehru to Nagaland, the divide only became sharper. On 18 September 1954, Phizo established the 'Republican Government of Free Nagaland'.[10] The Naga Federal Army (NFA) was created on a structure similar to the Army, with weapons provided by the British during World War II, and the die was cast.

Two guerrilla wings, under Thungti Chang and Kaito Sema, overwhelmed the local police and Assam Rifles, who were not only caught unaware but also underprepared for the violence. The raids on the police stations further augmented the armoury of the NFA. As the Assam Rifles were unable to break the resistance of the rebels, the Army was inducted after the Disturbed Areas Act was promulgated on 27 August 1955.[11] Counter-insurgency operations began soon thereafter.

The insurgency in the area, which went beyond the boundary of Nagaland, incorporating the hilly areas of Manipur and the southern-most districts of Arunachal Pradesh, went through a roller-coaster ride thereafter, witnessing a series of highs and lows. The 1950s and the 1960s saw the Naga insurgency gain strength with support in terms of training and weapons from China.[12] Over time, Pakistan also saw an opportunity in supporting militancy in the region.[13]

The conditions along the border, including weak or colluding groups, similarity of ethnic entities on both sides and limitations placed by thickly forested and mountainous terrain, placed constraints on operations by the security forces. However, military pressure and political initiatives continued in a bid to seek reconciliation.

Attempts at achieving a breakthrough were made by the government in the mid-1960s through initiatives, like granting statehood to Nagaland in 1963 and negotiating with a group of special emissaries which included Jaiprakash Narain, BP Chaliha and Reverend Michael Scott. However, these negotiations did not succeed and after the breakdown of talks sometime in 1968, operations continued from both sides.[14]

A major breakthrough was finally achieved with the surrender of 1,500 Revolutionary Government of Nagaland (RGN) guerrillas led by Scatu Swu and Zuheto. They were recruited into special Border Security Force battalions, commencing a very special arrangement to bring underground fighters back into the mainstream. This was followed by an agreement with the NNC in 1975, leading to the Shillong Accord.[15]

Hard-line groups, however, saw this as a sell-out and rejected the accord. Eventually, this led to the creation of the National Socialist Council of Nagaland (NSCN) in 1980, led by Isak Chisi Swu and Thuingaleng Muivah. The group further divided in 1988 into the Khaplang and Muivah factions, bringing in the element of internecine violence in addition to the existing counter-terrorism operations.

Yet another breakthrough was achieved with a ceasefire with the NSCN Isak-Muivah (NSCN-IM) faction in 1997, raising the possibility of peace after decades of violence. This was taken forward eventually through a framework agreement on 3 August 2015 between the NCSN-IM and the Government of India.[16] However, a final settlement on the basis of this agreement it still in the works.

Mizoram

A second violent movement, led by Laldenga, that challenged the state began in Mizoram on 28 February 1966. The situation in the area had been simmering with a rise in discontentment over time. However, allegations of neglect of the area came to the fore with the outbreak of 'Mautam', a rat famine caused by the flowering of bamboo plants. It began in 1958, but the food grain supplies to supplement the shortfall due to the famine only came in 1960. This was exploited by Laldenga, a fledgling political leader at that time. He started the Mizo National Famine Front (MNFF)[17] and tried his hand at electoral politics in 1962, but reality came to the fore when his party won only two seats.

This led to a hardening of approach and the MNFF converted to Mizo National Front (MNF), eventually raising a banner of revolt with the formal outbreak of violent movement in 1966. The MNF launched Operation Jericho, which was unique in many ways. It was a rare instance of an insurgent group commencing hostilities in multiple, simultaneous, near-conventional military raids on Assam Rifle posts and government establishments. The result was a near sweep of major towns, with only the Assam Rifles post at Aizawl standing its ground and denying the rebels a clean sweep. This was quickly followed with the induction of the Indian Army, led by 61 Mountain Brigade to include 8 SIKH and 2 PARA.[18]

Given the criticality of the situation, Aizawl was perhaps the only area which saw the employment of air power to control the precarious situation. The employment of air power did not have a severe physical effect in the area, but it did create a psychological impact. On the one hand, the region came face to face with the might of the Indian state and the kind of resources that were available if the need arose. On the other hand, it left an indelible impression on the people who continue to quote it as a harsh response on part of the state against them.[19]

After the induction of the Indian Army into the area, the MNF steadily got pushed out of the major population centres and into the outlying regions of the state. It also exploited the porous borders and the presence of Chin tribes across to seek sanctuaries. In addition to Myanmar, Bangladesh too was a safe sanctuary for the guerrillas. This continued for a few years, until the 1971 Indo-Pak War made their presence inside Bangladesh untenable. This came as a big blow to Laldenga, who barely managed to escape the Indian forces and moved to West Pakistan.

In the meanwhile, realising the futility of violence, which was unlikely to achieve any substantive results, the civil society, and especially the church, played the role of responsible intermediaries. Channels of communication were also opened with Laldenga, who began negotiations with emissaries. It was a matter of time before the MNF signed an agreement with the government. The settlement also paved the way for elections to be held and Laldenga swept into power as leader of the MNF. It was a rare case of an insurgent leader becoming the elected chief minister of a newly formed state; and an example that continues to reinforce the importance of a political settlement to resolve violent movements in the country.

Manipur

The insurgency in Manipur has proved to be the most complicated to resolve over the years. This is not as much because of the core demand of a particular group from the state, but more a result of competing rivalries amongst different groups themselves. The non-monolithic nature of the insurgency in the state has seen terror organisations pushing the interests of ethnic groups, which spill across district and state boundaries. This has further been aggravated by the hill–plains divide that exists between the Naga and the dominant Meitei tribes.

Manipur is one of the few states that can boast of a long, uninterrupted documented history and a rich cultural heritage. Post-independence, Manipur merged with India. This was resisted by certain sections, including Hijam Irabot Singh, the then maharaja's brother-in-law. He clearly had leftist leanings and after the merger slipped away into Myanmar. He eventually took up arms against central rule in the state.[20]

The dissatisfaction amongst a section of population was exploited and in 1964, the United National Liberation Front (UNLF) was created by Samarendra Singh, aimed at seeking national self-determination for the people of Manipur.

Immediately after the 1971 Indo-Pak War, Manipur was granted statehood in 1972. However, the insurgency that began in 1964 continued. In 1978, the People's

Liberation Army (PLA) was created by a breakaway leader of UNLF, Bisheshwar Singh, with the promise of support from China.[21] A number of other Meitei groups came up over time in addition to the initial ones. The situation further worsened with the NSCN-IM taking up the cause of Nagas in Manipur, who dominated the hilly regions of the state. When one adds to this the Kukis and a number of other smaller tribes, the resultant challenging security situation becomes evident.

Assam

Assam has witnessed multiple strains of insurgency in the state with specific and distinct causes. While the most prominent of these struggles was led by the United Liberation Front of Asom (ULFA), the state has also seen violence as a result of the Bodo movement.

The ULFA, an offshoot of All Assam Students' Union (AASU), was created on 07 April 1979.[22] Unlike a number of other organisations which took to violence immediately after their formation, the ULFA did not do so. This was also the time when the AASU was spearheading the agitation against illegal immigration into the state. The Assam Accord, signed in 1985, was the basis for identifying illegal migrants in the state. However, despite the Assam Gana Parishad (AGP)—formed by student leaders of the AASU—coming to power in 1985, the party failed to achieve the promised results.

Eventually, by 1988, the ULFA began its violent activities. The group also got in touch with some of the older militant organisations, like the NSCN, to seek weapons and support. What began as a relatively popular movement riding on the indigenous Ahom sentiment fast turned into a profit-making criminal activity. The ULFA started collecting large sums of money from traders, tea factory owners and the people. Over time, it became evident that there was a gap between the stated objectives of the group and the reality of their activities. This led to the launch of military operations by the Indian Army. What began with a moderately successful Operation Bajrang in 1990 was taken forward by a better planned and executed Operation Rhino.[23]

A combination of disillusionment with the ULFA, success of the military operations and division within the militant ranks finally led to a weakening of the movement. It was further challenged over time with India being able to foster better ties with neighbours, especially Bangladesh and Myanmar. This made it that much more difficult for groups like ULFA to seek shelter in the border areas.

While the ULFA fought for their Ahom identity and against foreigners, there were groups in the state which struggled for their respective rights. This includes the oldest inhabitants of the state, the Bodos. The Bodo struggle, though old, gained prominence with the creation of the All Bodo Students Union on 15 February 1967. What began with the demand for an autonomous council snowballed into the group seeking a separate state. By 1987, violent incidents began in the state. Unlike other areas, negotiations began soon thereafter and in 1993, the Bodo Accord was signed and the Bodo Volunteer Force laid down their arms as part of the settlement. In return, an autonomous council was established.[24]

However, as has been seen in other areas of the country, dissatisfied splinter groups came to the fore and continued with the violent movement and agitations. The Bodo agitation also saw a similar trajectory, with groups like the Bodoland Liberation Tigers Front and National Democratic Front of Bodoland emerging as the two opposing sides, divided along ethnic lines.

J&K

The incidents in J&K may have manifested into a violent movement in 1988, however its roots run deeper. In addition to the chequered history of the state prior to independence, which saw different groups dominate the region over centuries, including the Afghans, Sikhs and Dogra rulers, a sense of victimhood had become an abiding factor. Also, the disputed border between India and Pakistan and the latter's repeated attempts to employ force as a mechanism to resolve it further complicated the political and security situation in the area.

The delicate balance that was struck immediately after independence through the special status that the state was given in accordance with Article 370 was exploited by the local political leadership to retain political influence and question the issue of accession of Kashmir. Simultaneously, the special status of the state was diluted over a period of time. After covert military attempts by Pakistan in 1947–48 and 1965 to seek control over Kashmir failed to create an uprising within the state, conventional force was employed in a bid to wrest the region. This, however, did not yield the desired results. It led Pakistan to seek other options, including terrorism, as alternative proxy measures.

It is important to recall that Pakistan's ability to force a military decision on India was severely denuded after the decisive defeat in the 1971 Indo-Pak War. Commencing from 1979, the Pakistani state perfected the art of exploiting instruments of hybrid warfare in Afghanistan. They further honed it simultaneously against India in Punjab.

As a result, by the time a decision was taken in Islamabad to fight India yet again, the primary constituents of choice for waging war had undergone a change. Instead of conventional weapon systems, it was terrorism, subversion, information warfare and financing of terrorism that Pakistan chose to fall back upon. The policy of employing force was replaced by bleeding India through a thousand cuts.

Pakistan's support for violence and separatism began with its backing of groups like the Jammu and Kashmir Liberation Front (JKLF). However, it was soon realised that the agenda of an independent state did not suit Pakistan. Accordingly,

Hizbul Mujahideen (HM) was created, which pushed for the merger of the state with Pakistan. The differences between the groups were resolved through internecine clashes, which saw the JKLF virtually decimated.

With the HM also finding it difficult to stand up to the pressure exerted by the Indian security forces, a number of different terrorist organisations were created inside Pakistan, with members from both Afghanistan and Pakistan, directly trained, funded, supported and directed by the Pakistan Army.[25] Names like the Lashkar-e-Taiba (LeT), Harakat-ul-Ansar (HuA) and Al-Jihad, followed by the Jaish-e-Mohammed (JeM), came up with the common characteristic of support from Pakistan.

The pinnacle of their terror activities was witnessed with the attack on the Indian Parliament in 2001, followed by the sensational terrorist strike at Mumbai in 2008, nearly pushing India to war with Pakistan.[26]

Even as intermittent terrorism continued, a shift in the Indian government's approach became evident through its declaratory policy of counter strikes against Pakistan. While the first strike across the Line of Control (LoC) took place in 2016 as a reaction to Pakistan-guided attack on the Uri Army camp[27], the second took place in 2019 after a suicide attack against a convoy at Pulwama in 2019. The air strike at the JeM terrorist camp at Balakot, after the Pulwama attack, raised the bar of India's response and made the country's intent clear. It reinforced the policy of zero tolerance for terrorism.[28]

Punjab

The state witnessed the challenge of terrorism that emerged from an attempt to artificially exploit insecurities within a section of the population. These sentiments were promoted for seeking electoral advantage, until a stage was reached wherein the Sikh extremist views were hijacked by separatists, with support from Pakistan, to give rise to violence within the state.[29]

The first phase of the uprising got out of hand, after Jarnail Singh Bhindranwale took refuge with amassed weapons and militant volunteers inside the Golden Temple. It culminated with Operation Blue Star. This operation saw the Indian Army being given the unenviable task of evicting terrorists armed with sophisticated weapons, including medium machine guns and rocket launchers, from the Golden Temple at Amritsar in 1984.[30] The operation was successfully completed, though with heavy losses being suffered by the security forces.

The follow-up period witnessed the continuation of terrorism, which steadily transformed into a criminal activity, thereby losing the limited support it had. The second attempt at taking over the Golden Temple by terrorists led to a more clinical operation. As part of Operation Black Thunder in 1988, the surrender of terrorists was ensured after their protracted isolation inside the temple.[31]

The atrocities by the terrorists, sustained capacity building of the police force under Julio Ribeiro and KPS Gill, and support from the Indian Army and the political leadership saw the terrorism movement being decimated by the early 1990s, bringing the bloody chapter of violence in the state to a closure.

Left-Wing Extremism (LWE)

After independence, India's tryst with LWE began immediately with the Telangana uprising, which began in 1946 and continued till 1952.[32] Despite the violence and loss of lives that the struggle caused, it failed to successfully challenge the might of the Indian state, both pre- and post-independence.

Though left-wing struggles predate independence in 1947, more often than not, the Naxalbari uprising by a group of poor peasants against their landlords in 1967 is considered as the commencement of LWE in India. This peasant struggle made limited gains, but it became symbolic of peasant revolt against injustice and exploitation. It also led to similar struggles being waged in other states, like Bihar, Jharkhand, Chhattisgarh, Maharashtra, Andhra Pradesh and West Bengal. Over time, a number of splinter groups emerged, with little in terms of synergy in their actions. This changed in 2004, when the Maoist Communist Centre merged with the People's War Group to form the Communist Party of India (Maoist).[33] This led to a major surge in Maoist ranks and their ability to fight against the security forces. In 2006, Prime Minister Manmohan Singh termed the Maoist challenge as the most serious internal security threat.[34] This was reinforced by a series of major attacks by the Maoists thereafter, over the next few years.

The increasing spread of Maoist influence led to the description of a 'red corridor' from Pashupati to Tirupati, with a total of 220 districts of the country being affected by its impact at one time.[35] The government launched a two-pronged initiative aimed at development of areas impacted by Naxal violence and widespread deployment of security forces. This succeeded in curbing violence to a great extent commencing 2011. The graph of LWE violence has since been on the decline, even though the threat persists over a reduced yet significant area of the country, covering approximately 53 districts by 2020.[36]

The LWE example illustrates the successful employment of alternative security forces instead of the Army in a direct role.

Analysis of Insurgency and Terrorism in India

The constraints of space limit the details that can be provided for each of the insurgency or terrorist movements fought by the state and its constituents. However, this brief backdrop of some of the major insurgencies provides some important conclusions. These, in turn, help understand the nature and character of sub-conventional violence that has been witnessed in India, as also the distinguishing characteristics that define them. This is especially relevant since each of these challenges required a distinct approach. Indeed, this is perhaps one of the most important lessons that can be learnt from India's experience in countering terrorism and insurgency.

Past experience with violent movements in India suggests that insurgencies were a preserve of the periphery, which had remained comparatively neglected in the past. Its emergence in other areas of the country clearly suggested that dissatisfaction, real or perceived, irrespective of its location, can potentially give rise to such movements.

India's experience also suggests that the role of the armed forces was far more involved with such movements than should have ideally been the case. In some instances, it continues to remain so. This is despite the fact that a large number of organisations have seen their capacities enhanced, as is the case with the Central Reserve Police Force (CRPF) or even the state police organisations. Other specialist organisations have been raised specifically to fight terrorism, like the Rashtriya Rifles.[37] Yet, the Army remains involved in fighting these movements. While fighting terrorism is considered a secondary responsibility of the Army, how it affects the primary role of fighting external threats and challenges has often been the subject of discussion over the years.[38]

The incidence of foreign involvement in India's insurgencies is also not new. In the 1960s and 1970s, China provided active support to groups in North-East India.[39] Pakistan too was involved since the same period. While its efforts received a setback after the loss of East Pakistan in 1971, the policy of employing terrorism as a state instrument continues till date.[40] In fact, in the case of Pakistan, this support, from being peripheral to the larger fight against India, became central since the late 1980s. In that context, the involvement of the Army and the description of sub-conventional operations underwent a shift. Increasingly, actions of Pakistan in J&K, and other parts of the country as well, were viewed more as a hybrid war against India, than merely as terrorism.[41]

Despite the involvement of the Army, it needs to be emphasised here that the resolution of such violent movements was always seen through the perspective of a politically negotiated settlement. The employment of the Army, or for that matter, the security forces, was only to create conditions for a democratically elected government to undertake its mandated responsibility.[42] This was evident in the case of Mizoram, Punjab and to a great extent, in each of the regions where terrorism emerged in a major way in the country.

The nature of India's federal structure, where law and order are state subjects, created understandable but real challenges to fight violent movements. In a number of cases, the states did not have the requisite capacity in terms of training and equipment profile of the police. This led to a number of movements spiralling out of their control even prior to the central forces being employed. One of the most dangerous situations was created in Mizoram in 1966, when the MNF was able to nearly take over the state security apparatus in a surprise attack. This led to the immediate deployment of the Army to control the fast-deteriorating security situation.[43] Further, in a number of cases, the upswing in violence went beyond the ability of even the central police organisations, as was the case in J&K.[44] However, this trend has seen a degree of correction, with police and central police organisations being employed to counter violence in LWE areas with an appreciable degree of success.

A closer look at the causes of violent movements in India indicates a variety of reasons for the same.[45] While some movements had their roots in India's historical legacy prior to its independence, as has been repeatedly asserted by the Nagas and the Kashmiris, others were due to insufficient attention to local sensitivities and demands, as seen in Mizoram and Manipur. In the case of the former, the mishandling of the Mautam famine became the tipping point, while in case of the latter, the failure to recognise the rich cultural and historical legacy of the state provided dissenters with the very reason that they could exploit. Similarly, in Kashmir, the perception of election rigging in 1987 added to the dissatisfaction amongst a section of people within the state.

Amongst the differentiating factors associated with different violent movements in India is the manner in which they financially supported themselves. While the model of early insurgencies indicates a localised form of collecting funds, latter-day terrorism has been more globalised in this respect. The insurgencies in the North-East, as also LWE, were supported by collecting funds through an illegal taxation system or different forms of extortion. This included levies on businesses, transportation services, industries and even criminal activities, including kidnapping. On the contrary, in the later years, in areas like J&K, a vast majority of funding emanated from Pakistan through state support, fake Indian currency notes (FICN) printed there, drug money funnelled, charities and fund raisers that were allowed to function with impunity. This suggests peculiar models for specific areas. However, as a country, India has experienced a hybrid model of terror funding with multiple sources of funding.[46]

Doctrinal Evolution

Having seen a brief historical perspective of low-intensity conflicts in India, as well as some of the salient takeaways, it would be useful to attempt an understanding of India's doctrinal thought that accompanied the trajectory of these movements.

The absence of open and public articulation of India's counter-terrorism doctrine raises a challenge for identifying fundamental trends that have guided the actions of the state. Even when attempts have been made to articulate doctrines in the past, these have come at the behest of individual state entities, like the Army, without necessarily the complete involvement of other state agencies. The Indian Army brought out its sub-conventional doctrine both within the classified and unclassified domains.[47]

Commencing with pre-independence handling of sub-conventional military operations, it becomes evident that the initial focus of operations undertaken by the state was on suppression of rebellious, violent tribes on the periphery of the British Indian Empire. This included not only the Afghans but also North-East India.

The tactical guidelines laid down clearly suggest the presence of a punitive policy for dealing with uprisings. The suggested measures addressed those who opposed the British government through violent means, and the villagers too, in a bid to pressurise the militant cadres. The inclusion of measures such as destruction of villages and crops represented steps that were aimed at instilling fear and caution amongst the tribes. These were quite obviously regressive in their intent and objective. It was certainly not the intent of the state to win over the population. The objective was to maintain control through penal policies. This was the first exposure for the British Indian Army in the fight against violent uprisings within the sub-conventional domain.

After the interlude of World War II, wherein the Indian Army performed admirably, though within the conventional military sphere, the post-independence period brought the first opportunity to fight internal conflicts in Nagaland. Unlike the guidance in the pre-independence period, this time, as brought out earlier, both the political and military leadership took measures to specially communicate with the troops. They reinforced the government's humane intent and policy outlook towards such violent uprisings and the people of the region.

This, in some ways, became the primary building block for security forces in general, and the Indian Army in particular, for the implementation of their mandate in the region. This is not to suggest that this guidance led to a blemish-free deployment of the security forces thereafter; and it is evident from some of the cases that came to the fore.[48] However, for an Army that was used to conventional warfare against an identified enemy, it was important to make this distinction. While the impact of this guidance may not have been immediate, over time its influence started becoming evident.

The conventional orientation of the Army also became evident in its tactical deployment and operations. From the size of sub-units deployed to the conduct of operations and the tactics employed, the teachings of conventional military operations clearly had an impact on how units operated. Lieutenant General (Lt Gen) Thomas Mathew says that 'none of the battalions that were from 61 Mountain Brigade had any experience of counter insurgency.'[49]

The commencement of Army's deployment in counter-insurgency was characterised by a policy of 'search and clear'.[50] This implied that the battalions that were deployed in these areas would venture out in a bid to conduct search operations on the basis of either intelligence about insurgent movement or as part of area domination. In either case, the presence of the Army patrols would deter insurgents from moving in those parts with impunity. Over time, the balance of domination by insurgents would shift to greater control by the security forces and by co-relation, of the state. This was seen as an essential prerequisite for ensuring the reimposition of state control in some of these areas.

However, when it was realised that a temporary—and at times, fleeting—presence of security forces was inadequate to maintain control over areas, this policy shifted to 'clear and hold' in the late 1960s and the early 1970s.[51] This implied that now instead of merely staying in an area for a short duration of time, the security forces created a temporary post or a temporary base in that area. It facilitated the presence of security forces at multiple locations, which made the domination of the area that much more effective. This system of creating a grid worked that much more effectively, especially given the dual responsibility of reinforcing state presence and domination in the area, thereby convincing the population of state control. It also facilitated faster reaction to information, given limited availability of fast mobility assets like helicopters. This was all the more relevant in areas of the North-East, with its thick jungles, where ground mobility remained a challenge at most times of the year.

Changes in the approach of the Army also became evident from a shift in policies that were inspired from successes in Malaya, where the British forces employed the concept of separated villages. This led to villages being created along road arteries, within the direct supervision of security forces. Further, it ensured that guerrilla cadres could not access these villages for sustenance and support, as was the case with smaller hamlets spread around the countryside.

This experiment was also attempted by the Indian government in Nagaland and Mizoram for similar reasons. Experience, however, showed that it caused grave inconvenience to the people, without accruing the intended benefits. Resultantly, the experiment was not repeated, indirectly acknowledging its limitations.[52]

Over time, the Army began relying more on intelligence-based operations that could be undertaken clinically, instead of merely area domination or large-scale cordon and search. Such operations not only gave better results, they also reduced the inconvenience to the local population. Also, in the long run, it facilitated better cooperation from the local people and simultaneously made operations more result oriented.

In addition to these changes at the operational level, certain clear doctrinal principles were established over a period of time. While subtle changes were made according to the specific area of operations, the broad parameters have remained consistent.

The first principle that has guided India's actions is the primacy of political solutions in resolving internal security conflicts. Military force has been applied only to bring down levels of violence to enable the democratic process to be reinvigorated. Examples of this policy are evident in Nagaland where the government entered into the Naga accord in 1975 with the NNC, even though it did not lead to lasting peace. Efforts in this direction continue with ongoing talks with major Naga militant factions, to seek peace in the region on the basis of the framework agreement signed. Similarly, the recommencement of the political process in Mizoram in 1986 resulted in the MNF getting back into the political mainstream and the rebel leader, Laldenga, getting elected as the Chief Minister of the state.

The second principle that has been established over a period of time is that of minimum force. The Indian Armed Forces, possibly with the exception of employing air power fleetingly in Mizoram in the initial phase of operations in an offensive role, have desisted from using all forms of heavy-calibre weapons, including air power and Artillery guns. This is in contrast to how armed forces have operated in India's neighbourhood as well as elsewhere in the world. The positive impact of this policy has been the ability to reduce collateral damage to the very minimum, thereby reducing alienation of the local population. However, often, the junior military leadership has had to pay a heavy price in terms of battle casualties, given the need to get closer to the source of fire to neutralise it.

The doctrine of distinction has also been a characteristic of the armed forces response and has fully been supported by successive governments. This has taken place at a number of levels. At the very fundamental level, the guidance of the 1950s remains paramount in counter-insurgency areas, wherein a clear distinction is made between the local population and those who pick up arms against the state and the people. It remains the endeavour of the security forces to limit the inconvenience to the locals, who often tend to become unwilling victims of the circumstances prevailing in disturbed areas.

Distinction is also made between local insurgents and foreign terrorists. This is primarily because the locals are seen as those who have deviated from the path of peace and can be brought back into the mainstream. Examples of this option have been quoted earlier. However, foreign terrorists who infiltrate across the borders come into the country only with the intent of causing death and damage to property. They do not have any intent to negotiate. It is the latter who leave little option for the security forces but to neutralise them. In contrast, the former are always provided with the option of surrender or negotiating a settlement.

A distinction is also made between the employment of terrorism by an external power to achieve its strategic ends and the use of violence by disgruntled elements from within the country. The example of Pakistan is most appropriate here to illustrate the employment of terror as a strategic tool, which has been evident for decades. To begin with, subversion and terrorism were employed to aid conventional military means, as was witnessed in 1947–48, 1965 and during the Kargil conflict in 1999. However, since 1988, a new reality was acknowledged by the military hierarchy in Pakistan. It was realised that the focus needed to shift towards sub-conventional means, instead of reliance on major wars, to achieve strategic objectives. The ongoing terrorism in J&K, as well as terror incidents across the country over the last three decades, illustrate this shift.

It is in the face of such challenges and threats that India's policy, and more specifically that of the Army, has also undergone a change. Commencing from 2016, it was decided that the Indian security forces will employ a punitive approach against cross-border terrorism. This manifested in the cross-border strike against terrorist camps after the attack on the Uri military camp in 2016.[53] Thereafter, in 2019, after the terrorist strike at Pulwama, a cross-border air strike was undertaken at Balakot, yet again against a terrorist camp.[54] These actions were aimed at sending a clear message to terrorists and their handlers that India reserved the right to hit back at the perpetrators of terrorism at a time and place of its choosing.

By raising the force level on the escalatory ladder and making such responses a part of its declaratory policy, India changed its approach towards terrorism from reactive to proactive. In the past, the people and the government could only wait for the next major strike, unclear of its location and intensity. As a result of the changed policy, it was Pakistan that was unsure of the scale and scene of India's strike. India's actions also called out Pakistan as a state employing terrorism. This was accompanied by a call to major powers to support India's right to protect its people in self-defence. With the expected exception of China, India succeeded in achieving the support of major powers for its right to strike terrorists in self-defence.[55]

India's diplomatic success has not been limited to support for its counter-terrorism strategy. It has also been evident within the United Nations, wherein major terrorist groups, like the LeT, Harkat-ul-Mujahideen (HuM) and JeM, have been put on the list of proscribed terrorist organisations;[56] in some cases, despite resistance from China.

Pakistan also has come under pressure from the Financial Action Task Force (FATF), a body which lays down guidelines to safeguard the international financial system from money laundering and terrorism finance.[57] The mutual evaluation of Pakistan's existing structures, procedures and enforcement reveals major gaps, as a result of which the country has been consistently placed on the 'grey list'. This puts pressure on it to not only bridge existing systemic gaps but also take action against proscribed terrorist groups and leaders. The potential financial impact of such listing and the international humiliation suffered for being highlighted repeatedly for its omissions and commissions has achieved appreciable results in the fight against terrorism and its sponsorship by Pakistan.

Conclusion

India has experienced over seven decades of low-intensity conflicts and has been fighting insurgency and terrorism. A brief account of the experiences reveals that despite these being within the confines of the same country, there has been variance in the causes, trajectory and culmination of each. Others continue to remain a challenge despite decades of violence.

The historical survey also indicates that in spite of being the instrument of last resort, the Indian Army has often been at the forefront for fighting these movements. In doing so, there has been an evolutionary process to the approach adopted by the Army. Valuable lessons have been learnt and these, in turn, have enhanced the quality and impact of the Army's presence in disturbed areas.

Despite the evolving nature of the Army's approach, a common thread is evident in how over the decades, the institution has remained an integral contributing element to national security and nation building. Right from the time of India's independence, there was clarity amongst the Army's senior leadership that its role, in terms of providing aid to civil authorities, was merely to support, aid and strengthen the national framework of democracy. More than 70 years later, this thought is deeply imbibed into the Army rank and file and has contributed, to a great extent, to the institution being as successful as it has been. It is looked up to for stability and peace, whenever a crisis situation develops and is beyond the control of the local authorities.

Due to the absence of a national sub-conventional doctrine, it may not be easy to formally define the Indian way of fighting such conflicts. Yet, this chapter clearly suggests that an Indian model for seeking peace and reconciliation does exist. It also suggests that India's model, and the Army's role as a part of it, has a number of lessons that can be drawn for deriving best practices. These do not only emerge from the successes but also from the failures suffered over the years.

One of the most important takeaways is the need for an open and free assessment of such experiences and the desirability to document them to ensure that requisite learning value can be derived. It will also assist in building the strengths and eliminating, or at least limiting, the weaknesses observed during Army's deployment in low-intensity conflicts.

Notes

1. The first doctrine of the Indian Army dealing with counter-insurgency, given its scope, was referred to as *Doctrine for Sub Conventional Operations*. See Integrated Headquarters of Ministry of Defence (Army), *Doctrine for Sub Conventional Operations*, Shimla: Headquarters Army Training Command, December 2006.
2. For an explanation of these and some additional associated terms, see Ibid., pp. 64–65.
3. The subversive movement in Nagaland commenced prior to India's independence; however, violent insurgency began in 1955.
4. For a more detailed analysis of Pakistan's employment of different constituents of war, see Vivek Chadha, 'Pakistan's Hybrid War in South Asia: Case Study of India and Afghanistan', in Vikrant Deshpande (ed.), *Hybrid Warfare: The Changing Character of Conflict*, New Delhi: Pentagon Press, 2018, pp. 37–61.

5. See Great Britain War Office, General Staff, *Field Service Regulations, Part I: Operations*, London: Harrison and Sons, 1909, pp. 191–212.
6. Ibid, p. 191.
7. Ibid, pp. 191–92.
8. Sarvepalli Gopal, *Jawaharlal Nehru: A Biography, Vol. 2, 1947–1956*, Cambridge MA: Harvard University Press, 1979, p. 212, quoted in Rajesh Rajagopalan, *Fighting Like a Guerrilla: The Indian Army and Counterinsurgency*, New Delhi: Routledge, 2008, pp. 143–44.
9. Rajagopalan, *Fighting Like a Guerrilla*, n. 8, p. 147.
10. BG Verghese, *India's Northeast Resurgent: Ethnicity, Insurgency, Governance, Development*, New Delhi: Konark Publishers Pvt. Ltd, 1996, p. 88.
11. Nirmal Nibedon, *Nagaland Night of the Guerrillas*, New Delhi: Lancer, 1983, p. 73.
12. Vivek Chadha, *Low Intensity Conflicts in India: An Analysis*, New Delhi: Sage, 2005, p. 296.
13. DB Shekatkar, 'India's Counterinsurgency Campaign in Nagaland', in Sumit Ganguly and David P Fidler (eds), *India and Counterinsurgency: Lessons Learned*, London: Routledge, 2009, pp. 14–15.
14. Chadha, *Low Intensity Conflicts in India*, n. 12, p. 295.
15. For a text of the accord, see 'Shillong Agreement between the Government of India and the Underground Nagas', Shillong, 11 November 1975, available at https://peacemaker.un.org/sites/peacemaker.un.org/files/IN_751111_Shillong%20Agreement_0.pdf.
16. Prabhash K Dutta, 'Naga Sovereignty Claim and 2015 Deal', *India Today*, 17 August 2020, available at https://www.indiatoday.in/news-analysis/story/naga-sovereignty-claim-and-2015-deal-explained-1712194-2020-08-17.
17. Chadha, *Low Intensity Conflicts in India*, n. 12, p. 332.
18. Based on an interview with Lt Gen Mathew Thomas, quoted in Chadha, *Low Intensity Conflicts in India*, n. 12, p. 340.
19. Based on the interaction of the author with the people of the area during a field trip.
20. Irabot Singh's direct impact on leading a violent movement remained limited with his death in 1951.
21. 'People's Liberation Army', South Asia Terrorism Portal (SATP), at https://www.satp.org/satporgtp/countries/india/states/manipur/terrorist_outfits/pla.htm.
22. 'United Liberation Front of Asom', SATP, at https://www.satp.org/satporgtp/countries/india/states/assam/terrorist_outfits/ulfa.htm.
23. Chadha, *Low Intensity Conflicts in India*, n. 12, pp. 249–51.
24. See 'Memorandum of Settlement (Bodo Accord)', Guwahati, 20 February 1993, at https://www.peaceagreements.org/viewmasterdocument/30.
25. VG Patankar, 'Insurgency, Proxy War, and Terrorism in Kashmir', in Sumit Ganguly and David P. Fidler (eds), *India and Counterinsurgency: Lessons Learned*, London: Routledge, 2009, pp. 68–69.
26. For a detailed account of the attack, see Sandeep Unnithan, *Black Tornado: The Three Sieges of Mumbai 26/11*, New Delhi: HarperCollins, 2014.
27. Nitin Gokhale, 'The Inside Story of India's 2016 "Surgical Strikes"', *The Diplomat*, 23 September 2017, at https://thediplomat.com/2017/09/the-inside-story-of-indias-2016-surgical-strikes/.

28. Ministry of External Affairs, 'Statement by Foreign Secretary on 26 February 2019 on the Strike on JeM Training Camp at Balakot', 26 February 2019, at https://www.mea.gov.in/press-releases.htm?dtl/31091/Statement_by_Foreign_Secretary_on_26_February_2019_on_the_Strike_on_JeM_training_camp_at_Balakot.
29. Ved Marwah, 'India's Counterinsurgency Campaign in Punjab, in Sumit Ganguly and David P Fidler (eds), *India and Counterinsurgency: Lessons Learned*, London: Routledge, 2009, pp. 94–95.
30. For a military account of the operation, read KS Brar, *Operation Blue Star: The True Story*, New Delhi: South Asia Books, 1993.
31. For an account of Operation Black Thunder, see Ved Marwah, *Uncivil Wars: Pathology of Terrorism in India*, New Delhi: HarperCollins India, 1998.
32. The LWE began in 1946 in the Telangana area in response to the discontentment of poor farmers in the area.
33. Sumit Bhattacharjee, 'A Merger that Changed the Maoist Threat Perception', *The Hindu*, 22 September 2020, at https://www.thehindu.com/news/national/andhra-pradesh/a-merger-that-changed-the-maoist-threat-perception/article32664122.ece.
34. See 'India's Deadly Maoists', *The Economist*, 26 July 2006, at https://www.economist.com/news/2006/07/26/indias-deadly-maoists.
35. Anoop AJ, 'Assessment of Left Wing Extremism, 2010', Vivekanand International Foundation, 8 April 2011, at https://www.vifindia.org/article/2011/april/8/Assessment-of-Left-Wing-Extremism-2010.
36. See Ministry of Home Affairs, 'Lok Sabha Starred Question No. 389', 23 March 2021, at http://164.100.24.220/loksabhaquestions/annex/175/AS389.pdf.
37. The CRPF is considered the primary counter-terrorism security force in India. Having been raised on 27 July 1939, the force has 246 battalions, indicating the increase in size over the years. See CRPF, 'Introduction & Role of CRPF', at https://crpf.gov.in/role-of-crpf.htm.
38. See Kanwar Sandhu, 'Government Seeks to Counter Terrorism by Retaining Army in Punjab', *India Today*, 30 November 1992, at https://www.indiatoday.in/magazine/indiascope/story/19921031-government-seeks-to-counter-terrorism-by-retaining-Army-in-punjab-767090-1999-11-30; and Vijay Oberoi, 'Need for Holistic Restructuring of the Indian Military', *Journal of Defence Studies*, Vol. 2, No. 1, Summer 2008, available at https://www.idsa.in/jds/2_1_2008_NeedforHolisticRestructuringoftheIndianMilitary_VOberoi.
39. See G Ramchandra Reddy and M Sasikala, 'Insurgencies in Northeast India and the Role of China', in G. Jayachandra Reddy (ed.), *India and China Relations: Historical, Cultural and Security Issues*, Tirupati: UGC Centre for Southeast Asian and Pacific Studies, Sri Venkateshwara University, 2016, pp. 267–82.
40. The focus of insurgencies in India remained largely in the North-East, until terrorism emerged in Punjab. As a result, Pakistan also focused its efforts at fomenting trouble for India through the erstwhile East Pakistan till the 1971 Indo-Pak War led to the creation of Bangladesh.
41. For a detailed analysis of Pakistan's hybrid war against India, see Chadha, 'Pakistan's Hybrid War in South Asia', n. 4, pp. 37–61.

42. See Integrated Headquarters of Ministry of Defence (Army), *Doctrine for Sub Conventional Operations*, n. 1, p. 17.
43. See Vivek Chadha, 'India's Counterinsurgency Campaign in Mizoram', in Sumit Ganguly and David P Fidler (eds), *India and Counterinsurgency: Lessons Learned*, London: Routledge, 2009, pp. 29–44.
44. See Patankar, 'Insurgency, Proxy War, and Terrorism in Kashmir', in Ganguly and Fidler (eds), *India and Counterinsurgency*, n. 37, pp. 65–78.
45. For a detailed analysis of causes of various insurgencies in India and their comparative analysis, see Chadha, *Low Intensity Conflicts in India*, n. 12.
46. For an assessment of different sources of terror financing in India and the counter-terrorism finance strategy, see Vivek Chadha, *Lifeblood of Terrorism: Countering Terrorism Finance*, New Delhi: Bloomsbury, 2015.
47. The unclassified doctrine for sub-conventional operations was published by the Army in December 2006. However, subsequent volumes have remained classified and are not in public domain. See Integrated Headquarters of Ministry of Defence (Army), *Doctrine for Sub Conventional Operations*, n. 1.
48. See 'India: Top Court Orders Manipur Killings Inquiry', Human Rights Watch, 15 July 2017, at https://www.hrw.org/news/2017/07/15/india-top-court-orders-manipur-killings-inquiry.
49. Lt Gen Mathew Thomas, quoted in Chadha, *Low Intensity Conflicts in India*, n. 12, p. 342.
50. See SP Anand, 'Counter Insurgency Theory and Practice in Mizo Hills', *USI Journal*, Vol CI, No. 423, 1971, p. 154.
51. See Vijendra Singh Jafa, 'Insurgencies in North-East India: Dimensions of Discord and Containment', in S.D. Muni (ed.), *Responding to Terrorism in South Asia*, New Delhi: Manohar Books, 2006, p. 96.
52. See Vivek Chadha, *Even If It ain't Broke Yet, Do Fix It: Enhancing Effectiveness through Military Change*, New Delhi: Pentagon Press, pp. 88–97.
53. See 'India's Surgical Strikes across LoC: Full Statement by DGMO Lt Gen Ranbir Singh', *Hindustan Times*, 29 September 2016, at https://www.hindustantimes.com/india-news/india-s-surgical-strikes-across-loc-full-statement-by-dgmo-lt-gen-ranbir-singh/story-Q5yrp0gjvxKPGazDzAnVsM.html.
54. Ministry of External Affairs, 'Statement by Foreign Secretary on 26 February 2019 on the Strike on JeM Training Camp at Balakot', n. 28.
55. The most visible change was evident in West Asia, where countries like Saudi Arabia and United Arab Emirates (UAE) came out in support of India's actions, in contrast to the past when a number of fugitives chose to seek support in these countries.
56. United Nations Security Council, 'United Nations Security Council Consolidated List', at https://www.un.org/securitycouncil/content/un-sc-consolidated-list.
57. See 'Jurisdictions under Increased Monitoring—March 2022', FATF, at https://www.fatf-gafi.org/publications/high-risk-and-other-monitored-jurisdictions/documents/increased-monitoring-march-2022.html#pakistan.

7

Indian Army and UN Peace Operations

MAJOR GENERAL (DR) AK BARDALAI (RETD)

Introduction

Since its inception, the United Nations (UN) has undertaken a total of 71 Peacekeeping Operations (PKOs).[1] Indian troops have been present in 49 of the 71 UN Peacekeeping missions around the world. These include conventional PKOs to stabilise the security situation between warring states, for example, Egypt and Israel (United Nations Emergency Force [UNEF I]) in 1956, and complex operations, like United Nations Transitional Authority in Cambodia (UNTAC) in 1991; military interventions in Somalia, that is, Unified Task Force (UNITAF) in 1992 and United Nations Operations in Somalia (UNOSOM II) in 1993; and United Nations Assistance Mission for Rwanda (UNAMIR) in 1994. The PKOs have also been established in the Democratic Republic of the Congo (DRC), Liberia and Cote d'Ivoire to contain conflict and pave the way for peace. Unfortunately, not many of these missions can be said to have succeeded.[2]

A variety of reasons explain why states contribute to PKOs. National interest has traditionally been the foremost concern influencing a state's decision to either participate in or support a UN-authorised peace operation. Further, it has been argued that a government's foreign policy decision is guided by the perceived interests of that government.[3] However, disagreeing with this thought process, David Gibbs states that, among other factors, economic and strategic considerations also play a part while deciding to participate in PKOs.[4] Meanwhile, after examining 14 PKOs from 2001–08, Brian Urlacher concluded that countries had myriad reasons for participating in PKOs, ranging from financial benefits to establishing or advancing a position within the international community, asserting influence on the world stage and preserving peace and security.[5] However, essentially, more than the desire to restore global peace, the self-interest of the states is the primary driver in the decision-making process for participating in PKOs.

In terms of numbers, troops from the South Asian region presently dominate the UN peacekeeping missions. The only exception perhaps is the United Nations Interim Force in Lebanon (UNIFIL), where participation from European nations is the highest, that is, nearly half of the entire mission strength.[6]

This chapter traces how the Indian Army's approach to UN peacekeeping has evolved over a period of time, side by side with the difficult journey of UN peace operations over the decades. A brief overview of the country's participation in various PKOs is given, along with the rigorous training and selection process followed for the Indian peacekeepers as well as a few facts about India's position on the development of the UN peacekeeping doctrines.

Climate change and its impact on security is a new and urgent concern of the international community. Hence, besides peacekeeping, this chapter will also briefly touch upon the Indian Army's experience in providing assistance to civil authorities during natural disasters and how these can come in handy in conflict zones.

India and UN Peacekeeping[7]

Since the inception of the first UN peacekeeping mission in 1948, the Indian Armed Forces have been participating in some of the most difficult peacekeeping missions in the world. Lieutenant General (Lt Gen) P S Gyani and Lt Gen Dewan Prem Chand are some of the prominent figures who tenanted appointments in UN. The first peace operation in which India participated was in Korea (1950–54),[8] even though it was not a classical UN PKO. India contributed a medical unit and Parachute Field Ambulance. The Parachute Field Ambulance was tasked to operate as two entities: the principal part commanded by Lieutenant Colonel (Lt Col) AG Rangaraj, to provide medical support to multinational troops in the battle zone and the remaining unit under Major (Maj) NB Banerjee to aid the South Korean Field Hospitals in the strategic town of Taegu. A total of 17 officers, nine junior commissioned officers JCOs, and 300 other ranks ORs participated in this mission. This was followed by a Custodian Force of 231 officers, 203 (JCOs), and 5,696 (ORs) under the command of Major General (Maj Gen); (later Lt Gen) SPP Thorat for the Neutral Nations Repatriation Commission of which the Chairman was Lt Gen (later General) KS Thimayya.[9] While he was engaged in the peacekeeping efforts in Cyprus, General Thimayya suddenly expired on 18 December 1965. The medical unit's exemplary contribution was recognised by the Minister of War of Great Britain, wherein a tribute was paid to the unit and the Commanding Officer in the House of Commons. The unit had the unique distinction of receiving a 'Meritorious Unit Citation' from the United States (US) Army as well. For their gallant and exemplary actions, the personnel of the unit were honoured with numerous awards, including the Maha Vir Chakra (MVC) to Lt Col AG Rangaraj.[10]

Korea was followed by participation in Gaza (UNEF I) in 1956 and later in Congo (ONUC) in 1960. Its participation in the initial peace operations led to a pool of military officers seconded to the UN. Maj Gen IJ Rikhye was the first Military Adviser to the UN Secretary-General between 1960–1967. According to Lt Gen Satish Nambiar, 'India also contributed significantly to the Indo-China Supervisory Commission deployed in Cambodia, Laos and Vietnam from 1954 to 1970; a medical detachment from 1964 to 1968, and 970 officers, 140 JCOs and 6157 ORs over the period 1954 to 1970.'[11]

After the end of the Cold War, India participated in several missions only with unarmed observers and with formed units in Angola (UNAVEM), Somalia (UNOSOM), Sierra Leone (UNAMSIL), and Liberia (UNMIL) with a female-formed police unit (FFPU).[12] Currently, Indian peacekeepers are participating in the United Nations Organization Stabilization Mission in the Democratic Republic of the Congo (MONUSCO), United Nations Mission in South Sudan (UNMISS), UNIFIL and the United Nations Security Force in Abyei (UNISFA) with effect from 2022.[13]

Like other troop-contributing countries (TCCs), India's participation in peacekeeping is guided by its strategic interests, which are decided on a case-to-case basis. However, India does believe in adhering to the core principles of peacekeeping, as enshrined in the 'Capstone doctrine'.[14] Despite inherent ambiguity in the interpretation of the principles of peacekeeping, India, by practice, tries to take a clear stand when it comes to applying these principles in mandate implementation.[15] Nevertheless, as every situation is different in armed conflicts, it is problematic to legislate how to deal with each arising situation. Besides, even though enshrined in the Capstone doctrine, the peace operations doctrine is also still evolving.

India's position on important developments that impact the effectiveness of peace operations can be inferred from its stated positions in the UN as well as its practices in the field. The country's opinion on central issues that are intricately connected to mandate implementation of the peace operation has been summarised by the Permanent Mission of India (PMI) to the UN:

> India is of the view that the international community must grasp the rapid changes that are underway in the nature and role of contemporary peacekeeping operations. The Security Council's mandates to UN peacekeeping operations need to be rooted in ground realities and correlated with the resources provided

> for the peacekeeping operation…[T]troop and police-contributing countries must be fully involved at all stages and in all aspects of mission planning. There should be greater financial and Human Resources for peacebuilding in post-conflict societies where UNPKOs have been mandated.[16]

Indian Peacekeepers

Asoke Mukerji, a former Indian Ambassador to the UN, has noted that 'India's contributions to UN peacekeeping Operations (UNPKOs) have been underscored by the experience and professionalism of India's armed forces.'[17] Nearly half of India's Army is involved in internal security duties or counter-terrorist operations within the country. Years of experience in such operations have taught the Indian Army the need for patience, maturity and compassion. Therefore, Commanders of the Indian Army Contingents prefer the use of deterrence, negotiation, control measures, protection, warning and security of their areas as an alternative to the use of force against belligerents. To this end, a lot of importance is given to the selection, training and equipping of the individual as well as contingent members before their induction into the mission areas.

The 'selection' process for the Indian Army's peacekeepers is very elaborate. The officers and personnel below officer rank, who aspire to participate in peacekeeping missions in an individual capacity, undergo a stringent merit-based selection system. Professional competence, grades obtained in various courses of instruction, integrity, loyalty and the potential to hold higher ranks or assignments in the future are only a few of the criteria that decide the nomination of a candidate for UN peacekeeping. Similar criteria are followed while selecting individual police peacekeepers and police contingents. The selection process of troop contingents is equally strict. Past performance of these units in battlefield conditions is an important criterion for them to be called upon to be part of UN peacekeeping missions. Additionally, Indian troop contingents are always based on single homogenous units, thereby retaining their cohesiveness. For example, the core of a battalion group in the Indian Army is always a single Infantry battalion. All other non-Infantry elements are only by way of support of the Infantry for better logistic sustenance.

The first stage of peacekeeping training for the officers begins at the military academies—the National Defence Academy, Indian Military Academy, and the Officers Training Academy. This training is gradually augmented as an officer goes through his mandatory and selected courses in various training institutions. For other ranks, a soldier gets his basic training at the battalion level. The second stage or advanced training is conducted as part of the national pre-deployment training curriculum before induction into the mission. In addition, all officers, selected as staff officers/

unarmed military observers or forming part of a contingent, are made to go through a detailed training programme at the Centre for United Nations Peacekeeping (CUNPK), New Delhi, which is the Indian Army's premier institution for peacekeeping. For the training to be meaningful, training content and methodologies are carefully worked out and oriented towards the mission.

The training and the stringent selection process have proved to be of particular use in the PKOs. It is probably the Indian peacekeepers' decades of experience and understanding of the nuances of peacekeeping, selection of the peacekeepers and preparation before participation in PKOs that makes them acceptable anywhere in the world. Before discussing India's position on the UN peacekeeping doctrine, we will take a look at some key missions, the experience of which laid down the foundation of future peacekeeping. India has also participated in some of the missions being discussed here. The background of the missions will help us to better understand the ambiguities related to the doctrinal development of UN peace operations.

Peacekeeping Missions: Past and Current

UNEF I

The UNEF I was a seminal operation, the strategy of which laid down the framework for future UN PKOs and the identification of three principles of peacekeeping. Post the Arab–Israel War of 1948, the United Nations Truce Supervision Organization (UNTSO), the first UN PKO, was created to preserve ceasefire along the armistice lines. However, UNTSO was found to be ineffective during the Suez Crisis of 1956. This came in the wake of the nationalisation of the Suez Canal by Egyptian President, Gamal Abdel Nasser, on 26 July 1956. Based on a secret agreement between Israel, the UK and France, Israel invaded Egypt on 29 October 1956.[18]

Recognising the challenging situation arising due to the crisis, the United Nations Security Council (UNSC) adopted a resolution calling for an emergency meeting of the General Assembly.[19] Since a collective enforcement action became politically impossible, on 2 November 1956, the UN General Assembly passed a resolution calling for a ceasefire and withdrawal of forces.[20] On 04 November, the General Assembly passed a landmark resolution—Resolution 998—authorising the Secretary-General to set up 'an emergency United Nations international force to secure and supervise the cessation of hostility'[21]—UNEF I. While adopting the resolution, the General Assembly did not elaborate on the strategy, or the employability of the force or the composition, which was left to the Secretary-General. The strategy adopted by the Secretary-General was later described in his report to the General Assembly.[22] The key elements of this strategy were the identification of the three cardinal principles of peacekeeping, called the 'holy trinity'—consent, impartiality and use of force.[23] The Indian contingent that participated in UNEF consisted of Headquarters, Infantry Battalion, Platoon of Army Service Corps, Detachments from the Corps of Signals, Ordnance, Medical, Military Police and Army Postal Service. The Indian contribution accounted for the bulk of the UN forces and more than 12,000 Indian troops took part in UNEF, involving 393 officers, 409 JCOs, and 12,383 ORs over the course of 11 years, with Maj Gen PS Gyani and Brig IJ Rikhye as Force Commanders for the mission. The Indian contingents were actively involved in exchange of prisoners, monitoring the withdrawal of Israeli forces and acted as an effective buffer between the opposing forces. In the Indian Sector, several posts were set up to observe the boundary line and the troops had to routinely negotiate anti-personnel and anti-tank mines, and sustained 27 fatal casualties.[24]

After the UK, France and Israel pulled back, the Suez Canal—under Egyptian control—was reopened in April 1957 to international traffic, and UNEF settled down into its monitoring role on the Egyptian side of the armistice line. On 17 June 1967, at the request of the Egyptian government, the UNEF operation formally ended.

United Nations Operations in the Congo (ONUC)

Congo was a Belgian colony from 1908 until it gained its independence on 30 June 1960. The internal situation in the Democratic Republic of Congo (DRC) started to deteriorate soon after its independence, with violent clashes in certain areas and mutinies by Congolese soldiers against Belgian officers. Soon, Belgian military reinforcements arrived to restore order and protect Belgian citizens, but this was done without the permission of the Congolese government. Simultaneously, Moise Tshombe, the head of the provincial government of Katanga, declared independence of Katanga on 10 July 1960, further compounding the situation.

All these developments prompted the Congo's new leaders to appeal to the UN on 12 July 1960 for assistance.[25] Recognising the urgency of the situation, Secretary-General Dag Hammarskjold exercised his power under Article 99 of UN Charter XV and called for an immediate meeting of the UNSC. On 17 July, the Congolese President and the Prime Minister informed the Representative of the Secretary-General in the Congo that if the UN was unable to ensure the withdrawal of the Belgium troops within 48 hours, they would be forced to request the intervention of the Soviet Union.[26] This created a decision dilemma in the UNSC. For the West, the reports of Belgium's involvement were a matter of concern, and so were the political and economic implications of the situation. For the Eastern bloc, more specifically the Soviet Union, it was a good opportunity that could be used to highlight the imperialistic idea of the West if no action was taken. Overall, everybody wanted to do 'something'. Hammarskjold dominated most of the discussions that followed and indirectly forced the hands of the Security Council to act.[27]

On 14 July 1960, the ONUC was established via UNSC Resolution 143, which called for the withdrawal of Belgium troops and authorised the Secretary-General 'to take all necessary steps' to provide the government with 'such military assistance as may be necessary' until the national security forces are able 'to meet fully their tasks'. A total of five resolutions were adopted by the UNSC associated with the withdrawal of the Belgian military and mercenaries and the goals of internal stability.[28]

The deployment of the peacekeepers was rather quick, with Tunisian troops reaching the area immediately, followed by the Swedish Force Commander Maj Gen Carl Von Horn, who was seconded by UNTSO and troops from Africa. Despite some improvement, the security situation in Katanga deteriorated further and things came to head when, in mid-February 1961, Prime Minister Patrice Lumumba was killed. Eventually, ONUC was forced to launch two military operations—Operation Rumpunch on 28 August 1961 and Operation Morthor on 13 September 1961—and, later, another operation on 28 December 1961, which led to the restoration of order with full control of Katanga achieved on 17 January 1963. The ONUC was terminated on 30 June 1964.

India's contribution to the military operation with a brigade-size group was notable. The 99 Infantry Brigade Group was deployed in Congo, consisting of three Infantry Battalions, an Armoured Squadron, a Heavy Mortar Battery, an Engineer Company, a Machine Gun Company, Field Ambulances as well as six Canberra aircraft of the Indian Air Force (IAF). It was here that Captain (Capt) GS Salaria sacrificed his life in an operation against the Katangese gendarmerie on 28 December 1961. Salaria was posthumously decorated with the Param Vir Chakra, India's highest gallantry award, for his actions in Congo.

The ONUC was the first PKO to use force beyond self-defence. In this mission, 135 personnel lost their lives, which is the highest in any UN military operation so far. On a positive note, Secretary-General Hammarskjold played a hands-on role throughout the crisis. His initiative, personal involvement in all discussions and finally, being able to convince the Security Council to act is something that would probably be never forgotten in the UN's peacekeeping history. The ONUC's experience also foreshadowed the current challenges of intra-state conflict to the UN.[29]

United Nations Protection Force (UNPROFOR—Bosnia Herzegovina)

The Indian Army did not participate in the peace operations in the former republic of Yugoslavia other than Lt Gen Satish Nambiar, who was the UNPROFOR's first Head of the Mission and Force Commander (although India contributed to the International Police Task Force [IPTF] from 1996–2001[30]). However, the lessons learnt from the mission with special reference to the application of the principles of peacekeeping, mainly *the use of force,* are still relevant for the current peace operations. For a good understanding of how UN peacekeeping has evolved over the past several decades, it is important to be aware of the events that gradually unfolded following the extension of the mandate of UNPROFOR from Croatia to Bosnia and Herzegovina, to cope with the growing instability between Bosnian Serbs, Muslims and the Croat population.

UNPROFOR had a difficult mandate based on the consent and cooperation of numerous belligerent groups. Its efforts in Bosnia Herzegovina were thwarted by endless hostilities amongst the fighting factions and other operational shortcomings. Subsequently, its mandate was expanded to provide protective support for the United Nations High Commissioner for Refugees (UNHCR) humanitarian convoys but without any mention of Chapter VII. The UNPROFOR was to operate according to the traditional peacekeeping rules of engagement (RoE) and was authorised to use force only in self-defence.

The fighting continued to intensify mostly in small pockets of territories around Srebrenica, Zepa and Gordaze, which were crowded with Muslims, many of whom had fled there from the surrounding countryside. Poorly defended by Bosnian government soldiers, these areas were attacked by Bosnian Serb forces assisted by paramilitary units. Such attacks resulted in heavy loss of life among the civilian population and severely impeded UN humanitarian relief efforts in that area. Fighting slowly spread to other parts of the country, with increasing attacks on other 'safe areas' and UNPROFOR personnel. The UNPROFOR found itself short of troops to deal with the emerging security situation. Different perceptions about safe areas could also be attributed to the continuous attacks on the safe areas. Safe areas were a temporary mechanism where some vulnerable populations were to be protected pending a comprehensive negotiated political settlement. Since the safe areas contained not only civilians but also Bosnian government troops, the Serb forces considered them to be legitimate targets in the war.

The period from March to November 1995 witnessed an unprecedented level of military activities, including offensives by all sides, mass-scale movements of refugees and displaced persons, and gross violations of human rights. Continued lack of diplomatic activities and failure on the part of the international community resulted in a new wave of 'ethnic cleansing' by the Bosnian Serbs in western Bosnia, which later spread to central Bosnia and then on to Sarajevo. In Sarajevo, Bosnian Serbs ignored the UN threat of airstrikes and went to the extent of taking 300 UNPROFOR personnel as hostages to use them as human shields to deter any airstrikes. Images of some of the hostages, chained and used as human shields were broadcast worldwide. One of the observation posts, lost to Bosnian Serbs during the clash, was later recaptured by UNPROFOR though at the cost of the lives of a few peacekeepers. The hostage crisis was, however, resolved through negotiations.

In mid-1995, several events dramatically changed the dynamics of the war. On 11 July 1995, the Bosnian Serb Army overran Srebrenica, taking 150 Dutch peacekeepers as hostages and forcing some 40,000 people to flee. Meanwhile, in the largest massacre in Europe since World War II, Bosnian Serb forces killed some 7,000 people, virtually all of them men or boys, mostly Muslims. Days after the fall of Srebrenica, Serb forces overran Zepa, another so-called safe area. In early August, the Croatian Army retaliated against the Bosnian offensive by a massive military offensive involving some 100,000 troops and overran all Serb-controlled areas in western and eastern Croatia. As a result, some 200,000 Serb civilians fled, most of them going to the Federal Republic of Yugoslavia, with a small number remaining in the Serb-controlled parts of Bosnia and Herzegovina. Paying no heed to the North Atlantic Treaty Organization (NATO) air threats, the Croatian Army's attack was immediately responded to by Serb forces by firing at the busy marketplace in Sarajevo, killing civilians and injuring dozens more. To deter any more attacks on the safe areas, NATO airstrikes were conducted against Bosnian Serb positions. Bolstered by the airstrikes, Croatian and Bosnian government forces mounted a joint offensive in Bosnia and Herzegovina and took back a third of the territory held by the Bosnian Serb forces. Finally, the continuous diplomatic effort resulted in the Dayton Peace Agreement in Paris on 14 December 1995, and the replacement of UNPROFOR with a 60,000 strong multinational military Implementation Force (IFOR) on 20 December 1995. Subsequently, this new mission in Bosnia Herzegovina came to be known as the United Nations Mission in Bosnia and Herzegovina (UNBIH).

UNOSOM II

Following the downfall of President Siad Barre in January 1991, a civil war broke out in Somalia, leading to widespread death and destruction. The UN became engaged in providing humanitarian aid, in cooperation with relief organisations. Given the circumstances of the civil war, there was no effective government to give the consent, so the UN faced difficulties in carrying out humanitarian activities. As a result, the UN, in cooperation with the Organization of African Unity (OAU) and other organisations, sought to resolve the conflict. In January 1992, a UN envoy, with a team of senior officials, visited Somalia. During the visit, all faction leaders expressed support for a UN peace role. This led the Security Council to approve the establishment of UNOSOM I with 50 unarmed observers in April 1992.[31] On 12 August 1992, the Special Representative of the Secretary-General (SRSG) obtained the consent of all parties for the deployment of 500 peacekeepers in Mogadishu.[32]

Later, on the recommendation of the Secretary-General, the Security Council approved an enlarged deployment of a total of 3,500 peacekeepers.[33] This enraged the leader of one of the factions in Somalia, who considered it a breach of faith, leading to increased violence. As a result, acting under Chapter VII, the Security Council authorised the US-led coalition—also called the United Task Force (UNITAF)—to use force to secure a conducive environment for the distribution of humanitarian aid in Somalia.[34]

In 1993, the UNSC passed a resolution on the transition from UNITAF to UNOSOM II, with a strength of 22,000 and a mandate to cover all of Somalia.[35] Even though the US handed over responsibility to UNOSOM II on 4 May 1993, a sizeable number of its troops stayed back in support of UNOSOM II. India contributed one Infantry Brigade Group with three Infantry Battalions, one Mechanised Infantry Battalion, an Independent Armoured Squadron, an Artillery Battery, an Engineer Company, a Signals Company, a Field Ambulance and other supporting elements to UNOSOM II. Apart from the Indian Army deployment, the Indian Navy also deployed a maritime task force consisting of six ships for the delivery of humanitarian assistance. The violence continued and clashes with the UN peacekeepers as well as the US forces increased.

The UNSC extended the mandate of UNOSOM II till November 1993, allowing more time for an in-depth study of the Somali situation.[36] On 4 February 1994, the Security Council significantly downsized UNOSOM in terms of its strength and mandate, to 'traditional peacekeeping' only in the assistance role, till March 1995.[37] The UNOSOM II was finally closed on 2 March 1995.

UNIFIL

The Lebanese civil war, which began in 1975, led to a power vacuum and confrontation between Israel and its Lebanese proxies on one side, and the 'Joint Forces' of the Palestine Liberation Organization (PLO) and Progressive Lebanese Movement on the other. This resulted in a series of offensive actions by militias supported by Israel along the Lebanon–Israel border, which continued for almost two years. It ended with the US-backed (and Israeli-approved) deployment of the Arab Deterrent Force (ADF), a peacekeeping force mostly comprised of troops from the Syrian Army.[38] However, later, Egypt, under President Sadat, broke away from its Arab allies and made peace with Israel on 26 March 1979, becoming the first Arab nation to forge a diplomatic relationship with Israel. Soon after, Israel increased its cross-border raids on Lebanon.[39]

The UNIFIL is the result of Israel's first major invasion of Lebanon on 14–15 March 1978.[40] On 19 March 1978, the UNSC adopted Resolutions 425 and 426 calling for the immediate withdrawal of Israeli forces and authorising the establishment of UNIFIL.[41] The initial contributions to UNIFIL came from France, Nepal, Norway, Iran, Senegal, Nigeria, Ireland and Fiji. Resolution 425 mandated UNIFIL to: confirm the withdrawal of Israeli forces from Lebanese territory; restore international peace and security in the border area; and assist the Government of

Lebanon in ensuring the return of its effective authority in the area. The UNIFIL was thus established as a traditional mission to broker peace between Lebanon and Israel.[42] Further, the UNIFIL was established in a hurry for political reasons, to avoid derailing Camp David Accords that President Carter was pushing at that time.[43]

Following Hezbollah's kidnapping of two Israeli soldiers in a cross border raid, Israel invaded Lebanon again in July 2006, which lasted for 34 days. Finally, amidst immense public outcry and with full support from the US and France, on 11 August 2006, the Security Council unanimously adopted Resolution 1701 (co-drafted by the US and France), giving shape to the present structure of UNIFIL.[44] In addition to the mandate under Resolutions 425 and 426, UNSC Resolution 1701 authorised UNIFIL a strength of 15,000 troops.

India has participated in UNIFIL since December 1998. Until now, more than 40,000 peacekeepers have already participated in UNIFIL. Currently, there is a Battalion Group, one Level II Hospital, and more than 20 staff officers deployed in UNIFIL.

Principles of Peacekeeping

Peacekeeping has been undertaken under the aegis of the UN since the 1950s. Each conflict and its political and diplomatic resolution is unique. So too is the nature and requirement of peacekeeping given the specific context. In some cases, UNPKOs have led to the resolution of conflict and the operation is formally closed. In others, such as UNIFIL for example, the requirement of peacekeeping remains as the conflict is ongoing and there appears to be no resolution on the horizon. In the past seven decades, there have been numerous doctrinal developments vis-à-vis UN Peacekeeping and PKOs. The following sections shed light on a few facts about India's position on the doctrines of UN peacekeeping.

The principles which India adheres to while participating in peacekeeping missions are enshrined in the UN's 'doctrine' for PKOs—which is based on strict adherence to the core principles of peacekeeping.[45] These principles are always carefully considered when deciding on India's participation in any PKO. Once deployed, correct understanding and adherence to the basic principles of peacekeeping—consent, impartiality and neutrality and use of force—continue to remain the central elements that guide the day-to-day operational activities of Indian contingents. However, there have been times when India's decision to participate, or not, in the PKOs has been guided by other considerations. For instance, India decided against contributing troops to the United Nations–African Union peacekeeping mission in Darfur, possibly to not lose the support of Sudanese President Omar Hassan Ahmad al-Bashir.

India's position has always been consistent with regard to the principles of peacekeeping. There were widespread speculations about the actual motive of India's pulling out from UNAMSIL.[46] However, according to the Indian official spokesman, though India did pull out of UNAMSIL, the decision was not motivated by any political reason but by the fact that it was part of the routine rotation, to give an opportunity to other TCCs.[47] There was another reason that prompted India to pull out from UNAMSIL.[48] It was related to the UN Charter. When India decided to participate in UNAMSIL, the mission was mandated under UN Charter VI (UNSC Resolution 1270). Later, because of the developing security situation in Sierra Leone, the mandate was revised to act under Charter VII (UNSC Resolution 1289).[49] It was felt that since the revised resolution impacted mandate implementation and those who were to implement it, this revision should have been taken in consultation with major TCCs like India.

In May 2000, the security situation deteriorated in Sierra Leone and the rebels took several peacekeepers hostage, which included a sizeable number of Indian peacekeepers.[50] The official reports of the Secretary-General, however, referred to it only as 'detention'. This notwithstanding, in one of the biggest UN military operations of the time which was launched by the Indian Army—Operation Khukri—all hostages were rescued. Post Operation Khukri, the Indian government pulled out from UNAMSIL.[51] At the time of pulling out India's position, as stated earlier, was because it would not participate in peace operations mandated under Chapter VII of the UN charter.

India considers impartiality as an important ingredient of peacekeeping and its actions are independent of the stand of parties to a conflict; it is based on an assessment of the situation as well as an intent to be just, while not taking sides. On the other hand, the neutral entity is much more passive.[52] Former UN Secretary-General Kofi Annan further reinforced this vision in May 1998, during his visit to Rwanda, when he stated: 'In the face of genocide, there can be no standing aside, no looking away, no neutrality—there are perpetrators and there are victims; it is evil and there is evil's harvest.'[53]

To establish impartiality, 'use of force' may be necessary to implement the mandate. However, the history of UN peacekeeping demonstrates that whenever force has been used, there has always been retaliation, endangering the security of peacekeepers.[54] This, however, has not deterred the Indian peacekeepers from using force to save innocent lives and restore peace. For instance, in the DRC, MONUSCO (the current UNPKO in the DRC) used Indian gunships against rebel groups who were determined to derail the peace process.[55] Even in Sierra Leone, force was used to rescue the hostages from rebels. The multinational operation was led by the Indian Force Commander, Major General Vijay Jetley, and the Indian peacekeeping contingent was in the lead.

As mentioned earlier, the next section will highlight Indian Army's experience in handling natural calamities while providing aid to the civil authorities, which come in handy in implementing certain non-mandated tasks while deployed in peacekeeping operations.

Humanitarian Assistance and Disaster Relief (HADR)

The Indian subcontinent is prone to earthquakes, floods, droughts, cyclones, etc. Over the past decade and more, the region has seen massive earthquakes in the Himalayan belt (Kashmir 2005, Nepal 2015), recurrent floods (Assam), cyclones (1999 Orissa), avalanches in the higher Himalayas, and even freak natural and climate-induced disasters such as the one that occurred in Uttarakhand in 2013. Given this, there has been a conscious effort to work out and adopt a multi-dimensional, multi-disciplinary and multi-Sectoral approach to disaster management. The Indian Armed Forces constitute a significant resource available to the Government of India for disaster response and providing relief to the affected populace.

Thus, beyond its primary duty to protect the nation's borders, and its role in counterinsurgency and internal security, the Indian Army—along with the other Services and paramilitary and security organisations—also provides aid to civil authority. The Disaster Management Act of 2005 has ensured that the Army's role in disaster response remain focused on critical issues, with optimal utilisation of dedicated resources. Its structure, organisation and spread, and training ensures that it is capable of reaching out to the remotest of areas and terrain under the most difficult conditions. In terms of disaster relief, the Army can respond instantaneously and mobilise self-contained, composite task forces to any part of the country, even overseas, in conjunction with the Indian Navy and the Indian Air Force (IAF).

Since Independence the Indian Army has been amongst the first responder in most HADR operations across the country in varied terrain and the performance of the Indian Army has been remarkable and they have always delivered. The presence of the Army conducting HADR operations has raised the morale of the affected people in that area and they have carried out the tasks assigned to them with the utmost professionalism and dedication. Over the past two decades, the Indian Army has provided assistance and relief during the following instances. The range of HADR operations that the Army has been involved in is too vast to be discussed in detail here. Therefore, a few operations from the past two decades have been discussed below to provide readers with a brief view of the Indian Army's role and activities in HADR.

2004 Indian Ocean Tsunami

The Indian Army was able to deploy its columns in the first six to nine hours following the Indian Ocean Tsunami in 2004. This was followed by a systematic build up over long distances, in conjunction with the Navy and the Air Force. Around 8,300 troops were immediately mobilised and grouped into task forces for rescue and relief operations. These task forces were sent not just to locatiions within India—Tamil Nadu, Pondicherry and Kerala, but also overseas in the Andaman and Nicobar Islands and to neighbouring Sri Lanka.

Around 27,986 persons were rescued/evacuated under extremely hostile conditions. Around 60 relief camps were established, 41,080 patients were treated in mobile field hospitals/camps, over 990 dead bodies were recovered, debris cleared and essential rations, food packets, medicines, clothing, blankets and kerosene oil provided to the traumatised populace. The task forces were, thereafter, involved in rehabilitation and reconstruction operations for a sustained period of six to nine months, including restoration and manning of essential services, restoration of surface communications to include launching of bailey bridges and operation of ferries, erection of temporary dwelling units and toilets, enforcement of hygiene and sanitation measures to prevent an epidemic outbreak, trauma and psychological counseling, as also informative classes on employment and recruitment opportunities for youth, among others.

Kashmir Earthquake 2005

Despite the loss of 45 personnel and many other injured, the Indian Army, by virtue of its location in Kashmir, was able to immediately assume the role of the primary agency for rescue and relief effort after the 2005 earthquake in Kashmir. The Army's rescue teams were the first to reach the isolated, inaccessible areas. A total of 52 columns, comprising 2,600 troops, along with 39 medical teams, and 31 tonnes of medicine and specialised mountaineering equipment, were mobilised for the rescue and relief operation, known as Operation Imdad. The Army set up 40 relief camps, rescued 1,200 people, treated 6,000 civilian patients, and distributed around 150 tonnes of rations and 18,000 food packets to the affected populace.

Disease and Floods in Kerala

Consequent to the outbreak of vector-borne diseases like Dengue and Chikunguniya in Kerala in June 2007, the Indian Army's services were requisitioned by State Government. Medical and Health Teams with the requisite fogging and spray equipment were thus deployed to aid the state authorities. Army personnel carried out extensive fogging and spray of anti-larval pesticides was carried out at Amburi,

Patnamthitta, Kollam and Thalachira. Additionally, a Research Team comprising of an Entomologist, a Virologist and and Epidemiologist was also deployed for investigation and advice. A Neuro Physician, formerly with the Military Hospital Southern Command, Pune, also visited the affected areas.

In 2018, the state was also witness to heavy rainfall in the northern districts which also resulted in landslides. The Indian Army was involved in rescue operations in Idukki, Wayanad, Kannur, and Kozhikode districts of Kerala under Operation Sahyog. The Army dispatched ten flood relief columns, ten Engineer Task Forces (ETF), with approximately 40 personnel each were dispatched from Jodhpur, Bhopal, Pune, Bangalore and Secunderabad. Around 53 military boats were used to evacuate civilians from flood affected areas.

Nepal Earthquake 2015

In aftermath of the massive earthquake in Nepal in April 2015, the Government of India and the Indian Armed Forces launched Operation Maitri, a rescue and relief operation. The Indian response was instantaneous and began on 26 April 2015. Within three days of the operation, working in conjunction, the Indian Army and the IAF had evacuated 170 foreign nationals belonging to US, the UK, Russia and Germany from Nepal, and brought back over 5,000 Indians using IAF and civilian aircraft. India sent 18 medical teams (comprising 20 people each), and 12 engineer teams of about 60 people to assist in recovery and relief operations.

Conclusion

India has a rich history of participating in UN peace operations. Currently, the country is one of the leading TCCs and its peacekeepers are deployed, amongst others, in the two most difficult peace operations—MONUSCO and UNMISS.[56] India believes in the UN Charter and adhering to the three cardinal principles of peacekeeping in their true spirit. Even though India's doctrine for peace operations has not yet been legislated in writing, it is influenced by the articles of faith in its Constitution. It endorses the peacekeeping principles; wholeheartedly believes that PoC is the core obligation of the UN; that it is the responsibility of the host state to protect its civilians; and has reservations about the spirit and intent of the concept of R2P. The question, however, is how has its rich history (past and present) made India relevant in UN peacekeeping?

For quite some time India has been one of the top TCCs and it takes pride and claims that India deserves much more than what it has. There is a misnomer that the UN is desperate to have Indian peacekeepers because we are the best and they cannot do without us. There is no doubt that Indian peacekeepers are some of the best in peacekeeping operations. Because of their unique approach to peacekeeping, the Indian peacekeepers' local legitimacy and credibility are higher than their counterparts from developed nations. But whether the UN cannot do without Indian peacekeepers is questionable. Those who take important policy decisions do not participate in difficult operations. To them, it is not looking for the best but someone like Indian peacekeepers and a few other nations from the Global South, that are ever ready to implement the plan of a few developed nations. Capable peacekeepers undoubtedly help to bring stability to the conflict zone. However, for the peace process to move forward and for sustainable peace, there is a need to build the capability of peacekeeping to make it more effective.

In this context, while India takes pride in its contribution to peacekeeping and the ultimate sacrifices it has made in past in the name of peace, the developed nations have surged ahead by investing in the capability-building of peace operations. The list of the elements that can contribute to capability building is not complete. It can range from troop contribution, mandate, financial support, extracting support from host states, approach to the concept of peacekeeping and policy formulation by the UN, or anything that enables the peace operations and encourages the peacekeepers to deliver on the field. For example, when Butros Butros Ghali introduced the concept of *Agenda for Peace* in 1992, he underlined the need to use peace-making to remove the source of danger that could produce conflict, engage in peacekeeping to resolve issues that have led to the conflict, and, thereafter, standby to assist in peacebuilding in different contexts.[57] In the largest sense, to address the deepest causes of conflict, contribution to the concept of Agenda for Peace at different levels would help capability building of peace operations. However, since these three elements—*peace-making, peacekeeping* and *peacebuilding*—are not sequential, they work in tandem in the conflict zone with inter se priority shifting from one arm to another depending on the situation. The UN peace operation in Cambodia is an example of maintaining a good balance of this triangle. In that case, peace-making was done by the French, peacekeeping was by the peacekeepers, and most of the peacebuilding activities were undertaken by Japan, Australia, and France. The United Nations Trans Assistance Mission in Cambodia (UNTAC) is, therefore, often quoted as a successful mission. It is time for India to revisit its contribution to peace beyond the uniformed peacekeepers.

To begin with, in the short term and at the operational level, India can think of enhancing its contribution of the enabling units like engineering construction units, hospitals, air assets, demining teams, etc., and share intelligence. The Indian Army's combat engineers do not undertake humanitarian demining other than operational demining, but the government can always encourage Indian non-governmental organisations (NGOs) that are already in this field. What is important is that the government can identify such assets, encourage them, and support their cases in the UN. Regarding intelligence sharing, gone are the days when the word 'intelligence' was considered taboo, but for intelligence sharing, India will have to build its national capability first.

Being one of the largest democracies, there is potential for India to be a good peacemaker. But it will take the extra mile for actual peace-making. To cite an example, during the Ukraine crisis, many national leaders volunteered to mediate, but only a very few physically visited the war zone and talked to both Presidents to find a solution to the conflict.

As for peacebuilding, India is already doing a lot in developmental activities under different programmes, even though this might not always be in the name of peacebuilding. All that is required is to step up its overseas activities mostly in the areas where countries are trying to recover from the after-effects of the intra-state conflicts, and give it a name that the world wants to hear. In this regard, Yeshi Choedon has underlined India's approach to development/peacebuilding assistance as means to bring about sustainable peace in the conflict areas.[58]

Besides, the Government of India should encourage more scholarly contributions to the doctrinal development of UN peacekeeping. If the availability of finances to support academic research is a constraint, professional engagement between former and current peacekeeping practitioners, bureaucrats who are in the business of taking policy decisions of the nation's contribution to peacekeeping, and well-known Indian think tanks would give India more international visibility in the UN. Until then India will be able only to boast of its past glory of the sacrifices made in peacekeeping operations. As the interest of the other nations in contributing to peace operations grow more and more, there will be a time even our past glory will be consumed by history.

Besides the mandated tasks, being able to quickly respond to the natural disasters that may occur as the consequences of climate change has become a new challenge in peacekeeping missions. The need to train the peacekeepers by the TCCs to face the new challenge has become the subject of discussion mostly amongst the European nations. On the other hand, for Indian peacekeepers, the experience they have gained during their tour of duty in varieties of terrain is unique and would probably remain unmatched by many other TCCs.

Notes

1. UN Department of Peace Operations, 'Peacekeeping Operations Fact Sheet', 30 September 2021, available at https://peacekeeping.un.org/sites/default/files/peacekeeping_missions_fact_sheet_244_sept_2021_en.pdf.
2. UN General Assembly, *Report of the Panel on United Nations Peace Operations*, A/55/305-S/2000/809, 21 August 2000.
3. P Bennis, *Calling the Shots: How Washington Dominates Today's UN*, New York: Olive Branch Press, 1996.

4. D Gibbs, 'Is Peacekeeping a New Form of Imperialism?', *International Peacekeeping*, Vol. 4, No. 1, 1997, pp. 122–28.
5. Brian Urlacher, 'Answering the Call: A Study of Major Contributions to UN Peacekeeping Missions', 2008, available at https://www.academia.Edu, accessed on 17 October 2015.
6. UN, 'United Nations Peacekeeping', available at https://peacekeeping.un.org/en/troop-and-police-contributors; United Nations Security Council (UNSC) Resolutions 425 and 426, 19 March 1978, and Resolution 1701, 11 August 2006.
7. This section has been extracted from Joachim A Koops, Norrie Macqueen, Thierry Tardy and Paul D Williams (eds), *The Oxford Handbook of United Nations Peacekeeping Operations*, Oxford: Oxford University Press, 2015; and *The Blue Helmets: A Review of United Nations Peacekeeping*, New York: UN, 1996.
8. Permanent Mission of India (PMI), 'India and United Nations: Peacekeeping and Peacebuilding', available at https://www.pminewyork.gov.in/pdf/menu/49151pkeeping.pdf.
9. Satish Nambiar, 'India's Role in UN Peacekeeping Operations', Ian Cardozo (ed.), *Indian Army: A Brief History*, New Delhi: USI, 2007, p. 233.
10. "Indian Army's participation in United Nations Peacekeeping Ops," available at https://indianArmy.nic.in/Site/FormTemplete/frmTempSimple.aspx?MnId=b08QWgdzCCD3Ml376nw03BvP+Mxerdr3gadTyyO31M8=&ParentID=aLZn9p6YEorQgWsg4mdbXw==&flag=8CKP966uzg96kLov0aWdfQ==
11. Ibid.
12. Asoke Kumar Mukerji, 'UN Peacekeeping: India's Contributions', *Ministry of External Affairs,* 8 November 2019, at https://mea.gov.in/articles-in-indian-media.htm?dtl/32014/UN_Peacekeeping_Indias_Contributions.
13. 'Troop and Police Contributors', at https://peacekeeping.un.org/en/troop-and-police-contributors.
14. *United Nations Peacekeeping Operations: Principles and Guidelines*, New York: UN Department of Public Information, 2008; also known as the 'Capstone doctrine'.
15. AK Bardalai, 'Ambiguity in Normative UN Norms: A Challenge to UN Peace Operations', under publication by the Integrated Headquarters (HQ) of the Army, Ministry of Defence; and John Karlsrud and Kseniya Oksamytna, 'Norms and Practices in UN Peacekeeping: Evolution and Contestation', *International Peacekeeping*, Vol. 26, No. 3, 2019, pp. 253–54.
16. PMI, 'India and United Nations: Peacekeeping and Peacebuilding', n. 8.
17. Mukerji, 'UN Peacekeeping: India's Contributions', n. 12.
18. Briefly, the plan was for Israel to invade Egypt first, followed by an intervention by the UK and France forcing Israel to withdraw, while the latter would stay back and wrest full control of the canal from the Egyptians. For details see Manuel Frohlich, 'The Suez Story', in Carsten Stahan and Henning Melber (eds), (*Peace Diplomacy, Global Justice and International Agency,* Cambridge: CUP, 2015, pp. 305-40.
19. UNSC Resolution S/RES/119 (1956), 31 October 1956; and UN General Assembly, 'Annexure: Decisions deemed Procedural', A/RES/267 (III), 14 April 1949.
20. UN General Assembly, A/RES/997 (ES-1), 2 November 1956.
21. UN General Assembly, A/RES/998 (ES-1), 4 November 1956.

22. UN, *Summary Study of the Experience Derived from the Establishment and Operation of the Force: Report of the Secretary-General*, A/3943, 9 October 1958.
23. Paul F Diehl, 'First United Nations Emergency Force (UNEF I)', in Koops et al. (eds), *The Oxford Handbook of United Nations Peacekeeping Operations*, n. 7, p. 151.
24. 'Indian Army's participation in United Nations Peacekeeping Ops', at https://indianArmy.nic.in/Site/FormTemplete/frmTempSimple.aspx?MnId=wyMF29cycvxRfT9V0WhFjQ==&ParentID=vAtF1yvYPMqnPt8/dtcGGA==&flag=8CKP966uzg96kLov0aWdfQ==. Also see UN, 'Peacekeeping Fatalities', at https://peacekeeping.un.org/sites/default/files/stats_by_nationality_mission_2_73_march_2022.pdf.
25. 'Cable dated 12 July 1960 from the President of the Republic of the Congo and Supreme Commander of the National Army and the Prime Minister and Minister of National Defence Addressed to the Secretary-General of the United Nations', UNSC, S/4382, 13 July 1960.
26. 'Questions Relating to the Situation in the Republic of Congo (Leopoldville)', available at https://www.un.org/depts/dhl/dag/docs/congo60.pdf.
27. Eşref Aksu, 'The UN in the Congo Conflict: ONUC', in *The United Nations, Intra-State Peacekeeping and Normative Change*, Manchester, England: Manchester University Press, 2018, pp. 100–29, available at https://doi.org/10.7765/9781526137906.00009.
28. UNSC Resolutions: S/RES/143, 14 July 1960; S/RES/145, 22 July 1960; S/RES/146, 9 August 1960; S/RES/161, 21 February 1961; and S/RES/169, 24 November 1961.
29. Jane Boulden, 'United Nations Operations in Congo (ONUC)', in Koops et al. (eds), *The Oxford Handbook of United Nations Peacekeeping Operations*, n. 7, pp. 167–68.
30. For details see, Satish Nambiar, *For the Honour of India: A History of Indian Peacekeeping*, New Delhi: CAFHR, USI, 2009, p. 494.
31. UNSC, S/RES/751 (1992), 24 April 1992; and *Report of the Secretary-General on the Situation in Somalia*, S/24343, 22 July 1992.
32. UNSC, *Report of the Secretary-General on the Situation in Somalia*, S/24480, 24 August 1992.
33. UNSC, S/RES/775 (1992), 28 August 1992.
34. UNSC, S/RES/794 (1992), 3 December 1992.
35. UNSC, S/RES/814 (1993), 26 March 1993.
36. UNSC, S/RES/878 (1993), 29 October 1993; and S/RES/885 (1993), 16 November 1993.
37. UNSC, S/RES/897 (1994), 4 February 1994.
38. Laurie Zittrain Eisenberg, 'From Benign to Malign: Israeli Lebanese Relations, 1948–78', in Clive Jones and Sergio Catignani (eds), *Israel and Hezbollah: An Asymmetric Conflict in Historical and Comparative Perspective*, New York: Routledge, 2010, p. 21; and Imad Salamey, *The Government and Politics of Lebanon*, New York: Routledge, 2013.
39. Salamey, *The Government and Politics of Lebanon*, n. 38.
40. UN, 'UNIFIL Background', available at https://unifil.unmissions.org/unifil-background, accessed on 18 November 2020.
41. United Nations Security Council (UNSC) Resolutions 425 and 426, 19 March 1978.
42. Grant T Hammond, 'The Perils of Peacekeeping for the US: Relearning Lessons from Beirut to Bosnia', in Edward Moon Brown (ed.), *A Future for Peacekeeping*, London: Macmillan Press 1998, pp. 74–75.

43. Marrack Goulding, 'The Evolution of United Nations Peacekeeping', *International Affairs*, Vol. 69, No. 3, 1993, p. 453. Also see AK Bardalai, *United Nations Interim Force in Lebanon: Assessment and Way Forward*, 2021, available at https://research.tilburguniversity.edu/files/50853309/Bardalai_UNIFIL_1_07_2021_correct.pdf.
44. Raffaella A Deal Sarto, *Israel under Siege: The Politics of Insecurity and the Rise of the Israeli Neo-Revisionist Right*, Washington, DC: Georgetown University Press, 2017.
45. *United Nations Peacekeeping Operations: Principles and Guidelines*, n. 14.
46. Colum Lynch, 'India to Withdraw Large UN Force from Sierra Leone', *The Washington Post*, 21 November 2000, available at https://www.washingtonpost.com/archive/politics/2000/09/21/india-to-withdraw-large-un-force-from-sierra-leone/33c46528-678d-4014-b8b2-8aa299a3658b/.
47. 'India Pulling Out of Sierra Leone', *CBS News*, 20 September 2000, available at https://www.cbsnews.com/news/india-pulling-out-of-sierra-leone/.
48. The author, who was then posted at the Army HQs and was handling various subjects related to the Indian Army's participation in peace operations, was privy to the internal discussions between the Ministry of External Affairs, Ministry of Defence and the Army HQs regarding the decision to pull out of UNAMSIL.
49. UNSC Resolution, S/RES/1270 (1999), 22 October 1999; and S/RES/1289 (2000), 7 February 2000.
50. Douglas Farah, 'UN Rescues Hostage in Sierra Leone', *The Washington Post*, 16 July 2000, available at https://www.washingtonpost.com/archive/politics/2000/07/16/un-rescues-hostages-in-sierra-leone/e17f58e7-ec24-4222-8acc-bb78faddcee3/; and UNSC, *Report of the Secretary-General on the United Nations Mission in Sierra Leone*, S/2000/455, 19 May 2000.
51. For more details see, VK Jetley, '"Op Khukri" – The United Nations Operation Fought in Sierra Leone Part-I and Part-II,' *Journal of the USI of India*, Vol. CXXXVII, 2007, at https://usiofindia.org/publication/usi-journal/op-khukri-the-united-nations-operation-fought-in-sierra-leone-part-ii-2/?_sfm_journal_author=Lieutenant+General+V+K+-Jetley,+PVSM,+UYSM+(Retd).
52. D Donald, 'Neutrality, Impartiality and UN Peacekeeping at the Beginning of the 21st Century', *International Peacekeeping*, Vol. 9, No. 4, 2002, p. 22.
53. Ibid., p. 23.
54. AK Bardalai, 'United Nations Peacekeeping Operations: Causes for Failure and Continuing Relevance', *Journal of Defence Studies*, Vol. 12, No. 4, 2018, pp. 5–34.
55. Jonny Hogg and Louis Charbonneau, 'Insight—Getting Tough in Congo: Can Risk Pay off for UN Forcers?', *Reuters*, 29 August 2013, available at https://www.reuters.com/article/uk-congo-un-insight-idUKBRE97S0PZ20130829.
56. From the time of its establishment in 2011, India's participation in UNMISS until now has been significant, comprising over 40,000 peacekeepers. The figures for MONUSCO are around 90,000 peacekeepers, approximately.
57. Butros Butros Ghali, *An Agenda for Peace*, A/47/277-S/24111, New York: The United Nations, 1992.
58. Yeshi Choedon, 'India's Engagement in Development and Peacebuilding Assistance in the Post-Conflict States: An Assessment', *Frontiers in Political Science*, 31 May 2021, at https://doi.org/10.3389/fpos.2021.637912.

8

Indian Army

Ethos, Values and Training

MAJOR GENERAL IAN CARDOZO*(RETD)

Ethos and Values

The Indian Army represents a diverse nation and draws its ethos from the philosophy and beliefs of the society that it serves and of which it is an integral part. India's civilisational values have shaped the ethos and moral code of the Indian Army, which is an amalgam of diverse philosophies, traditions and beliefs drawn from the rich tapestry of histories, myths and cultures of various races that make up India's heterogeneous whole.

The beliefs and value systems of the Marathas, Sikhs, Dogras, Garhwalis, Tamils, Malayalees, Andhraites, Kashmiris, Kodavas, Assamese, Manipuris, Punjabis, Jats, Rajputs, Nagas, Bengalis, Mizos, Oriyas, Gorkhas, the residents of the Konkan coast, and many other clans, tribes and communities have all contributed to the ethos of the Indian Army to make it truly representative of the Indian nation. It is this fusion—of diverse cultures, philosophies and traditions—that continues to be the bedrock of the

*This chapter is an updated and rewritten version of two of the author's previous works: 'The Ethos of the Indian Armed Forces', *Journal of the United Service Institution of India*, Vol. CL, No. 622, October-December 2020, and 'Ethos, Valus, Training', in Maj Gen Ian Cardozo, AVSM, SM (ed.), *The Indian Army: A Brief History*, New Delhi: USI, 2007.

attitude and behaviour of the soldier that teaches him how to live and behave in peace and how to fight and die in war.

The fate of a nation in war depends on how well its soldiers fight. Indeed, the true quality of an Army and the nature of its soldiers becomes evident only in war. It would, however, be foolish to wait for war to discover the proficiency and potential of the Army. It is here that ethos plays a vital part in shaping the Army before it goes to war. This includes an emphasis on sound leadership, high moral code, good training and high morale.

How well soldiers fight depends much on how well they are trained, motivated and led. Leadership at every level plays a critical role in translating the ethos of the Indian Army into performance in peace and war. The selection of leaders is thus very important. Recruiting officers and soldiers using time-tested methods that analyse their character, sense of duty, commitment, integrity and self-discipline is more likely to yield men of moral and physical courage, weeding out candidates that do not have the necessary characteristics that make a good soldier. Therefore, selection systems have to be built in such a way that they are able to identify persons who possess the requisite qualities—qualities that will make them think and act beyond self and for the good of larger causes and institutions, like the country and the people of India.

The moral force that drives the conduct of soldiers in war is based on love—for India, for its people, for the Regiment, for adventure and for a way of life that has no equal. Love may not be a very military word, but it is on the altar of love that men and women in uniform place their lives in the line of fire and, if necessary, make the ultimate sacrifice.

The destiny of a nation during times of war often hangs in balance on the outcome of a battle, which depends on the courage and competence of its soldiers. Regimental spirit is one of the primary motivators that makes men fight without considering the cost. In the history of the Indian Armed Forces, there have been many instances where men have performed outstanding acts of courage for the sake of their Regiment; the honour of the Regiment has always been placed higher than their own lives. The Regimental spirit of the units of the Indian Army, including the traditions which have nurtured them, is the strength of the fighting arms, particularly in times of war. It is this 'cause', larger than the 'self', that is the ultimate of all motivators that has fortified men against death and put 'duty above fear' and 'death above dishonour'. Any meddling with the composition of our Regiments can, therefore, jeopardise the nation's safety.

Leading men into battle is a privilege given to very few. It is an overwhelming responsibility because both the officer and the men he leads are aware that some of them may not come back alive. As the officers of the Indian Army lead from the front, percentage wise, the casualty rate of officers is very high. For instance, my own Battalion, that is, 4th Battalion, the 5th Gorkha Rifles (Frontier Force), entered the

1971 war with 18 officers and only seven survived unscathed at the end of the 14-day war—four officers were killed and seven were badly wounded.

Undoubtedly, the Indian soldier is amongst the best in the world. He is imbued with the quality of putting the country above all else. He follows his officers unquestioningly and undergoes great discomfort, in unbelievably difficult circumstances, without complaint, because he knows that his officer is there right in front facing maximum danger and setting the right example.

The ethos of the armed forces is the lifeblood of its members and inspires them to carry out extraordinary acts of courage. A few examples of leadership and the outcomes that it generates would be useful to understand the important part that honour, courage, self-sacrifice and personal example play in translating these beliefs into action.

Leading by Example

A classic example of leadership linked with the honour of the Regiment is the battle of Dograi. In the 1965 Indo-Pak War, 3 JAT, led by Lieutenant Colonel (Lt Col) Desmond Hayde, captured Dograi across the Ichhogil Canal. It was a hard-fought battle in which many soldiers were killed and wounded. However, as the brigade was not able to provide reinforcements, 3 JAT was ordered to withdraw from the area it had captured. The Battalion followed the orders, but it was unhappy and considered this to be a slur on its honour. Therefore, when Dograi had to be recaptured, 3 JAT volunteered to be at the forefront. For them, it was a matter of honour!

However, by then, the Pakistanis had reinforced Dograi with armour and Infantry, making its capture even more difficult. On the eve of the battle, the commanding officer (CO) addressed the men in Haryanvi. He made it clear that the battle would be tough and that many would be killed and wounded. Then he said: 'I will be leading you into battle and if I die, I want you to carry me to Dograi because I want to be there with you—dead or alive!' He further added: 'Where will we be tomorrow morning?', and the Battalion roared, 'In Dograi!'

In the epic battle that followed, many soldiers were killed and many more wounded, but Dograi was recaptured by the invincible 3 JAT. What was it that made 3 JAT so invincible? The answer is Regimental spirit and morale.

As an instructor at the Indian Military Academy (IMA), Captain (Capt) Desmond Hayde had constantly grilled into our young minds: 'Battles are won or lost in the minds of men, before they are won or lost on the ground!' He made this happen at Dograi, under impossible conditions, and therefore, this battle continues to remain an outstanding example of Regimental honour and courage, exemplifying what the ethos of the Indian Army is all about.

Self-sacrifice is another characteristic of leadership that inspires the soldier to go beyond the call of duty. During the 1971 war, Indian Navy carried out two attacks on Karachi harbour, sinking a destroyer and a mine-sweeper and a few others, thus restricting the Pakistan Navy's fleet. However, their submarine arm was far superior to ours and it was successful in sinking *INS Khukri*. Capt Mahendra Nath Mulla, the captain of *Khukri*, went down with the ship. He had the choice of saving his own life, but it was not part of his character to do so when his men were trapped on the sinking ship. In fact, he gave his own life jacket to a sailor who was without one. As a leader, he practised what he believed. Personal acts of cold courage like this are rare to come by, and when they do, they shake the world by their heroic content and epitomise the moral code which is so much part of the ethos of the armed forces. The way he lived and died has become part of the folklore of the Indian Navy and a guiding light not only to the officers and sailors of the Navy but also to all personnel of India's armed forces.

Another example of self-sacrifice is what happened in a raid across the border by the Indian Air Force during the 1965 Indo-Pakistan War. Squadron Leader 'Tubby' Devayya set a strong example of cool courage and diehard determination in the face of impossible odds. On an attack on the Pakistani airfield at Sargodha, he was faced with the option of returning to his air base in India or engaging in combat with a supersonic Pakistani Starfighter, which was far superior in weapons and avionics to his subsonic Mystere. His orders were to return to base because his fuel was just enough to hit Sargodha and return. However, being the last aircraft of his wave, it was also his duty to protect the other aircraft of the team. So, he turned around and took on the Pakistani Starfighter in an unequal combat setting. Though the Pakistani pilot was able to damage his aircraft, Devayya continued to take on the Starfighter and managed to destroy it, but was killed in the process. He lies today buried in a corner of a farmer's field in Pakistan. His action is an outstanding example of self-sacrifice of the highest order in keeping with the moral code he was taught as a young pilot officer in the Indian Air Force.

There are many such stories that exemplify the spirit of the armed forces. This account would, however, be incomplete if one does not look at the conduct of Lieutenant (Lt) Manoj Pandey and Capt Vikram Batra, whose exemplary conduct during the 1999 Kargil War typifies the code of conduct of the armed services officers groomed at the defence academies, the cradles of leadership.

Lt Manoj Pandey constantly and persistently volunteered for the most difficult missions. In his diary, he had noted before the commencement of the war, 'If death strikes before I prove my blood—I promise I will kill death.' Philosophical words from one so young! He continued to lead mission after mission on the snow-covered slopes of Kargil mountains. When he was mortally wounded on his last mission, he said, 'I regret that I have only one life to give up for my country.'

Capt Vikram Batra became an icon well before the termination of the Kargil War. Due to his many skirmishes with the enemy, he was nicknamed 'Sher Shah' by the Pakistanis. His quote, 'Dil mange more' (the heart wants more), typifies the spirit of the Indian Army. Prior to his last mission, he said, 'Either I will come back after hoisting the tricolour or I will come back wrapped in it but I will be back for sure!' Prophetic words, because that is what happened. After a series of missions in which he displayed uncommon qualities of leadership, sacrifice and love for his country and men, he died saving the life of another soldier. Both the officers were awarded the Param Vir Chakra, India's highest award for gallantry in war.

Embracing all Faiths

The ethos of the Indian Army is against divisiveness caused by religion. It is spirituality that shapes the attitude and behaviour of the officers and soldiers towards God. With religion being considered as a personal matter, the focus of the Army is on the integration of men of all faiths. The Army, thus, emphasises unity in diversity and the ability to work closely despite differences.

In single-class units, like the Sikhs, the Gorkhas, the Garhwalis and the Kumaonis, religion continues to be a motivating factor in both war and peace. In such units, religious functions are attended by officers and men of other faiths as part of their military duties. This helps in cementing Regimental bonds and the officer–men relationship. In mixed-class units, mandir, masjid, gurdwara and *girja ghar* are often seen separately but also together under one roof, with men of different faiths attending each other's religious functions. In the Indian Army, all religions are respected and there is no difference whatsoever in consideration of creed, cast and community. In fact, in all the wars that India has fought before and after independence, soldiers of different faiths have fought shoulder to shoulder with outstanding results.

It needs to be remembered that in the Indo-Pak War of 1971, though the majority of the Generals were of the Hindu faith, the Indian Army had a Parsi Chief, a Sikh Army Commander, a Jew as the Chief of Staff of Eastern Command, an Anglo-Indian as the Director of Military Operations, and three Christian officers commanding Infantry Divisions spearheading offensive operations on both fronts. It is this unity in diversity that makes the Indian Army one of the finest in the world.

As mentioned earlier, the ethos of the Indian Armed Forces draws its inspiration from the beliefs of its people and therefore, the government elected by the people of India needs to reflect the beliefs and aspirations of the people of India in its policies, programmes and strategies. India is a spiritual country and people of various faiths believe that belief in God and a high moral conduct are essential for progress of the country in peace and war. This belief permeates into the conscious mind of every person of the armed forces, from the Chief to the junior-most soldier, sailor and airman. This consciousness translates into a habit because habits transform attitude, which affects behaviour, and this in turn affects conduct. This 'conduct' motivates personnel of the armed forces to put country first, courage beyond fear and death above dishonour.

This now brings us to the important aspect of training, especially operational training, and the institutes where this training is imparted.

Training in the Indian Army

Currently, India boasts not only of the largest standing volunteer Army in the world but also one of the most experienced ones. The Indian Army has vast experience ranging from wars to counter-insurgency operations, as well as fighting in and holding terrains as varied as the high mountains to dry deserts and riverine deltas. One of the most well-trained armies, it is in constant readiness to take upon itself any challenge cohesively. Indeed, in the seven decades and more since independence, the readiness of the armed forces has been tested consistently. Since 1947, India has gone to war five times to defend her territorial and national integrity, with practical experience showing that strength in the military dimension is essential to prevent outside forces from taking advantage of a perceived weakness.

The purpose of training is to prepare for the eventuality of war. Training is, therefore, an important factor to ensure that a country is militarily strong. It focuses not only on the human resource but also on how the capacity of the soldier can be multiplied by other factors. In this 'information age', technology has gained primacy, but it is the 'man' who continues to be the most critical element in war. Consequently, leadership continues to be an important aspect of soldiering. Quantum jumps in technology have revolutionised warfare and therefore, technological training is being increasingly prioritised. It has also become apparent that we are functioning in a world of interdependency and that military capacity increases exponentially when all branches of the armed forces, the paramilitary forces, civil defence forces and the essential services work as a team. Moreover, as with other militaries the world over, the Indian Armed Forces too are leaning towards jointness and integration, with the move towards theatre commands being one such step. In the present context, training is necessary so that success is achieved in the shortest possible time, with minimum loss of life.

In India, training has been an essential part of the military way of life since time immemorial. One of the oldest treatises on statecraft, Kautilya's *Arthashastra*, mentions the importance of training. Guerrilla warfare was also first conceptualised by Chhatrapati Shivaji. He trained his Army in this kind of warfare, to fight the Mughals, and was highly successful. Further, the Marathas won battles against the Mughals, the Portuguese and the other Indian princes because they were mobile, hardy and united. The arrival of the Europeans in India in the mid-eighteenth century led to a new approach towards war and the profession of arms. The British and the French, in particular, supplemented their own very small forces by training Indians in the new methods. This came in rather handy in the two World Wars.

In 1914, at the start of World War I, the Indian Army was armed with outdated rifles, aircraft were unknown and it had virtually no artillery. However, it was a highly professional and efficient Army. Though mechanisation came to India late, it was one more change in the life of the rank and file. The Indian soldier—adaptable, intelligent and well trained—managed to cope and was soon as good as his British counterpart. By 1945, when World War II ended, the men were trained in jungle and desert warfare, along with trench warfare. They knew how to drive tanks and armoured carriers, and operate artillery of all kinds. They were also trained in amphibious operations from ships and in parachute jumps. This Indian Army, once it was properly trained and equipped, showed that its troops were equal to any in the world.

India's independence in 1947 came along with the partition of the former colony into two antagonistic states. Partition destroyed part of the ethos of the old Indian Army, that is, the concept of brotherhood between soldiers of all faiths, communities and creeds. Troops who had fought shoulder to shoulder on battlefields all over the world were now to be separated and would soon to be fighting against each other. However, the Indian Army rebuilt its ethos and came together to fight wars with both Pakistan (multiple times) and China.

In peacetime, the most challenging task for the Indian Army is 'training'. This training for war, which is the Army's primary role, tends to get disrupted due to other national needs, like counter-insurgency and aid to civil authorities during flood, drought, etc. However, the Army takes this as a form of 'hands-on' training and as part of its contribution to national development. Every year, the Indian Army inducts about 70,000 soldiers and 1,000 officers to maintain operational capacity against wastages. Their training is intensive and focuses on preparing them for their roles. Training in the Indian Army is thus an ongoing process for both officers and men—an activity which keeps their skills honed at all times.

Among the many reforms undertaken in the Indian Army in the recent past, the most important reform relating to training in the Army has been the setting up of the Army Training Command (ARTRAC). This command is a high-powered organisation that formulates training policies; plans, coordinates and monitors all aspects of training; and reviews, evolves and disseminates concepts and doctrines for the entire Army, thereby maximising operational readiness. The ARTRAC, which came into being on 1 October 1991 at Mhow in Madhya Pradesh, was subsequently shifted to Shimla in March 2002. This command is headed by an Army Commander of the rank of Lieutenant General. Apart from formulation and dissemination of concepts and doctrines of warfare in the fields of strategy, tactics, logistics, training and human resource development, ARTRAC also acts as the nodal agency for all institutional training in the Army.

In essence, the training philosophy of the Army, as laid down by ARTRAC, is to develop forces that will win in combat; and that no officer or soldier should ever lose his life or limb in combat because he was inadequately trained. It is only intelligent, imaginative and innovative training that produces good soldiers, officers and cohesive units and formations. The training philosophy focuses on building three major components, namely, force structure, material and doctrine, to create a combat-ready force.

Operational Training

The Indian Army requires its soldiers, officers and units to be ready to deploy, fight and win in combat at any intensity level, anywhere and at any time. Operational training prepares the Army to meet such requirements. It consists of all training in field formations which is planned, coordinated and conducted under formation/unit arrangements. Individual training, sub-unit and unit training, collective training, field firing, all form part of operational training. The training standards achieved during operational training determine the fighting efficiency of the Army. The Indian Army's training cycle is normally on a yearly basis and the training year is from July to June.

The Army Headquarters (HQ) issues the Army Training Directive, which lays down the training policy. It generally contains the key result areas which are to be achieved in training. The directive is based on training reports of the previous year, annual inspection reports, personal observations and reports from various sources. Based on this, subordinate formation commanders issue their own training directives and instructions. Since conditions vary in each command and formation, Army HQ directs and coordinates training only in very broad terms. The responsibility of implementing training policies devolves on the command HQ. At lower levels, training becomes more and more specific and focuses on the particular needs of formations and units concerned.

The Indian Army is the fourth largest Army in the world with approximately one million personnel in uniform. In the post-independence era, in addition to Kargil, the Army has fought four major wars; it continues to hold live and sensitive borders; and it has been engaged in sustained counter-insurgency in certain parts of the country. High standards of effectiveness demand rigorous and imaginative training of our officers and men from the time they join the Army as cadets or recruits till they leave the service. Technology has also changed the pace and concept of warfare, which is a major challenge that the Army has had to face. This includes taking on board new technological concepts and balancing it against its relevance in our battlefield scenario.

Training Tailored to Specific Needs

The subcontinent encompasses a wide variety of terrain, ranging from the thick forests of the North-East to the flat obstacle-ridden plains of the Punjab and from the arid mountains and high-altitude deserts and glaciers of snow and ice of the Ladakh

Sector to the sandy deserts of Rajasthan. Training, therefore, has to encompass the environment, technology and the threat perception. This includes the threat of terrorism from across the border that has thrown up a new dimension for the Army to tackle.

As before, training within units and formations continues to be achieved through individual and collective training. Outside of units and formations, training extends to 'institutional' training, which includes training imparted on induction of an individual into the Army, technical training and tactical training. This is imparted initially at the training centres, and subsequently at schools of instruction, respectively. Over the past few years, officers of the Army have been encouraged to go to selected universities and academic institutions in India and abroad, to take advantage of opportunities to acquire the latest advances in the art and science of war.

Training Institutions

National Defence Academy (NDA)

The NDA is the premier Joint Services Training Institution of India. It is located at Khadakwasla, near Pune. The idea of a joint services academy in India was conceived after World War II and before independence, that is, in 1945. Accordingly, it was designed for the education and joint basic training of future officers of the three services. A sum of 1,000 pounds was given by the Government of Sudan for the construction of a suitable war memorial in appreciation of the services rendered by the Indian Army in liberation of their country. This was used towards the construction of the NDA, which, in fact, is a living war memorial. In 1954, the Joint Services Wing (JSW) shifted from Clement Town to Khadakwasla and the NDA started its first term in January 1955. The syllabus of the NDA meets the required national education format of 10+2+3 and on passing out, the cadets are granted BA or BSc degrees from Jawaharlal Nehru University, New Delhi.

Indian Military Academy (IMA)

The founding of the IMA is part of India's struggle for freedom and its birth was the culmination of a long-drawn-out battle fought in forums such as the Central Legislative Assembly and the Round Table Conference, by stalwarts like Sir Sivaswamy Aiyar, Pandit Motilal Nehru, Mohammad Ali Jinnah, and Lala Lajpat Rai, among others. Leaders of all political parties were united and unanimous in their demand for the establishment of a military academy in India. The political significance of this battle is that the Army, at last, was open to commissioning Indians as officers in the Indian Army.

The IMA came into being on 01 October 1932. The first course of 40 gentlemen cadets (GCs), known as the 'Pioneers', had on its rolls Sam Manekshaw, Smith Dun and Mohammad Musa, later to be Chiefs of the armies of their respective countries, that is, India, Burma and Pakistan. Field Marshal Sir Philip Chetwode, Bart, GCB, KCMG, GCSI, DSO formally inaugurated the Academy on 10 December 1932. Chetwode delivered the inaugural address in the hall, which has been named after him, and the present IMA credo has been adopted from this address. Between December 1934 and May 1941, 16 regular courses passed out of IMA and 524 GCs were commissioned. Consequent to the German invasion of France, there was a surge in the intake, with 3,387 Indian and British GCs being commissioned between August 1941 and January 1946.

Independence in 1947 brought about a change in the command of the Academy. The first Indian Commandant was Brigadier Thakur Mahadeo Singh, DSO. The bifurcation of the Indian Army on independence led to redefining training needs. The new scheme for training officers brought about the establishment of the Armed Forces Academy in 1949, with the IMA as its nucleus. As part of the IMA, JSW was opened in 1950, which later became the NDA. In 1954, after the NDA shifted to its present location at Khadakwasla, Pune, the IMA reverted to its original identity and role.

In the aftermath of the Chinese aggression in 1962, the Academy expanded. From November 1962 to November 1964, a total of 4,051 GCs were granted emergency commission. During this period, peak strength of 3,090 GCs was reached in July 1963. In 1977, Army Cadet College, the progeny of Kitchner College, Nowgong, shifted to the Academy campus; it now functions as a wing of the IMA. The IMA was presented Colours in 1934 in recognition of its services to the British Empire. After independence, the first Indian Colours were presented to the IMA in 1962 by the then President, Dr S Radhakrishnan. The current Colours were presented to the Academy in 1976 by the then President, Shri Fakhruddin Ali Ahmed.

The IMA has grown from strength to strength over the years. It celebrated its silver jubilee, golden jubilee and diamond jubilees in 1957, 1982 and 1992, respectively. The spirit of the Academy is symbolised by its crest and colours. The crest is composed of crossed swords with a flaming torch symbolising knowledge, all superimposed in the middle by the *Dharama Chakra* of Ashoka, against the background of steel grey and blood red. The scroll bears the inscription 'Veerta aur Vivek', meaning 'Valour and Wisdom'. Regarding the colours, the steel grey denotes strength and resilience, and blood red signifies the ultimate sacrifice in devotion to duty.

The IMA has five main entry streams: the NDA Cadets from Khadakwasla, Pune; the Army Cadet College (for servicemen only); the Graduate Direct Entry Scheme from colleges; the Technical Graduates Entry Scheme from technical institutions/colleges; and the University Graduates Entry Scheme. The duration of training is one year, except for the Direct Entry Scheme, for which it is one-and-a-half years.

Leadership and character development is the prime concern of the Academy. The essence of duty and honour is constantly impressed upon a GC to make him a responsive leader and dignified citizen of the nation.

The art of war, miniaturised to the level of a platoon, is the essence of service training at the Academy. Whilst gaining knowledge of basic tactical training at the platoon level, a GC learns the use of ground and fire and movement tactics. Supporting arms and services are co-opted to develop the concept of an integrated all-arms battle philosophy. Training in the various nuances of low-intensity conflict operations forms an important segment of the syllabus. Tactical exercises develop leadership and independent thinking, while laying greater stress on endurance and team building.

The Academy encourages and provides opportunity for adventure activity because it helps GCs to understand the elements of risk, chance, fortune and luck. Each GC is encouraged to pursue at least one adventure sport. The range of activity spans river rafting, para jumping, rock climbing, trekking, mountaineering and desert safaris.

As all GCs are graduates on joining the Academy, academic training aims at their overall development. The main objectives are to provide a broad education base essential for future development; enhance their powers of analysis, reasoning and expression, both verbal and written, in English and Hindi; and provide scientific orientation to keep abreast of technological advancements in warfare.

Since 1951, the Academy has trained GCs from friendly countries such as Angola, Afghanistan, Bhutan, Botswana, Burma (Myanmar), Ghana, Iraq, Jamaica, Malaysia, the Maldives, Mauritius, Nepal, Nigeria, the Philippines, Seychelles, Singapore, Sri Lanka, South Africa, Tanzania, Tonga, Uganda, Yemen and Zambia.

For nine decades, the IMA has produced officers who have served the nation with pride, élan and dedication. To meet new challenges, it has been constantly improving the quality of training, administration and infrastructure. 'Valour and Wisdom', the motto of the IMA, is manifested in the deeds of the alumni of the Academy. That the Army has given a good account of itself, both in peace and war, is a tribute to the Indian Army's gallant officers who have always led from the front. A large share of the credit for the leadership of the Army can be given to the IMA.

Officers Training Academy (OTA)

Originally raised as an Officers' Training School in 1963, at Madras (Chennai), the institute was redesignated as the Officers Training Academy (OTA) in 1988. OTA Gaya was raised as a new institute in 2011. Initially, the main task of the OTA was to train GCs for Short Service Commission. The OTA has made history by admitting and training lady cadets (LCs) since 1992. The OTA trains 500 cadets every year, of which 50 are LCs. The motto of the OTA is 'Serve with Honour', which is signified by the crossed swords that depicts the profession of arms and the Ashoka Chakra that represents honour.

Army War College (AWC)

The College of Combat, located at Mhow, was renamed as the AWC in 2003. It is one of the premier institutes of the Army and the country. It imparts training in the art of leadership, strategy and tactics to Army officers, ranging from Captains to Generals. The AWC also imparts integrated all-arms training to officers, promotes inter-service jointmanship and encourages doctrinal research on military subjects. The College trains over 1,200 officers every year. About 100 officers from friendly countries are also trained every year at the middle and joint levels of command. It is the nodal instructional agency for all-arms training at the tactical, operational and higher levels.

It provides commanders with knowledge on the employment of all arms and services, so as to facilitate the ability to fuse them together into a single battle-winning machine. It originates tactical doctrines and carries out continuous study to keep abreast of tactical and technological developments, both at home and abroad. It also conducts research on tactics, logistics and contemporary studies.

Armoured Corps Centre and School

The outbreak of World War II and the consequent mechanisation of the Indian Cavalry necessitated the establishment of a training institute for officers, junior commissioned officers (JCOs) and men of the Armoured Corps. The Fighting Vehicles School was consequently established at Ahmednagar. The School of Armoured Warfare, which is part of the Armoured Corps Centre and School, trains personnel from all combat and supporting arms so that they have the capability to assume scales of responsibility from troop to Regimental levels; it trains all ranks in the tactical and technological aspects of armoured warfare.

School of Artillery

The School of Artillery for the British Indian Army was established at Quetta in 1919, and later shifted to Kakul in 1923, both now in Pakistan. On 1 January 1941, the School of Artillery moved into its permanent home at Deolali, near Nasik in Maharashtra. The School is the seat of learning of the various disciplines of artillery warfare.

Air Defence and Guided Missile School

The Indian component of the Anti-Aircraft School which was at Karachi moved to Deolali in 1947, where it was merged with the School of Artillery as the Anti-Aircraft Wing. It was later designated as the Air Defence Wing. The Air Defence Wing moved to Gopalpur, Orissa, in October 1989, to become the nucleus for the raising of the Air Defence and Guided Missile School. It became fully functional on 1 November 1989. The School imparts technical and tactical training in all aspects of air defence gunnery to officers, JCOs and non-commissioned officers (NCOs); evaluates tactical and training doctrines related to Army Air Defence; conducts trials on air defence equipment; and produces suitable notes and pamphlets concerning the handling of Army air defence weapons. It also acts as a centre of excellence on all matters concerning air defence artillery.

College of Military Engineering

Prior to 1934, officers of the Corps of Engineers attended courses in military Engineering at the School of Military Engineering, Chatham, United Kingdom (UK), and attended a mechanical science course at Cambridge University, UK. From 1934 to 1939, officers commissioned from the IMA, Dehradun, were attached to the Bengal Sappers and Miners and attended a civil Engineering course at Thomson College, Roorkee. As the requirement of Engineer officers began to increase during the war, Officer Cadet Training Units were established at the three Engineer centres at Bangalore, Roorkee and Kirkee, where cadets were given military as well as Engineering training for service in Engineer units. The School of Military Engineering was established at Roorkee in September 1943.

After World War II, it was evident that centralised training of officers and other personnel of the Corps was essential. Therefore, the School of Military Engineering at Dapodi, Pune, was established. Subsequently, in view of the increased responsibilities and training facilities provided, the name of the school was changed to the College of Military Engineering in November 1951. This was also in keeping with the higher status of the degree Engineering courses run by the school and their recognition by the Institution of Engineers (India). The College imparts technical and tactical training on all Engineering subjects; carries out trials, analysis of Engineer data, testing of equipment and stores relating to Engineering matters, research in various Engineer projects; and acts as a centre of excellence on improvised explosive devices. In addition, it has a faculty of combat, civil, electric and mechanical Engineering; a faculty of nuclear, biological and chemical (NBC) protection; and runs courses on NBC warfare.

Military College of Telecommunication Engineering (MCTE)

The MCTE at Mhow is the premier training institution of the Corps of Signals. The erstwhile Indian Signal Corps School, established in 1946, was later named as the School of Signals in 1948. In keeping with the advanced technical training being imparted at this institution, it was redesignated as the MCTE in 1967. The MCTE trains all ranks in the tactical and technical aspects of combat communications, electronic warfare, automatic data processing systems, electromagnetic interference and electromagnetic compatibility.

Infantry School

The Infantry School is the largest and oldest military institution in India. Originating as the School of Musketry at Changla Gali in 1888, it has changed names and locations several times over the years. Some of these are listed below:

1. School of Musketry in Satara and Belgaum;
2. Small Arms School in Pachmari and Ahmednagar;
3. Indian NCO Training School, Jhansi;
4. Indian Platoon Commanders School, Faizabad; and
5. Battle School for Tactics and Administration, Dehradun.

Since 1948, the Infantry School has been located at Mhow. The College of Combat was carved out of it in February 1971. The Army Marksmanship Unit, which has earned great laurels in India and Asia, was raised in December 1993. The Infantry School conducts various courses of instruction; develops new tactical doctrines, battle techniques and battle drills pertaining to Infantry; studies and evaluates the latest trends in the development of Infantry tactics, weapons, ammunition and equipment; prepares training manuals pertaining to Infantry; carries out trials on weapons, equipment and ammunition; and trains the Army and national shooting teams. The School has been split into two locations. The HQ, the Young Officer's Wing, the Support Weapons Wing, the Platoon Weapons Wing, the Faculty of Study and Trials, along with the Army Marksmanship Unit, are located at Mhow. The Junior Leaders Wing, comprising the Commando and Platoon Commanders Wings, is located at Belgaum.

High Altitude Warfare School

The High Altitude Warfare School was initially set up in Gulmarg as a Formation Ski School. The training imparted consisted mainly of skiing techniques, mountain lore and patrolling on skis. On 8 April 1962, the School was designated as a Category 'A' establishment and renamed as the High Altitude Warfare School. It has the distinction of being the only training institution in the country which has participated in active military operations during war. It is also the nodal centre for winter sports in the country.

Qualified mountaineering experts train the officers and soldiers of the Indian Army in high-altitude warfare. The students are trained to traverse crevasses, scale steep ice walls, handle snow craft to rescue companions and handle specialised weapons. The school has trained a large number of mountaineers who have scaled various peaks in the high Himalayas. Training instils confidence and stamina, besides defrosting the fear of the unknown. The men are taught to integrate with the environment so that they can guard the Himalayan frontiers effectively.

Counter Insurgency and Jungle Warfare School (CIJWS)

The CIJWS was established in 1967 as a Jungle Training School at Mynkre, near Jowai in Meghalaya. This was later designated as the Eastern Command Counter Insurgency Training School in 1968. Two years later, the School became a Category 'A' establishment. It was relocated at Vairengte, in Mizoram, on 1 May 1970. Over the years, progressive upgradation in all facilities has made CIJWS the centre of excellence in low-intensity combat. The School, according to its motto, teaches students to 'fight the guerrilla like a guerrilla'. The CIJWS functions as the Indian Army nodal instructional facility and a centre of excellence for training in counter-insurgency and related aspects of jungle warfare. The CIJWS also participated in the 1971 Indo-Pak War and takes part in counter-insurgency operations and psychological warfare when called upon to do so.

Other Training Institutions

There are, in addition, a number of other training institutions. These are the Army Service Corps Centre and College, Bangalore; the College of Material Management, Jabalpur; the Military College of Mechanical Engineering (MCEME), Secunderabad; the Military Intelligence Training School, Pune; the Army Medical Corps Centre and School, Lucknow; the Remount and Veterinary Corps Centre and School, Meerut; the Corps of Military Police School, Bangalore; the Institute of Military Law, Delhi the Army Education Corps Training College and Centre, Pachmari; the Army School of Physical Training, Pune; and the Army Airborne Training School, Agra.

Besides these training establishments, there are joint service training institutions, namely, the Defence Services Staff College, the College of Defence Management, and the National Defence College, that have a considerable impact on the Army.

Defence Services Staff College (DSSC)

The DSSC is one of the most prestigious military institutions in India. It was set up in 1905 at Deolali as the Army Staff College. In 1907, it shifted to Quetta. On Partition, the Indian element moved to Wellington in south India. It has since been imparting training to middle-level officers of the three Services, Army, Navy and Air Force. A few officers from the civil services, paramilitary forces and friendly countries also attend the DSSC. The focus of the course is to train officers of the three services in operational and staff functions in peace and war in their own service, inter-service and joint service environment, and generally related education to enable them to perform effectively in staff appointments tenable by Majors to Lieutenant Colonels and their equivalents in the Indian Navy and the Indian Air Force.

The College enjoys international recognition as a premier military training institution. A large number of developed and developing countries seek vacancies on the course for their defence officers every year.

College of Defence Management (CDM)

The CDM was set up in Secunderabad in 1970 as the Institute of Defence Management. It was renamed as such in 1980. The College is the national centre for defence management. In addition to the instructional courses that are run, the CDM also carries out research in the field of defence management and provides consultancy services to the three services to find optimal and practical solutions to organisational problems.

National Defence College

Located in New Delhi, the NDC was established in 1960 on the lines of the Imperial Defence College of the United Kingdom (now the Royal College of Defence Studies). The College is India's apex institution of learning for the study and practice of National Security and Strategy. The NDC is attended by selected officers of the rank of Brigadier in the Indian Army and its equivalents in the Indian Navy and the Indian Air Force. The NDC course is highly competitive and is also attended by civilian officials of the Government of India as well as military officers from friendly foreign nations. The participants of the NDC course are selected and trained for positions of higher leadership and responsibilities.

Conclusion

The training philosophy of the Indian Army is designed to meet its present and future threats. The sophisticated combat environment of the future battlefield would be replete with the latest technological advancements. Advanced systems, modern techniques and improved training methodologies would facilitate the deployment of battlefield support systems and force multipliers. These would necessitate the evolution and reorientation of operational concepts, tactics and techniques in preparing the Indian Army to meet the challenges of the twenty-first century. These, in turn, demand changes in the force structure, organisations and training philosophy to ensure optimal use of advanced techniques for the efficient application of combat power. Increasingly, the move is towards integration and jointness in terms of both training and doctrines.

The Indian Army training philosophy is designed to:

1. Retain a high state of operational readiness.
2. Maintain a strong dissuasive defence, while retaining strategic offensive capability—deterrence being the key.
3. Ensure defence capability against NBC threats and support the acquisition of a strategic deterrence.
4. Continue to have the capability to combat insurgency and/or proxy war.
5. Ensure out-of-area capability to support friendly littoral states.
6. During peace, the thrust is to enhance military education and to develop bold and competent leaders capable of 'getting things done'.

Training is basically a means to ensure that the performance of the soldier in combat is enhanced. The Indian Army faces numerous challenges in its endeavours to conduct quality training. The transitions in society, the changes in technology, coupled with the problems of technological assimilation and the rapid obsolescence of weapons and equipment, shrinking defence budgets and fiscal constraints, are only some of the issues. The variety of operational roles and commitments, the need to conserve expensive equipment, along with the vastly different approaches to train various components of the arms and services demand a new orientation and outlook. The Indian Army has opened windows to the future, to maintain its cutting edge, to sustain its proficiency and to conduct performance-oriented training. Ever in the service of the nation, the Indian Army continues to strive for professional excellence in the controlled application of force.

General Service Medal
1947 with clasp LADAKH
1962

Originally instituted in 1937 as the 'Order of Merit' the Indian Order of Merit (IOM) is the oldest gallantry award in the Commonwealth
Source: USI of India.

Instituted in 1858 by Queen Victoria to commemorate acts of gallantry in the Crimean War. Indians became eligible to receive the VC in 1911
Source: USI of India.

Sepoy Khudadad Khan, 129th Duke of Connaught's Own Baluchis, was the first Indian to receive the Victoria Cross for acts of bravery during the Battle of Ypres in 1914

Naik (later Subedar) Darwan Singh Negi, 1/39th Garhwal Rifles, was awarded the Victoria Cross for bravery in the Battle of Festubert, 1914

Param Vir Chakra
Source: USI of India.

Maha Vir Chakra
Source: USI of India.

Vir Chakra
Source: USI of India.

Ashok Chakra
Source: USI of India.

Kirti Chakra
Source: USI of India.

Shaurya Chakra
Source: USI of India.

Major Somnath Sharma, PVC, Op Battle of Badgam, 1947

Naik Jadunath Singh, PVC, Indo-Pak War, 1947-48

2/Lt Rama Raghoba Rane, PVC, Indo-Pak War, 1947-48

Company Havildar Major Piru Singh, PVC, Indo-Pak War, 1947-48

Lance Naik Karam Singh, PVC, Indo-Pak War, 1947-48

Capt Gurbacahan Singh Salaria, PVC, Congo Ops, 1961

Major Dhan Singh Thapa, PVC, Sino-Indian War, 1962

Subedar Joginder Singh, PVC, Sino-Indian War, 1962

Major Shaitan Singh, PVC, Sino-Indian War, 1962

Company Quatermaster Havildar Abdul Hamid, PVC, Indo-Pak War 1965

Source: USI of India.

Lt Col AB Tarapore, PVC, Indo-Pak War, 1965

Lance Naik Albert Ekka, PVC, Indo-Pak War, 1971

Lieutenant Manoj Kumar Pandey, PVC, Op Vijay, 1999

2/Lt Arun Khetarpal, PVC, Indo-Pak War, 1971

Major Hoshiar Singh, PVC, Indo-Pak War, 1971

Nb Subedar Bana Singh, PVC, Op Rajiv, 1987

Major Ramaswamy Parmeswaran, PVC, Op Pawan, 1987

Grenadier Yogendra Singh Yadav, PVC, Kargil War, 1999

Rifleman Sanjay Kumar, PVC, Kargil War, 1999

Capt Vikram Batra, PVC, Kargil War, 1999

Source: USI of India.

Located near Neuve Chapelle in an area that was central to the operations of the Indian Corps during 1914 and 1915, the Memorial commemorates around 4,700 Indian war dead who fell in France and Flanders
Source: CWGC.

The India Gate, an iconic symbol of New Delhi, was built in 1931 to commemorate Indian battle casualties during World War I as well as the Third Anglo-Afghan War. Out of over 83,000 Indians who laid down their lives, the monument bears 13,516 names
Source: CWGC.

The Kirkee Memorial commemorates 1,805 casualties of World War I
Source: CWGC.

Teen Murti in New Delhi commemorates the 15th Imperial Service Cavalry Brigade that fought in the Middle East during the First World War. It also serves as the Indian Cavalry Memorial

Source: CR Elderton.

Many thousands of Indian soldiers wounded on the Western Front passed through Brighton & Hove Hospitals during the Great War. The Chattri Memorial was erected on the exact site where 53 Hindu and Sikh soldiers were cremated according to their faith, while 21 Muslim soldiers were buried in nearby Woking
Source: CWGC.

The Rangoon Memorial bears the names of more than 26,000 World War II servicemen—almost 20,000 of them served with the Indian forces. The Taukyan Cremation Memorial commemorates a further 1,000 World War II casualties whose remains were cremated in accordance with their faith. The majority of these men were casualties of the campaign in Burma (now Myanmar)
Source: CWGC.

Of the more than 11,000 casualties commemorated on the Alamein Memorial, over 1,800 of them served with Indian forces, who fought in campaigns across North Africa and the Eastern Mediterranean
Source: CWGC.

The Kohima War Cemetery, Kohima, Nagaland
Source: CWGC.

Kargil War Memorial at Dras, UT of Ladakh

This memorial commemorates the war dead of the Kapurthala Imperial Service Infantry who served in East Africa between 1914 and 1917, and also in the Third Afghan War
Source: Sukhjit Singh.

National War Memorial Obelisk, New Delhi

9

Gallantry and War Memorials

NEHA KOHLI

Introduction

Conflict and warfare are undeniable realities of human history and societies. Similarly, remembrance is also part of human nature and all human societies, from prehistoric times till date, have come up with unique ways and means of remembrance and memorialisation. Victories in battles have been commemorated in legends, stories and ballads, on stone and paper, in the memories of civilisations. Memorials to victory as well as sites of battles and tombs or cenotaphs marking the sites of cremation/burial of kings and warriors are found throughout the length and breadth of India in the form of commemorative *stambhas* (pillars), *dwaras* (gates), *chhatris* (cupolas) and 'hero stones'. The rise of the individual, and the accompanying modernisation and democratisation of society, led to the role, valour and sacrifice of the individual soldier becoming significant and finding an expression of acknowledgement in official despatches and rewards. We begin to see this during colonial times, in particular, when two significant practices: of marking the valour of a soldier in battle by the grant of an official gallantry award, and recording the names of individual 'other ranks' who had performed exceptionally well in the field in the official dispatch sent by the Commander to government, now known as being 'mentioned in despatches', both originated in the Indian Army.[1]

The 'Indian Order of Merit' (IOM), originally instituted by the East India Company in 1837 as the 'Order of Merit', has the distinction of being the oldest gallantry award in the Commonwealth. It was later taken over by the British Crown in 1858. The IOM predates the Victoria Cross (VC) by 19 years. The IOM was the Indian equivalent of the VC and the highest gallantry award that could be won by an Indian soldier until 1911, when Indians were made eligible for the latter decoration following King George Vs proclamation at the Delhi Durbar that year.[2] By this time, around 3,000 Indian soldiers had been awarded the IOM, including 47 awards of the first class of the Order, equivalent of being awarded the VC with two bars.[3]

Post-independence, the British Honours System was replaced with an Indian system of gallantry awards beginning 1950 with the adoption of the Constitution that made India a sovereign republic. A series of awards were instituted to recognise the bravery of those who made the supreme sacrifice for the nation and to inspire the next generation to serve honourably. Gallantry Awards in India are classified into two categories: those awarded in wartime or for gallantry in the face of the enemy; and those awarded during peace time or for gallantry other than facing the enemy. Of the former, the first three gallantry awards—the Param Vir Chakra (PVC), the Maha Vir Chakra (MVC) and the Vir Chakra (VrC)—were instituted by the Government of India on 26 January 1950 with retrospective effect from the 15 August 1947. The PVC replaced the pre-independence Victoria Cross, and was designed by Savitri Khanolkar on the request of then Adjutant General, Major General Hira Lal Atal. Khanolkar went on to design other bravery medals, including the Mahavir Chakra, the Vir Chakra and peacetime gallantry medals such as the Ashok Chakra, Kirti Chakra, and the Shaurya Chakra.

Awards for bravery not only honour and commemorate the actions of those who have served beyond the call of duty but also inspire each generation to pick up the mantle to defend our treasured freedoms.

Apart from gallantry awards the Yuddh Seva and Vishishth Seva series of medals in three grades recongnised distinguished services in times of war and peace respectively, while the Sena Medal can be awarded for gallantry as well as for distinguished services.

Gallantry Awards in India

British Honours System

Prior to independence in 1947, the Indian government as well as the military followed the British Honours System. As mentioned earlier, the oldest military and civilian decoration instituted in India was by the East India Company—the IOM in 1837. This was taken over by the British Crown in 1858. Its name was changed to the 'Indian Order of Merit' in 1902. The IOM had three classes—the first, second and third—in the military decoration until Indians became eligible for other medals such as the VC. The IOM classes were as follows:

1. Third Class: This was an eight-pointed dull silver star with blue circle, surrounded by silver laurels, in the middle, with crossed swords and the words 'Reward of Valour'. The medal featured a dark blue ribbon flanked by two red stripes of about a sixth of the width. The IOM Third Class was awarded for a 'conspicuous act of individual gallantry on the part of any Native Officers or Soldiers, in the Field or in the attack or defence of a Fortified place, without distinction of rank or grade.'
2. Second Class: This featured an eight-pointed shiny silver star with blue circle, surrounded by gold laurels in the middle, with crossed swords and the words 'Reward of Valour'. This was changed to 'Reward of Gallantry' in 1944. The medal featured a dark blue ribbon flanked by two red stripes of about a sixth of the width. The IOM Second Class could be obtained by those who already possessed the third class till 1911, and for similar services thereafter.
3. First Class: This was an eight-pointed gold star with blue circle, surrounded by gold laurels in the middle, with crossed swords and the words 'Reward of Valour'. This was changed to 'Reward of Gallantry' in 1944. The medal featured a dark blue ribbon flanked by two red stripes of about a sixth of the width. This class of IOM could be obtained in like manner only by those who possess the third and second classes.

The VC was originally instituted by Queen Victoria in 1856 to honour acts of valour during the Crimean War. The medal is awarded for an act of the most conspicuous bravery, or some daring or pre-eminent act of valour or self-sacrifice, or extreme devotion to duty in the presence of the enemy. The medal is a bronze cross pattée, 41 mm high and 36 mm wide, bearing the crown of Saint Edward surmounted by a lion, and the inscription 'for valour', with a 38 mm wide crimson ribbon. Until 1911, when Indian servicemen became eligible for the VC, the IOM was the highest decoration which Indians serving in the Indian Army could be awarded.

The first Indian to be awarded the VC was Subedar Khudadad Khan for acts of bravery during the Battle of Ypres in 1914. The official citation of Khan's award published in the London Gazette dated 7 December 1914 reads:

> His Majesty the KING-EMPEROR has been graciously pleased to approve of the grant of the Victoria Cross to the undermentioned soldier of the Indian Army for conspicuous bravery whilst serving with the Indian Army Corps, British Expeditionary Force: —
>
> 4050, Sepoy Khudadad, 129th Duke of Connaught's Own Baluchis.
>
> On 31st October, 1914, at Hollebeke, Belgium, the British Officer in charge of the detachment having been wounded, and the other gun put out of action by

a shell, Sepoy Khudadad, though himself wounded, remained working his gun until all the other five men of the gun detachment had been killed.

The Distinguished Service Order (DSO) was instituted by Queen Victoria in 1886. It is awarded for meritorious or distinguished service by officers of the armed forces during wartime, typically in actual combat. General KS Thimayya, Chief of Army Staff of the Indian Army from 1957–1961 was awarded a DSO during the Second Arakan Campaign in Burma in the Second World War.

Table 9.1 Victoria Cross Awardees from Indian Army

S/ No	Name	Unit	Year	Battle	Place
1.	Khudadad Khan	129th Duke of Connaught's Own Baluchis	1914	First World War	Hollebeke, Belgium
2.	Darwan Singh Negi	39th Garhwal Rifles	1914	First World War	Festubert, France
3.	Mir Dast	55th Coke's Rifles (Frontier Force)	1915	First World War	Wieltje, Belgium
4.	Kulbir Thapa	3rd Queen Alexandra's Own Gurkha Rifles	1915	First World War	Fauquissart, France
5.	Gabbar Singh Negi	39th Garhwal Rifles	1915*	First World War	Neuve Chapelle, France
6.	Shahamad Khan	89th Punjabis	1916	First World War	Beit Ayeesa, Mesopotamia
7.	Lala	41st Dogras	1916	First World War	El Orah, Mesopotamia
8.	Chatta Singh	9th Bhopal Infantry	1916	First World War	Wadi, Mesopotamia
9.	Gobind Singh	2nd Lancers	1917	First World War	Épehy, France
10.	Karanbahadur Rana	3rd Queen Alexandra's Own Gurkha Rifles	1918	First World War	El Kefr, Egypt
11.	Badlu Singh	14th Murray's Jat Lancers	1918*	First World War	River Jordan, Palestine
12.	Ishar Singh	28th Punjabis	1921	Waziristan campaign (1919-1920)	Haidari Kach, India

S/ No	Name	Unit	Year	Battle	Place
13.	Premindra Bhagat	Royal Bombay Sappers and Miners	1941	Second World War	Metemma, Abyssinia
14.	Richhpal Ram	6th Rajputana Rifles	1941*	Second World War	Keren, Eritrea
15.	Gaje Ghale	5th Gurkha Rifles	1943	Second World War	Chin Hills, Burma
16.	Parkash Singh	8th Punjab Regiment	1943	Second World War	Donbaik, Burma
17.	Lalbahadur Thapa	2nd Gurkha Rifles	1943	Second World War	Rass-es-Zouai, Tunisia
18.	Chhelu Ram	6th Rajputana Rifles	1943*	Second World War	Djebel Garci, Tunisia
19.	Ganju Lama	7th Gurkha Rifles	1944	Second World War	Ningthoukhong, Burma
20.	Tulbahadur Pun	6th Gurkha Rifles	1944	Second World War	Mogaung, Burma
21.	Agansing Rai	5th Gurkha Rifles	1944	Second World War	Bishenpur, Burma
22.	Bhandari Ram	10th Baluch Regiment	1944	Second World War	Arakan, Burma
23.	Kamal Ram	8th Punjab Regiment	1944	Second World War	Gari River, Italy
24.	Nand Singh	11th Sikh Regiment	1944	Second World War	Maungdaw-Buthidaung Road, Burma
25.	Umrao Singh	Royal Indian Artillery	1944	Second World War	Kaladan Valley, Burma
26.	Yeshwant Ghadge	5th Mahratta Light Infantry	1944*	Second World War	Upper Tiber Valley, Italy
27.	Thaman Gurung	5th Gurkha Rifles	1944*	Second World War	Monte San Bartolo, Italy
28.	Abdul Hafiz Khan	9th Jat Infantry	1944*	Second World War	Imphal, India
29.	Ram Sarup Singh	1st Punjab Regiment	1944*	Second World War	Kennedy Peak, Burma
30.	Netrabahadur Thapa	5th Gurkha Rifles	1944*	Second World War	Bishenpur, Burma
31.	Sher Bahadur Thapa	9th Gurkha Rifles	1944*	Second World War	San Marino, Italy

32.	Bhanbhagta Gurung	2nd Gurkha Rifles	1945	Second World War	Snowdon East, Tamandu, Burma
33.	Lachhiman Gurung	8th Gurkha Rifles	1945	Second World War	Taungdaw, Burma
34.	Ali Haidar	13th Frontier Force Rifles	1945	Second World War	Fusignano, Italy
35.	Namdeo Jadhav	5th Mahratta Light Infantry	1945	Second World War	Senio River, Italy
36.	Gian Singh	15th Punjab Regiment	1945	Second World War	Kamye, Burma
37.	Fazal Din	10th Baluch Regiment	1945*	Second World War	Meiktila, Burma
38.	Karamjeet Judge	15th Punjab Regiment	1945*	Second World War	Meiktila, Burma
39.	Sher Shah	16th Punjab Regiment	1945*	Second World War	Kyeyebyin, Burma
40.	Prakash Singh	13th Frontier Force Rifles	1945*	Second World War	Kanlan Ywathit, Burma

Source: Indian Army.
Note: * indicates posthumous award.

Indian Honours System

In the Indian Honours System, the following paragraphs briefly describe on the series and order of gallantry awards. Post-independence, over 4,000 members of the Indian Armed Forces have been awarded for acts of bravery and gallantry during times of war and peace.

Param Vir Chakra

The PVC is the highest gallantry award in India and was instituted to replace the VC, which was awarded prior to independence. The medal is made of bronze and is in the form of a circle with a diameter of 1.4 inches. On the obverse side, it features four replicas of Indra's Vajra, which encloses India's national emblem. On the reverse, the words 'PARAM VIR CHAKRA' are embossed in Hindi and English. Between the words in Hindi and English on the reverse of the medal, lotus flowers are visible on each side. The medal ribbon is purple in colour.

The PVC is awarded for most conspicuous bravery or some daring or pre-eminent act of valour or self-sacrifice, in the presence of the enemy, whether on land, at sea, or in the air. The decoration may be awarded posthumously.

Major Somnath Sharma of 4 KUMAON was the first awardee of the PVC (Posthumous) on 26 January 1950. Only 21 PVCs have been awarded since 1947 of which 20 have been earned by the Indian Army and one by the Indian Air Force.

Mahavir Chakra

The MVC is the second-highest gallantry award in the country, awarded for bravery in the face of enemy. The award replaced the former British DSO. The MVC features a circular medal of 1.4 inches diameter, which is made of standard silver. On the obverse, the medal features a five-pointed heraldic star along with the national emblem embossed on the domed central piece. On the reverse, the medal features the words 'MAHA VIR CHAKRA' in Hindi and English, separated by lotus flowers. The medal ribbon is half-white and half-orange.

The medal is awarded for gallantry in the presence of the enemy on land, at sea or in the air. The decoration may be awarded posthumously.

Lt Col Dewan Ranjit Rai of 1 SIKH was the first recipient (Posthumous) of the Maha Vir Chakra for his courageous actions in the 1947–48 India-Pakistan War.

Vir Chakra

The VrC is the third-highest gallantry award in India. The medal, made of standard silver, is circular in shape with a diameter of 1.4 inches. It features a five-pointed heraldic star and the state emblem along with the motto at the centre on the obverse. On the reverse, the words 'Vir Chakra' are written in Hindi and English and separated by a flower on each side. The medal ribbon is half-blue and half-orange. The VrC is awarded for acts of gallantry in the presence of the enemy, whether on land or at sea or in the air, and may be awarded posthumously.

Ashok Chakra

The Ashok Chakra was instituted on 4 January 1952 and renamed on 27 January 1967. It is the highest peacetime gallantry award in the country that recognises most conspicuous bravery or some act of daring or pre-eminent act of valour or self-sacrifice other than than in the face of the enemy, and can be awarded posthumously. The Ashok Chakra can be awarded to both uniformed personnel as well as civilians. On the obverse, the chakra features a replica of the Ashoka Chakra encircled by a lotus garland. On the reverse, words 'Ashoka Chakra' are imprinted in English and Hindi, with lotus flower between them on each side. The medal ribband is dark-green silk of 3.2 cm with an orange vertical line through the centre.

Kirti Chakra

The Kirti Chakra is the second-highest peacetime gallantry award in peacetime and was first instituted on 4 January 1952 as the Ashoka Chakra Class-II. It was redesignated as the Kirti Chakra on 27 Jan 1967. The silver medal is circular with a diameter of 1.38 inches, with rims on both sides. The obverse features the Ashoka Chakra enclosed by a lotus wreath, and on the reverse the medal is imprinted with the words 'Kirti Chakra' in English and Hindi. The words are separated by a lotus flower on each side. The ribband is green, of 3.2 inches width with two orange vertical lines divide the riband into three equal parts. The medal is awarded for conspicuous gallantry otherwise than in the face of the enemy. The decoration may be awarded posthumously.

Shaurya Chakra

The Shaurya Chakra was instituted on 4 January 1952 as the Ashoka Chakra Class-III and renamed on 27 January 1967. It is the third-highest peacetime gallantry award, awarded for gallantry otherwise than in the face of the enemy. The decoration may be awarded posthumously. The Shaurya Chakra medal is circular, with a diameter of 1.4 cm made of bronze with the obverse similar to that of the Ashoka Chakra. On the reverse, the words 'Shaurya Chakra' are imprinted in Hindi and English, and separated by lotus flowers. The 3.2 inch wide riband accompanying the medal is divided into four equal parts by three orange vertical lines.

Table 9.2 Param Vir Chakra Awardees from the Indian Army

S/ No	Name	Rk	Regiment	Date	Battle	Place
1.	Somnath Sharma	Major	Kumaon Regiment	3 November 1947*	Battle of Badgam	Badgam, Jammu and Kashmir, India
2.	Jadunath Singh	Naik	Rajput Regiment (now 4 GUARDS)	6 February 1948*	Indo-Pakistani War of 1947	Naushera, Jammu and Kashmir, India
3.	Rama Raghoba Rane	Second Lieutenant	Bombay Sappers	8 April 1948	Indo-Pakistani War of 1947	Naushera, Jammu and Kashmir, India

4.	Piru Singh	Company Havildar Major	Rajputana Rifles	17 July 1948*	Indo-Pakistani War of 1947	Tithwal, Jammu and Kashmir, India
5.	Karam Singh	Lance Naik	Sikh Regiment	13 October 1948	Indo-Pakistani War of 1947	Tithwal, Jammu and Kashmir, India
6.	Gurbachan Singh Salaria	Captain	1 Gorkha Rifles[d]	5 December 1961*	Congo Crisis	Élisabethville, Katanga, Congo
7.	Dhan Singh Thapa	Major	8 Gorkha Rifles	20 October 1962	Sino-Indian War	Ladakh, Jammu and Kashmir, India
8.	Joginder Singh	Subedar	Sikh Regiment	23 October 1962*	Sino-Indian War	Tongpen La, North-East Frontier Agency, India
9.	Shaitan Singh	Major	Kumaon Regiment	18 November 1962*	Sino-Indian War	Rezang La, Jammu and Kashmir, India
10.	Abdul Hamid	Company Quarter Master Havildar	The Grenadiers	10 September 1965*	Battle of Asal Uttar	Khemkaran, India
11.	Ardeshir Tarapore	Lieutenant Colonel	Poona Horse	11 September 1965*	Battle of Chawinda	Phillora, Sialkot, Pakistan
12.	Albert Ekka	Lance Naik	Brigade of the Guards	3 December 1971*	Battle of Hilli	Gangasagar, Agartala, India
13.	Arun Khetarpal	Second Lieutenant	Poona Horse	16 December 1971*	Battle of Basantar	Barapind-Jarpal, Shakargarh, Pakistan
14.	Hoshiar Singh Dahiya	Major	The Grenadiers	17 December 1971	Battle of Basantar	Basantar River, Shakargarh, Pakistan
15.	Bana Singh	Naib Subedar	Jammu and Kashmir Light Infantry	23 May 1987	Operation Rajiv	Siachen Glacier, Jammu and Kashmir, India

16.	Ramaswamy Parameshwaran	Major	Mahar Regiment[e]	25 November 1987*	Operation Pawan	Sri Lanka
17.	Manoj Kumar Pandey	Lieutenant	11 Gorkha Rifles	3 July 1999*	Operation Vijay	Khaluber / Juber Top, Jammu and Kashmir, India
18.	Yogendra Singh Yadav	Grenadier	The Grenadiers	4 July 1999	Battle of Tiger Hill	Tiger Hill, Jammu and Kashmir, India
19.	Sanjay Kumar	Rifleman	Jammu and Kashmir Rifles	5 July 1999	Kargil War	Kargil, Jammu and Kashmir, India
20.	Vikram Batra	Captain	Jammu and Kashmir Rifles	7 July 1999*	Operation Vijay	Kargil, Jammu and Kashmir, India

Table 9.3 Ashok Chakra Awardees from the Indian Army

S/ No	Year	Rk	Name	Org
1.	1952	Naik	Narbahadur Thapa	Indian Army
2.	1952	Havildar	Bachittar Singh *	Indian Army
3.	1956	Lance Naik	Sundar Singh	Indian Army
4.	1957	Lieutenant Colonel	Jagannath Raoji Chitnis *	Indian Army
5.	1957	Second Lieutenant	Pollur Mutthuswamy Raman *	Indian Army
6.	1957	Havildar	Joginder Singh *	Indian Army
7.	1958	Captain	Eric James Tucker *	Indian Army
8.	1962	Subedar Major	Kharka Bahadur Limbu *	Indian Army
9.	1962	Captain	Man Bahadur Rai	Indian Army
10.	1962	Cadet	Shri Amrat Lal Mehra	NCC
11.	1969	Captain	Jas Ram Singh	Indian Army
12.	1972	Captain	Ummed Singh Mahra *	Indian Army
13.	1974	Naib Subedar	Gurnam Singh *	Indian Army
14.	1981	Second Lieutenant	Cyrus Addie Pithawalla	Indian Army
15.	1985	Lance Havildar	Chhering Mutup	Indian Army
16.	1985	Naik	Nirbhay Singh *	Indian Army
17.	1985	Naik	Bhawani Datt Joshi *	Indian Army
18.	1985	Lieutenant	Ram Prakash Roperia *	Indian Army
19.	1985	Captain	Jasbir Singh Raina	Indian Army
20.	1985	Major	Bhukant Misra *	Indian Army

21.	1992	Captain	Sandeep Sankhla *	Indian Army
22.	1993	Second Lieutenant	Rakesh Singh *	Indian Army
23.	1994	Colonel	Neelakantan Jayachandran Nair *	Indian Army
24.	1995	Major	Rajiv Kumar Joon *	Indian Army
25.	1995	Subedar	Sujjan Singh *	Indian Army
26.	1995	Lieutenant Colonel	Harsh Uday Singh Gaur *	Indian Army
27.	1996	Captain	Arun Singh Jasrotia *	Indian Army
28.	1997	Second Lieutenant	Puneet Nath Datt *	Indian Army
29.	1997	Lieutenant Colonel	Shanti Swarup Rana *	Indian Army
30.	2000	Major	Sudhir Kumar Walia *	Indian Army
31.	2002	Subedar	Surinder Singh *	Indian Army
32.	2002	Naik	Rambeer Singh Tomar *	Indian Army
33.	2003	Subedar Major	Suresh Chand Yadav *	National Security Guard
34.	2004	Lieutenant	Triveni Singh *	Indian Army
35.	2004	Paratrooper	Sanjog Chhetri *	Indian Army
36.	2007	Captain	Radhakrishnan Nair Harshan *	Indian Army
37.	2007	Naib Subedar	Chuni Lal *	Indian Army
38.	2007	Colonel	Vasanth Venugopal *	Indian Army
39.	2008	Major	Dinesh Raghu Raman *	Indian Army
40.	2009	Havildar	Bahadur Singh Bohra *	Indian Army
41.	2009	Havildar	Gajender Singh Bisht *	NSG
42.	2009	Major	Sandeep Unnikrishnan *	NSG
43.	2009	Colonel	Jojan Thomas *	Indian Army
44.	2010	Havildar	Rajesh Kumar *	Indian Army
45.	2010	Major	D Sreeram Kumar	Indian Army
46.	2010	Major	Mohit Sharma *	Indian Army
47.	2011	Major	Laishram Jyotin Singh *	Indian Army
48.	2012	Lieutenant	Navdeep Singh *	Indian Army
49.	2014	Major	Mukund Varadarajan *	Indian Army
50.	2014	Naik	Neeraj Kumar Singh *	Indian Army
51.	2016	Lance Naik	Mohan Goswami *	Indian Army
52.	2017	Havildar	Hangpan Dada *	Indian Army
53.	2019	Lance Naik	Nazir Ahmad Wani *	Territorial Army (Indian Army)

Source: Indian Army.
Note: * indicates posthumous award.

War Memorials

In the heart of New Delhi, the capital of India, stand two war memorials. The iconic India Gate, was built in 1931 to 'commemorate the Battle Casualties (Fatal) of India during World War I as well as Third Anglo-Afghan War. Out of over 83,000 Indians who laid down their lives, India Gate bears 13,516 names, etched all over the monument.'[4] The Amar Jawan Jyoti was built under the India Gate arch to commemorate India's victory in the Indo-Pak War of 1971 and to pay tribute to India's brave soldiers/sailors/airmen who laid down their lives in service of the nation. The Amar Jawan Jyoti features an inverted bayonet with a helmet structure on a black marble platform. This has now been moved to the National War Memorial.

Post-independence, India has fought four major wars as well as seen many instances of conflict. Its armed forces have participated in a number of operations both within the borders of the country and beyond, ranging from peacekeeping missions to counter-insurgency and counter-terrorism as well as facing an ongoing proxy war. Over 26,000 personnel from the Indian Armed Forces have laid down their lives for the sovereignty and integrity of the nation.

There were many local, 'area/battle specific memorials' across the country but the need was felt to have a war memorial in the capital to record for posterity the bravery and gallantry of those who have served the nation. While the demand for a National War Memorial has been around since 1961, the process got momentum in 2015 when the 'Union Cabinet approved construction of a National War Memorial and Museum (NWM&M)...[t]aking into consideration the existing ceremonial practices at India Gate and AJJ, area East of the India Gate around the Canopy at "C" Hexagon in New Delhi was found to be the most suited site for the Memorial.'[5] The National War Memorial was inaugurated on 25 February 2019 by the Prime Minister.

War Memorials: A Brief History

The Saragarhi Memorials at Amritsar and Ferozpur are some of the earliest modern memorials built in India to honour collective gallantry and sacrifice. These mark the last stand of a detachment of the 36 Sikhs, numbering 21 men, that faced a 10,000–12,000 strong tribal lashkar, in a battle at Saragarhi, a small outpost on the Samana range in September 1897. The soldiers fought to the last man and each was posthumously admitted to the IOM for gallantry.

It was, however, World War I (1914–1918) that led to the marking of the sacrifice of individual soldiers of all ranks by universally according an official recognition in the form of a grave or memorial located in the theatre of war where the soldier had died. Of the many Hindu and Sikh soldiers who fought in the war, and whose remains were cremated and who had no known grave, their details were recorded on common collective memorials. Examples of such memorials are the India Gate at New Delhi and the memorial at Neuve Chapelle in France.

It is the Commonwealth War Graves Commission (CWGC) in the United Kingdom (UK) which 'has the responsibility for recording details, maintaining the memorials, and the numerous graves and cemeteries. The cost is shared by partner governments—Australia, Canada, India, New Zealand, South Africa and the UK—in proportions based on the numbers of their graves. All members of the forces who died in service or as a result of service within the two war periods designated by the participating governments—between 4 August 1914 and 31 August 1921, and 3 September 1939 to 31 December 1947, are considered as war dead and recorded as such.'[6]

India's contribution to both World Wars was immense: over 1.4 million Indians served during the First World War; in the Second World War, between 1939 and 1945, the Indian Army grew from a strength of 1,95,000 in 1939 to over 2.5 million men by the end of the war, the largest volunteer force in the history of human conflict. 'The 160,000 war dead of undivided India are buried and commemorated in over 60 countries. India's massive volunteer Army suffered by far the heaviest losses, but the Second World War also saw men of the Royal Indian Navy and the Royal Indian Air Force play a significant role, with many of their number also falling in the line of duty.'[7]

War memorials thus provide a focus for memory and for commemoration both nationally and internationally, as well as a space where friends and relatives can remember the sacrifice of their loved ones. Broadly speaking, three kinds of memorials/war graves exist in India and abroad:

1. Memorials/war graves commemorating the war dead of undivided India. These are of the pre-Independence period and most of these memorials are under the care of the CWGC.
2. Memorials of post-Independence era constructed within military stations, cantonments and field areas with government sanction; as well as memorials to Indian soldiers/peacekeepers in other countries.
3. Memorials constructed by civic bodies and state governments within India.

At the end of World War I, a large number of Memorial Tablets were installed by government in villages and towns across the country. Post-independence, a number of specific memorials were constructed and maintained across the country. Nationally, it was the India Gate that served as the premier war memorial until the inauguration of the National War Memorial in 2019.

Pre-Independence Wars and Memorials

World War I

World War I, also known as the 'Great War', was fought between 1914–1918. It was a seminal event in modern world history and changed the social and political map of the world forever. The repercussions of the war can be felt even today, with many current conflicts originating from the impact of the war. As Great Britain entered the war on 4 August 1914 in response to the German violation of the sovereignty of Belgium', its colonies were also pulled into the war.

At the time, the only regular forces available to Britain were its own Army and the Indian Army. The Indian Army was not organised, trained or equipped for a major war of the type that was to take place, but it was the only reserve that was immediately available. Mobilisation commenced on 8 August 1914, just four days after the declaration of war by Great Britain. Within India, the National Movement was gathering pace and the Indians actively supported the war effort in a bid to gain Dominion status. 'The overwhelming majority of mainstream political opinion in 1914 was united in the view that if India desired greater responsibility and political autonomy, it must also be willing to share in the burden of Imperial defence. As a result, India contributed immensely to the war effort in terms of both men and material.'[8]

'Indian soldiers served in battlefields around the world: in France and Belgium, in Aden, Arabia, East Africa, Gallipoli, Egypt, Mesopotamia, Palestine, Persia, Salonica, Russia, and even in China. By the end of the war 1,100,000 Indians had served overseas at the cost of 60,000 dead. They earned over 9,200 decorations for gallantry including 11 Victoria Crosses. These figures include the contribution of over 26,000 Imperial Service troops who were a part of the Indian States Forces.'[9] Between 1914 and 1918, the Indian Army expanded sevenfold. Overall, around 1.2 million men were mobilised for the Indian Army and 0.3 million for non-combat duties.[10]

The Indian Army was divided into seven expeditionary forces and broadly deployed as stated below:

1. Indian Expeditionary Force (IEF) A: Northern Europe, in France and the Low Countries.
2. IEF B: East Africa.
3. IEF C: East Africa.
4. IEF D: Mesopotamia
5. IEF E: Egypt and Palestine
6. IEF F: Egypt
7. IEF G: Gallipoli

The Indian soldier was not trained for trench warfare, nor were the troops equipped for the European weather. The Army, prior to the war, was designed and trained to police the frontiers of empire in the Indian Subcontinent and in other outposts of the British Empire. Still, they acquitted themselves admirably in the war.

A number of war memorials commemorate the participation and sacrifice of Indian soldiers and officers in the Great War. Presented below is a brief description of some key memorials.[11]

Europe

France

The Neuve Chapelle Memorial The Neuve Chapelle Memorial was erected in France by the Imperial War Graves Commission (IWGC) on 7 October 1927 by then Secretary of State for India, Lord Birkenhead. It is in the form of a sanctuary enclosed within a circular wall. Carved Indian symbols as obtained in Indian shrines adorn the railings. In the middle of the railing is a column approximately 15 metres high similar to the columns erected by the Emperor Ashoka all over India. The Memorial is located close to the village of Neuve Chapelle in an area that was central to the operations of the Indian Corps during 1914 and 1915. The Memorial was designed by Sir Herbert Baker, and its cost shared between Britain, India and the rest of the Dominions.

The rear of the Memorial is a solid wall on which the names of the 'Missing' are inscribed including those who were cremated but for whom no grave stone or tablet exists. Where the railing meets the solid wall are two stone 'chattris 'which are found in sacred burial places in northern and central India.

In addition to the names of 4,742 of the Indian war dead who fell in France and Flanders are the names of two Indian VC winners—Lieutenant Bruce McCrae of the 59 Scinde Rifles and Rifleman Gabar Singh Negi of the 39 Garhwal Rifles who were killed in the battles of Givenchy and Neuve Chapelle respectively.[12]

Meerut Military Cemetery The Meerut Military Cemetery is located towards the south of the French port of Boulogne and is linked to the fact that the Meerut Stationary Hospital was located here and it is here that over 300 Indian casualties are commemorated, including 287 from the 1914–15 period. This Memorial also includes a Memorial to 32 Indian Army officers and men who were cremated in the cemetery in 1915.[13]

Zelobes Indian Cemetery The Zelobes Indian Cemetery is located at Lacouture, north west of Bethune, and was used by Field Ambulances from November 1914 to October 1915. It contains the graves of 73 Indian casualties including that of Subedar Hashmat Dad Khan, who was killed at Windy Corner, south of Festubert and is described as 'a very fine Indian Officer remarkable for his fatalistic contempt for danger'. He was awarded the Indian Distinguished Service Medal (IDSM) for his courage.[14]

Mazargues Cemetery The Mazargues Cemetery is just three miles from Marseilles, which was the base for the Indian Army during its stay on the Western Front and thereafter. It contains the graves of 127 Indian soldiers who died between 1914–1915, and many others who died subsequently. These casualties cover a range of Regiments and corps fighting in the north and also large numbers from support units such as the Mule Corps, the Indian Veterinary Corps, the Indian Ordnance Department, the Army Bearer Corps, and the Indian Subordinate Medical Corps. The majority of casualties after the departure of the Indian Corps for Mesopotamia, Palestine and Egypt are from the Indian Labour Corps, of which there are 420 graves and Memorials. In addition, are the graves of personnel of the Artillery and Cavalry units who were retained on the Western Front after the Indian Corps departed at the end of 1915. This cemetery commemorates a total of 994 Indian dead.[15]

Gorre British and Indian Cemetery The Chateau at Gorre was only about two miles from the front in 1914–15 and was occupied during this time by the Indian Corps. The cemetery contains 80 Indian graves from the 1914–15 period.[16]

Ayette Indian and Chinese Cemetery This cemetery is located in the village of Ayette in France. It remained in British hands from March 1916 to 27 March 1918 when it was captured by the Germans. The cemetery was begun in September 1917 and used till April 1918, and again in September and October 1918. Thirty five Indians are buried here.[17]

Etaples Military Cemetery Seventeen Indian soldiers are buried in this cemetery at Etaples, in France which saw a number of Commonwealth reinforcement camps and hospitals during World War I.[18]

Merville Communal Cemetery The headquarters of the Indian Corps, and the Meerut and Lahore Casualty Clearing Stations were located here in 1914–15. Ninety-seven Indians are buried here.[19]

Neuville-Sous-Montreuil Indian Cemetery This Indian Cemetery was made between December 1914 and March 1916 by the Lahore Indian General Hospital. Twenty-five Indian soldiers are buried here.[20]

Belgium

Menin Gate The Menin Gate War Memorial focuses on the soldiers who were listed as missing in the battles at France and Flanders and for whom no grave exists. It was unveiled on 27 July 1927. Menin was chosen for the memorial because it was through here that hundreds of thousands of soldiers passed through on their way to the battlefields of the Ypres Salient.

The design of the memorial is on the lines of the classic Roman triumphal arch with its three central passageways. The exterior is of red brick and faced with Portland stone which is the material used for the headstones of all graves which are part of all IWGC cemeteries. The central passageway has a semi-circular arch. The central memorial hall, the stairwells and the galleries record the names of soldiers missing, believed killed, in the region before 15 August 1917. Those who died after this date are mentioned in the Tyne Cot Memorial or at the Memorial at Ploegsteert. On the South side of the Memorial to the missing is the Indian Forces Memorial which was opened in March 2011 and is dedicated to the 130,000 troops of the Indian Forces who served in France and Flanders during the Great War. The existing stone was replaced by the more imposing Ashoka Lions marker in November 2011.[21]

Germany

Durnbach War Cemetery The Durnbach War Cemetry contains the graves of 41 Indian soldiers who died as prisoners of war in various places in Germany.[22]

Zehrensdorf Indian Cemetery This cemetery contains the graves of 206 Indian soldiers who died during the First World War at a prisoner-of-war camp at Zossen, south of Berlin.[23]

Britain

The Chattri Memorial, Brighton Around 12,000 wounded Indian soldiers passed through Brighton and Hove Hospital during the Great War. The Chattri Memorial was erected on the exact spot where 53 Hindu and Sikh soldiers were cremated according to their faith.[24]

Patcham Down Memorial This memorial commemorates 53 Indian casualties of the First World War who died in the United Kingdom, many of them at the Indian Army hospital established at the Royal Pavilion in Brighton. These men were cremated in accordance with their faith and were initially commemorated on the Hollybrook and Neuve-Chappelle Memorials to the Missing. However, it was later decided that as these casualties were not 'missing' and therefore it would be better to commemorate them on a memorial at their cremation site. The Memorial bears an inscription written in Hindi, Punjabi and English that reads: 'IN HONOUR OF THESE SOLDIERS OF THE INDIAN Army WHOSE MORTAL REMAINS WERE COMMITTED TO FIRE'.

Malta

Pieta Military Cemetery The Pieta Military Cemetery commemorates 28 Indian servicemen who died from their wounds in the hospitals of Malta and Gozo chiefly from the campaigns in Gallipoli and Salonika, 20 of whom were prisoners of war.[25]

Romania

Slobozia Military Cemetery The Slobozia Military Cemetery was made in 1920 by the Rumanian (Romania) Government for the reburial of those Indian soldiers, captured by the Germans and sent to work in Rumania and who later died in captivity.[26]

Greece

Monastir Road Indian Cemetery This cemetery was used from 1916 for the burial of those Indians who served in Salonika and commemorates the remains of Indian servicemen who were cremated in accordance with their faith.[27]

Africa

Kenya

Maktau Indian Cemetery Maktau was a fortified camp, reinforcement depot, and an Indian clearing hospital during World War I and was established in 1915. The cemetery was used from March 1915 to May 1916.[28]

Nairobi British and Indian Memorial In 1914, Indian Expeditionary Force 'B' arrived at Mombasa to take part in operations against German East Africa. The memorial commemorates many of those who died before the advance to Rufiji in January 1917 and who have no known grave. The Memorial commemorates 1,151 Indian soldiers who fell in this campaign.[29]

Middle East

Egypt

Abbasiya Indian Cemetery Cairo was the headquarters of the British Garrison in Egypt at the start of World War I. It subsequently became the main base and hospital centre for operations in Gallipoli, Egypt and Palestine. The cemetery at El Abbasiya was established in May 1918 and used till December 1920. Seventy-five Indian soldiers are buried here.[30]

Port Tewfik Memorial The original Port Tewfik Memorial stood at the southern boundary of the Suez Canal. The canal itself was perhaps even more important during the two World Wars than it is today—linking the Mediterranean with the Red Sea and beyond, connecting Great Britain with its colonies in East Africa, Asia and the Pacific.

During the First World War, it was a prime target for the Ottoman Empire, who launched several attacks towards the canal in 1915. These attacks were successfully repulsed, and the canal remained in British hands. British forces, including Australian, Indian and New Zealand units, would go on the offensive in late 1916 and by 1918 had captured large swaths of Ottoman territory in the Eastern Mediterranean.

Indian troops played a large part in the war in Egypt and the Eastern Mediterranean. In the 1920s, the Port Tewfik Memorial was built to commemorate the Indian servicemen who lost their lives in this theatre of war and who have no known grave. Unfortunately, the memorial suffered severe damage during the Israeli-Egyptian conflict of 1967–73, and was eventually demolished. A replacement memorial was later erected at Heliopolis War Cemetery and commemorates more than 3,700 Indian servicemen of the First World War.

Israel

Haifa War Memorial The Haifa War Memorial commemorates those who fell in the Cavalry charge by the Jodhpur Lancers of the 15 Imperial Service Cavalry Brigade on 23 September 1918 on fortified Infantry defences at Haifa. A commemorative service is now held annually at the Memorial attended by members of the diplomatic corps and representatives of the Indian Armed Forces.[31]

Jerusalem Indian War Cemetery This cemetery was used from July 1918 to June 1920 for Indian servicemen killed during the Palestine campaign of World War I.[32]

Lebanon

Beirut Maronite Cemetery Beirut was occupied by the 7th (Meerut) Indian Division on 8th October 1918 and the 32nd and 15th Clearing Hospitals were sent to this town. The majority of those buried in this cemetery died in October 1918.[33]

Turkey

Helles Memorial, Gallipoli This memorial commemorates the death of 20,834 killed at Gallipoli, 1,516 of who were Indian. The height of the memorial is the same as that of the Colossus of Rhodes so that the monument of the missing dead would be visible by the ships sailing in those seas.[34]

India

India Gate

India Gate is a memorial that is a landmark in New Delhi, India. This memorial commemorates 12,357 Indian soldiers whose names are inscribed on the bricks of the walls of this edifice. The inscription at the top of the arch reads as given below:

> To the dead of the Indian Armies who fell and are honoured in France and Flanders, Mesopotamia and Persia, East Africa, Gallipoli and elsewhere in the Near and Far East and in Sacred Memory also of those whose names are here recorded and who fell in India and on the North West Frontier and during the Third Afghan War.

Teen Murti Memorial

The Teen Murti memorial stands close to India Gate and is a part of the landscape conceived by Edward Lutyens. 'Teen Murti' is the local name given to this memorial and literally means 'Three Statues'. The memorial commemorates the 15th Imperial Service Cavalry Brigade that fought in the Middle East during the First World War. It also serves as the Indian Cavalry Memorial and a memorial service is held here every year by the Indian Cavalry Association on Cavalry Day. The names of the Cavalrymen who fell in the Great War are inscribed on the memorial.

Kapurthala State Forces War Memorial

This memorial commemorates the war dead of the Kapurthala Imperial Service Infantry who served in East Africa between 1914 and 1917, and also in the

Third Afghan War. This monument is also known as the Captain Jhaggar Singh Memorial.[35]

Kolkata 49th Bengalis Memorial

This memorial pays tribute to the 49th Bengalis—a remarkable unit which happens to be the only Army unit to be composed entirely of Bengalis. The unit was raised in 1917 and was deployed on active service in Mesopotamia.[36]

Kolkata Lascar Memorial

This memorial commemorates the Indian Lascars who replaced British sailors, and made up to 20 per cent of the British maritime force by the end of the war. Their contribution to the war is also recorded in the Tower Hill Memorial, UK which honours allied merchant seamen who lost their lives in both World Wars.[37]

Chennai Victory Memorial

This memorial is located along the Sea Beach Road locally known as the 'Marina Beach', which faces the Bay of Bengal and is close to Fort St George. It was constructed by prominent citizens of Madras to commemorate the victory of the allied armies during World War I.[38]

Kirkee 1914–18 Memorial

This memorial commemorates 1,805 casualties of the First World War. It consists of a series of walls on which are inscribed the names of those who fell during the Great War, with the dedicatory inscription in Hindi.[39]

Patiala State Forces Memorial

The memorial commemorates the dead of the military units of the erstwhile princely state of Patiala during the First World War (1914–18).[40]

In addition to the memorials mentioned above, memorial plaques and tablets to commemorate those who fell in the First World War have been installed in towns and villages across India. They record the number of men who went to war and the number who did not return. Regimental memorials also occupy pride of place in Regiments and Battalions of the Indian Army. They are sacred symbols and figure prominently in units and figure prominently in the ceremonies that celebrate battle honour days.[41]

World War II

The First World War ended with the armistice on 11 November 1918. During the course of the war, over 9 million soldiers were killed and another 15 million wounded.[42] 'Four great empires had fallen to pieces: Russia...; Germany...; Austria-Hungary...' and the Ottoman Empire.... The old international order had gone forever.'[43] The Treaty of Versailles, signed on 28 June 1919, which formally ended the state of war between Germany and the Allied Powers. It 'held Germany responsible for the war' and imposed upon it heavy repatriations to the Allies. This led to resentment by the German people and created conditions that led to the rise of Adolf Hitler who took over as Chancellor of Germany in 1933 and set about rapidly [militarising].... 'On 13 March 1938 he annexed Austria and occupied Czechoslovakia. The British and the French, fearful of another world war, took no action but realized that German military expansion had to be stopped.'[44] On 01 September 1939, Germany attacked Poland; on 03 September, Great Britain declared war on Germany owing to its treaty obligations with Poland, and the Second World War began. The war would last for six years and be the most destructive conflict of its time.

At the start of World War II in 1939, the Indian Army had a strength of 194,000 personnel, with 96 Infantry Battalions and 18 Cavalry Regiments. 'Modernisation had yet to start. The Cavalry had no tanks; the Infantry had no mortars as anti-tank weapons. Wireless sets were available only at brigade headquarters and above.... By the time the war ended, the Indian Army had expanded to over 2.5 million men and had fought on both the Western and Eastern fronts. These figures include units of the Indian State Forces. Indian soldiers were deployed in Persia, Iraq, East Africa, North Africa, in Sicily, Italy and France and in Burma, South East Asia and Indonesia. The Indian Army of the Second World War was the largest volunteer Army in the history of human conflict.'[45] An interesting bit of trivia about the war is that 'four Indian Animal Transport Companies that supported the British Divisions in France took part in the retreat at Dunkirk, impressing all with their discipline in difficult circumstances.'[46]

Indian troops saw action in almost all theatres of the war: in Europe, North Africa, in Burma and South-east Asia. 'In the Second World War [the Indian Army] had fought against two of the finest armies of the world—the Germans and the Japanese—and had proved its worth. Towards the end of the war it was led by its own officers at unit and sub-unit level.... The myth of the martial classes was also finally broken. The rapid wartime expansion of the Indian Army from a strength of 2,00,000 to 20,00,000 forced recruitment from all classes. The officer cadre expanded from 1000 to 15,740.' Thus by the end of World War II the Indian Army was truly representative of all areas and classes of the country. The Indian Army earned '[n]early 6,300 awards... including 31 Victoria Crosses, 4 George Crosses, 252 Distinguished Service Orders, 347 Indian Orders of Merit and 1,311 Military Crosses.'[47]

According to *The Last Post*, published as a commemorative volume during the centenary celebrations of the First World War, over '62,000 Commonwealth war dead of the two world wars are commemorated by the CWGC in India. During the First World War, many soldiers died on the North West Frontier or in garrison outposts, and, as it was not possible to maintain all the civil, cantonment and outpost cemeteries in which many of them were buried, their names are recorded on Memorials in the war cemeteries at Delhi, Madras and Kirkee, and on the Memorial Arch in New Delhi (today known as the India Gate). During the Second World War, cemeteries for hospitals and lines of communication were established at Ranchi, Kirkee, Madras, Digboi and Guwahati, and for the battlefields at Imphal and Kohima. Delhi War Cemetery was established after independence to accommodate wartime graves from cantonments in Northern, Western and Central India.'[48]

World War II Memorials Commemorating Indian Soldiers

Rangoon Memorial

Located at the heart of Taukkyan War Cemetery, the Rangoon Memorial bears the names of more than 26,000 World War II Servicemen—almost 20,000 of them served with the Indian forces. The Taukyan Cremation Memorial commemorates a further 1,000 World War II casualties whose remains were cremated in accordance with their faith.

The majority of these men were casualties of the campaign in Burma (now Myanmar). In 1942, in the face of the invading Japanese forces, the British Burma Army retreated from Burma into India. The country would remain under Japanese control until the winter of 1944-45, when a Commonwealth force returned to liberate the country from the Japanese.

A fierce campaign followed, culminating in a race to Rangoon, where Commonwealth troops hurried to secure the vital port before monsoon season set in. Within the week of the recapture of Rangoon, Germany formally surrendered to the Allies—and with Japanese influence in Burma all but eradicated, the end of the war was in sight.

Alamein Memorial

The two battles of El Alamein arguably feature as one of the key turning points of the Second World War. Not only did they mark one of the first major Allied successes of the war, but they were the first step towards eventual victory in the North African campaign, which in turn was vital for the securing control of the Mediterranean. At times during the conflict the desert was as much an enemy as the opposing troops.

Swelting days and freezing nights in a vast bleak desert, which meant supply lines could be precariously long, and populated by biting flies.

Of the more than 11,000 casualties commemorated on the Alamein Memorial, over 1,800 of them served with Indian forces, who fought in campaigns across North Africa and the Eastern Mediterranean. A further 600 Indian casualties are listed on the Alamein Cremation Memorial as their remains were cremated during the war, in accordance with their faith.

Singapore Memorial

Japanese forces launched a devastating surprise attack against British Malaya (Malaysia) in December 1942. British and Commonwealth forces where quickly driven back down the peninsular and by February had retreated across the straits to Singapore. Japanese forces besieged the island on 15 February 1943. Singapore, the key stone of British imperial defence in southeast Asia, fell and some 80,000 Commonwealth troops became prisoners of war.

The Singapore Memorial commemorates more than 24,000 Commonwealth casualties, more than 12,000 of whom are Indian. Some of the those commemorated here died during the defence of Malaya and Singapore, but most died while in captivity as a result of brutal treatment by the Japanese. The Singapore Cremation Memorial commemorates almost 800 casualties, mostly Indian forces, who were cremated in accordance with their religious beliefs.

War Memorials in India

As already noted in Chapters 3 and 4, post-independence, India has fought four major wars with its neighbours, China and Pakistan. In addition, The Indian Armed Forces have participated in a number of key operations both domestically and abroad, including in UN Peacekeeping missions. Counter-insurgency and internal security are some of the other key tasks that have been placed upon the armed forces, in particular the Indian Army.

Until the inauguration of the National War Memorial in 2019, India Gate and the Amar Jawan Jyoti served as a space of national memorial to honour the sacrifices of the brave Indian men and women who gave their lives in service of the nation. Additionally, there are a number of smaller memorials across the country, many of which are located within cantonments, that commemorate the gallantry and bravery of the Indian Armed Forces. Table 9.4 is an exhaustive list of such memorials, state-wise.

Table 9.4 List of War Memorials in India

No.	State		Location	Name of War Memorial
1.	**Andhra Pradesh**	1	Secunderabad	Bison War Memorial
2.		2	Hyderabad (Mehdipatnam)	Basantar War Memorial
3.		3	Secunderabad Cantonment (1 EME Centre)	1 EME Centre War Memorial
4.		4	Secunderabad (AOC Centre)	AOC Centre War Memorial
5.		5	Secunderabad (Army Training Ground)	Veerula Sainika Smarak
6.	**Arunachal Pradesh**	1	18 Km from Walong	Helmet Top War Memorial
7.		2	Manmao Post	Manmao War Memorial
8.		3	Nuranang (25 km from Tawang)	Jaswantgarh War Memorial
9.		4	Tawang	Tawang War Memorial
10.		5	Walong	Walong War Memorial
11.		6	Walong	Hut of Remembrance
12.		7	Tilam	Memorial at Namti
13.		8	Lumpo	War Memorial
14.		9	Hathong La	War Memorial Hathong La
15.		10	Tawang	War Memorial New Khingzemane
16.		11	Surwa Samba	War Memorial Surwa Samba
17.		12	Bum La	Sub Joginder Singh, PVC War Memorial
18.		13	Phudung	Brig Hoshiar Singh War Memorial
19.		14	Rupa	Brig Hoshiar Singh War Memorial
20.		15	Nyukmadung	Nyukmadung War Memorial
21.	**Assam**	1	Dibrugarh	DAH War Memorial
22.		2	Likabali	War Memorial
23.		3	Silchar (On top of Kheba Hills)	Amar Jawan War Memorial
24.		4	Tezpur (HQ 4 Corps)	4 Corps War Memorial

25.	**Bihar**	1	Danapur (Bihar Regimental Centre)	Bihar Regiment War Memorial
26.	**Delhi**	1	New Delhi (Teen Murti Road)	Teen Murti Memorial
27.		2	New Delhi (Rajpath)	India Gate
28.		3	New Delhi (Rajputana Rifles Regimental Centre)	Rajputana Rifles War Memorial
29.		4	New Delhi	War Memorial, Delhi Area
30.		5	New Delhi (India Gate, C Hexagon Road)	National War Memorial
31.	**Gujarat**	1	Ahmedabad Cantonment	Golden Katar War Memorial
32.		2	Ahmedabad (Shahibaugh, near State Guest House)	Ahmedabad War Memorial
33.		3	Bhuj (Rajaram Park, Military Station Bhuj)	Bhuj War Memorial
34.		4	Gandhinagar (Chiloda Military Station)	Parbat Ali War Memorial
35.	**Haryana**	1	Chandimandir Cantt	Veer Smriti Western Command War Memorial
36.		2	Gurgaon (John Hall)	Gurgaon Martyr's Memorial
37.		3	Hissar (Inside MD University Campus)	Amar Jawan War Memorial
38.		4	Jhajjar (At Sainik Rest House)	Jhajjar War Memorial
39.		5	Jind (Opposite District Court on Gohana Road)	Jind War Memorial
40.		6	Narwana (Navdeep Stadium)	Narwana War Memorial
41.		7	Bahadurgarh (On Rohtak road)	BahadurgarhWar Memorial
42.		8	Rohtak (Inside ManasaSarowar Park)	Yudh Shahid Samarak
43.	**Himachal Pradesh**	1	Dharmasala	Dharamsala Martyrs Memorial

44.		2	Jutogh Cantonment, Shimla (Right of gate No 1 bisecting National Highway at Toute)	3rd Mountain Artillery Brigade War Memorial (WW-1)
45.		3	Subathu (14 GTC)	14 GTC War Memorial
46.		4	Hamirpur	Capt Mridul Park Memorial
47	**Jammu & Kashmir and Ladakh (UT)**	1	Baramulla	1 Sikh War Memorial
48.		2	Baramulla	Dagger Memorial
49.		3	BB Cantt, Srinagar	Op Rakshak Memorial
50.		4	Karu, Ladakh (UT)	Trishul War Memorial
51.		5	Jammu (Bahu Wali Rakh)	Balidan Stambh
52.		6	Jammu (Tiger Park opposite St Mary's Public School)	Tiger War Memorial
53.		7	Rezang La, Ladakh (UT)	Rezang La War Memorial
54.		8	Leh, Ladakh (UT)	Leh (1962, 1965, 1971) War Memorial
55.		9	Leh, Ladakh (UT)	Leh (1947–48) War Memorial
56.		10	Machhal	Sahi Memorial Hospital
57.		11	Poonch (In front of 171 MH link road from NH-1 to Village Sangwali Mandi)	Lok Bahadur Stadium Memorial
58.		12	Ladakh (UT)	Hall of Fame
59.		13	Siachen, Ladakh (UT) (Siachen Base Camp)	Siachen War Memorial
60.		14	Daulat Beg Oldi, Ladakh (UT)	Joint Memorial, DBO, Advance Landing Ground (SSN)
61.		15	Srinagar (HQ 15 Corps)	15 Corps War Memorial
62.		16	Srinagar	The JAK Light Regt War Memorial
63.		17	Leh, Ladakh (UT)	Ladakh Scouts Regt War Memorial
64.		18	Uri, Baramulla	War Memorial
65.		19	Uri, Baramulla	Nand Singh War Memorial

66.		20	Gurez Valley	Gurez War Memorial
67.		21	Tithwal	Tithwal War Memorial
68.		22	Trehgam Garrison	Hajipir War Memorial
69.		23	Sonapindigali	Sonapindigali War Memorial
70.		24	Machhal	Machhal War Memorial
71.		25	Chowkibal	Chowkibal War Memorial
72.		26	Quila Darhal	War Memorial at Saheed Garh
73.		27	Poonch	War Memorial Naman Sthal
74.		28	Jhangar	Usman War Memorial
75.		29	Naushera	Naik Jadunath Singh, PVC War Memorial
76.		30	Naushera	Butalia Memorial
77.		31	Udhampur	Dhruva Shaheed Smarak
78.		32	Chushul, Ladakh (UT)	Chushul War Memorial
79.		33	Dras, Kargil, Ladakh (UT) (Bimbat)	Bimbat 8 Mountain Division Kargil War Memorial
80.		34	Gumri, Ladakh (UT)	Zoji La War Memorial
81.		35	Samba (On link road from NH-1A to Village Katli)	3 Madras Memorial
82.		36	Samba (Cremation ground)	2/Lt Arun Khetrapal PVC War Memorial
83.		37	Samba (On NH-1, approx 7 kms on Samba road towards Pathankot)	Major RS Rajwat Memorial
84.		38	Satwari Cantonment (Manekshaw Marg, opp Tiger CSD Canteen)	Jammu and Kashmir State Forces War Memorial
85.	**Jharkhand**	1	Ramgarh Cantonment (Sikh Regimental Centre)	Saragarhi War Memorial
86.		2	Ramgarh Cantonment (Sikh Regimental Centre)	Sikh Regiment War Memorial
87.		3	Ramgarh Cantonment (Punjab Regimental Centre)	Punjab Regiment War Memorial
88.		4	Ranchi (Depatoli Cantonment)	Jharkhand War Memorial
89.	**Karnataka**	1	Bangalore (Along Central Parade Ground, MEG & Centre)	Madras Sappers War Memorial

90.		2	Bangalore (ASC Centre and College)	Army Service Corps War Memorial
91.		3	Bangalore (ASC Centre and College)	Army Transport Animals Memorial
92.		4	Bangalore (CMP Centre & School)	Corps of Military Police War Memorial
93.		5	Bangalore (End of Brigade Road, near junction between Brigade & Residency Roads)	Pioneer Corps War Memorial
94.		6	Bangalore	The Parachute Regiment War Memorial
95.		7	Bangalore (MEG & Centre)	British War Memorial
96.		8	Belgaum (Maratha LI Regimental Centre)	Maratha Light Infantry War Memorial
97.	**Kerala**	1	Cannanore District (DSC Centre)	Defence Security Corps Gaurav Sthal
98.		2	Cannanore	Defence Security War Memorial
99.		3	Thiruvananthapuram (Pangode: on Vazhuthakad-Thirumala Main Road opposite 91 Inf Bde)	The Bogra Memorial Hut
100.	**Madhya Pradesh**	1	Bhopal (3 EME Centre)	No. 3 EME Centre War memorial
101.		2	Saugor	Shahbaaz War Memorial
102.		3	Saugor	The Mahar Regiment War Memorial
103.		4	Pachmarhi	Army Education Corps War Memorial
104.		5	Bhopal (HQ 21 Corps Complex)	Sudarshan Chakra War Memorial
105.		6	Jabalpur (1 Military Training Regiment, 1 Signal Training Centre)	Corps of Signals War Memorial
106.		7	Jabalpur (Grenadiers Regimental Centre)	The Grenadiers War Memorial
107.		8	Jabalpur (Jammu and Kashmir Rifles Regimental Centre)	Jammu and Kashmir Rifles War Memorial
108.		9	Jabalpur (CMM)	KanglaTongbi War Memorial
109.		10	Mhow	Infantry Memorial

110.	**Maharashtra**	1	Ahmednagar (Armoured Corps Centre and School	Armoured Corps War Memorial
111.		2	Southern Command AOR (Ranjit Ground in front of HQ 94 Armoured Brigade)	45 CAV War Memorial
112.		3	Ahmednagar (Mechanised Infantry Regimental Centre)	Mechanised Infantry Regiment War Memorial
113.		4	Khadakwasla, Pune (NDA)	Hut of Remembrance
114.		5	Kirkee (Training Battalion 1 Area, BEG & Centre)	Bombay Pioneers Memorial (WW-1)
115.		6	Kirkee (Entrance to Parade Ground, BEG & Centre)	Bombay Sappers War Memorial
116.		7	Nasik Road Camp	Regiment of Artillery War Memorial
117.		8	Kamptee	Brigade of The Guards Regiment War Memorial
118.		9	Mumbai (Military Station, facing Colaba Navynagar Road, behind Afghan Church, Colaba)	Subedar Joginder Singh PVC Memorial
119.		10	Nasik Road Camp (Artillery Centre)	Artillery Centre War Memorial
120.		11	Pune Cantonment (Morwada Junction)	Morwada War Memorial
121.		12	Pune	Intelligence Corps War Memorial
122.	**Manipur**	1	Imphal (Khenjang Village)	Kangla Tongbi War Memorial
123.		2	Leimakhong	Shantivan War Memorial
124.		3	Khongjam	War Memorial
125.	**Meghalaya**	1	Shillong (58 Gorkha Training Centre)	58 GTC War Memorial
126.		2	Shillong (Happy Valley, Assam Regimental Centre)	Assam Regiment War Memorial
127.		3	Shillong	1971 War Memorial
128.	**Nagaland**	1	Zakhama Military Station	Orchid Memorial
129.	**Orissa**	1	Gopalpur	Army Air Defence War Memorial

130.	**Punjab**	1	Amritsar (Military Station Khasa)	Dograi War Memorial
131.		2	Amritsar (Near Rattoke Gurudwara)	5 Gorkha Rifles War Memorial
132.		3	Amritsar (Pulkanjri, Dhanaya Kalan)	Pulkanjri War Memorial
133.		4	Asal Uttar (Tarn Taran Sahib)	CQMH Abdul Hamid PVC Memorial
134.		5	Asal Uttar (Tarn Taran Sahib, on road Khemkaran-Valtoha)	7 Grenadiers War Memorial
135.		6	Bhura Kuhna, Tarn Taran District	2/Lt JP Gaur Memorial
136.		7	Bhura Kuhna, Tarn Taran District	2 Madras Memorial
137.		8	Bhura Kuhna, (On Road Bhikhiwind Khemkaran near village Bhura Kuhna)	Sapper Harak Singh Memorial
138.		9	Ferozepur Cantt	Sehjra 1971 Memorial
139.		10	Ferozepur	Barki 1965 Memorial
140.		11	Ferozepur	Saragarhi Memorial
141.		12	Ferozepur (Golden Arrow House crossing)	Satluj Campaign War Memorial
142.		13	Ferozepur (Mehdipur Village)	6 Mahar War Memorial
143.		14	Ferozepur (Golden Arrow House crossing)	VI K E O Cavalry War Memorial
144.		15	Ferozepur (Golden Arrow House crossing)	Brownlow's Punjabis War Memorial
145.		16	Ferozepur (Near Golden Arrow House crossing)	19, 22 & 24 Punjabis War Memorial 1914–1919
146.		17	Ferozepur (Cantonment General Hospital Family Wing)	Gallipoli Memorial tablet
147.		18	Gurdaspur (Batala)	Batala War Memorial
148.		19	Gurdaspur (Dera Baba Nanak)	Dera Baba Nanak 1971 War Memorial
149.		20	Hussainiwala, Ferozepur	National Martyrs' Memorial at Hussainiwala
150.		21	Jullundhar	Virjila Sthal, War Memorial

151		22	Kapurthala	Lieutenant Jhaggar Singh War Memorial (WW-1)
152.		23	Fazilka (Asafwala Village)	Asafwala 1971 War Memorial
153.		24	Kapurthala (Kapurthala-Kanjili-Kartarpur Road at Tri junction near Station Headquarters)	Imperial State Forces War Memorial (WW-1)
154.		25	Patiala (Stadium Road near Polo Ground)	Patiala State Forces Memorial
155.		26	Patiala (YPS Chowk)	Black Elephant Division Memorial
156.		27	Patiala	Cenotaph War Memorial
157.	**Rajasthan**	1	Alwar (Company Garden)	Alwar War Memorial
158.		2	Churu (District Mukhyalaya Sainik Basti, Sector No 2 on main road Churu)	Shahid Smarak Memorial
159.		3	Jaipur	Sadhewala War Memorial
160.		4	Jaipur (MI Road)	Shahid Smarak War Memorial
160.		5	Jaipur (Raj Path Road near State Legislative Assembly)	Amar Jawan Jyoti War Memorial
161.		6	Jodhpur (Next to the Umaid Bhavan Palace at the northern entrance to the cantonment)	Konark War Memorial
162.		7	Jodhpur (Paota Circle, Jodhpur)	Major Shaitan Singh PVC Memorial
163.		8	Laungewala	Laungewala War Memorial
164.		9	Laungewala Sector	War Memorial BP 638
165.		10	Laungewala (Adjacent to Laungewala War Memorial)	168 FD Regt War Memorial
166.		11	Sriganganagar (Karanpur Town)	Nagi War Memorial
167.	**Sikkim**	1	Tumulpur	Jaswant Baba, MVC War Memorial
168.		2	Nathu La	Nathu La BMP Hut War Memorial

169.		3	Sherathang	Sherathang War Memorial
170.		4	Gangtok	Baba Harbhajan Singh Shrine
171.	**Tamil Nadu**	1	Tiruchirapalli (Gandhi Market)	Tiruchirapalli WW-1 Memorial
172.		2	Wellington (Madras Regimental Centre)	Madras Regiment War Memorial
173.	**Tripura**	1	Agartala	Agartala War Memorial
174.		2	Agartala	Albert Ekka War Memorial
175.	**Uttar Pradesh**	1	Allahabad (Hall of Fame located at Old Cantonment)	4 Infantry Division War Memorial
176.		2	Agra	Shatrujeet War Memorial
177.		3	Bareilly (Jat Regimental Centre)	Jat Regiment War Memorial
178.		4	Faizabad	CMP & 7 Infantry Brigade War Memorial
179.		5	Faizabad (Dogra Regimental Centre)	Dogra War Memorial
180.		6	Faizabad (HQ Madhya UP Sub Area, HQ 7 Infantry Brigade)	HQ 7 Infantry Brigade War Memorial
181.		7	Farrukhabad, District Fatehgarh (SIKH LI Regimental Centre)	Sikh Light Infantry War Memorial
182.		8	Fatehgarh (Rajput Regimental Centre)	Rajput Regiment War Memorial
183.		9	Lucknow	Mangal Pandey War Memorial
184.		10	Jhansi Cantt	White Tiger War Memorial
185.		11	Kunraghat, Gorakhpur (Gorkha Recruiting Depot)	Gorkha Brigade War Memorial
186.		12	Lucknow, (AMC Centre and College)	Armed Forces Medical Services War Memorial
187.		13	Lucknow (Mahatma Gandhi Road)	Smritika War Memorial
188.		14	Lucknow	War Memorial of Kiranti Lines
189.		15	Lucknow (11 GR Regimental Centre)	11 Gorkha Rifles War Memorial
190.		16	Mathura (HQ 1 Corps)	1 Corps War Memorial

191.		17	Meerut	Dugal Dwar& Naik Dwar
192.		18	Meerut Cantonment	Col KH Sharawat, SM Memorial
193.		19	Meerut Cantonment	Maj Ranbir Singh, VrC Memorial
194.		20	Meerut Cantonment	Pine Division War Memorial
195.		21	Meerut Cantonment	Saragarhi Memorial
196.		22	NOIDA (Opposite Army Public School)	NOIDA Shaheed Smarak
197.		23	Shahjahanpur	CQMH Abdul Hamid, PVC Memorial
198.		24	Shahjahanpur	Nk Jadunath Singh, PVC Memorial
199.		25	Shahjahanpur	Shahjahanpur War Memorial
200.		26	Varanasi (39 Gorkha Training Centre)	39 Gorkha Training Centre War Memorial
201		27	Baghpat	War Memorial, Baoli
202.	**Uttarakhand**	1	Lansdowne (Garhwal Rifles Regimental Centre)	Garhwal Rifles War Memorial
203.		2	Pithoragarh	Maharajke Memorial Park
204.		3	Ranikhet (Kumaon Regimental Centre)	Kumaon Regiment War Memorial
205.		4	Roorkee	Bengal Sappers War Memorial
206.		5	Dehradun (Indian Military Academy)	Indian Military Academy War Memorial
207.		6	Dehradun (Lal Gate)	Lal Gate War Memorial
208.		7	Dehradun	Khalanga War Memorial
209.		8	Dehradun	Memorial of Ghagora
210.		9	Tehri Garh	War Memorial Late Rfn Kuldeep Singh, VrC
211.	**West Bengal**	1	Binnaguri (Binnaguri Military Station)	Bogra War Memorial
212.		2	Darjeeling	Batasia Loop War Memorial
213.		3	Howrah (Bank of River Hooghly)	Lascar War Memorial

214.	4	Kolkata (Red Road)	The Glorious Dead War Memorial
215.	5	Kolkata (College Square)	49th Bengalis War Memorial
216.	6	Kolkata (Fort William)	Purvi Kaman Vijay Smarak
217.	7	Sukna Military Station (Near Siliguri)	33 Corps Vijay Smarak War Memorial

Notes

1. Rana TS Chhina, *The Last Post: Indian War Memorials around the World*, New Delhi: USI, 2014, p. 1.
2. Ibid.
3. Ibid.
4. See https://nationalwarmemorial.gov.in/about-memorial#memorialHistory for more information.
5. See https://nationalwarmemorial.gov.in/about-memorial#memorialHistory.
6. Rana TS Chhina, 'Introduction', in *The Last Post*, n. 1, p. 6.
7. Ibid.
8. Ibid., p. 16.
9. Chhina, *The Last Post*, n. 1, p. 18.
10. Kaushik Roy, *The Indian Army and the First World War: 1914-1918*, New Delhi: Oxford University Press, Kindle edition.
11. The description text for the memorials has been sourced from Maj Gen (Retd) Ian Cardozo, AVSM, SM, *The Indian Army in World War I, 1914-1989*, New Delhi: USI and Manohar, 2019, pp. 216–231; and from Chhina, *The Last Post*, n. 1.
12. Simon Doherty and Tom Donovan, *The Indian Corps on the Western Front- A Handbook and Battlefield Guide*, New Delhi: United Service Institution of India, New Delhi, 2014.
13. Ibid., p. 156.
14. Ibid.
15. Ibid., p. 155.

16. Ibid., p. 156.
17. Chhina, *The Last Post*, n. 1, p. 61.
18. Ibid. p. 62
19. Ibid., p. 66.
20. Ibid., p. 70.
21. Doherty and Donovan, *The Indian Corps on the Western Front*, n. 12, pp. 154, 155.
22. Chhina, *The Last Post*, n. 1, p. 72.
23. Ibid., p. 73.
24. Ibid., p. 121.
25. Ibid., p. 108.
26. Ibid., p. 111.
27. Ibid., p. 78.
28. Ibid. p. 105.
29. Ibid., p. 106.
30. Ibid., p. 55.
31. Ibid., p. 96.
32. Ibid., p. 97.
33. Ibid., p. 107.
34. Ibid., p. 119.
35. Ibid., p. 83.
36. Ibid., p. 88.
37. Ibid., p. 90.
38. Ibid., p. 77.
39. Ibid., p. 85.
40. Ibid., p. 92.
41. Ibid., p. 8.
42. Margaret MacMillan, *The War that Ended Peace: How Europe Abandoned Peace for the First World War*, London: Profile books, Kindle Edition.
43. Ibid.
44. Chhina, *The Last Post*, n. 1, p. 30.
45. Ibid.
46. Ibid.
47. Ibid., p. 40.
48. Ibid., p. 43.

About the Contributors

Maj Gen (Dr) AK Bardalai (Retd) is a veteran of the Indian Army and a graduate of the Defence Services Staff College, Wellington (India). During his service in the Army, he held various command and staff assignments at different levels, including the command of an Infantry Division. He was also the Commandant of the Indian Military Training Team in Bhutan from October 2011 to January 2014. Earlier, he served as a Military Observer in the United Nations Verification Mission in Angola from 1991 to 92. He was awarded the Ministry of External Affairs Fellowship at the United Services Institution of India for the year 2003–2004 for his research on 'Changing Global Security: Its implications for UN Peacekeeping Operations'. He also served in Lebanon as the Deputy Head of the Mission and Deputy Force Commander of UNIFIL from 2008 to 2010. Post-retirement from the Army on 30th April 2014, he is actively engaged with the academic study of UN Peace Operations. The author holds a PhD from Tilburg University, the Netherlands for his research on 'United Nations Interim Force in Lebanon: Assessment and Way Forward'.

Maj Gen Ian Cardozo, AVSM, SM (Retd) was educated at St Xavier's School and College, Mumbai. At the National Defence Academy, he was awarded the gold and silver medals and is the first officer of the Indian Army to be awarded the Sena Medal for gallantry on a patrol on the Sino-Indian border. He has taken part in three wars. Not deterred at losing a leg in 1971, he went on to command a Battalion, Brigade and Division in the Army. He retired as Chief of Staff of a corps in the North East. After retirement, Gen Cardozo worked in the disability sector and was chosen by the prime minister to head The Rehabilitation Council of India. His books—*Param Vir*, *The Sinking of INS Khukri*, *Indian VCs of World War I* and *The Indian Army in World War I: 1914–1918*—have been widely acclaimed. He was an elected member of the USI Council for a number of years and has been the Chairman of the Board of Management of USI-CMHCS.

Col Vivek Chadha (Retd), was commissioned in 8 MARATHA LI and commanded 1 Maratha LI (Jangi Paltan). He served in the Indian Army for 22 years prior to taking premature retirement to pursue research. He joined the Institute for Defence Studies and Analysis in November 2011 and is a Research Fellow at the Military Affairs Centre. He has served in active counter terrorism zones to include Sri Lanka (Op Pawan), Northeast India to include Assam, Nagaland, Manipur and Jammu and Kashmir. Colonel Chadha's areas of research are counter terrorism and military studies. His single author books on counter terrorism include *Low Intensity Conflicts in India: An Analysis*; *Lifeblood of Terrorism: Countering Terrorism Finance* and *Company Commander in Low Intensity Conflicts*. His single author books on military subjects include: *Even if Ain't Broke Yet, Do Fix It: Enhancing Effectiveness Through Military Change*; *Kargil: Past Perfect: Future Uncertain; CDS and Beyond: Integration of the Indian Armed Forces*. He was part of the team that wrote the Indian Army's first Sub Conventional Doctrine in 2006. He also serves on the Editorial Board of the *Journal of Defence Studies*.

Col PK Gautam (Retd), a veteran of 1971 war in Bangladesh, was a former Research Fellow at the Institute for Defence Studies and Analysis, New Delhi, and later a consultant to the project 'Indigenous Historical Knowledge' at the Institute. He has authored numerous works, including *Composition and Regimental System of the Indian Army: Continuity and Change* and monographs on Kautilya's *Arthashastra*, Kamandaka's *Nitishastra*, and the *Thirukural*. He has written extensively on environmental security, water, climate change, military affairs and Tibet. He is currently an Honorary Distinguished Fellow at Centre for Military History and Conflict Studies, USI. His present research is on the *Sukraniti*.

Neha Kohli is currently Senior Research Fellow at the Centre for Military History and Conflict Studies, USI. She is also Executive Editor of *Maritime Affairs*, the journal of the National Maritime Foundation, New Delhi. Prior to this, she was Associate Editor of the *Journal of Defence Studies,* published by the Institute of Defence Studies and Analysis, New Delhi from 2012-2020. She has worked with reputed academic publishing houses such as Oxford University Press and Sage Publications. She has also worked in the print media, with *The Pioneer*, *The Financial Express* and *The Indian Express* newspapers. At the IDSA, she authored and co-authored articles and book chapters as part of the Institute's projects.

Maj Gen VK Singh (Retd) has varied interests include adventure sports, military history and journalism. He has participated in the Himalayan Car Rally thrice, from 1982–84. He is a regular contributor to magazines and journals, and many of his short stories and poems were published in the *Illustrated Weekly*, *Filmfare*, *Femina*, and *Eve's Weekly* in the 1970s and 1980s. In later years, he took to professional writing and has authored a number of books—*Through: Saga of the Corps of Signals, Leadership in the Indian Army: Biographies of Twelve Soldiers, History of the Corps of Signals: Volume II, India's External Intelligence: Secrets of the Research and Analysis Wing*, and Contribution *of the Armed Forces to the Freedom Movement in India*, among others.

Maj Gen PJS Sandhu (Retd) was commissioned into 8th Light Cavalry on 15 June 1966 and later commanded 47 Armoured Regiment. He retired from the Army as Chief of Staff, 1 Corps on 31 July 2003 after 37 years of service. During his military service, he commanded an armoured Regiment, an Independent Armoured Brigade, and an Armoured Division. He participated in the 1971 India-Pakistan War in the Shakargarh Sector and also served as a deputy commander of an Infantry brigade on the LOC in J&K. He also served as Deputy Director General of Military Operations (DDGMO) at the Army HQ nad the GOC of Bengal Area. Gen Sandhu was formerly the Deputy Director and Editor at the USI of India. He has been a regular contributor to the *USI Journal* and was the edtitor of the USI Study titled *1962: A View from the Other Side of the Hill.*

Maj Gen Jagatbir Singh VSM (Retd), is a second generation Army Officer. who was commisioned into 18th Cavalry, a Regiment he subsequently commanded. He has had wide ranging command, staff and instructional appointments across the country and has also served in the UN Mission in Iraq and Kuwait between the two Gulf wars. He commanded an Armoured Brigade where he was responsible for its conversion to Arjun Tanks and the prestigious 1 Armoured Division. He has been an instructor at IMA as well as at Defence Services Staff College and the PM of a Mountain Brigade and served in the Military Secretary's Branch amongst others staff appointments. He is currently a Distinguished Fellow at the United Services Institute of India, India's oldest think tank. He has been publishing various articles related on Defence related issues in magazines and newspapers and has co-autored Armour 71.

We also wish to place on record the following people who have assisted in compiling and editing this book - **Sqn Ldr Rana TS Chhina, MBE (Retd), Maj Gen Mandip Singh, SM, VSM (Retd), Ms Shefali Oberoi, Ms Niharika Tarneja** and **Mr Rakesh Agnihotri.**

Index

1965 India-Pakistan war, 127
  assessment, 137–141
  background, 127–128
  ceasefire and Tashkent accord, 136–137
  smokescreen *see* Rann of Kutch incident
  Sino-Soviet split, 127
1971 India-Pakistan war
  background, 141–144
  Barmer sector, 168–169
  central Punjab sector, 165–166
  Chhamb and Jammu sector, 163–164
  Chittagong sector, 156–157
  eastern front, 147–150
  Fazilka sector, 166–167
  Indian forces and plans, 159–160
  Jaisalmer sector, 167–168
  Kargil sector, 161
  Kutch sector, 169
  northern and eastern sectors, 153–155
  northern Punjab sector, 165
  north-west sector, 152–153
  Pakistani forces and plans, 157–158
  Punch sector, 162–163
  Shakargarh Bulge area, 164–165
  south-west sector, 150–152
  strategies and forces, 144–147
  Sylhet area, 155–156
  Tangdhar and Uri sector, 161–162
  Turtok sector, 160–161
  western front, 157

A

advance landing ground (ALG), 118
Air Defence Information Zone (ADIZ), 193
Animal Transport Companies, 76
armies
  composition, mid-nineteenth century, 3
  presidency around 1796, 3
Ashok Chakra, 276
Assam
  Assam Accord, 221
  Operation Bajrang, 221
  post-independence deployment in Indian Army, 221–222
  ULFA, 221
Assam accord, 221
Auchinleck Committee, 72
Australian and New Zealand Army Corps (ANZAC), 69

B

Battle of Festubert, 50, 52
Battle of Neuve Chapelle, 51, 52
Battle of Se La and Bomdi La, 116–118
Battle of Shalateng, 101
Battle of Ypres, 51
Battles on Pangong Tso, 111–112

Burzil Forces, 194

C

Central Treaty Organisation (CENTO), 10
Central Treaty Organization (CENTO), 136
Changez Khan, 166
Chatfield Committee, 72
Chinese People's Liberation Army (PLA)
  marched into Tibet, 9
Chumik Glacier, 196
College of Defence Management (CDM), 270
combat effectiveness, 21–22
Combined Defence Services Exam, 24
Counter Insurgency and Jungle Warfare School (CIJWS), 269

D

Dardanelles campaign
  Indian Army units and Indian state forces, 70
Defence Services Staff College (DSSC), 269–271
Dhola, 9, 108
Distinguished Service Order, 276

E

East Africa, 57, 60–61
  Indian Army units and Indian state forces, 62–64
East India Company (EIC), 1
  mid-1700s, 2
Egypt and Palestine
  Indian Army units and Indian state forces, 66–69
  World War I, 61, 64–65
Esher Committee, 71

F

Financial Action Task Force (FATF), 230
Force K6, 76

G

Gallipoli
  ANZAC, 69
  MEF, 69
Gilgit Scouts, 101

H

High Altitude Warfare School, 268
Hizbul Mujahideen (HM), 223
Humanitarian and Disaster Relief (HADR), 246
  disease and floods in Kerala, 248
  Indian Ocean Tsunami, 2004, 247–248
  Kashmir Earthquake 2005, 248
  Nepal Earthquake 2015, 248

I

Imperial Cadet Corps, 4, 73
India
  EIC, 1
  seventeenth and eighteenth century, 1–2
  UN peacekeeping, 249–250
India-Pakistan war, 1965
  background, 127–128
  Rann of Kutch, 128–131
Indian 11 Corps Offensive (Operation Riddle), 133–134
Indian 1 Corps Offensive in Sialkot Sector (Operation Nepal), 134–135
Indian Army
  aftermath of World Wars, 87
  armoured regiments, composition of, 25

Assam, post-independence deployment in, 221–222
class regiments, 24
combat arms, 22
combat effectiveness, 21–22
combat support arms, 22
conflicts, 4
contribution to freedom struggle, 34–38
customs and traditions, 29–30
doctrinal evolution, 226–230
future, 2010–2020, 20–21
historical perspective, 216
infantry regiments, composition of, 25–27
inter-war period, 71–74
J&K, post-independence deployment in, 222–223
Manipur, post-independence deployment in, 220–221
Meghdoot Operation, 1984, 192
Mizoram, post-independence deployment in, 219–220
Nagaland, post-independence deployment in, 215, 218–219
new communities recruited, 46
new millennium, 18–20
Operation Polo 1948, 177
origin, 1–6
Peel Commission's suggestion, 3–4
pre-independence era, 43
Punjab, post-independence deployment in, 223–224
recruitment and composition, 24, 28
regimental system, 21
regiments, composition of, 28–29
reorganisation, 71–72
restructuring, 4
services, 22
Sikkim: Skirmish at Nathu La 1967, 185
since 1947, 6
small wars, 87–89
social composition, 1912, 45
structure, 23
UN peace operations, 235
unit/battalion level structure, 22, 24
Vijay Operation 1961, 181
War of Austrian Succession, 1
wartime growth phases, 77
World War I, 5–6
World War I eve, 44–46
World War II, 6, 8

Indian Army since 1947, 6
Armed Forces Reconstitution Committee, 7
Army Partition Scheme, 7
consolidation, 8–9
division, 7
internal security gains momentum, 16–18
modernisation challenges and domestic turmoil, 14–16
new millennium, 18–20
Operation Gulmarg, 7
two fronts conflict, on, 9–11
victory and move to modernise, 12–14

Indian counter-offensives, 133–135
Indian General Staff, 5
Indian Ocean Tsunami, 2004, 247–248
Indian Order of Merit, 273–274
Indian peacekeepers, 238
ONUC, 240–241
training, 238
UNEF I, 239–240
UNIFIL, 244–245
UNOSOM II, 243–244
UNPROFOR, 241–243

India-Pakistan war, 1965, 127
air forces, 135
Barmer sector operations, 135
casualties and territory, 136
Chhamb–Jaurian sector, 132
Indian counter-offensives, 133–135
Indian Navy, 136

Indo-Sri Lankan Accord, 198
Infantry School, 268
Integrated Headquarters (IHQ), 19
Inter-war period

Indian Army, 71–74

J

Jammu and Kashmir (J&K), 204
Jammu and Kashmir Liberation Front (JKLF), 17, 222
Jangi-Azadi Gilgit-Baltistan, 101
J&K
 Hizbul Mujahideen (HM), 223
 JKLF, 222
 post-independence deployment in Indian Army, 222–223

K

Kameng Frontier division
 Battle of Se La and Bomdi La, 116–118
 Chinese military strategy, 115
 fall of Tawang, 116
 Namka Chu Battle, 115–116
 trigger, 114–115
Kanjarkot, 129
Kargil, Operation Vijay 1999
 background, 204–205
 chronology of Kargil war, 209–210
 crisis, 205
 execution, 207–208
 intrusions and response, 205–207
 Kargil conflict, 208
Kargil Review Committee (KRC), 19
Kashmir conflict, 1947–48
 August-October 1947, 98
 ceasefire, 104–105
 division of armed forces, 95–97
 geography and administration, 94–95
 historical background, 93–94
 late October 1947, 98–99
 May-December 1948, 102–104
 October-November 1947, 99–100
 Pakistan's plan, 97–98
 winter and spring offensives, 101–102
Kashmir Earthquake 2005, 248
Kirti Chakra, 280

L

Left-wing Extremism (LWE), 224
Lohit Frontier Division, 118
 6 KUMAON attack, 119–120
 Build-up by China, 119
 preliminary operations, 118–119
 reorganisation by India, 119
Low-intensity conflicts
 historical perspective, 216–218

M

Mahavir Chakra, 279
Maldives, 202
 NSS, 202
 Operation Cactus, 202–204
Manipur
 Army, post-independence deployment in Indian, 220–221
 PLA, 220–221
 UNLF, 220
Mediterranean Expeditionary Force (MEF), 69
Mesopotamia, 55–57
 Indian Army units and Indian state forces, 58–60
Military customs and traditions, 29–30
 Cariappa's influence, 30
 invitation, 33
 martial races, 30–31
 matter of honor, 31
 musical traditions, 31–32
 officers's mess, 31
 regimental, 33–34
 reverence for dead, 33
 salutation, 33
 sanctity, 32–33
 service dresses and accoutrements, 32
Mizo National Famine Front (MNFF), 219
Mizoram

MNFF, 219
Operation Jericho, 219
post-independence deployment in Indian Army, 219–220

N

Naga Federal Army (NFA), 218
Nagaland
NFA, 218
NSCN, 219
post-independence deployment in Indian Army, 218–219
Namka Chu Battle, 115–116
National Defence College, 270
National Security Service (NSS), 202
National Socialist Council of Nagaland (NSCN), 219
Nepal Earthquake 2015, 250
NSCN Isak-Muivah (NSCN-IM), 219

O

Operation Ablaze, 131
Operation Bajrang, 221
Operation Cactus, 202–204
Operation Desert Hawk, 130–131
Operation Grand Slam, 132
Operation Hammer, 102
Operation Jericho, 219
Operation Kabadi, 130
Operation Meghdoot, 1984, 192
background, 192–194
Bana Post, battle for, 195–196
Chumik Glacier, 196
commencement, 194–195
Operation Pawan, 196
Operation Pawan, 196
assessment, 202
background, 196–198
divisions, 200
heliborne operation, 200
Jaffna Sector, 199
launch date, 199
military operations in Sri Lanka, 199
Sri Lanka's political crisis, 201
Trincomalee Sector, 199
Operation Polo 1948, 177
background, 177–179
formal accession, 181
ground operations, 179–181
Operation Poomalai, 198
Operation Vijay 1961, 18, 181
action, 185
background, 181–182
Daman and Diu, 183
Goa, 183–185

P

Pakistan Muslim League (PML), 18
Pakistan People's Party (PPP), 18
Param Vir Chakra, 278
Peacekeeping
principles, 245–246
People's Liberation Army (PLA), 220–221
People's Liberation Organisation of Tamil Eelam (PLOTE), 202
Permanent Mission of India, 237
Phoney War, 76
Punjab
Operation Blue Star, 223
post-independence deployment in Indian Army, 223–224

Q

Quaid Post, 195

R

Race to the Sea, 50
Rann of Kutch incident, 128–131
Desert Hawk-I, 130–131
historical background, 128–129

intrusion, 129–130
Revolution in Military Affairs (RMA), 21
Royal Indian Air Force (RIAF), 35
Royal Indian Military College. *see* Rashtriya Indian Military College (RIMC)
Royal Indian Navy (RIN), 35
Rue du Bois attack, 52

S

Sepoy Mutiny, 3
Shaurya Chakra, 280
Siang sector, 121–122
Sikkim: Skirmish at Nathu La 1967, 185
assessment, 191–192
background, 185–187
event-11 September 1967, 189–191
lead-up to the Skirmish, 187–189
Sind Reserve Police (SRP), 129
Sino-Indian Conflict, 1962, 107–108
air aspects, 122–123
Chinese war aim and grand strategy, 109
end of diplomacy, 108
Indian POWs in Chinese custody, 123
Kameng Frontier division, 114
Lohit Frontier Division, 118
Mao's armed co-existence, 108
Nehru's Forward Policy, 108
Operation Ablaze, 131
Operation Gibraltar, 131–132
spark, 108–109
War in Ladakh, 109
Skeen Committee, 74
Small wars
defined by Col CE Callwell, 87–88
India's north-eastern jungles, 88
North-West Frontier, 88
purposes, 88
South East Asia Treaty Organisation (SEATO), 10
South East Asia Treaty Organization (SEATO), 136
Southeast Asia, World War II, 81
Italy, 85–87
Subansiri Frontier Division, 121

T

Tamil United Liberation Front (TULF), 197
Terrorism in India, 224–226

U

Union Public Service Commission (UPSC), 24
United Liberation Front of Asom (ULFA), 221
United National Liberation Front (UNLF), 220
United Nations (UN)
formation, 9
United Nations Operations in the Congo (ONUC), 240–241
United Nations Protection Force (UNPROF-Bosnia Herzegovina), 241–243
United Nations Trans Assistance Mission in Cambodia (UNTAC), 250

W

War in Ladakh, 109
China prepares, 110
Chinese plan, 110
Indian dispositions, 109–110
Indus Valley operations, 112–113
opening attacks, 111
Pangong Tso, 111–112
second Chinese offensive, 113–114
War balance sheet
air forces use, 106
casualties, 105
land forces, 105
militias, 106–107
War Memorials, 284-296
World War I, 47–48
causes, 46–47, 74–75

East Africa, 57, 60–61
Egypt and Palestine, 61, 64–65
Gallipoli, 65, 69–71
imperial service troops, 49
Indian Army, 44–46
Indian Army division, 48
Indian Army units and Indian state forces, 58–60
inter-war period, Indian Army, 71–74
Mesopotamia, 55–57
New middle class in India, 73
new communities recruited in Indian Army, 46
Northern Europe, 48–53
order of battle, 54–55
World War II
causes, 74–75
end, 6
Hitler, 76
impact on Indian Army, 6
Indian Army, 75–77
India's entry, 75
Indianisation, 76
Indian soldiers, 35
Munich Conference, 76
recruitment in Indian Army, 77
Southeast Asia, 81
theatres Indian Army, 32, 78
volunteer-driven army, 8